WORK AND THE FAMILY
A Study in Social Demography

This is a volume in
STUDIES IN POPULATION

A complete list of titles in this series appears at the end of this volume.

WORK AND THE FAMILY
A Study in Social Demography

VALERIE KINCADE OPPENHEIMER

Department of Sociology
University of California, Los Angeles
Los Angeles, California

ACADEMIC PRESS
A Subsidiary of Harcourt Brace Jovanovich, Publishers
New York   London
Paris   San Diego   San Francisco   São Paulo   Sydney   Tokyo   Toronto

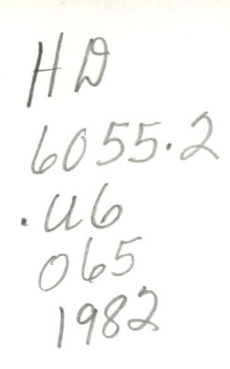

COPYRIGHT © 1982, BY ACADEMIC PRESS, INC.
ALL RIGHTS RESERVED.
NO PART OF THIS PUBLICATION MAY BE REPRODUCED OR
TRANSMITTED IN ANY FORM OR BY ANY MEANS, ELECTRONIC
OR MECHANICAL, INCLUDING PHOTOCOPY, RECORDING, OR ANY
INFORMATION STORAGE AND RETRIEVAL SYSTEM, WITHOUT
PERMISSION IN WRITING FROM THE PUBLISHER.

ACADEMIC PRESS, INC.
111 Fifth Avenue, New York, New York 10003

United Kingdom Edition published by
ACADEMIC PRESS, INC. (LONDON) LTD.
24/28 Oval Road, London NW1 7DX

Library of Congress Cataloging in Publication Data

Oppenheimer, Valerie Kincade.
  Work and the family.

  (Studies in population)
  Bibliography: p.
  Includes index.
  1. Wives--Employment--United States. 2. Mothers--
Employment--United States. 3. Children of working
mothers--United States. 4. Cost and standard of living--
United States. 5. Family--United States. 6. United
States--Population. I. Title. II. Series.
HD6055.2.U6065   306.8'5'0973   82-3909
ISBN 0-12-527580-3   AACR2

PRINTED IN THE UNITED STATES OF AMERICA

82 83 84 85   9 8 7 6 5 4 3 2 1

To Tony and Chris

Contents

PREFACE xi
ACKNOWLEDGMENTS xv

I
AN OVERVIEW

1
Analytical Goals and Conceptual Tools 3

    I. Economic Squeezes 6
    II. Career and Family-Cycle Stages 9
    III. Relative Economic Status as a Conceptual Tool 12
    IV. Extension of Model 19
    V. Changing Sex-Role Attitudes 28
    VI. Data Sources 31
    VII. Conclusion 32

2
Conceptual and Methodological Issues 37

    I. An Intermediate Classification of Occupations 37
    II. Conceptual and Methodological Issues in Life-Cycle Analyses 42

II
LIFE-CYCLE SQUEEZES AND THEIR COMPONENTS

3
Career Cycle and Occupational Differentials in Men's Earnings — 65

    I. Age–Earnings Profiles of Men by Occupation: 1959 and 1969 Similarities — 66
    II. The Lower White-Collar Squeeze — 78
    III. 1959–1969 Changes in Age and Occupational Patterns of Earnings: A Description — 84
    IV. Explaining Changes in the Age Patterns of Earnings — 90
    V. Prospects for the 1980s — 103
    VI. Conclusion — 121

4
The First Life-Cycle Squeeze — 123

    I. The Cost of Setting up a Household — 124
    II. Marriage and the First Squeeze — 135
    III. Conclusion — 162

5
The Second Life-Cycle Squeeze — 165

    I. The Cost of Children — 169
    II. The Overall Picture — 173
    III. Occupational Differentials — 188
    IV. Conclusion — 209

III
THE NATURE OF WIVES' SOCIOECONOMIC CONTRIBUTION TO THE FAMILY

6
The Effect of Socioeconomic Pressures and Deterrents on Wives' Labor-Force Participation — 215

    I. The Role of Income and Occupation — 220
    II. Past Marital Instability as a Factor in Wives' Labor-Force Participation — 238

III. Family-Cycle Stage	244
IV. Conclusion	252

7
Wives' Potential Socioeconomic Contribution and Their Labor-Force Status — 255

I. The Sociology of Women's Economic Role in the Family	255
II. The Labor-Force Impact of the Potential Socioeconomic Advantage of Wives Working	265
III. Conclusion	287

8
Socioeconomic and Demographic Implications of Wives' Employment — 289

I. Educational Attainment	290
II. Economic Impact of Wives Working	309
III. Conclusion	348

IV
EPILOGUE

9
Life-Cycle Squeezes and Adaptive Family Strategies — 355

I. Conceptualization	355
II. Group I and II White-Collar Families	363
III. Group III and IV Blue-Collar Families	372
IV. Group III and IV White-Collar Families	391
V. Implications	396

APPENDIXES

Appendix A
Occupations Classified by Peak 1959 Median Earnings within Major Occupation Groups — 403

Appendix B
Total Male Population in Selected Age Groups — 423

Appendix C
Dollar Estimates of Expenditures on Children 425

Appendix D
Multiple Regression Models of Wives' Labor-Force Status in 1970 437

Appendix E
Time Demands of Children 445

Appendix F
Median Income of Husbands and Families by Age and Occupation 449

References 453

References to Government Documents 464

SUBJECT INDEX 471

Preface

This book grew out of a continuing interest in women's changing economic behavior in American society. In previous research I have stressed the role of the rapid postwar rise in the *demand* for workers in female occupations as a major factor in explaining the sharply increasing labor-force participation of older women during this period (Oppenheimer 1970). On the *supply* side, I have focused particularly on sociodemographic factors that had actually reduced the size of population groups from which most female workers had traditionally been drawn—emphasizing especially the role of the low fertility of the Great Depression, the rising school-leaving age, and earlier marriage and childbearing. With regard to factors affecting labor supply, in the sense of who does or does not decide to work, I largely relied on the work of others in my earlier research. This had indicated that women do respond to rising job opportunities with increased labor-force participation.

The present book was initially inspired by a desire to explore for myself the question of factors influencing women's labor-supply decisions. I wanted to investigate the relationship of women's work behavior to variations in lifestyle aspirations and needs associated partly with the family cycle and also with husband's socioeconomic position. In addition, I wished to examine the nature of the joint socioeconomic characteristics of husbands and wives and their impact on wives' work behavior. However, over the course of the study, my focus gradually shifted to viewing women's economic behavior as only one of a *variety* of behavioral mechanisms for dealing with variations in actual or potential economic stress. Increasingly, I became concerned with marital and fertility behavior, as well as women's labor-force participation, and became intrigued by the heuristic value of focusing on the family as the major unit of analysis rather than on women alone.

The investigation was primarily based on the Public Use Samples of the 1960 and 1970 U.S. Censuses of Population. If used somewhat imaginatively, by their very size, such large data sets provide the opportunity for empirical approximation of theoretical constructs. I took advantage of this opportunity to focus on socioeconomic differentials in the interaction of family and career cycles. To accomplish this I have used the age and occupation of men as the major devices for distinguishing differences in socioeconomic position and of simultaneously examining career- and family-cycle behavior and characteristics. My fundamental objective in this approach has been to use empirical research to develop a general theoretical perspective on family socioeconomic and demographic behavior. And, indeed, one of the most rewarding aspects of the research was the constant interplay between empirical analysis and theoretical development, which at times led me somewhat afield of my original research goals. But this in itself represents part of the adventure of undertaking research—taking advantage of an opportunity to seize upon a potentially fruitful area of investigation and, by employing relatively simple statistical procedures, further develop the theoretical statement. It is also a way of developing social theory that maintains close ties with the empirical world.

In essence, then, this book reports on an exploratory study as it uses an empirical analysis to develop a theoretical approach. It is also one which, I hope, reflects the convergence of research on family behavior by scholars from a wide variety of disciplines, most notably economics and history as well as social demography. Certainly I found that one of the most intellectually exciting aspects of the analysis was to search the historical literature for—and find—a preliminary confirmation of hypotheses I had developed using modern data. In addition, microeconomic theories and research on economic and demographic behavior have been significant in developing my ideas—first, because they focus on the household as a major unit of analysis; and second, because of their emphasis on the substitutability of one kind of behavior for another in achieving any particular goal. To social demography and occupational sociology I owe a long-term debt for the deep interest they early inspired in me for the analysis of family and career cycles, on the one hand, and relative economic deprivation as a major motivating force, on the other. This study, then, is aimed at the wide audience of demographers, sociologists, economists, and historians who are interested in family socioeconomic and demographic behavior. It is also intended to appeal to readers at all levels of methodological sophistication—whether professionals or graduate students.

The book is organized into four parts. Part I (Chapters 1 and 2) introduces the theoretical model to be used and the major objectives of the research (Chapter 1). It also discusses important conceptual and methodological problems involved in life-cycle analysis and the use of occupation as a major analytical tool (Chapter 2). Part II (Chapters 3–5) examines life-cycle squeezes—structured sources of economic stress arising out of the interaction of family and career cycles. Chapter 3 discusses the career-cycle effect on men's earnings and how this is related to different types of occupational careers. Chapter 4 focuses particularly on the economic squeeze of early adulthood. It also examines occupational differences in the severity of this squeeze and age at marriage as one type of response to these difficulties. Chapter 5 investigates the economic squeeze associated with the peak child-dependency period, how this has changed over time, and the implications of these changes for the relative economic position of various subgroups. It also describes occupational differences in the timing of the peak child-dependency period and discusses whether these differences may present an adaptive response to different occupational career patterns. Part III (Chapters 6–8) examines the nature of wives' socioeconomic contribution to the family. Chapter 6 investigates the sensitivity of wives' labor-force participation to estimates of various types of economic pressures, while Chapter 7 looks at the effect of wives' potential socioeconomic contribution on their labor-force status. Chapter 8 examines the impact of wives' employment on their families' socioeconomic positions and its possible feedback effects on wives' future labor-market and demographic behavior. Part IV (Chapter 9) essentially sums up the theoretical implications of the analyses conducted in Chapters 2 through 8 and represents a more formal theoretical statement of the issues in terms of adaptive family strategies. As a test of its theoretical generality, a preliminary analysis of the relevance of this formulation to historical as well as contemporary family patterns is also undertaken.

Acknowledgments

This research was supported by a grant from the Russell Sage Foundation. I owe a considerable debt of gratitude to the Foundation for soliciting this research and for its extreme patience during the many years it has taken to complete the study. Second, I am extremely grateful to those who, over the years, provided me with invaluable programming assistance—most particularly Ken Ong, Rene Baca, Andrew Cherlin, and Rita Engelhardt. I am indebted to Judith Blake for a copy of the 1960 Public Use Samples and to Dualabs for selecting my samples from the 1970 Public Use Samples. My thanks go to numerous colleagues who provided valuable critical comments, and to unknown reviewers of this book as well as of earlier articles based on preliminary versions of some of the material included. Regardless of whether I always agreed with their comments, they always made me think more deeply about what I was trying to accomplish as well as how I might do it better.

Some of the material in this volume has appeared in various forms at previous times. Permission to reprint revised versions of part or all of the following publications is gratefully acknowledged: "The Life-Cycle Squeeze: The Interaction of Men's Occupational and Family Life Cycles," *Demography* 11 (May 1974); "The Easterlin Hypothesis: Another Aspect of the Echo to Consider," *Population and Development Review* 2 (September–

December 1976); "The Sociology of Women's Economic Role in the Family," *American Sociological Review* 42 (June 1977); "Structural Sources of Economic Pressure for Wives to Work: An Analytical Framework," *Journal of Family History* 4 (Summer 1979); "The Changing Nature of Life-Cycle Squeezes: Implications for the Socioeconomic Position of the Elderly," in *Aging: Stability and Change in the Family*, edited by Robert W. Fogel, Sara B. Kiesler, and Ethel Shanas (New York: Academic Press 1981).

WORK AND THE FAMILY
A Study in Social Demography

I

AN OVERVIEW

1

Analytical Goals and Conceptual Tools

For many years demographers have debated the nature of the causal processes involved in the empirically observed relationship between wives' work and reproductive behavior. Recently, however, the number of socioeconomic and demographic variables that are being considered appropriate to include within a single analytical framework has been greatly expanded, largely through the influence of economic theories of household decision making. By far the most fully developed theoretical models tying together a variety of economic and demographic factors are those of microeconomists and they rely heavily on notions of household utility-maximizing behavior, given certain exogenous economic constraints. While many social demographers may object to the notion that the family can legitimately be treated as a *homogeneous* decision-making group, the increased emphasis on the family as a theoretically important unit of analysis should be a welcome development for the sociologist–demographer who has traditionally stressed its analytical importance for marriage and fertility behavior.

As beneficial as the growing emphasis on the family is in the study of an expanded set of socioeconomic and demographic variables, microeconomic models of family decision making have posed certain fundamental problems for social demographers. There have, accordingly, been a number of critiques of these models by sociologists and demographers (as well as by other economists), particularly as they are applied to fertility behavior. Some of these criticisms will be discussed in subsequent pages, but two will exemplify the types of problems such models raise. One is the assumption of neoclassical economists that "tastes" are either invariant or vary randomly over time and among people at one point in time. Hence, tastes are, in effect, usually relegated to the error term in most microeconomic regression analyses. Since variables such as social norms and institutions fall under the rubric of "tastes," these models offer little for the sociologist, qua sociologist, to do.

Another problem is the static nature of many, though not all, microeconomic models. The assumption is that a number of major and permanent decisions are made simultaneously at marriage—decisions such as the number of children a couple will have, their "quality," and the life-time labor-market input of the wife. Such static models are often created for convenience—to facilitate the creation, in turn, of manageable mathematical models—rather than because economists really believe people make most of their important decisions in young adulthood and then stick to them for life. However, these oversimplified operating assumptions are sometimes accepted as empirically true without the benefit of any direct empirical data ever being brought to bear on the issue. In any event, demographers are often, if not usually, deeply involved in the analysis of change and hence static models tend to have a somewhat limited appeal on these grounds alone.

At issue at the moment is not whether some models, such as the microeconomic model, are "wrong" whereas others are "right." Rather, there are two points to be made here. They both arise out of the fact that, especially in the early developmental stages, all analytical models have to make certain simplifying assumptions. These assumptions are sometimes even central to the paradigm out of which the model arises and hence are strongly resistent to modification. I suspect this is very much the case with the neoclassicist's view on "tastes." The first point is that if sociological variables, such as norms or social institutions, do have any theoretical and empirical utility in social research, then a major way in which sociologists can make a unique and useful contribution to the joint analyses of socioeconomic and demographic behavior is through developing analytical models in which such variables form an organic part of the theory. Second, the fact that most models involve certain simplifying—and often *over*simplifying—assumptions implies that a heuristically healthy research development would be the creation of a variety of models that utilize different types of assumptions. Some of these models may ultimately fall by the wayside. Others will be further developed and refined, perhaps converging over time. In short, my basic argument is that different types of models are needed and that social demographers can and should contribute to this model-building process by developing theories that are sociodemographic in character. The present study represents just such an effort.

The original goal of this study was to investigate the nature of women's economic role in the family and the factors that have been operating to change this role. However, the analysis progressively developed into a somewhat broader investigation of the relationship between the economic and family systems of our society and the consequences of this relationship for several types of socioeconomic and demographic behavior. In particular, I felt that a rather neglected aspect of the study of work and family roles was the economic dimension of both men and women's familial roles—that is, the couple's responsibility for providing the means of maintaining or achieving a given standard of living for the family. It was this particular aspect of an adult's familial economic responsibilities, and the conditions affecting the ease with which such responsibilities are discharged, that seemed likely to provide a fruitful way of linking family and economic systems.

One of the major strategies I have employed to explore the changing relationship of family and economic behavior has been to utilize the notion of economic pressures for additional income in families, aside from that provided by the husband—paid employment of the wife being one among several obvious responses to such pressures. For convenience, these pressures are often referred to as *economic squeezes*. Relevant to the issue of exploring economic squeezes, three overall questions have dominated the study. First, what structural sources of economic pressure could be detected in our society?[1] Second, is there evidence of behavioral responses to these economic squeezes? To the extent there is such evidence, the notion of economic pressures should be a useful research tool. Third, what socioeconomic and demographic factors have been contributing to the changing severity of such pressures over time, including the feedback effects of various responses to these pressures? These questions will be explored in detail throughout the book, using published Census and Current Population Survey (CPS) data but primarily relying on data on whites from the Public Use Samples of the 1960 and 1970 U.S. Censuses (PUS). By virtue of their large sizes, these samples permit detailed comparisons among rather narrowly defined subgroups in the population. Let us start, however, with a discussion of the analytical framework developed to investigate economic squeezes.

---

[1] By *structural* sources of economic pressure is meant pressures that arise out of the basic social and economic organization of our society. This organization is assumed to be relatively stable though changes in it will, of course, be occurring over time. Hence, stability is partly a function of the time framework being employed.

I. ECONOMIC SQUEEZES

The Components of Economic Squeezes

I will define economic squeezes as an imbalance among three components. One consists of those life-style aspirations that lead to a desire to consume certain market-produced goods and services. A second is the cost of these aspirations, focusing primarily on the "factor" rather than the "time" intensity of these costs—that is, the component of life-styles that is purchased on the market (see Smith 1977). Economists sometimes maintain that most families are faced with the same price structure at any point in time, due allowances being made for geographical differences in prices. Hence, differences in expenditures simply reflect differences in tastes or income. Over time, of course, there is the problem of the role of inflation in changing the cost of certain consumption aspirations. However, the situation is more complex than this as cost changes can occur that have little to do with price inflation. For example, the cost of consuming certain items of a given "constant" quality will vary by the age of a child. Keeping a boy in Levi's will involve considerably different outlays when he is 14 years old than when he is 4. Quantities as well as the sizes of a good which are consumed can also vary considerably, depending on the age of a child. A child of 14 can certainly consume more hamburger than a child of 4. It is hard to view such expenditure differences as indicative of a variation in taste. Rather, what they reflect are the problems of translating more general consumption goals into a particular shopping list. How these general goals get specified more exactly will often depend on a number of factors. In the example used here, the age of the child is one major factor affecting the cost of maintaining a given standard for children of different ages in the population at one point in time or of a given child as he or she matures. In sum, a second important component of the economic-pressure variable is the market cost of achieving certain life-style aspirations. In this study it is the cost of setting up and maintaining a household as well as the cost of supporting and socializing one's children over the family cycle that will receive particular attention.

The third component of the economic-pressures variable is the economic resources the family has (other than the wife's income) to achieve its consumption aspirations, given their cost. The major source of such economic resources has traditionally been the husband. Incomes of husbands will vary considerably at one point in time and over time for a host of reasons and unless the variations are always perfectly matched with variations in consumptions aspirations and costs, these three factors are likely to get out of balance at times with the result that, given costs, consumption aspirations will sometimes exceed the economic purchasing ability of the husband. It is when this happens that economic squeezes may develop.

I. Economic Squeezes 7

One of my major goals has been to explore some of the conditions under which such economic pressures do arise by studying the circumstances that produce variations and changes in: (*a*) life-styles (and hence consumption aspirations); (*b*) the husband's economic ability to achieve desired consumption aspirations; and (*c*) the cost of achieving these aspirations. By analyzing these three components separately and together to see how they balance out, I hope to achieve a deeper and more detailed understanding of family demographic behavior and of the major factors promoting changes in the nature of the wife's economic role in the family.

Given the desire to analyze the economic-pressures variable via an analysis of its components, the question is how to approach this complex problem—especially in view of the fact that direct data on life-style aspirations and their costs are lacking in the Census. Fundamental to the analysis has been the use of the sociological concept of reference groups (Merton 1957: Chapters 8 and 9). My strategy has been to try to distinguish different socioeconomic reference groups that will help pin down the role of life-style aspirations as well as that of costs and the husband's economic resources to achieve these aspirations. I think this can be done via the joint analysis of the husband's occupation and his life-cycle stage as this applies to a man's working (his career cycle) and to his and his wife's family life (their family cycle).

Occupation as a Conceptual Tool

Working at a given occupation is, first, the major source of a man's income and thus of his family's income. Occupations vary, of course, in their rates of remuneration. Hence, differentiating men by their occupation, classified partly according to the typical earnings level of the occupation, is one way of differentiating families according to the resources the husband usually can provide for achieving any particular consumption goal.

In addition, occupations are important reference groups, providing life-style models and values. Thus college professors are more likely to use each other as a reference group for life-styles than the businessmen or craftsmen they occasionally encounter in the course of their daily activities. The well-known push for public servants in certain occupations—such as firemen or policemen—to maintain or achieve economic parity with others in the same occupation in different areas is another example.[2] Second, occupation is the

[2] Evidence of this is found in the 1975 strike of San Francisco policemen to achieve economic parity with the Los Angeles police force and the 1975 Kansas City strike of firemen to achieve equal pay with policemen.

major determinant of one's socioeconomic position in society and, as such, it provides a reference group for the establishment of status-determined lifestyles.

If a man's own occupation group often constitutes a positive reference exhibiting life-style models that he and his family will desire or feel constrained to emulate, then this provides a means of studying one type of relative economic deprivation that might produce economic squeezes. We can measure this by comparing the actual earnings of the husband to the general earnings level of men in his occupation. The extent to which his earnings are below average for his occupation would then be an indication of the degree of relative economic deprivation he and his family might be experiencing. This, in turn, should be related to the wife's labor-force behavior as well as to other behavioral responses.

This is a stratified society and families use as a reference group not only other families whose husbands are in similar occupatons. They also make comparisons between themselves and others outside their own occupational reference groups. For one thing, people have perceptions about how the "average" American family lives and the relative position of their own occupational reference group in comparison. These comparisons, in turn, may result in a positive or negative evaluation of their own relative economic position. This process should lead to an inverse relationship between occupations classified by earnings level and the degree of economic pressure experienced.

Again, since this is a stratified society, people often perceive themselves as having a certain place in this stratification system. However, this "place" may, at times, be threatened by income similarities among differentiated reference groups and may result in economic squeezes. Thus, college professors might experience at least a slight twinge of discomfort when they read in the newspaper that the garbage collectors of some cities have comparable incomes. More important, however, I would hypothesize that families of men in white-collar occupations have certain shared life-style aspirations that sometimes involve more expensive consumption patterns than those considered obligatory among manual workers' families. One example of this is the relatively high educational attainment children of white-collar workers need to achieve in order to avoid downward occupational mobility. However, families of men in lower-paid white-collar occupations are not in any better position economically to achieve these white-collar life-styles than many blue-collar worker families. Hence, families of men in lower white-collar occupations are likely to find themselves in a chronic squeeze—caught between relatively high life-style aspirations and the very limited economic resources of the husband to achieve these aspirations.

In sum, then, the husband's occupational-earnings group can provide a multifaceted tool for analyzing sources of economic pressures. On the one hand, it is an indication of the husband's general economic level and hence of his usual ability to achieve certain consumption goals. On the other hand, an occupational classification of men and their families will provide us with a variety of reference groups—both positive and negative. A knowledge of these, the typical income level of the occupation, and the husband's particular income should go a long way towards helping us detect situations of relative economic deprivation, with resulting responses in socioeconomic and demographic behavior.

II. CAREER AND FAMILY-CYCLE STAGES

The second analytical tool that I think is indispensable in the detection and specification of sources of economic squeezes is the concept of life-cycle and life-cycle stages. We can apply this concept to both an individual's family life and to his working life. We think of each of these as forming a cycle—a family cycle and a career cycle. In the case of the family cycle, there are actually two such cycles since most people are involved in at least two families during their lives—their family of orientation and their family of procreation. From the point of view of the individual, the cycle in the family of orientation can be divided up into a number of stages—how many depending partly on our analytical interests. The cycle in the individual's family of procreation can also be divided up into a number of stages (see also Glick 1977; Glick and Parke 1965; and Uhlenberg 1974). For example, there is the period before the birth of the first child when the young couple are alone, then the period of childbearing and early childrearing when there are very young children in the home, followed by the period when all children are of school age but are still preadolescents. This stage will gradually develop into the stage when most or all children are adolescents and then into the period when they start to leave home and become financially independent. Finally, there is the stage when the couple is again alone until death eventually ends the cycle. How long each stage lasts and how sharply the stages are demarcated will depend on the number and spacing of children, on the one hand, and the advent of divorce or death, on the other. High fertility and/or wide-spacing of children will tend to prolong some stages and make them run together, whereas close spacing and/or low fertility will tend to lead to relatively sharply defined stages, some of which are short in duration. And, of course, the family cycle can be terminated or transformed at any stage by death or divorce.

Career cycles will also involve several stages. First entry into the labor force, or perhaps when the man makes a relatively permanent commitment to working, signals the start of the career cycle. He will be a beginning worker and will gradually gain experience and skills that will affect his status and earning in the occupation as he ages. Finally, death or retirement ends the career cycle.

The concepts of family cycles and career cycles are essential analytical tools in studying all three components of the economic-pressure variable. To begin with, family-cycle and career-cycle stages are themselves a source of reference group comparisons as well as a means of modifying other reference group expectations. In addition, earnings vary considerably by age so that the resources needed to achieve a given life-style are not constant over the life-cycle or among men at different life-cycle stages. Hence, life-cycles present several interesting analytical possibilities.

For example, one's family of orientation should provide an important reference for life-style aspirations—especially among young adults who have only recently left home and who have not yet "collected" many other additional reference groups. Richard Easterlin has approached the problem of relative economic deprivation from this perspective. Easterlin argues that the consumption aspirations of young people are formed during adolescence in their parents' households. Given this premise, his concern has been to estimate the extent to which economic and demographic conditions have operated to instill high or low consumption aspirations for particular cohorts and how these conditions have made it easy or difficult to attain these consumption goals on the young husband's income alone (Easterlin 1968, 1973). Easterlin's major interest is in the explanation of fertility but, as he has also pointed out, an additional concomitant of this kind of relative economic deprivation is the increased labor-force participation of young wives (Easterlin 1973). Hence, Easterlin's rationale provides us with another way of investigating sources of economic pressure, since one might try to approximate intergenerational comparisons by comparing the 1960–1970 changes in the relative economic position of younger and older males.

Career-cycle stage will also operate to modify reference groups based on occuption alone by creating new reference groups within the larger occupational group. Thus few people will have the normative expectation that young men just entering an occupation will earn as much as when they are older and more experienced. By and large, I would argue that there is a general feeling in our society that the level of living families should not decline with age, even if reality sometimes disappoints us in this respect. Moreover, another manifestation of this attitude is the additional feeling on the part of somewhat older men and their families that they ought to be able to maintain a comparable or even sometimes higher life-style than

II. Career and Family-Cycle Stages

younger, less experienced men in the same general occupational reference group. In other words, people's ideas about how their level of living should change over their life course get translated into ideas about how levels of living should vary across age groups at one point in time. As a consequence, they set up reference group comparisons that not only include their own past and presumed future, but also *contemporaneous* reference groups consisting of others at different stages of the career and family cycles.[3]

This hypothesis certainly seems consistent with the considerable emphasis among government, management, labor, and the public on the importance of rewarding seniority on the job and greater occupational experience with higher income and greater job security. In the process, however, age differentials in rewards almost invariably occur and become legitimized. Moreover, age-related differentials in rewards are seen as part of the incentive system in most work organizations. This is why across-the-board absolute increases in salaries or wages are often considered detrimental to morale as they operate to reduce the relative rewards among various levels in the hierarchy. Similarly, shortages of qualified young workers put an upward pressure on beginners' wages but this, in turn, puts pressure on the whole wage structure of an organization. Consequently, management must choose between raising the whole wage structure or paying "disproportionately" high salaries to new entrants (the young, usually). The latter strategy not only might affect people at higher levels (who will feel that their experience and years of service are no longer being adequately rewarded relative to that of beginners), but it also affects the new entrants who tend to use the experience of more senior personnel as the model for their future expectations. As a consequence, if the age profile of earnings gets rather flat, the organization becomes less attractive to them on a long-run basis. Hence, norms regarding lifetime changes in consumption almost inevitably come to include normative expectations regarding age differences in consumption levels at one point in time. In sum, career-cycle stages provide positive and negative reference groups for people and modify occupationally determined life-style aspirations. In addition, the resources to achieve consumption goals vary over a man's career cycle and among men at different career-cycle stages.

Switching our focus now to family-cycle stages, it is possible to see that they too can help produce economic squeezes because they will strongly

---

[3]As demographers who teach should be well aware, understanding the distinction between real and synthetic cohorts does not come too naturally to people. There seems to be a very strong tendency to interpret age differences in a phenomenon in life-cycle terms and the fact that the experiences of a real cohort can be quite different from those of a synthetic cohort is something that is not readily perceived.

affect both consumption aspirations and their cost. This is because the type of life-style (e.g., the type of household) people desire varies over the family cycle and so does the cost of setting up and maintaining a household. In general, there appear to be at least two peak periods of expense over the family cycle in contemporary American society. The first occurs when (and if) the young couple is trying to set up a household suitable for childbearing. At that period the investments in housing and heavy household consumer durables are likely to be high—or least the desire to invest in them is strong. Since the direct money costs of children vary considerably by age and indications are that adolescent children are the most expensive to support, the second peak period of costs should arise when families are at a later stage of the family cycle with adolescent children in the home.[4]

In sum, consumption goals vary by life-cycle stage and hence so do their cost and so does the income required to achieve such goals. An important research question then is not only how each of these three factors vary individually over the life-cycle and among groups at different life-cycle stages, but also how they balance out. Do income variations parallel variations in the cost of maintaining or achieving desired living levels or are there predictable life-cycle stages where the family's consumption goals are likely to exceed the husband's economic ability to achieve these goals, and families find themselves in what Wilensky has called the "life-cycle squeeze" (Wilensky 1963)? Furthermore, do these life-cycle squeezes, if they exist, affect some occupational groups more seriously than others? To the extent we can specify such life-cycle squeeze points and the occupational groups they affect more strongly, we can again, identify situations where a variety of adaptive behavioral strategies may be observed and used as tests of the life-cycle squeeze hypothesis.

III. RELATIVE ECONOMIC STATUS AS A CONCEPTUAL TOOL

Reference Group Theory and Related Sociological Concepts

The notion that people evaluate their well-being by comparing their position with significant others is commonly used in the sociological literature. It cuts across a wide variety of sociological perspectives, ranging

---

[4]At least one additional life-cycle squeeze seems intrinsic to the socioeconomic organization of contemporary Western society. This is the economic squeeze that often occurs when the husband and his wife if she has been working retire from market employment. This is the third squeeze of old age when income may drop precipitously because of the loss of earnings.

III. Relative Economic Status as a Conceptual Tool

from social-psychological to structural–functional approaches. However, the reference-group concept formulated by Merton and Rossi has been especially influential in the present study (Merton 1957: Chapter 8). Five of their hypotheses about reference-group processes have been particularly useful. The first is that people evaluate their position in comparison to important reference groups and, on the basis of this comparison, they may (or may not, depending on the circumstances) experience feelings of relative deprivation. Second, a number of reference groups rather than just one may be influential in the evaluation of one's position (Merton 1957: 241ff). Third, reference groups may consist of people in the same or different social statuses (or categories) and they may involve those who do or do *not* belong to the same membership group (Merton 1957: 231–234). Fourth, reference groups may provide negative as well as positive standards of comparison (Merton 1957:300–301). Fifth, reference group standards may often have a strong normative component (Merton 1957: 283ff, see also Turner 1956).

Recent formulations in the area of social exchange theory and distributive justice indicate that the notion of evaluating one's position relative to certain significant others continues to be an important theoretical orientation (Berger, Zelditch, Anderson, and Cohen 1972). Thus, one of the arguments that Berger and his colleagues make is that individuals are likely to experience feelings of injustice when the allocation of rewards is not commensurate with the normative expectations of established "referential structures," despite a similarity of characteristics between the individual(s) and the "generalized others" of the referential structure. For example, an airline mechanic will experience feelings of distributive injustice if his hourly wages are below those of airline mechanics in general, even though his qualifications and experience are not below average. Such ideas obviously have a strong resemblance to Merton's notion of reference-group comparisons and relative deprivation. While Berger *et al.* are talking about distributive *justice*, it is clear that those who are experiencing injustice are also probably experiencing feelings of relative deprivation. However it does not necessarily follow that the reverse is true. A man may earn less than others in the same occupation because he is somewhat less well trained or in poor health or for a variety of other reasons. Under such conditions, he may not feel the victim of injustice. Nevertheless, if certain group life-style standards have some normative backing to them, then despite extenuating circumstances relative deprivation may still be experienced though not necessarily with feelings of distributive injustice. Hence, in a sense, Berger and his coworkers are focusing on a special case of one type of reference-group comparison process. However, I am more concerned with the broader concept of relative deprivation, whether or not distributive injustice is also involved.

Nevertheless, one aspect of the status value formulation of the problem of distributive justice holds considerable interest for the present analysis. This is the notion that when distributive justice does *not* occur, an imbalanced situation arises and "imbalanced status situations produce tensions and pressures for change [Berger *et al.* 1972: 145]." One might extend this notion to all situations of perceived relative deprivation, while recognizing that the tensions and pressures for change that are thereby produced are most acute when the relative deprivation also involves a perceived injustice in distributive rewards.

In general, all these hypotheses concerning the process of relative deprivation have played a fundamental role in the development of an analytic framework for the present study. Thus, the basic operating assumptions involve, first, the notion that families compare their economic position to groups in which the husband is in a different type of occupation and to groups in which the husband is in the same occupation. Second, families will compare their economic well-being to reference groups represented by their own past experiences and their presumed future as well as to contemporaneous reference groups of people at different stages of the life-cycle, but with other characteristics in common such as the occupation of the husband. Given this analytical approach, the study is then particularly concerned with trying to determine whether the tensions that arise when relative deprivation is probably experienced do, in fact, lead to observable behavioral changes, provided the opportunities for change arise.

Relative Economic Status and Research on Fertility

While sociologists have been very active in the conceptualization of the "reference other orientation," as Schmitt has called it (1972), there has been relatively little empirical work done on the possible consequences of relative economic deprivation when *occupational* reference groups are at issue. In fact, to my knowledge, little seems to have been done on occupational reference groups at all. More pertinently, the reference-group perspective, as such, has not been extensively exploited by sociologists in the analysis of demographic behavior or the related problem of wives' labor-force participation. A major exception to this is Banks's book, *Prosperity and Parenthood* (1954). Essentially, this is a study of the growing difficulties the Victorian middle classes were experiencing in maintaining a life-style appropriate to their own social-class reference group and the implications of these growing difficulties for fertility behavior. However, although relatively uncommon in social-demographic research, economic concepts that are related to the logic of reference-group analysis have been extensively used in demographic research by economists, as well as by a number of social demographers who have been influenced by economic perspectives.

The concept of relative economic status has been most frequently employed by economists and more economically oriented demographers in the analysis of fertility. Easterlin's work is one outstanding example (Easterlin 1968, 1973, 1978). In his research, Easterlin uses socialization experiences in the parental household as the source of consumptions standards that young people may or may not have trouble emulating, depending on their relative economic position during the early reproductive period. Their fertility behavior will, in turn, be positively or negatively affected by their relative economic status, depending on how favorable that status is (Easterlin 1968, 1969, 1973).

However, an individual's life-style aspirations, or preferences, are not entirely determined by his experiences in his parent's household. Nor are preferences acquired in youth immutable throughout life. As Easterlin remarks:

> one's preference system at any given time may be viewed as molded by heredity and past and current environment. The process starts with birth and continues through the life cycle. Religion, color, nativity, place of residence, and education enter into the shaping of tastes. So, too, does one's childhood and adolescent experience in one's own home with material affluence and family size. One reaches family-building age with preferences already molded by this heritage, but these preferences are subsequently modified by ongoing occupational, income, and family building experiences, among others [1969:135].

One task of the present study is to propose reference groups that, in addition to the parental household, will shape consumption aspirations and, as a result, affect socioeconomic and demographic behavior. This has been done to some extent by others in the area of fertility research (Freedman 1963; Freedman and Coombs 1966; Bean and Wood 1974; Bernhardt 1972; Reed, Udry, and Ruppert 1975; Leibenstein 1974). My own efforts in setting up a variety of reference groups are basically an extension and elaboration of these approaches, as well as of the theoretically based sociological concept of reference groups.

Empirical Status of Reference-Group-Based Attitudes

The major sources of data for this study are the 1960 and 1970 Public Use Samples. These data greatly facilitate the exploration of several types of problems. By virtue of their large sample sizes, it is possible to make a number of reference-group comparisons that I have hypothesized are important in assessing relative economic status—for example, the economic position of lower-income white-collar workers compared to craft workers, the economic position of men with adolescent children to support versus that of those with less expensive children. However, there are a number of factors involved in the analytical framework that cannot be explored with the PUS data employed here. One obvious example arises because several possibly important reference groups cannot be empirically identified with this data base—kin, neighbors, work companions, friends, etc. Furthermore, some reference groups will necessarily be very crudely measured. For example, occupations are, of necessity, highly grouped. In addition unmeasured geographical variations introduce other measurement problems that cannot be resolved.

A more fundamental problem, however, is that there are a number of basic assumptions that are critical to the analytical framework but which cannot be empirically validated with the PUS data. One concerns what might be called the social–psychological "glue" that holds the theory together. This is the notion that people do, in fact, compare their personal situations with those of others in important reference categories, that unfavorable comparisons do lead to subjective feelings of relative deprivation (or injustice) and that these, in turn, influence behavior. Given the enormous and growing literature in sociology concerning reference-group theories and distributive justice as well as the economic literature dealing with relative income, the social–psychological assumptions used here do not appear highly controversial. Nevertheless, while "reference other" concepts and theoretical formulations are common, their empirical documentation is much less frequent—especially outside of a laboratory setting.

Another serious concern is the exact nature of the reference groups, comparisons people make. Are inter- and intra-occupational comparisons often made? How important are they as a source of feelings of relative deprivation? To what extent is this true for life-cycle comparisons as well? Unfortunately, there is not much detailed empirical documentation of whether such comparisons are actually common—perhaps because they appear so self-evident to people that they hold little intrinsic research interest. Hence much of the evidence relevant to the question of occupational and life-cycle comparisons is fragmentary and often tangential to the major issues of concern here. Nevertheless, what data do exist indicate that occupation and life-cycle stage form a meaningful point of comparison, especially with regard to the appropriateness of differential rewards.

Research by Jasso and Rossi (1977) on distributive justice indicated that their respondents thought differential earnings were just, given differences in a number of selected characteristics such as occupation, marital status,

III. Relative Economic Status as a Conceptual Tool

number of children, sex, education, and earnings. This implies that people who see themselves in a different position within an occupational hierarchy will have certain predictable expectations about their "just" rewards. These expectations would, furthermore, be based on two sorts of comparisons. One would be their "just" rewards relative to those in occupations at both higher and lower levels. The other would be rewards they would expect to have by virtue of membership in a particular occupational group. In other words, both inter- and intraoccupational comparisons of earnings would be involved.

A similar relationship regarding the evaluation of just differentials in rewards was found by Jasso and Rossi for educational attainment as well as for occupation—the higher the educational level, ceteris paribus, the more likely respondents were to feel that the individual was underpaid. To the extent some occupations are characterized by relatively high educational attainments but relatively low earnings (a feature of a number of white-collar occupations), this suggests that a certain amount of relative deprivation is inherent in a system characterized, on the one hand, by such notions of distributive justice and, on the other, by the earnings actually observed for lower level white-collar occupations.

Jasso and Rossi's findings showed that differentials in rewards according to life-cycle stage were also considered just. Thus, other things being equal, respondents were more likely to feel that married people were underpaid compared to single. Furthermore, the greater the number of children, the more likely an individual or couple was thought to be underpaid. All this indicates that the respondents felt that differentials in familial responsibilities justify differentials in rewards.

Further evidence that people use others in the same group or similar occupational groups as appropriate reference standards was the previously mentioned tendency of government employees to try to achieve parity with similar occupational groups in the same or different localities. This tendency was also noticeable in a study of agreements involving state and local government employees by the Bureau of Labor Statistics (BLS) in the 1970s (U.S. Bureau of Labor Statistics 1975a: 26, 1976a: 39).[5] BLS studies of collective bargaining agreements in private industry and in public employment also indicate that job experience or seniority are important factors in promotions and wages (U.S. Bureau of Labor Statistics 1970a, 1976a: 39). This suggests general support for the notion that rewards should not deteriorate with age but, if anything, improve.

Returning to the question of *inter*occupational reference group com-

---

[5]In addition, to the extent reference groups are, in part, based on the frequency of association, a study by Mackenzie of skilled craftsmen, clerks, and managers indicated that the leisure-time companionship of these three occupational groups were largely separate (Mackenzie 1973: 153).

parisons, Blau and Duncan's study provides some evidence—albeit indirect—that blue-collar occupations provide a negative reference group for white-collar workers in spite of the sometimes higher earnings of manual jobs. What they found was an apparent boundary limit of inter- and intragenerational downward mobility between white-collar and blue-collar occupations (Blau and Duncan 1967: 58ff). They attributed this to an unwillingness on the part of downwardly mobile males of white-collar origins to move into blue-collar jobs but to settle, instead, for poorer-paying white-collar jobs (Blau and Duncan 1967: 63).[6] The extent to which white-collar status is so important for some men that they choose lower paying white-collar jobs, as opposed to better paying blue-collar ones, influences the acuteness of the economic squeeze experienced by such men and their families. For surely it is not just the white-collar status of the occupation alone that is at issue with them but a whole white-collar life-style as well. If so, then their economic ability to achieve this is severely hampered by an earnings level that is not only low relative to white-collar standards but relative to the actual earnings levels exhibited by many men in manual occupations as well. In short, the ability to maintain a social distance between themselves and manual workers must be particularly difficult.[7]

Finally, numerous studies seem to indicate that at least in the case of the

---

[6]However, many such men may not really have the option of moving into higher-paying blue-collar occupations. They would probably not have access to blue-collar job networks—especially in the crafts—and many of the same characteristics that make some sons of higher-level white-collar fathers unsuccessful in white-collar employment probably also make it unlikely that these sons can make a go of it in higher-level manual jobs. Hence, the choice to remain a white-collar worker may not be based primarily on status considerations but on economic ones as well. In any event, to the extent white-collar life styles are important to these men—especially white-collar mobility aspirations for their children—their position does appear rather unenviable.

[7]Runciman found some support for the notion that English workers in different classes employed different reference groups to evaluate their relative economic status (Runciman 1968). For example, he found that middle-income *non*manual workers were more likely than middle- or higher-income *manual* workers to believe that others were doing noticeably better than themselves. Runciman interpreted this to mean that since manual workers tended to compare themselves to other manual workers, they experienced less relative deprivation despite lower actual income than did nonmanual middle-income workers who compared themselves to others within the nonmanual group (Runciman 1968: 209). Furthermore, Runciman had some interesting responses to the following question: "What income do you think is necessary for you (your husband) in order to maintain a proper standard of living for people like yourself? [Runciman 1968: 215]." By and large, he found that a much larger proportion of the manual than nonmanual workers would be satisfied with roughly the same income. For example, 56% of the highly paid manual workers and 26% of the medium paid fell into this category compared to 42% and 26% respectively of the nonmanual workers (Runciman 1968: 217). This is despite the fact that the high-income manual workers of his study had much lower incomes than the high-income nonmanual workers. Once again this indicates that the manual and nonmanual families seemed to operate in different reference groups. How well these findings would hold up for the United States, however, is not at all certain.

professions, socialization into a profession involves the growth of strong group identifications with the particular profession plus the development of well-defined ideas of what it means to be a professional in general. It is tempting to believe that such group-based norms also involve the development of life-style patterns and standards—especially with regard to the socialization of one's children. I would surmise that such life-style aspirations might even tend to transcend particular professions, especially in those clusters of professions and semiprofessions that interact on a frequent basis in the work organization. An outstanding example would be the numerous professional and technical occupations involved in the delivery of health care. And, in general, one might hypothesize that one source of interoccupational comparisons, especially ones that may lead to the diffusion of certain life-style aspirations, may be found among diverse occupational groups whose members are involved in frequent or daily interactions in the course of doing their jobs. This would again be much more likely to lead to interoccupational reference group comparisons within white-collar occupations and blue-collar occupations separately rather than across this dividing line since manual workers and white-collar workers are relatively insulated from each other.[8] One can also see, furthermore, how within the white-collar group rather acute feelings of relative deprivation might sometimes arise among lower-paid white-collar workers since they may often interact during the work day with much higher level workers (e.g., medical technicians and nurses with physicians).

In conclusion, although the data are frustratingly incomplete and often annoyingly tangential, they do suggest that life-cycle as well as inter- and intraoccupational reference-group comparisons are a common feature of social life—perhaps so common that it has not seemed very interesting to document their prevalence. However, it is hoped this study can indicate that people behave as if they are making certain reference-group comparisons. If it does, perhaps other sociologists will then find it important to conduct a more rigorous empirical investigation of the validity of these important assumptions. Unfortunately, it is beyond the scope of this analysis to do so.

IV. EXTENSION OF MODEL

Given an economic squeeze approach, the study's initial focus on factors affecting wives' economic role in the family gradually evolved into an

---

[8]An important exception to this would be a number of manual types of occupations that involve production of goods or services for white-collar families directly, for example, house painters and other construction and service workers that get a more intimate glimpse of "how the other half lives." In addition, it would be interesting to study the types of reference-group standards that families of blue-collar workers develop when the wife is in a white-collar occupation.

analysis of more general socioeconomic and demographic characteristics and behavior. After all, if wives' economic behavior is affected by economic squeezes, then we must also study the characteristics of other family members besides the wife and how families, and the constraints under which they operate, vary among different subgroups in the population and over time.[9] Second, if wives' labor-force participation can be viewed as one response to economic squeezes, this naturally raises the possibility of other additional or even alternative behavioral responses to the same squeezes. Some of these responses will include a variety of behaviors on the part of the wife and some will involve the behavior of other family members. For example, such responses could include postponed marriage (by men and/or women), moonlighting or overtime work by husbands, delayed and/or restricted childbearing, and so on. The lack of economic pressures, or their amelioration may, in turn, elicit a reversal in such responses or obviate them entirely.

In sum, as the analytical model developed, concentrating solely on wives' economic behavior increasingly appeared to be highly arbitrary and unnecessarily limited the generalizability of the model. As a consequence, the focus of the study gradually shifted to the family as the more appropriate unit of analysis, including a much broader range of interrelated socioeconomic and demographic behaviors rather than just limiting itself to the analysis of wives' labor-force participation. As a result, two additional types of behavioral patterns will also be investigated. One is occupational differences in men's age at marriage and the changes in this over time. For the second, we will pay some attention to fertility behavior, including the spacing and number of children, how this has changed over time, and how patterns vary by the husband's occupation.

Microeconomic Models

The expansion of the theoretical model used in this study to include marriage and fertility behavior as well as wives' economic behavior is, of course, quite consistent with recent trends in demographic and microeconomic analyses of fertility and women's work behavior. But it also differs significantly from the microeconomic model of a number of economists now working in this area (Ben-Porath 1974; Cain and Dooley 1976; Mincer 1963; Schultz 1975; Willis 1974). For example, Mincer had argued:

[9]The economic role of family members other than the husband and wife should also be considered. However, for analytical simplicity this was ignored in the empirical analysis of this study.

IV. Extension of Model

that the choices of labor and family size are not causally related to one another. Rather, these choices are simultaneously determined by the same basic economic variables. The higher the female wage rate and the lower the husband's earning power, the higher the labor-force rate and the smaller the fertility rate. The relation between fertility rate and labor-force participation is not autonomous; it does not provide new insight once the two structural relations are specified [1963: 78–79].

More recently, Willis developed a rather elaborate model based on essentially the same argument as Mincer's (Willis 1974). According to Willis, at the outset of marriage, husband and wife adopt a utility-maximizing lifetime plan for (a) the number of children they will have; (b) the expenditures of time and money they will make on these children; as well as (c) the expenditures of time and money they will make on other sources of parental satisfaction not related to children; and (d) the wife's amount of life-time labor supply after marriage—to the market and in the home. This utility maximization model is made possible, furthermore, by the analytical assumption that the couple will "possess perfect foresight concerning all relevant demographic and economic variables over the course of their marriage . . . [Willis 1974: 28]." Hence, in this model of wife's labor supply, fertility, and a number of other variables are all endogenous. The only explicitly recognized exogenous variables are: (a) the husband's life-time income; (b) the wife's stock of human capital at the outset of marriage; and (c) the life-span of the wife after marriage (Willis 1974: 46). It is not clear how "tastes" fit into this model but they certainly do not seem to be treated as explicitly exogenous factors.[10]

Now, if the wife's life-time labor supply and fertility are both determined at the outset of marriage, one might argue, I suppose, that parents have made these decisions with the full knowledge of the costs involved and will not be subject to the kind of "life-cycle squeezes" proposed in this study. As a consequence, the couple's utility-maximization procedure ought to enable them to avoid "squeeze" situations. To begin with, I am not sure this is true. Even if one accepts all the assumptions of Willis's model, it is not clear how much my approach is in conflict. Willis is, after all, talking about decisions regarding *total* numbers of children and the wife's *total* labor supplied over her married life, whereas my analysis could be interpreted as trying to get at how wives' presumed preset total labor supply tends to be distributed over

---

[10]"Tastes" seem to be a class of variables that economists often, though not always, feel uncomfortable about handling. As Bowen and Finegan remark, "in most [presumably economic] studies, 'tastes' is the emptiest of conceptual boxes [Bowen and Finegan 1969:19]." However, "tastes" (though not known by this term) are, in part, what sociology is all about.

the family cycle and why one particular labor-supply allocation pattern will be observed rather than another.[11]

Nevertheless, there is little doubt that the overall approach of the present investigation is incompatible with the Willis model in a number of major respects.[12] Most important is the difference in the assumptions about the analytical place of consumption aspirations or "tastes." In the present study tastes regarding "parental satisfaction other than children" are important exogenous factors to be explicitly taken into account. This is not to say that there is no discretionary element—even a large one—in taste formation or persistence. However, the fundamental assumption here is that tastes are learned through childhood and adult socialization and hence are partly determined by group membership and the consumption behaviors and standards of such groups. In a related fashion, the so-called quality of children is also not considered an entirely discretionary variable, but is partly determined by the general standard of living of the parents and will vary for parents in different socioeconomic groups. Furthermore, it is assumed that child quality cannot vary markedly among children in the same family, at least in a way that is entirely up to the discretion of the parents.[13]

My approach is also partly based on the assumption that consumption aspirations are not immutable over time—either from generation to generation or over the individual or couple's life-cycle. Socialization experiences, as Easterlin argues, can result in generational differences in life-style aspirations. Furthermore, couples have numerous experiences over their adult life-time that will alter these consumption aspirations in ways not anticipated when they were in their twenties.

In order to understand the full analytical implications of these alternative views of the function of tastes, it is important first to have a clear understanding of how different the variables *fertility* and *wives' labor-force participation* are. For one thing, some fertility decisions, once acted upon, are irrevocable. Futhermore, Americans in the twentieth century, at least, tend

---

[11]For some economic discussions of this issue, see Mincer (1962) and Smith (1977). In addition, in light of the empirical analysis in the main body of this book, we return to the question of wives' work patterns over the life-cycle, as to other issues, in Chapter 9 on family strategies.

[12]For discussions and criticisms of the utility-maximization model that are oriented toward its fertility implications see Blake (1968), Cramer (1979), Hout (1978), Leibenstein (1974), Namboodiri (1972), Turchi (1975a, 1975b).

[13]For a discussion of the problem of determining child quality and its possible variability among children within the same family and among different families see Ben–Porath (1974: 218), Blake (1968), Duesenberry (1960), Namboodiri (1972), Okun (1960), Turchi (1975a, 1975b). For a criticism of adopting a one-period life-time optimization plan including the determination of both the number and quality of children and the life-time labor-force participation of the wife, see Turchi (1975a: 48–49, 67–68; 1975b: 115–116).

IV. Extension of Model

to have their children relatively early and over a short period of years, though in recent years delayed childbearing has been on the rise. When we turn to wives' labor-force participation, however, we have a rather different situation. Labor-force decisions and behaviors *are* reversible. Furthermore, labor-force decisions can be made and remade over a rather long period of time as compared to the relatively brief childbearing period, though we may hypothesize that some labor-force decisions become less reversible as the woman ages.[14] Finally, we must remember that child care (at least the care of young children) and work have traditionally competed for women's time.

As a conseqence of the nature of the fertility and labor-force variables, on the one hand, and the different set of assumptions regarding tastes, on the other, fertility and wives' labor-force participation cannot reasonably be treated as typically endogenous variables in this study. For example, even if we could assume that most families engage in the kind of utility-maximization behavior posited by the microeconomic model (while moving some taste variables into an explicit exogenous category), if consumption aspiration can change over time, then families will often desire to rethink their utility function. However, once children are born, couples are no longer entirely free to rethink their decisions about fertility. But it is still possible to modify the couple's decision about the wife's labor-force behavior—both her total labor supply over the life-cycle and how it will be distributed. Since young children are an impediment to mothers' working and older children involve expenditure commitments (including previously unanticipated ones), then at this point in the revamping of the utility-maximization plans, number and ages of children become exogenous to wives' labor-force behavior.

There are numerous circumstances that might arise and affect wives' labor-force behavior after fateful fertility decision have already been made and carried out—circumstances that put the numbers and ages of children in the position of affecting wives' labor-force participation in ways not anticipated in the hypothesized "original" utility maximization plan. For example, a young couple may in all sincerity (and also in all innocence) decide they will prefer to "consume" children as opposed to other consumption goods and that the wife will not work after the birth of her first child. They then have these children. But over the years, experiences with

---

[14]However, part-way into the childbearing process couples may still be able to alter their completed fertility decisions. That this is a distinct possibility forms one critique of the microeconomic model (see, for example, Blake 1968; Namboodiri 1972: 198). Moreover, the notion that couples make final fertility decisions at the outset of marriage seems unlikely in view of past research on short- and long-term instabilities with regard to desired family size, expected family size and preferences versus completed family size (see Bumpass and Westoff 1970; Freedman, Combs, and Bumpass 1965; Lee 1980; Westoff, Mishler, and Kelly 1957; Westoff, Potter, and Sagi 1963).

new social groups (work-related friends, neighbors, etc.) they knew nothing about at the time of their fertility decisions, may operate to change their preference structure. They cannot, of course, send their children back at this point and they will be under some normative constraints to raise them according to certain minimum standards (even in the event they did not wish to do so). But they might also like to go to Europe as their next-door neighbors did last year (something which may never have occurred to them as possible or desirable when they were 25). In effect, 15 years later they find out they would like to have their cake and eat it too. Futhermore, they also find out they may be able to do just that if they reassess their earlier decision about the wife's life-time labor-market behavior and she goes out to work.

Another factor to consider is the monolithic character of the family which is presumed under the one-time utility-maximizing model. Without even raising the issue of the possibility of conflicting goals between spouses, there is no consideration of the dynamic element inherent in the very process of having a family.. As most parents come to realize, children develop rather decided preferences of their very own, and these preferences are not entirely a function of the socialization experience within the parental household but are, in addition, strongly influenced by peers and numerous other factors. Children's preferences should therefore impinge on parental consumption decisions regarding themselves and their children—whatever the presumed original trade-offs between consumption goods and children that the couple was willing to make when its fertility decisions were made and carried out. In short, the dynamics of family life, except perhaps under the most rigidly patriarchal conditions, will inevitably lead to some changes in "tastes" over time. The complete cast of characters usually do not make their appearance until after the first act.

To take another example, the price of achieving certain child "qualities" will change over time so that decisions made earlier in adult life on the basis of perceptions of prevailing price structure can no longer be transformed into behavior several years hence. Thus, parents' goals for children may involve the desire to invest sufficient inputs of market goods and services so that children are not downwardly mobile from their parents' general socioeconomic position. However, the price of the inputs necessary to enable children to maintain "parity" may go up over the years. Thus a high-school education is now virtually mandatory and a college degree is increasingly important to enter many white-collar occupations, a situation that was neither true nor foreseeable when some cohorts were presumably making their youthful utility-maximizing life-time plan. As Crowley pointed out in discussing the professional job market some years ago, prospects are not as favorable as they used to be for those with B.A. degrees or better. One consequence, he points out, is that professional and technical occupations are

IV. Extension of Model

increasingly becoming monopolized by those with at least a B.A. degree and, furthermore, college graduates are entering other fields such as management and sales to a much greater extent than they did in the past. This, in turn, results in or reflects rising entry requirements in a number of occupations, which probably limit opportunities for those with lower educational attainments (Crowley 1972).

In sum, the more sociological approach of this study differs considerably from that of microeconomic household utility models. A major effort is made here to deal explicitly with tastes—both taste differentials among population subgroups and changes in taste over time. Moreover, imperfect knowledge and changing constraints and the resulting sequential decision-making these often entail are of major research interest.

The Easterlin Hypothesis

A major advantage of extending the economic-sqeeze model to a variety of behaviors, in addition to wives' labor-force participation, is that it permits a close examination of theories of marriage and fertility that also emphasize the causal role of relative economic status. The major example of this is Easterlin's work and more recently that of Wachter (Easterlin 1968, 1969, 1973, 1978, 1980; Wachter 1977). Basically, Easterlin argues that in the United States during the period following World War II, young people entering the labor market had developed their consumption preferences in households that were hard-hit by the depression of the 1930s and by the shortage of consumption goods during the war years. As a consequence, their consumption aspirations were presumably more modest than those of young people raised in a time of greater prosperity. However, these same young people who were entering the labor market in the postwar period were a relatively small cohort—they were, as Easterlin puts it, the "echo" of the low depression fertility. Because of the small size of these depression cohorts plus the high demand for labor due to the extended postwar prosperity (among other factors), the market position of young men was highly favorable. As a result, their economic status improved over time relative to the economic status of their parental household during their adolescent years. According to Easterlin, this improvement in the relative economic status of young men encouraged early marriage and early childbearing in the postwar period.

The reverse situation, Easterlin argues, has been occurring in more recent years, with a resulting negative effect on the birth rate. First, another echo effect is operating—the entry into the labor market of the large baby-boom cohorts of the postwar period. Second, these young people were brought up in households that had experienced the long-term prosperity of the postwar

United States, and hence they have developed high consumption aspirations. However, for a variety of reasons—the large size of these cohorts being the main one—the economic position of such young men has been less than ideal. Over time, their economic position has been deteriorating relative to the economic position of the households in which their adolescent years were spent. One response to this deterioration in their economic position has been marriage and birth postponements which, in turn, have caused a decline in the birth rate and a rise in young wives' labor-force participation. However, when the small *baby-bust* cohorts now being born reach working age, this, in turn, will set the stage for another baby boom (Easterlin 1978). Thus, according to Easterlin, fertility fluctuations have started a cyclical process that should presumably keep repeating itself over time, barring the intervention of other, as yet unspecified, circumstances.

Both Easterlin's research and the present study rely heavily on the concept of reference-group comparisons and the role of relative economic deprivation in behavior. In particular, there is a common focus on the impact of changes in young men's relative economic status. Because both approaches stress the importance of relative economic deprivation as a causal factor and because wives' labor-force participation, as well as marriage and family formation, provide several of the possible responses to changes in relative economic status, the present investigation provides an opportunity to explore Easterlin's theories in some detail. This is achieved primarily through the evaluation of the theoretical and empirical status of the causal variables themselves. For example, does the present study lead to the same conclusions as Easterlin's regarding the relative economic status of various subgroups in the population and changes in this status over time? If it does, then this is additional confirmation of at least one aspect of Easterlin's theory—namely, that the relative-economic-status variable behaved in the way he proposed. However, if the results of my analysis of relative economic status are not similar to those of Easterlin, then this too has implications for the long-swing theory. Contradictory findings mean that, even if there is agreement on the presumed demographic effects of relative deprivation, some questions may arise about a theory whose independent variables do not quite behave as originally proposed.

Although there are several major points of similarily between Easterlin's theoretical model and the one developed here, there are also important differences. As will become apparent in the course of this analysis, these differences lead to findings and predictions that are not entirely compatible with those of Easterlin. Although the contrasts between the two approaches will be discussed in some detail at relevant points in the study, a preliminary comment is in order now.

First of all, the present study is characterized by a far more elaborate set of

IV. Extension of Model

reference-group comparisons. By and large, Easterlin limits his analysis of relative economic status to the presumed comparison young people make between their own actual economic position and that of the parental household during adolescence. Theoretically, Easterlin seems to argue that other relevant comparisons do arise as people get older;[15] however, he does not attempt to specify any of them or study their effects. I have argued that a number of contemporaneous (as well as longitudinal) occupational and age-related reference groups are important in the assessment of relative economic status (see also Leibenstein 1976). By and large, I have *not* found that in cross-section the trends in the relative income position of males over time have led to exactly the same conclusions as the findings based on the lagged-relative-income variable used by Easterlin. Nor do I think that the evidence indicates that the relative income position of young men will in the 1980s return to the favorable conditions of the 1950s as Easterlin has recently argued (Easterlin 1978; see also Oppenheimer 1979). However, this question will be discussed at length in Chapter 3.

A second important divergence in perspective has to do with whether income alone is an adequate proxy for economic status. Easterlin tends to assume, as do other economists, that this is the case. However, as I have already argued at length, there is reason to doubt this assumption. With reference to the Easterlin hypothesis in particular, it is important to consider whether the cost of attaining and maintaining similar life-styles changes over time and varies among age groups, depending on a variety of factors. If this is the case, then a proper evaluation of changes in the relative economic position of young adults should take into account changes in cost that may offset or enhance their relative income position. Such a discussion is undertaken in Chapters 4 and 5.

Perhaps one of the major differences between the present analysis of relative economic status and that of Easterlin has to do with the role of wives' labor-market behavior in assessing relative economic status. Easterlin does not explicitly consider the role of wives' contribution to the family as a possibly exogenous variable. He views it primarily as a response to relative economic deprivation. However, wives' economic behavior is a central variable in this study. Hence, I have focused on the economic roles of women quite explicitly and rather carefully, in terms of both the determinants and *consequences* of their labor-market behavior. In particular, I will argue that wives' economic behavior has an impact on the relative economic position of younger and older families, an impact that Easterlin largely ignores. As a

---

[15]Easterlin's statement, as quoted on p. 15 of this chapter, certainly seems to indicate that he considers the possibility of additional reference groups as reasonable.

consequence of this impact, changes in wives' economic behavior will result in certain feedback effects. These feedback effects may, in essence, be instrumental in changing women's work behavior further still. Thus, one issue we will consider in Chapter 8 is whether, given a relative deprivation model, changes in wives' labor-force participation have not started a different kind of self-generating process than that proposed by Easterlin—one that continually produces socioeconomic pressures for the further increase in wives' work involvement.

Finally, with regard to the relevance of this study to the Easterlin hypothesis, it is worthwhile pointing out that the PUS data used here have one important advantage over the published CPS data used by Easterlin. This is the ability to organize the data in terms of the socioeconomic characteristics of the husband and to look at the characteristics of husbands and wives jointly. Since what is at issue in Easterlin's theory is the fertility behavior of couples and how this is influenced by the *husband's* socioeconomic characteristics (as well as the wife's), the PUS data provide a valuable research opportunity. The disadvantage, of course, is that samples of only two censuses could be studied, thus limiting time-series analysis sharply.

V. CHANGING SEX-ROLE ATTITUDES

By and large, I have not tried to deal directly with sex-role norms or changes in them over time in this study. This is particularly true with regard to the question of sex-role attitudes as potentially important *determinants* of wives' economic or family behavior. There are a number of reasons, both practical and substantive, for this research decision. On the practical side, the major data sources for this study are from 1960 and 1970 PUS plus published data from the CPS. These do not include information on sex-role attitudes; nor did it seem likely that a good proxy for such attitudes could be found in data of this type. Hence, there was no way to test hypotheses about the possible effect of sex-role norms on women's economic and sociodemographic behavior.

In addition to these practical constraints, there were important substantive reasons for not putting a major emphasis on the possibly exogenous nature of sex-role attitudes. There is considerable empirical evidence indicating that such attitudes have not been the major, or even an important, underlying determinant of American women's changing work patterns, much less their

V. Changing Sex-Role Attitudes

demographic behavior.[16] This is most clearly indicated by comparing the timing of behavioral changes to the timing of attitudinal changes.

The early postwar period saw very substantial shifts in the pattern and extent of married women's labor-force participation. Between 1940 and 1950 the proportion of married women (husbands present) who were in the labor force rose from 14 to 22%; between 1950 and 1960 it rose still more to 31% (Oppenheimer 1970: 11). By 1970 it was 39% (U.S. Bureau of the Census 1973a: Table 216). Even more impressive was the changing relationship between female labor-force participation and the family cycle. In 1940, as in 1900, the work rates of women were highest for the young and declined steadily with age. Starting some time in the 1940s, however, this traditional pattern was transformed. One major departure was the entry, or reentry, of women past 35 into the labor force—those whose children had usually reached school age. For example, in 1940, of married women (husband present), only 15 and 11% respectively of 35–44- and 45–54-year-olds were in the labor force. By 1950, these proportions had risen to 26 and 23%, and in 1960 they were all the way up to 36 and 39% (Oppenheimer 1970: 11). By 1970, the proportions were 46 and 47% (U.S. Bureau of the Census 1973a: Table 216).

A second major postwar trend was the increased labor-force participation of younger married women, including women with preschool children. While, initially, not as dramatic a rise as that exhibited by older women, the increases were still substantial, especially in view of the sizable baby boom occurring at the same time. The 1940 work rates for married women in the 20–34 age groups was rather low. Consider married women aged 25–29, for example. In 1940, only 18% of them were in the labor force. This rose to 22% by 1950 and went up to 27% by 1960—a rise of 50% in the work rate during the 1940–1960 period (Oppenheimer 1970: 11). It then increased substantially again, to 38% in 1970 (U.S. Bureau of the Census 1973a: Table 216). These shifts do not reflect merely compositional changes in the proportions with preschool children in the home. The work rates of women with preschool children also rose substantially during this period. For 25–29-year-old married women with preschoolers in the home, it increased from 7% in 1940 to 12% in 1950, to 19% in 1960. It then rose rapidly to 28% in 1970.[17]

---

[16] For an opposing view of the effect of changes in sex-role attitudes on fertility, see Scanzoni (1975, 1976). Scanzoni's analysis is based on cross-sectional rather than longitudinal data. This makes it very difficult to ascertain the causal ordering of variables, particularly those involving attitudes.

[17] Data for 1940, 1960, and 1970 include only married women with husbands present whereas the 1950 data refer to all married women. Data for 1940 and 1970 refer to women with children under 6 (U.S. Bureau of the Census 1943: Table 2; 1955: Tables 46 and 47; 1963a: Table 8; and 1973a: Table 216).

There is no evidence that these substantial shifts in women's labor-force participation were precipitated by prior changes in sex-role attitudes. On the contrary, the data show that although shifts in attitudes occurred, they lagged behind behavioral changes, indicated that changes in behavior have gradually brought about changes in sex-role norms rather than the reverse.[18] Moreover, the evidence clearly indicates that the start of the rapid changes in women's labor-force behavior greatly preceded the rebirth of the feminist movement. Betty Frieden's book *The Feminine Mystique* was not published until 1963, the same year that the Report of the President's Commission on the Status of Women was published. The Civil Rights Act, including Title VI which prohibited discrimination on the basis of race or sex, was not passed until 1964 and the National Organization for Women (NOW) was not organized until 1966 (Freeman 1973). Thus, feminism as a movement did not really get under way until the mid or late 1960s, long after women had been moving into the labor-force in unprecedented numbers.[19]

In general, then, the evidence suggests that sex-role attitudes, and feminism perhaps too, have been important *consequences* rather than major *causes* of the enormous postwar changes in women's economic behavior. This is not to say that more equalitarian sex-role attitudes and a feminist ideological perspective are not major motivating forces in the lives of many women today, especially young middle-class women. What seems likely, however, is that these attitudes reinforce and provide an ideological rationale (or normative justification) for processes that have important underlying structural determinants. Hence, the study of these structural determinants should not be seriously impaired by the inability to incorporate sex-role attitudinal variables as exogenous factors. Rather, a structural analysis, such as this study is, should shed light on the determinants of attitudinal change, in

---

[18]For detailed review of opinion polls and other attitudinal surveys covering the period from the 1930s to the early 1960s, see Oppenheimer (1970: Chapter 2). I found little evidence that major shifts in attitudes regarding wives' working preceded the substantial changes in labor-force behavior of the early postwar period. By and large, attitudes tended to lag behind behavior. Even in 1969, when about 39% of married women were in the labor force, 40% of the adults in a Gallup Pole disapproved of a "married woman earning money in business or industry if she has a husband capable of supporting her"; 55% approved and 5% were undecided (Gallup 1969: Part 1). The 1970 National Fertility Survey of "ever-married woman under age 45" indicated that women's sex-role attitudes remained remarkably conservative given the extensive change in their labor-market behavior in the previous 30 years. For example, 78% of the respondents agreed with the statement: "It is much better for everyone involved if the man is the achiever outside the home and the woman takes care of the home and family [Mason 1973: 138]." Neither were there significant differences in the responses between women under age 30 and those over 30, which would have been indicative of major cohort shifts in sex-role attitudes (Mason and Bumpass 1973: Table 1; see also Mason, Czajka, and Arber 1976).

[19]Neither is there evidence that the movement had a substantial impact on sex-role attitudes in the 1960s and early 1970s. See Mason, Czajka, and Arber 1976.

spite of the lack of such data in the censuses and the CPS. For example, the discussion in Chapter 8 of the feedback effects of the rise in women's labor-force participation suggests an important mechanism by which behavioral changes can produce changes in social norms and attitudes.

VI. DATA SOURCES

While data from the CPS have been employed for certain purposes in this study, most of the analysis rests on 1960 and 1970 Public Use Samples of white couples. The data involved are from two samples each for 1960 and 1970. For 1960 we have a 1/1,000 sample of white couples (excluding Spanish surname) where the husband was 18–64 years old and currently or last reported in a non-farm occupation. There is also a 1/1,000 sample of white males (all marital statuses combined) with the same socioeconomic characteristics as the men in the sample of couples. The original 1960 Public Use Sample was employed, not the sample more recently issued to accompany the 1970 PUS (U.S. Bureau of the Census, no date). Parallel samples were drawn for 1970 from the 5%, Country Group Sample. However, the sampling ratio was increased to 3/1,000 and the sample of couples were limited to those where the husband was the household head.[20] Spanish descent, rather than Spanish surname, was used to exclude Hispanics from the sample (U.S. Bureau of the Census 1972a).

Using the PUS has considerable advantages, as well as a few disadvantages. One disadvantage, already mentioned, is the lack of any attitudinal data. While attitudes, such as reference-group-based aspirations, form an important aspect of the model, they cannot be directly observed although they may enter into the empirical analysis indirectly—for example, as in my use of occupational and age groups as proxies for various reference groups. In this respect, one major advantage of the PUS is that the large sample sizes, combined with the considerable detail available on some of the variables, such as occupation, permit very detailed comparisons of hypothetical positive and negative reference groups with regard to income, marital, and family characteristics. Another important advantage is that the PUS permit a far more extensive analysis of the single and joint characteristics and behavior of both husbands and wives than would be possible using published data or surveys with smaller sample sizes.

It is true that although the analysis of change is stressed in this study the PUS only cover two points in time (1960 and 1970). Hence they do not

---

[20]The 3/1,000 sample was selected from the 1/100 PUS by DUALABS.

provide a long historical series, nor as firm a basis as would be desired to make generalizations about structural sources of economic pressure endemic to American society. Nevertheless, the temporal scope of the data is really larger than it first appears because a number of cohorts can be studied and some of their characteristics, such as cohort size, educational attainment, numbers of children ever born, and the ages of those present, tell us about the behavior and characteristics of those samples over a considerably more extensive time period than just 1960 and 1970.[21]

VII. CONCLUSION

In sum, this volume reports on the investigation of a variety of economic squeezes hypothesized to be characteristic of postwar American society. One is the lower white-collar squeeze where the attainment of white-collar lifestyle aspirations may be impeded by an income equivalent to that of many manual workers. The others are the two life-cycle squeezes: the squeeze of *early* adulthood when the desire to set up a household is hampered by the relatively low earnings of young men and the squeeze of *middle* adulthood when the cost of children is peaking but increases in the earnings of husbands may be slowing down with regard to those squeezes. There are three basic research questions that provide the underlying framework of the study. First is there empirical evidence supporting the existence of such structured economic squeezes? Is there evidence that the severity of life-cycle squeezes varies among occupational subgroups in the population? Second, if there is evidence for the existence of these squeezes, what factors seem to have been changing their severity over time? What are the prospects for the future? Third, what types of behavioral responses appear to represent adaptations to these squeezes and how are these responses likely to change, given variations in the severity of the squeezes? Moreover, do prior responses to one or more of the

[21]While the original plan of the study was to conduct a parallel analysis on blacks as well as whites, this goal was never achieved. The 1960 1/1,000 PUS on blacks proved too small to permit the replication of the analysis conducted on whites. Even a 3/1,000 sample of blacks in 1970 would not have been large enough due to the heavy concentration of black males in lower-level manual occupations. Hence, the analysis of both groups could not be conducted simultaneously. As it turned out, this was all to the better as the development of the model on whites indicated that a more complex conceptual framework would be more appropriate for blacks. For example, to simplify the conceptualization and analysis, the economic role of family members other than husband and wife was ignored. This has disadvantages for white families but appears to be singularly inappropriate for black families with their more complex and varied household structures. Hence, it seemed wiser to postpone any analysis of black families until more thought could be given to their particular characteristics.

VII. Conclusion

squeezes create feedback effects that change the severity of various squeezes, thereby producing further modifications in the response to squeezes?

These three basic questions will be explored in Chapters 3 through 8 of this book. Chapter 3 examines the income component of economic squeezes. At issue is whether age-earnings profiles and occupational differences in men's earnings provide partial evidence for the existence of the lower-white-collar and two life-cycle squeezes, and what evidence there is that earnings patterns have changed over time, thereby affecting the severity of the various squeezes? The last question to be explored is what are the reasons for these shifts and does the evidence suggest that they are of cyclical or secular nature?

Chapter 4 concentrates on the first life-cycle squeeze. Given the earnings characteristics of young men documented in Chapter 3, Chapter 4 uses CPS data to examine whether the consumption behavior of different age groups indicates that young families both aspire to and actually do invest in certain types of heavy consumer durables, in spite of the low earnings of young males. It also attempts a rough investigation of the role of inflation in disproportionately affecting young families. Second, using the PUS data once again, the chapter examines age at marriage as a response to the first squeeze and how this may vary among young men with different types of career trajectories.

Chapter 5 focuses on the second life-cycle squeeze, particularly the cost component and how it interacts with the age pattern of men's earnings documented in Chapter 3. A number of questions are explored in the effort to document the existence of the second squeeze as well as the variations in its severity. First, rough estimates of differences in the money costs of children by their age will be used to investigage the timing of peak child-dependency for men in all occupational groups combined and how this is related to the age patterns of men's earnings. Second, we will examine the changes in the severity of the second squeeze resulting from the postwar baby boom and the implications of this for the relative economic position of older and younger families. Third, the chapter considers occupational differences in the timing of the second squeeze and how this may itself represent an adaptive response to basic occupational differences in the age-earnings profile. Finally, we will look into occupational differences in observed changes in the severity of the second squeeze due to postwar shifts in fertility.

Chapters 3 through 5, as we have seen, will explore the various components of the economic squeezes as well as certain types of demographic responses to these squeezes such as variations in the age at marriage and the number and spacing of children. Chapters 6 through 8 focus primarily on women's economic behavior and its role in affecing the severity of the various squeezes. Chapter 6 is a regression analysis that investigates the sensitivity of wives' labor-force participation to estimates of various types of economic pressures. Chapter 7 explores wives' labor-force participation from a somewhat different perspective. Although economic pressures for wives to work is one factor affecting women's economic behavior, as is stressed in Chapter 6, it is not the only one. Not all families will respond to such pressures by having the wife enter the labor force. Whether she does or not depends on a number of other factors as well—factors that may also influence her labor-force behavior whether or not economic pressures to work have arisen. A major one is the wife's potential socioeconomic contribution to the household. All studies of wives' labor-force participation have shown that the higher the wife's estimated potential wage, the more likely she is to be working (e.g., Bowen and Finegan 1969; Cain 1966; Leibowitz 1975; Oppenheimer 1972; Sweet 1973). Chapter 7 will focus particularly on the impact of wives' potential absolute but especially their *relative* socioeconomic contribution on their labor-force participation, as measured via the educational attainments of husbands and wives.

If the potential relative socioeconomic contribution of wives is an influential factor in their economic behavior, how does this vary among families of men at different occupational levels? Although the educational level of wives may be positively associated with their husband's socioeconomic position, is there also such a positive relationship for their potential *relative* socioeconomic contribution? In other words, how does the relative advantage of wives working vary among socioeconomic groups? Chapter 8 tackles this important question. It also tries to gauge the actual economic impact of wives working. Here a number of important questions are addressed. One is whether wives' earnings seem to be a significant factor in easing the lower white-collar and two life-cycle squeezes. Is there, moreover, evidence that wives' earnings can provide a functional substitute for upward occupational mobility by the husband? Finally, are there possible feedback effects of wives' labor-force participation and, if so, what are the implications for future family economic and demographic behavior? The question here is whether wives' increased employment may not be changing traditional reference-group comparisons and thereby creating self-generating pressures for further increases in women's labor-force participation, with all the implications for demographic behavior this may involve.

Chapter 8 completes the empirical investigations of this study. At the point of finishing it, however, it appeared to me that the general theoretical implications of the analysis had not yet been fully developed. In Chapter 9, I have, therefore, tried to restate more formally some of the overall theoretical implications of the study's findings on life-cycle squeezes. In the process, it became clear that this formulation had implications going beyond the American experience of the 1950 through the 1980s period. In particular, I

VII. Conclusion

have tried to show the theoretical relevance of the life-cycle-squeezes perspective to historical work on American and English family socioeconomic and demographic behavior earlier in the industrialization process.

Since so much of this study is devoted to an analysis of economic squeezes among families of men at different life-cycle stages and in different occupational groups, it is essential to consider carefully how these important variables are to be measured. The task to which we now turn in Chapter 2 is to describe the occupational classification system used in this study and to discuss the conceptual and methodological problems involved in life-cycle analyses.

2

Conceptual and Methodological Issues

Whereas Chapter 3 will launch into the substantive analysis, the task of the present chapter is to discuss the problems involved in utilizing occupation and life-cycle variables in the study of economic squeezes. First I will describe the occupational classification system developed for this study. Then we will turn to the conceptual and methodological difficulties involved in life-cycle analysis and how these relate to the specific interests of this investigation.

I. AN INTERMEDIATE CLASSIFICATION OF OCCUPATIONS

In order to use the husband's occupation as a source of reference-group comparisons as well as a rough measure of typical socioeconomic position, it is essential to measure occupation in a way that is both meaningful and practical. This creates something of a dilemma since, on the one hand, the three-digit census occupational classification is much too unwieldy to use from either a methodological or a theoretical point of view; and, on the other hand, the major occupational groups are too internally heterogeneous. The professional and technical group and the managers, officials, and proprietors group are particularly poor in this respect, but the other groups are also far from homogeneous. The median 1959 earnings of male workers in the professional group varied from $14,561 for physicians and surgeons to $3,366 for dancers and dancing teachers and $3,033 for religious workers. Within the managerial category, median earnings varied from $12,757 for self-employed managers in banking and other finance activities to $4,283 for self-employed managers in food and dairy product stores (U.S. Bureau of the Census 1963b: Table 29). Large variations in education also existed. For example, the median school years completed of physicians in 1960 was 17.5, but it was only 13.7 for artist and art teachers and 12.9 for draftsmen. Managers in banking and finance had 13.7 median school years completed, but building managers and superintendents only had 9.4 years of schooling (U.S. Bureau of the Census 1963b: Table 9).

Since income and other socioeconomic characteristics vary so enormously within major occupational categories, such groups provide an extremely unsatisfactory classification system. Their use would obscure more than it could reveal about occupational differences in socioeconomic characteristics. Moreover, there are no minor modifications that seem to be more suitable. Take, for example, Blau and Duncan's 17 occupational groups (Blau and Duncan 1967: Chapter 2). In that elaboration of the major occupational groupings, the industry division within the craft, operative, and laborer categories increases the number of categories employed but not in a particularly relevant way for this study; and the divisions made in the other occupational categories still leave a lot of heterogeneity. Neither is the much more differentiated Duncan Socioeconomic Index (SEI) appropriate for my purposes (Duncan 1961: 109–138). There is no particular need or desire to force occupations into a single hierarchy nor to examine the socioeconomic characteristics of men with a socioeconomic score of 90 versus 82 or 50. Rather the goal is to study occupations themselves in order to understand how the various socioeconomic contingencies that are characteristic of particular types of occupations impinge on the families of men in such occupations. Furthermore, I want to investigate occupations where status inconsistencies exist—for example, those professions where educational attainment is typically high but average earnings are low. Thus, the interest is in examining which occupations overlap in some characteristics (e.g., educational attainment) but not on others (e.g., income) and what kinds of socioeconomic problems this raises for the family (e.g., the educational aspirations for the children versus the income needed to achieve these aspirations). The Duncan socioeconomic index, with its substitution of numbers for occupations and its averaging of education and income, is most unsuitable for such purposes, invaluable though it may be for the attainment of other research goals. Finally, it is impossible to view occupations scored

I. An Intermediate Classification of Occupations

according to the SEI as very meaningful reference groups for the individuals or families involved. The classification system used must have some subjective meaning for people if occupational reference group comparisons are going to be inferred.

If the Blau and Duncan classification systems are not especially appropriate for this study, the census major occupational categories too internally heterogeneous and the detailed categories too numerous to handle, what occupational classification can be used? Is it possible to construct a set of groupings in between the two extremes of the census system? The approach employed here was to utilize 1959 earnings as a variable differentiating detailed occupations within major occupational categories. Since one goal of the analysis is to examine how life-cycle earnings patterns vary among occupations, some method of occupational classification that would facilitate the use of the occupation variable as a major analytical and descriptive tool in a life-cycle analysis was desired. The first step in trying to develop such a classification system was to study the median earnings by age for each detailed occupation on which published data were available in the 1960 Census (1970 data were not yet available at the time).[1] Such an analysis indicated that different occupations had distinctive earnings patterns by age and that virtually all occupations had an age at which median earnings were at their maximum or peak vis-à-vis other age groups. Furthermore, as is well known, the shape of the age–earning profile and the age at which peak median earnings occur is related to the level of mid-life earnings in an occupation (see Becker 1975; Mincer 1974). Since this was the case, the peak median earnings appeared to be an excellent basis for classifying occupations within major occupational groups. For example, take the case of accountants and auditors. The age group that had the highest 1959 median earnings in this occupational category was 45–54, with median earnings of $7,615 (U.S. Bureau of the Census 1963b: Table 31). Hence, accountants and auditors were classified into the Group II Professions—those professional occupations with peak 1959 median earnings in the $7,000–8,999 range. All detailed non-farm occupational groups were classified in a similar way—into peak median earnings groups within major occupational groups.

This occupational classification schema was developed using published data on "detailed" occupations that include class-of-worker and industry as a means of further differentiating a large number of occupational categories. In this way I was able to take advantage of the fact that workers in the same

---

[1] Developing this classification schema on the basis of published data also had the advantage of utilizing a much larger sample of detailed occupations than would have been available in the 1/1,000 1960 PUS. See Appendix A for a more detailed description of the procedure and for tables showing how particular occupations were classified.

three-digit occupational group often have very different socioeconomic characteristics depending on these other variables. For example, the 1959 peak median earnings for salaried managers in manufacturing was $10,861 compared to $5,748 for self-employed managers in retail trade (Appendix A: Table A.3). Class-of-worker and industry information therefore increases the value of the occupational variable by helping to distinguish much more carefully those subgroups within occupations who had different levels of permanent income and who were likely to be operating in relatively distinct internal labor markets.

The net result of this classification process is an 18-category system in which no major occupational group has more than three subdivisions and several have only one or two. The men in the 1960 PUS sample were then classified into one of these categories on the basis of their current or last occupation. For the 1970 PUS, the same occupations were classified in exactly the same way, regardless of their 1969 earnings—at least to the extent this was possible given the numerous changes in the 1970 detailed occupational classification system (U.S. Bureau of the Census 1972b).

Four earnings groups were utilized in the creation of the peak median occupational classification based on the 1959 earnings patterns. However, to avoid confusion when discussing the 1970 data, due to the fact that earnings levels had changed considerably since 1960, the labels for the peak median groups were set as follows:

Group I, high earnings:
  Occupations with 1959 peak median earnings of $9,000+

Group II, medium high earnings:
  Occupations with 1959 peak median earnings of $7,000–8,999

Group III, moderate earnings:
  Occupations with peak 1959 median earnings of $5,000–6,999

Group IV, low earnings:
  Occupations with 1959 peak median earnings of less than $5,000

As a rough check on the accuracy of the classification system, Table 2.1 presents the 1959 and 1969 peak median earnings of all white males according to their peak median occupation group. As far as 1959 peak median earnings are concerned, in all but one category the peak median earnings, computed on the 1/1,000 sample of men after they were classified according to the present system, fall within the categories set up on the basis of published data used to estimate peak median earnings for detailed occupational categories. Since the published data included nonwhites and people of Hispanic heritage whereas these were excluded from the PUS used here, some discrepancy might be expected but it is quite small. The one

I. An Intermediate Classification of Occupations

TABLE 2.1
Peak 1959 and 1969 Median Earnings of White Males, by Peak Median Occupation Group (Current Dollars)[a,b]

Peak median occupation group	Peak median earnings 1959	Peak median earnings 1969
Professionals		
I	10,596	16,726
II	7,719	12,689
III	6,491	10,905
Managers		
I	9,500	15,534
II	7,896	12,368
III	6,133	10,374
Sales		
II	7,077	12,534
III	5,750	9,609
Clerical		
III	5,709	8,968
IV	4,906	7,860
Craft		
II	7,440	11,245
III	6,028	9,550
IV	5,080	7,857
Operatives		
III	5,284	8,282
IV	4,884	7,831
Service		
III	5,721	9,754
IV	3,935	6,731
Laborers		
IV	4,128	6,602

Sources: 1960 and 1970 Public Use Samples of White Males.

[a]See text and Appendix A for a detailed explanation of the occupational classification system used.

[b]White males, 18–64 years old in non-farm occupations.

exception was the Craftsmen IV group which had median earnings of $5,080, just above the cutting off point for Group IV occupations ($4,999). Even so, the peak median earnings of Group IV craftsmen was well below that of Group III craftsmen so that the proper ranking within the crafts group is maintained. In addition, the same rank ordering persisted in 1970 although absolute earnings shifted enormously, of course, because of large increases in money (and real) earnings.

Because the peak earnings were based on earnings *intervals,* there is a certain amount of variation between occupations within any one earnings interval. For example, in both 1959 and 1969 Operative III males had considerably lower peak median earnings than Craft III males and Clerical III males had lower earnings as well. However, Craft III males had lower peak median earnings than Professional III males, and so on. Hence, peak median earnings level is not really held constant in any rigorous sense and it will sometimes be important to keep in mind the systematic earnings differences between occupations in the same earnings group.

II. CONCEPTUAL AND METHODOLOGICAL ISSUES IN LIFE-CYCLE ANALYSES

As social scientists have become increasingly aware, the study of age–earnings profiles and how these change over time involves serious conceptual and methodological difficulties. The heart of the problem lies in the interpretation of data involving age as a major independent variable. When one views the age pattern of a variable at one point in time, two interpretations of any observed relationship are possible and often confounded. If, in addition, longitudinal comparisons are involved, *three* interpretations are possible and are sometimes very difficult to disentangle. These three interpretations, or effects, are commonly termed *age, period,* and *cohort effects* (Mason, Mason, Winsborough, and Poole 1973; Ryder 1965; Schaie 1967; Glenn 1976; Weiss and Lilard 1978). Age effects are those factors related to an individual's age per se—for example, fecundity, investments in and depreciation of human capital, physical strength. Period effects refer to the influence of the historical period on the behavior or characteristics of respondents at the time the observations are made. For example, economic growth will affect real income over time and can be considered a period effect, as are cyclical fluctuations in the business cycle which may affect earnings, the birth rate, the marraige rate, etc. in any particular year. Cohort effects are those that are tied to a particular birth cohort and that influence its behavior or characteristics aside from any effects that might be traced to age or period effects. Thus a number of investigators have argued that the size of a birth cohort will affect its economic chances later in life—large cohorts being in a chronically more difficult labor market position than small ones (Ryder 1965; Wachter 1977; Easterlin 1978). It is also possible that these different effects interact. Thus period effects may interact with age. For example, young people seem particularly vulnerable in recent years to downswings in the business cycle—a vulnerability that will probably not have a life-long (i.e., cohort) effect if the recession is relatively short.

Whereas it may be possible to make the conceptual distinction between age, period, and cohort effects, it is often very difficult to disentangle them empirically. Once a group of a particular age in a particular year is singled out, there is only *one* birth cohort that can be observed (Mason et al. 1973: 243). Conversely, once a particular cohort in a given period is selected, there is only one age group that can be observed for that cohort. As a consequence, age and cohort effects will be confounded in cross-sectional studies of earnings by age; age and period effects will be confounded in a longitudinal analysis of the earnings of a cohort over its life-cycle; and intertemporal comparisons of cross-sectional age patterns (e.g., the pattern in 1970 versus that observed in 1960) will confound all three effects.

The problems the confounding of these effects raises for the present investigation are serious. First, there is the difficulty of assessing the stability of the age pattern of earnings observed at any one point in time. If period and cohort effects "distort" the age pattern—and in unanticipated directions—then how can we adequately discuss whether certain earnings patterns by age are typical and whether there are systematic differences among occupations in earnings for men at different stages of their career cycle? Second, how do we interpret any observed differences in the age pattern of earnings between 1959 and 1969? Do these differences represent *changes* in the age pattern and, if so, are these changes transitory or more permanent? Or are the differences due primarily to the distortion of the age pattern introduced by "atypical" cohorts as they pass through the age structure?

In short, it becomes exceedingly difficult to arrive at meaningful interpretations of data on earnings by age unless we can achieve some success in sorting out age, period, and cohort effects. The question is how can this disentangling of the various effects be carried out. There have been several approaches employed to handle these problems. One common strategy in the past has been simply to assume that one of the effects is not operating, the cohort effect being a common choice. However, the ignored cohort effect may not, in fact, be trivial and if it is not then the effect will be incorrectly estimated and, because of this, the period effect will also be off as it is often measured in a residual fashion.[2] Moreover, to the extent that age

---

[2] For example, using data from the 1950 and 1960 censuses, Herman Miller developed estimates of age and period effects on men's income by ignoring cohort effects. Thus he found that the median income of the cohort of college graduates who were 25–34 in 1949 and 35–44 in 1959 rose by 127%. The age-effect component was estimated to be 76 percentage points—the relative difference between the mean income for 25–34- and 35–44-year-old college graduates in *1949*. The growth component (the period effect) was then the total increase for the cohort (127%) minus the age effect (76%) or 51% (Miller 1965).

and period effects interact in the short term—and in the long term as well—producing cohort effects, this approach does not appear to be an appropriate one to use here. Furthermore, it seems particularly risky to make such simplifying assumptions in assessing occupational differences in age-earnings patterns since there are good reasons for believing that interactions of age and period effects with occupation occur.

A second approach to the problem of disentangling age, period, and cohort effects is the one using multiple regression techniques proposed by Mason et al. (1973). They suggest that one conduct a multiple classification analysis which is methodologically possible provided "the analyst is willing to assume that at least two age groups, time periods or birth cohorts, have identical effects on the dependent variable [Mason et al. 1973: 248]." Such a strategy is not very practical in the present study, however, for two major reasons. For one thing, I do not have enough time periods or age groups to permit me to impose the constraints that are necessary. I have only data for *two* periods—1960 and 1970. This means, of course, that I can only observe any particular cohort at two points in time. Furthermore, I am utilizing only five age groups—primarily to achieve descriptive simplicity. Hence, I would have very little left to disentangle once I made the kinds of assumptions necessary to conduct a multiple classification analysis on these data. An even more intractable problem is that the model proposed by the Masons and their coworkers is additive whereas I have good reason to believe interactions can occur. For example, the interaction of age and period effects in the greater vulnerability of young people to recessions is one we will explore.

Another approach to the problem is more eclectic. It is to try to develop a theoretical and empirical rationale for which effects are expected to be operative and under what circumstances. This is the strategy followed in the present study. Although the results are statistically inelegant and unlikely to be definitive, this seems the most practical approach given the limitations of the data being analyzed. Furthermore, whatever drawbacks are encountered in this procedure are unlikely to be too serious since the purpose of the analysis is primarily descriptive rather than analytical—that is, to describe conditions under which relative economic deprivation may exist rather than to undertake a complete explanation of how such situations have come about. In addition, at this point, my major goal is to describe patterns and rather marked departures from these patterns rather than to develop precise mathematical estimates of the various effect. Hence a somewhat less rigorous approach does not appear to exact too high an analytical price. Nevertheless, I hope this analysis will provide a first step in the development of a model that can eventually be tested with much more sophisticated multivariate techniques.

Age Effects

There are numerous reasons for expecting a strong age effect on men's earnings. Becker's human capital theory not only provides an important rationale for an age effect on earnings but also for systematic occupational differences in the age–earnings profile (Becker 1975). According to Becker, foregone earnings are one of the major, though indirect, costs of investing in human capital. In the case of formal schooling, the individual partly pays for his education by not working and thus sacrifices the earnings he might have made were he not in school. Or he may work part time or at a very low-level temporary job that pays more poorly than jobs for which he is already qualified on the basis of past investments in human capital. In the case of on-the-job-training, the individual typically pays for it at least partially via lower earnings than he would otherwise have made if he were not simultaneously receiving training. Of course, the later returns from such human capital investments are higher earnings. Furthermore, Becker argues, the most extensive investments in human capital tend to be made in youth or young adulthood when the cost in foregone earnings is less. Early investments in human capital will also maximize the number of years during which the returns on such investments are reaped.

In short, human capital theory provides a rationale for age-related differentials in earnings and, indicates why the age effect should be strongly related to the skill level of an occupation.[3] The unskilled will tend to have relatively flat age–earnings profiles. Small amounts of skill investment will reduce earnings in youth but lead to early and relatively low peaks since investments in training are neither extensive nor prolonged. There may actually be some depreciation in human capital at more advanced ages resulting in declines in earnings. However, positive period effects such as economic growth usually offset the negative age effect in later life so that the earnings of cohorts do not, in fact, decline in the preretirement years. Highly skilled workers, though, will exhibit rather steep age–earnings profiles with peaks at older ages. This is because training is lengthy, involving extensive foregone earnings in youth. However, the income returns on such investments are considerable, leading to sharp increases from age group to age group with high peaks occurring for middle-aged or older men.

Other age-related aspects of human capital should also affect earnings. Health and physical strenth are negatively related to age. Deterioration of a man's health may be expected to lead to a leveling off or even a decline in

---

[3]That the age–earnings profiles of different educational groups, at least, actually behave in this way is well known. See, for example, Becker (1975: 216–217), Mincer (1974: 65ff).

earnings as the individual approaches retirement age. The effect of changes in strength can be expected to interact with occupation—those occupations where physical strength is more important may exhibit earlier peaks in earnings, followed by declines. Ross Stolzenberg found some evidence for this in an analysis of 1960 Census data using estimates of the physical demands of occupations developed by the U.S. Bureau of Labor Statistics (Stolzenberg 1975: 659–700).

Internal labor market theory leads us to expect age and occupation related patterns similar to those predicted by human capital theory—sometimes for the same reasons but not always.[4] First, many higher-paying jobs are at the top of promotion ladders within organizations and it takes time to ascend these ladders, not only because of the number of years required to invest in human capital but also because of the importance of seniority in promotion decisions. However, bureaucratic organizations are typically hierarchical in nature. As a consequence, the farther up one goes in the organization hierarchy the fewer the number of positions one finds at a similar rank; and practically no one makes it to the top. This situation will almost invariably lead to a leveling off of income with age. The older the age group considered, the greater number who have reached their maximum job level. Hence the older age groups in such occupations will have a disproportionate number of people who will no longer achieve any further upward mobility. Those who continue to be upwardly mobile will either move into other occupations or will constitute an ever decreasing proportion of the workers for each older age group. Offsetting this tendency is the fact that large organizations frequently reward seniority with higher earnings. Nevertheless, Rees and Schultz found that "the value of seniority increases at a decreasing rate [Rees and Schultz 1970: 154]." Hence, here too there should be some leveling off of earnings with age. However, the data used by Rees and Schultz are based on the experience of workers from a sample of establishments. The importance of the effect of seniority on income may not be so much due to any marked upward push on hourly earnings within the firm but in its prevention of job loss and the serious decline in income such a loss may precipitate (Parnes and King 1977).[5] This process may not be adequately picked up in a sample

---

[4]This discussion is in terms of internal labor market operations in a broad "neo-institutionalist" sense and is not limited to a dualist approach. For some of the relevant literature on these issues, see Kerr (1954), Dunlop (1957), Doeringer and Piore (1971), Wachter (1974), and Cain (1975).

[5]However, the other side of this coin may be an increased economic vulnerability of older men who are not involved in such protected internal labor markets or who have, for one reason or another, lost the protection of such a labor market (e.g., due to organizational mergers that may disrupt previous institutionalized practices). Such men will increasingly be "out in the cold" and the most practical thing to do may be to retire from the labor force—especially given the growing financial supports to do this (e.g., social security).

of work organizations unless these organizations frequently hire older workers with and without relevant specific training.

In sum, both human capital and institutional factors should produce certain distinctive age effects on men's earnings, effects that will, moreover, interact with occupation.

Period Effects and Their Interaction with Age Effects

If only a simple age effect were operating, age–earning profiles would remain constant over time (i.e., numerous cross-sectional "snapshots" taken at different time periods would be identical). Moreover, if one followed a cohort through time the longitudinal pattern of its members' earnings as they actually aged would be the same as the cross-sectional earnings profile observed at any one point in time. However, all other factors are not constant, of course. Consider first how period effects may complicate this initially oversimplified view of the effect of age on men's earnings, including the complications raised by the interaction of age and period effects.

If period effects occur without any interactions then the *pattern* of the age-earning profile in cross-section should be unaffected—at any one of several points in time in which it may be observed. However, the actual earnings of particular cohorts *over* time will no longer be identical to that of men of different ages at one point in time. In addition, the actual earnings of men in the same age group at different dates (e.g., 35–44-year-old males in 1970 versus 1960) will be different although their position relative to older and younger men will not change. But if interactions of period and age effect should occur, then the cross-sectional pattern of earnings at different time periods may vary. Hence, interactions of period and age effects may reduce the usefulness of any single cross-sectional age–earnings profile as a measure of the age effect, even without considering the additional complications of possible cohort effects. Keeping these problems in mind, let us consider the type of period effects that might distort comparisons of the 1960 and 1970 PUS data, thus hindering efforts to estimate the general nature of the age effect from this admittedly limited information.

INFLATION

An obvious period effect that will affect comparisons of earnings over time is inflation. I have made an effort to control for this by uniformly inflating 1959 earnings of all males, regardless of age or occupation, into 1969 dollars, using the consumer Price Index (CPI). However, this procedure will not necessarily give a true picture of actual changes in the buying power of different age groups. For one thing, changes in the cost of consumer items are not uniform over all commodities. For example, while the CPI rose 26% between 1959 and 1969 for all items combined, the increase for home ownership costs was about 37% and for medical costs it was 48% (U.S. Bureau of Labor Statistics 1975b: Tables 122 and 128; see also Morgan and Newman 1976). If consumption patterns vary by family-cycle stage, as seems very likely, then families at stages where they are more likely to purchase goods and services whose prices have been rising more rapidly than average will experience a greater loss of buying power than those families whose purchases are more concentrated in goods and services with more stable prices. Thus, rapidly rising home ownership costs should put a special burden on young couples entering the housing market for the first time and rapidly rising medical costs might have a greater effect on families in the childbearing and early childrearing stages as well as on the elderly population. Whether this unevenness in the rise in prices in the components of the CPI will tend to balance out is not readily apparent and there is no a priori reason to expect that it will. As a consequence, an empirical analysis of how consumption patterns vary by life-cycle stage coupled with changes in the cost of these consumption items would be desirable to evaluate properly how much inflation interacts with age in its effects on real earnings. Some effort will be made to investigate this issue with regard to the first squeeze in Chapter 4.

BUSINESS-CYCLE FLUCTUATIONS

Business cycles will also affect the interpretation of the comparison of earnings over time. In particular, first, since only two periods are involved (1960 and 1970), there is a danger of confusing cyclical with secular period effects. For example, if 1969 were a period of lower unemployment than 1959 (as indeed it was) then there is the possibility of arriving at rather misleading conclusions about "trends" in age and occupational patterns of earnings.

Second, business-cycle fluctuations can greatly affect our interpretation of the data if these cyclical conditions interact with age and occupation. For example, if some age groups are more vulnerable than others to business-cycle shifts (e.g., youths versus men in the prime working years) then the interpretation of observed "changes" in age patterns of earnings between 1959 and 1969 should take into account that the economy was not at comparable stages of the business cycle in the 2 years. Similarly, if some occupations (e.g., lower-level blue-collar occupations) are particularly sensitive to unemployment conditions then apparent improvements in the economic position of these occupations between 1959 and 1969 might be at

II. Conceptual and Methodological Issues in Life-Cycle Analyses

least partly the result of short-run lower unemployment in 1969 than in 1959 rather than primarily due to any long-run secular improvements in the average earnings of such occupations.

Since decennial census information on unemployment refers only to the reference weeks in April of 1960 and 1970, it is a poor measure of how contrasting cyclical conditions can affect 1959 and 1969 earnings. CPS data are much more illuminating. Figure 2.1 presents the monthly unemployment rate for the 1959–1960 2-year period and the 1969–1970 period. It reveals that unemployment was quite low throughout 1969 and fluctuated little. There were greater fluctuations in 1959 but the highs in the latter part of the year seemed to balance out the low unemployment rates from April through August. Nevertheless, despite fluctuations in the 1959 rates, the gap between the rates for 1959 and 1969 were fairly substantial—generally on the order of 2 to 2.5 percentage points or more. However, unemployment started to climb in January 1970 so that by March and April 1970 (the period during which the census reference week occurred), it was well above the rate for any month

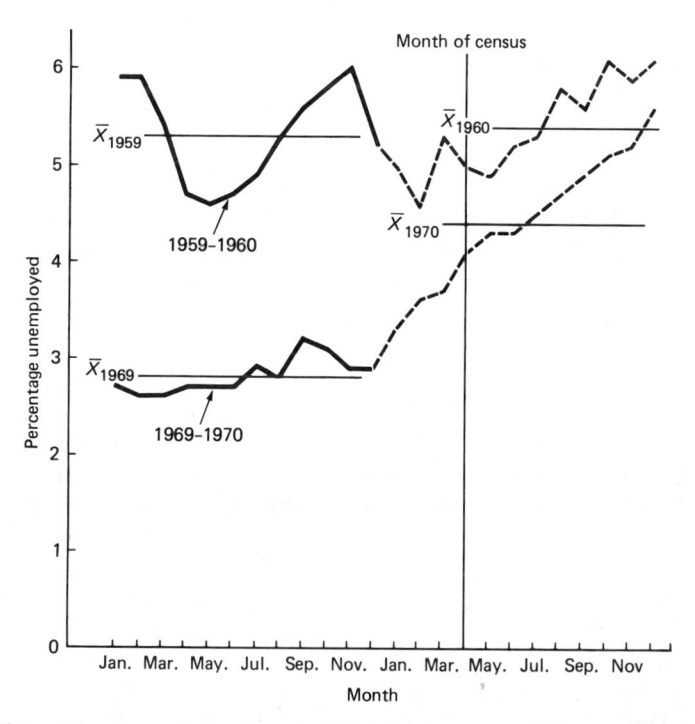

Figure 2.1. Percentage of all males aged 16 and older, who were unemployed, by month: 1959–1960 and 1969–1970. (Fourteen years and older in 1959–1960.) (*Sources*: U.S. Bureau of Labor Statistics 1960: Table A-1; 1961a: Table A-1; 1970b:Table 7; 1971b:Table 7.)

in 1969. However, in March and April, the *1960* unemployment rate was slightly *lower* than the annual average for 1959. As a consequence, the gap between the March–April 1960 and March–April 1970 rates were rather minimal—on the order of half a percentage point. Hence, the 1960 and 1970 census data on unemployment will understate the extent to which better employment conditions were operating in 1969 than in 1959 by about two percentage points. Furthermore, to the extent business-cycle conditions affect hours worked during a week, the census data will also tend to understate the difference between the "typical" hours worked in 1969 and 1959 because the census data on hours worked, like the unemployment data, also refer to the reference week and not to any week of the year to which the earnings data refer.

How seriously the census understatement of the different employment conditions in 1969 and 1959 should affect our interpretation of earnings differences is hard to judge. However, these measurement problems should be kept in mind when discussing changes that occurred between the two censuses, especially if trends are to be inferred.

With regard to the question of whether there is any interaction of unemployment with age, Figure 2.2 indicates that there certainly is (see also Bednarzik 1975a; Hedges 1976). Throughout the 1948–1976 period, unemployment was considerably higher for 18–19- and 20–24-year-old white males than for men in the 25–64 age groups who, by contrast, exhibited very similar rates. For example, in 1970 (a period of relatively higher unemployment) the unemployment rate for 18–19-year-olds was 12.0% and for 20–24-year-olds it was 7.8% while the rate for men in the 25–64 age groups varied from only 2.3 to 3.1%. Furthermore, business-cycle fluctuations seem to produce much larger absolute (though not relative) changes in the unemployment rate for younger men than for older men, undoubtedly producing fluctuations in earnings to match. Hence any observed improvements between 1959 and 1969 in median earnings can more readily be attributed to the business cycle for younger men than it can for older men.

Turning to the question of occupational differences in the vulnerability to unemployment, the CPS data provide some idea of gross occupational differentials in unemployment and these are substantial (Figure 2.3). Blue-collar workers typically have considerably higher unemployment rates than white-collar workers—even in times of prosperity (see also Badnarzik 1975b). For example, in 1961 the average unemployment rate for laborers was 14.5% as opposed to 1.7% for managers, officials, and proprietors—the group with the lowest unemployment rate in 1961. In 1975 laborers had an average unemployment rate of 15.8% as compared to 2.7% for managers. Furthermore, as with the age-group comparisons, business-cycle fluctuations apparently produce larger absolute fluctuations in the unemployment rate for

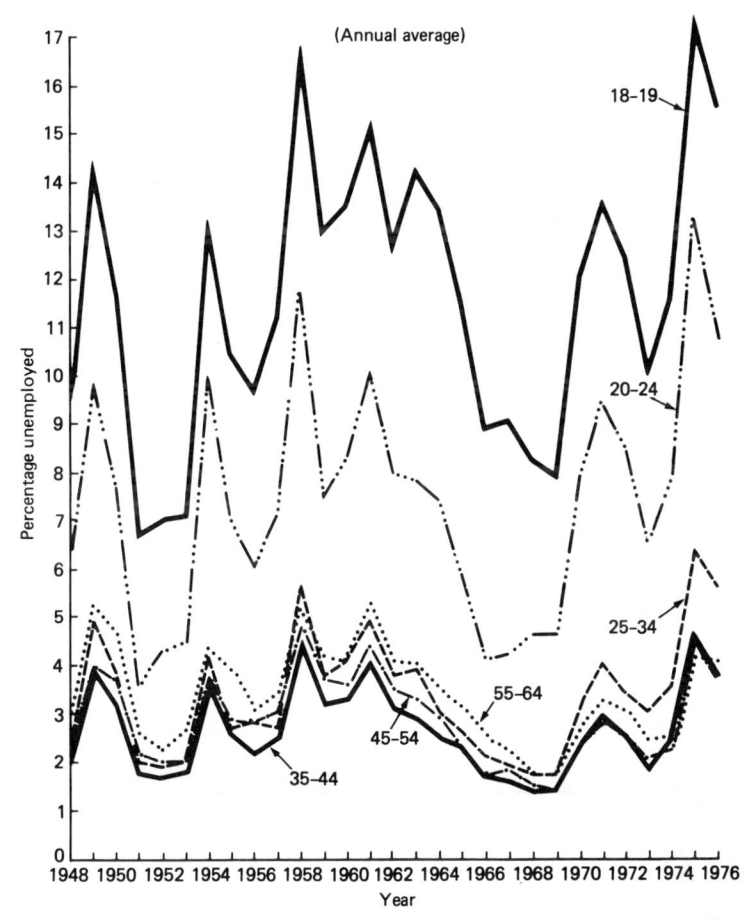

II. Conceptual and Methodological Issues in Life-Cycle Analyses 51

Figure 2.2. Percentage of white males who were unemployed, by age: 1949–1976. (*Sources*: U.S. Bureau of Labor Statistics 1973a: Table A-16; 1977a: Table 56; 1978a: Table A-3; 1979a: Table 3; 1980: Table 3; 1981b:Table 3.)

blue-collar workers than for white-collar and this must undoubtedly have a greater impact on earnings. Hence if unemployment is an important factor in earnings, the annual earnings position of blue-collar workers should be more closely connected to the business-cycle than that of white-collar workers so that 1959–1969 "improvements" in earnings for blue-collar workers would, in greater part, be attributable to the temporarily more favorable economic climate in 1969 rather than to long-run changes in the economic position of blue-collar workers.

Unemployment rates vary also by industry and this is partly why some

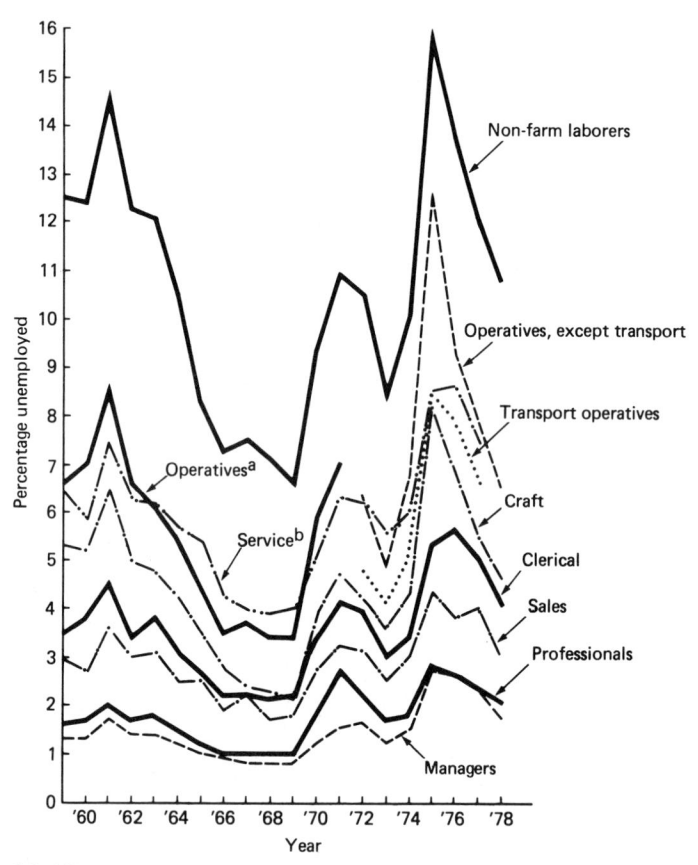

Figure 2.3. Percentage of males unemployed, by occupation of last job: 1959–1978. (*Sources*: U.S. Bureau of Labor Statistics 1960, 1961a, 1962, 1963, 1964, 1965, 1966a, 1970c, 1971a, 1972, 1973b, 1973c, 1974a, 1975c, 1976b, 1978a, 1979a, 1980, 1981b.)

[a] Starting with 1972, operatives were divided into two groups: "transport operatives" and "operatives, except transport."
[b] Service workers do not include private household workers.

occupational groups or some individual occupations are especially vulnerable to business-cycle fluctuations. Construction and goods-producing industries—especially some durable-goods industries—are particularly sensitive. For example, in the 1974–1975 recession, unemployment in automobile manufacturing rose by 13.6 percentage points between 1973 and 1975 compared to a total rise in male unemployment of 3.8 percentage points (U.S. Bureau of Labor Statistics 1975c: Table 9; 1976b: Table 9). Comparing 1959 with 1969, we find that the unemployment rate for workers in construction was 12.0% in 1959 but 6.1% in 1969. For males in motor vehicle and equipment, the unemployment rate was 10.1% in 1959 but 6.8% in 1969. This compares to the unemployment rates in services of 4.3% in

1959 and 3.0% in 1969 (U.S. Bureau of Labor Statistics 1960: Table F-2; 1971a: Table A-10). As a consequence, the special sensitivity of the construction and goods-producing industries to business-cycle fluctuations tends to affect blue-collar workers more than white-collar since the occupational composition of construction and goods-producing industries are much more heavily blue-collar than is the case with service industries.

SECULAR ECONOMIC CHANGE

If secular economic growth is an important factor in real earnings changes of men in the 1959–1969 period what are some of the factors involved in economic growth that may importantly interact with certain subgroups and thus affect this dimension of the period effect on men's earnings?

It seems likely that some long-term trends in economic growth may actually favor the income position of somewhat older workers to the disadvantage of the young. One feature of economic growth in our society has been the growth of large bureaucratic work organizations. If such work organizations involve internal labor markets, then these may disproportionately benefit prime-working-age and older males. For one thing, the greater their seniority, the less the chances of permanent job loss from the organization (and the income loss this may entail, especially given the difficulties of starting afresh at an older age). Second, an organization with a relatively protected internal labor market provides institutionalized paths of upward mobility that will help improve the incomes of at least some of the workers in these organizations. Third, there are typically institutionalized means of raising earnings without promotions—wage increases based on seniority alone and escalator clauses raise wages to keep up with inflation (see, for example, LeRoy 1978). Finally, such work organizations and their relatively senior employees may have a considerable amount invested in specific human capital that increases the costliness of turnover among such workers and operates to maintain job security for the more senior workers. In short, if internal labor markets such as this are an increasingly important setting for work in our society, then this should increase the relative vulnerability of the young to economic downswings because of their low seniority and their much smaller investments in human capital specific to a particular organization or type of organization.

Cohort Effects

What sorts of complications will be raised in our analysis by cohort effects?[6] First of all, just what is a cohort effect? We may think of it as those

---

[6]I will limit the discussion to the question of *birth* cohorts. One could, of course, focus on other types of cohorts as well—marriage cohorts, for example.

characteristic features of a cohort that modify its response to age and period effects in ways that distinguish it from other cohorts. Furthermore, these characteristic features are typically the consequence of a period effect that influenced the cohort at some critical point in its life-cycle (Ryder 1965: 844). For example, the period effect may be the socioeconomic circumstances that affected fertility in the years defining the birth cohort and thus determined the cohort's size. The cohort's size, in turn, may have a life-long effect on its socioeconomic characteristics (Ryder 1965: 845; Easterlin 1978). Or the characteristic features of the cohort may result from the historical circumstances existing at some strategic point in the cohort's life-cycle—for example, the health of the economy when the cohort was entering the labor market (Ryder 1965: 846).

If a cohort effect is, in fact, the consequence of the interaction of period and age effects, is there anything that distinguishes it from such interactive effects? Yes, I think it is that cohort effects persist over time. At one extreme, the interaction between age and period effects may produce very ephemeral results—for example, short-term high unemployment among youth in a mild recession. We may more properly term these pure interaction rather than cohort effects. However, if such interaction effects continue to have a distinctive impact on the same cohort over time, then we have what is more properly thought of as a cohort effect. Thus a prolonged depression at a critical state in a cohort's life-cycle may permanently handicap it economically. At the other extreme, then, interaction effects that are cohort effects may be permanent. However, it is possible to conceive of a cohort effect that is not permanent but gradually declines in importance over the life-span of the cohort. Thus, depending on the seriousness and length of a recession, it may have a negative effect on a cohort which is strongest during the period of the recession, persists for several years, but gradually diminishes over time. Or the reverse may be the case. For example, if each successive cohort has a higher educational attainment than the previous cohort, then the educational characteristics of a cohort may progressively hamper its economic position as it ages—that is, to the extent it is thrown into direct competition with much younger cohorts.

If cohort effects are the long-term results of the interaction of period and age effects on a given cohort, then an important question is the identification of the critical events at the critical stages of the life cycle whose intersection results in a cohort effect. In some cases, this identification is relatively easy. Thus, where cohort size is the cohort effect at issue, the important factor is typically the birth rate at the time period defining the cohort versus earlier and later birth rates. The occurrence of a devastating war while the cohort of males is of fighting age may also contribute to the effect of cohort size. However, it is not always so readily apparent what the critical stage of the

II. Conceptual and Methodological Issues in Life-Cycle Analyses

life-cycle is which, given certain historical circumstances, will lead to a cohort effect. Hence, one of the theoretical difficulties of cohort analysis lies in identifying critical points in the life-cycle for the different possible dependent variables. These critical points may be rather different for a variable such as life-cycle earnings patterns as opposed to marriage or divorce behavior or fertility. However, to the extent a cohort effect persists over time—and to the extent its effect is permanent—then early critical points will have a long-lasting effect than events which affect cohorts at later stages of the life cycle.

Given these theoretical problems, what are some of the socioeconomic conditions that may have a long-run impact on the earnings of a cohort of males? It is convenient to divide the circumstances affecting a cohort's economic situation into two types: (*a*) circumstances that affect its economic situation partly, at least, because they have affected the *size* of the cohort; and (*2*) circumstances that affect the economic position of the cohort more directly.

THE INFLUENCE OF BUSINESS CYCLES AND HUMAN CAPITAL INVESTMENTS

Both cyclical and secular economic change should have long-run effects on a cohort's earnings performance. Thus if periods of considerable prosperity occur at a strategic point in a cohort's life-cycle this will probably have a long-term positive impact on its earnings. The reverse would hold for periods of severe recession or depression. There are two initial problems in determining whether or not such cyclical changes will have a long-run economic impact on a cohort. One is how *much* of a down- or upswing is necessary to produce a long-run impact. The other is to determine those critical points in the life-cycle where business cycle fluctuations will leave a lasting impression. Let us focus particularly on downswings, assuming for simplicity's sake that upswings will just have the reverse effect.

We have hypothesized that the long-run impact of a recession on a cohort will vary, depending on the length and severity of the downswing. At one extreme, a very short and minor recession will probably not have a permanent impact on any cohort. Older cohorts will be relatively protected from unemployment by seniority and investments in specific human capital. Younger workers will bear the brunt of the unemployment but there is a lot of "natural" job instability in youth anyway, when tenuous attachments to the labor force are frequent. Hence, if the recession is short, it probably will not have a permanently disruptive effect on the cohorts of men in their early working years. As we get to more severe and more prolonged recessions, however, the cohorts that will first experience some long-term damage to their economic prospects should be those cohorts in the early years of their career cycle. Both human capital and internal labor market theory would lead to this expectation.

According to human capital theory, employers will often have more investments in specific human capital for older workers than for younger, investments that would be permanently lost if older workers were the first to be laid off (Becker 1975: 32ff). This should provide greater protection to older workers than to younger workers in times of recession. Second, investments in on-the-job training are more profitably made relatively early in the career cycle. If a prolonged recession postpones such investments for certain cohorts, then both employers and potential employees may be unwilling to make the same level of investment at a later date. From the employer's point of view, human capital theory argues that investments in specific human capital are not as profitable later on in the employee's life as when he was younger. Furthermore, younger cohorts of workers with more attractive human capital investment prospects may be arriving on the scene.

From the potential *employee's* point of view, investments at a later point in life will also have disadvantages and not only for the reasons Becker argues — that of, lower total returns on such late investments and their higher cost in terms of foregone earnings. If the recession and the unstable employment conditions resulting from it necessitated the postponement of marriage and family formation, then extensive investments in human capital, once prosperity is returning, may involve still further postponements of familial role involvements since such investments are partially paid for by foregone earnings. As a consequence, the familial "opportunity costs" of late human capital investments might be expected to loom large for such cohorts, other things being equal. Hence, it is possible that cohorts so affected may never achieve the same level of human capital investments as cohorts starting their career cycle at a more propitious point in the business cycle.

Internal labor market theory also implies that as the length and severity of the recession increases, cohorts at the early career cycle stage may suffer more long-lasting damage to their economic prospects than older cohorts. This is for two reasons. First, to the extent job security is tied to seniority, the older workers will be more protected from downswings in the business cycle than will younger workers. Certainly the comparison of unemployment rates by age in Figure 2.2 supports this view. Second, to the extent firms recruit workers from the outside primarily at entry level positions for which they desire young people, some cohorts may lose out on gaining a foothold in such firms because of poor labor market conditions. When the economy is again on the upswing, employers may give preference to younger workers. As a result, some of the men in the older cohort may never make up for the disadvantage of entering the labor market during a fairly severe recession.

How difficult their economic position will be depends on demographic factors such as the size of the labor supply from other cohorts and the speed and extent of the economy's recovery.

In sum, one might hypothesize that cohorts at early points in their career cycle will be the ones who are the first to experience long-term or permanent damage to their economic position as one moves from a consideration of short and mild recessions to longer-lasting and more severe downswings. However, as we get to still more severe and prolonged economic downswings such as the Great Depression of the 1930s, this can be expected to have long-term impacts on older cohorts as well, particularly in some occupations and industries. This is because in a very severe and prolonged depression institutional factors such as seniority will not necessarily continue to protect older men, especially in industries that are particularly sensitive to cyclical conditions and for moderate- or small-size firms which may not have the resources to weather a severe depression. Older men (in their 30s and older) who do suffer long-term unemployment or job instability because of a severe depression may, therefore, have even more difficulty in satisfactorily breaking back into the system than younger cohorts.[7]

I am not aware of studies that actually examine these hypothesized long-term economic effects on cohorts at different stages of the career cycle when economic downswings of varying severity have occurred. However, when examining the earnings by age data for the 1960 and 1970 PUS we should try to keep in mind which cohorts might bear the long-term traces of relatively severe economic fluctuations—especially cohorts that might have been affected by the Great Depression or by the period of postwar prosperity. However, as I shall discuss, there are serious problems involved in investigating such cohort effects in any rigorous fashion.

Since secular economic growth in our society has involved increased investments in human capital for each successive cohort that should produce strong cohort effects. Even more important may be qualitative changes in human-capital investments. Evidence that all this has been happening is the considerable growth in the number and size of the various professions and semiprofessions and the tendency to professionalize other occupations such as managerial occupations. Also, there has been a considerable increase over the years in educational attainment. If older cohorts have less invested in human capital, and less *relevant* investments, their cross-sectional "pure" age pattern of earnings will be distorted because of the human capital advantage of younger cohorts relative to older cohorts. How much distortion

---

[7]Here demographic factors might be of significance. If the younger workers are from small birth cohorts, then the economic prospects of somewhat older workers affected by a recession may not be as severely damaged.

occurs, however, will partly depend on the extent to which older, less educated men actually compete in the same labor market as younger, more educated men. Inter-cohort differentials in human capital investments will also presumably affect the longitudinal earnings patterns of earlier versus later cohorts but this will be impossible to consider here since only two periods are observed.

THE ROLE OF COHORT SIZE

A number of demographers have suggested that a cohort's size can have a long-run impact on its economic position (Ryder 1965). Easterlin, in particular, has maintained that the relative size of cohorts during the early working years has had and will continue to have a major impact on the relative economic position of young men. Thus he argues that the small size of the depression cohorts produced extremely favorable labor market conditions for these cohorts in their young adult years. Conversely, the large size of the baby-boom cohorts has led to considerably poorer labor market conditions for these later cohorts in their early working years (Easterlin 1968, 1973, 1978). Our discussion of earnings patterns by age will attempt to detect whether such cohort effects are observable in our data.

In concluding this preliminary discussion of cohort effects, we might briefly consider the possible impact of wars and other military actions. Wars—especially those involving large-scale mobilizations—could certainly have long-term economic effects on the cohorts of young males directly involved, and perhaps indirectly on other cohorts. If nothing else, a disruption in the usual course of career-cycle development is possible. The results of such disruptions might vary, however, depending on a number of circumstances. If only a minority of young males are involved, they could be put in a poor competitive position when they get out of the service as they will be entering the occupational world and engaging in on-the-job training at an older age than usual, and will also be competing with younger men for jobs. Their disadvantage in this respect may be compensated for or offset in a number of ways, however. For example, in some cases the training received in the military may be relevant to civilian jobs. G.I. benefits have also helped subsidize human capital investments for veterans and many organizations—especially governmental ones—give hiring and promotion preferences to veterans. If large numbers of men in a given cohort are involved, such as in World War II, then they may not be very handicapped as a group because so many are in the same boat. Certainly, World War II veterans did not appear highly handicapped economically but this is also probably due to the compensatory factors already mentioned and the small size of the younger cohorts coming on the labor market scene. Reductions in cohort size due to war-related causes of death would operate, of course, to improve the labor market position of those surviving.[8] However, this does not appear to have been a significant demographic factor for American males in World War II.[9]

I have tried to discuss some of the types of circumstances that may lead to a cohort effect on men's earnings. However, I do not believe it will be possible to do a very satisfactory job of empirically investigating most of these possibilities. One serious problem is that I only have data for the 1960 and 1970 PUS. Hence for no cohort can I even compare the difference in experience for the transition between the same two age groups. Thus a proper cohort analysis is obviously impossible. Second, the data were not organized in a way that would optimize the possibility of detecting cohorts effects even on cross-sectional comparisons. This is primarily because one of my major goals has been descriptive—showing variations in age patterns of earnings by occupation. Given an 18-category occupational variable, it was not practical to use very detailed age groups. This was partly because sample sizes—in 1960 especially—in some age and occupational group categories would have become too small. Second, it would have become too cumbersome for presentational tables. Hence, I mainly used 10-year age groups with the exception of the 18–24 age category. Furthermore, I used rather conventional age categories—primarily to facilitate the use of supplementary data from published sources. However, such conventional age categories are not necessarily the optimum ones for an analysis of cohort effects since some 10-year age categories can span cohorts with rather different characteristics and experiences. For example, men who were 35–44 in 1970 came from the cohort of 1926–1935. This was partly a depression cohort and partly not. Hence, once rather gross age categories are employed, it is almost impossible to arrive at a classification system that is equally useful for the analysis of age as well as cohort effects.

Summary

As we have seen, there are a number of age, period, and cohort effects (plus several interactions) that will probably affect the earnings of males in the 1960 and 1970 PUS. First, distinct age pattern of earnings that vary by occupation should be observable. Earnings would be low in youth, rising to a

---

[8]This does not take into account, of course, the labor market problems of those who were physically or mentally handicapped by combat experiences.

[9]A rough indicator of this is the number of battle deaths as a percentage of all personnel serving in World War II. The proportion was 1.8% as compared, for example, to 6.3% for the Union forces alone in the Civil War (U.S. Bureau of the Census 1972c: 258).

peak in the middle years, and leveling off or, in some occupations perhaps, declining with age. Occupations involving higher skills would experience greater rises in earnings for each age group and perhaps a later peak since investments in human capital (and hence returns from these investments) would occur for a longer period of time than in occupations at a lower skill level. Second, although age or cohorts effects might distort the age pattern of earnings somewhat, it seems reasonable to argue that if similar age–earnings profiles are observed for both 1959 and 1969, this reflects a more-or-less "true" overall age effect though period and cohort effects will create perturbations in the pattern that make exact measurement impossible—and perhaps meaningless.

As far as period effects are concerned, these natually divide themselves into cyclical and secular period effects. With regard to cyclical effects, the 1969 unemployment situation was considerably better than that of 1959. Hence real earnings of all men are higher in 1969 just because the latter period represented a more favorable stage of the business cycle. Furthermore, these cyclical conditions seem to interact with both age and occupation. Young males experience much higher unemployment rates during a recession than males 25–64 years old. Hence, that 1959 was a higher unemployment period than 1969, should operate to improve the apparent position of young men relative to older men in 1969 versus 1959. In addition, some occupations and industries are also particularly sensitive to business cycle fluctuations—manual as opposed to nonmanual occupations, on the one hand, and construction and durable-goods-producing industries compared to other industries on the other. These interactions of period with occupation and industry should improve the relative position of males in craft, operative, and laborer occupations in 1969 because of the more favorable economic climate during this year. Secular economic change and its interaction with age effects, should have improved the economic position of men 25 or 30 and older, given the trend toward the increased institutionalization of labor markets.

There are a number of possible consequences resulting from cohort effects and their interaction with period effects. First of all, cohorts who were in the early to middle working years of the Great Depression may exhibit a life-long economic disadvantage if difficulties in the early work years are likely to have a permanently damaging effect on their career prospects. But, the cohorts entering the labor market during the postwar economic boom might have a life-long advantage, especially since many of these males came from small depression cohorts. Conversely, the baby-boom cohorts entering the labor market in recent years may be at a considerable disadvantage—at least at this point in their career cycle. This is because they have the dual problem of large size and of entering the labor market at a time when economic growth has been slowing down but inflation has been accelerating.

Finally, both human capital and internal labor market theories suggest that certain cohort effects should result from secular change. Increasing educational attainment puts younger cohorts at an advantage over older cohorts. However, this is counteracted—to an unknown extent—by the importance of on-the-job training. Furthermore, an increasing institutionalization of labor markets would give older men an advantage over young workers with little seniority.

II

LIFE-CYCLE SQUEEZES AND THEIR COMPONENTS

3

Career Cycle and Occupational Differentials in Men's Earnings

The goal of this chapter is to explore the income component of economic squeezes as the first step in detecting structural sources of relative economic deprivation. Two types of squeezes are of major interest. One is the type of economic stress arising out of variations in the balance of familial consumption aspirations and men's earnings over the life-cycle—that is, life-cycle squeezes. Here, I will use age as the indicator of life-cycle stage, although, admittedly, it is a crude measure. The other type concerns the kinds of stress built into a differentiated occupational system characterized by a tension between occupationally-related consumption aspirations, on the one hand, and the earnings patterns of different occupational groups, on the other. This has two facets of particular interest. One is the contrasts in life-cycle contingencies among occupational groups—namely the interaction of life-cycle squeezes with occupation. The other is whether there is any evidence of a lower white-collar squeeze—relatively high white-collar consumption aspirations combined with an earnings level similar to many blue-collar occupations.

The chapter is divided into five major sections. First, we will consider life-cycle squeezes and occupational variability in the nature and severity of such squeezes, at least to the extent this can be done on the basis of earnings data alone. In the second section, evidence for the existence of a lower white-collar squeeze will be considered. The third and fourth sections describe and try to account for recent changes in the nature of life-cycle squeezes—especially the first squeeze of early adulthood. This naturally leads us to the final section in which we will consider some of Easterlin's work on trends in the relative economic position of young men, the reasons he gives for these trends, and prospects for the 1980s.

Although a good part of this study is about *married* men and their wives, it is inappropriate to use married males to analyze age differentials in men's earnings since the married are not representative of *all* men. The ability or desire to marry will itself be partly a function of a man's economic position. Hence the extent to which age–earnings patterns in an occupation facilitate or impede marriage formation is of analytical concern. For this reason, the sample used in this chapter is not limited to married men but includes white males in other marital statuses. The nature of what marital selectivity occurs and how it varies among occupational groups and according to career-cycle stage will be taken up in Chapter 4.

I. AGE–EARNINGS PROFILES OF MEN BY OCCUPATION: 1959 AND 1969 SIMILARITIES

Do men's age–earnings profiles indicate that certain life-cycle squeezes are an inherent feature of an economic system in which men would have the major economic role outside the home.[1] Is there evidence that, at any one point in time, it is possible for men in the same occupational group—but at different stages in the career cycle—to achieve similar life-styles, other things being equal? Of course, other things never really are equal. For example, an important factor is the man's marital and family status, which will affect what style of life a given income will purchase. However, we will postpone consideration of this complication until a later chapter. Hence, given this ceteris paribus assumption, when earnings vary among different age groups within the same occupational group, this will be taken as a preliminary indication of age differentials in the ability to achieve a common life-style—at least to the extent such a life-style is based on current earnings. A related question is whether there are systematic differences among occupational groups in age differentials in earnings.

[1]Since whether or not wives are likely to work is one of the questions at issue in this study, their role in the amelioration of squeezes is ignored for the moment while men's earnings characteristics are treated as exogenous. Moreover, earnings have not been adjusted for taxes.

I. Age–Earnings Profiles of Men by Occupation

The whole issue of age differentials in earnings is closely related to the question of the age effect on earnings, which I interpret as a career-cycle effect. As discussed in Chapter 2, there are a number of reasons for expecting a particular age or career-cycle effect on earnings and one that will vary systematically among occupations. Furthermore, cohort effects will distort the age effect at any single point in time and period effects will raise additional complications in comparing age patterns over time. Hence, any effort to achieve a precise numerical measurement of age effects is probably doomed to failure—if, indeed, such an effort is theoretically defensible as well as methodologically feasible. This is certainly the case in the present study since only two time periods are available. Nevertheless, it should be possible to obtain a general idea of the career-cycle effect from cross-sectional data because we do have these two periods to compare. If the overall age pattern of earnings, and occupation differences in these, are roughly similar in both 1959 and 1969, then it seems reasonable to argue that they represent an overall picture of the career-cycle effect on earnings during this general period. Then we will turn to a study of the differences between the two censuses, dealing with the question of period and cohort effects in a more systematic fashion.

There are several major points of interest when comparing age patterns of earnings. First, there is the extent to which youthful earnings resemble peak median earnings (which the reader will remember are the highest median earnings among the five age groups) and how this varies among occupational groups. The greater the discrepency between youthful and peak earnings, the greater the apparent improvement wrought by experience and seniority. But this also means that young men in such an occupation are at a greater economic disadvantage vis-à-vis more experienced men. The smaller the discrepancy between peak and youthful earnings, the less experience seems to "pay off" in the occupation, at least for the cohorts we are observing.

A second point of interest is the age at which median earnings generally peak in cross-sectional data and how this varies among occupational groups. If earnings consistently peak at a relatively young age, then perhaps greater experience is not, after a certain age, being translated into improved earnings. Hence older men may be at an economic disadvantage compared to younger men, unless their economic responsibilities are also lighter. It also indicates that if a man's earnings are to continue to increase throughout his working life, it will not be primarily due to career-cycle factors (unless the relationship between age and earnings changes drastically) but rather to other economic factors such as occupational mobility or continued secular improvements in real hourly earnings for his occupational group in particular or for all workers in general. If earnings typically peak at a late age this suggests that increased experience or seniority in the occupation continues to be an important factor in improving earnings until quite late in the career cycle.

A third important issue is the rate of "change" in earnings as we progress from the youngest to the peak-earnings age group and how occupations differ in this respect. In other words, between which age groups are the greatest differences apparent? If most of the youthful-to-peak increase in median earnings occurs when men are quite young—between the 18–24 and 25–34 age groups—then the economic returns from increased experience reach a state of diminishing returns rather early in the career cycle. But, if median earnings continue to rise significantly for each age group between 18–24 and the age at which the peak occurs, then experience probably continues to produce earnings improvements over a large part of the career cycle—just how large a part would depend on the age at which median earnings peak.

Finally, what is the relative position of older men vis-à-vis those in the peak earnings group or even younger and, again, how do occupations vary in this comparison? Is the earnings position of older men versus men in the peak-earnings group similar among occupations or are older men more seriously disadvantaged in some occupations than in others? If the earnings position of older men drops off only slightly in some occupations then the greater experience and/or seniority of the older workers in our samples has probably been enough to protect them from the competition of younger men who usually have superior formal training. If the earnings position of older men typically drops off sharply, however, then experience or seniority probably does not protect them from the adverse competition coming from younger men.[2] However, for some occupations, a greatly reduced earnings position among older men may reflect a voluntary reduction in number of hours worked.

Occupational Mobility

Given the emphasis on age differentials in earnings within occupations, what effect will well-known patterns of occupational mobility have on the validity of inferences about relative deprivation among men in the same occupational group? After all, occupational mobility is quite common, especially among new workers. Many young men are undoubtedly planning (or at least hoping) to move on to higher-level occupations and therefore might not consider older men in their current occupation as positive status-role models. Hence income comparisons between age groups within a

---

[2]This is, of course, a cohort effect rather than an age effect.

number of occupations may be of marginal relevance because of a lack of shared life-style aspirations. While this argument is superficially appealing, occupational mobility does not, in fact, pose as serious a threat to the analysis as one might suppose. This is partly because of the variety and nature of the reference groups used and partly because of the particular character of commonly observed occupational mobility patterns.

First, occupational mobility has a strong inverse relationship to age (Bancroft and Garfinkle 1963; Byrne 1975; Rosenfeld 1979; and Saben 1967). Many young men are to be found in occupations that, for one reason or another, provide them with but a temporary sojourn. Hence, the presumed invalidating impact of occupational mobility will be, at the worst, most serious when investigating relative economic deprivation among the young but it will decline in importance for older men with their lower mobility. But it is not even true that the kind of inferences I wish to make about the young are on particularly shaky ground. Typically, young men are in lower level occupations than older men and their mobility—at least their *planned* mobility—is usually upward rather than downward. The high mobility of young males will certainly bias the estimate of whether they are experiencing relative economic deprivation compared to the older men who really do represent a positive reference group. However, the bias will work *against* my argument that the young chronically experience relative deprivation. Comparing earnings of younger and older men in the *same* occupation, when it is really older men in a *higher-level* occupation who may provide the role model, will thus understate the relative disadvantage of the young. However, the poor intraoccupational "match" in reference groups becomes a greater problem when discussing the aspirational and cost components of the first life-cycle squeeze, especially when trying to look at behavioral adaptations to occupational differences in the nature of these squeezes. Hence, in Chapter 4, where the first squeeze is considered in greater detail, I undertake an analysis of occupational mobility among young males to show what it tells us about possible reference-group comparisons, the first squeeze, and age at marriage as a possible adaptive response.

It is important to remember that *negative,* as well as *positive,* reference groups have their analytical utility. In addition it seems psychologically reasonable to assume that people cannot help but be partially oriented toward their current reality, regardless of their past experiences or future expectations. Those in the same or similar occupations are usually a major part of the everyday reality of a working man, a reality to which he must relate in one way or another. If he also has other occupational reference groups that are on a higher socioeconomic level and provide positive role models, then those in the same occupational group in which he currently finds himself will tend to provide a *negative* reference standard. Hence, younger men in lower-level occupations with higher future aspirations may often view the life-styles of older men currently in the same occupation somewhat negatively. To the extent this is true, equal or lower earnings of the young should provide rather reliable evidence of an economic squeeze situation, ceteris paribus. Similarly, even if men in their forties and fifties anticipate future upward occupational mobility, part of their day-to-day reality is also composed of men of a variety of ages in the same occupational group. Moreover, they are likely to feel that older men should be earning more than younger men, whether or not they themselves have future upward mobility plans. For both these reasons, younger men should provide something of a negative reference group. Where earnings resemble each other, or older men are doing more poorly, then this too may indicate that perceived relative deprivation is being experienced.

Finally, much occupational mobility may not have a significant impact on earnings or a man's overall career trajectory—that is, in the *economic* sense of the term. There is a considerable amount of overlap in earnings levels and patterns across major occupational groups so that apparently significant mobility (as measured by traditional socioeconomic indices such as the Duncan SEI) may not be very significant from an income point of view. The very fact that I could construct the same or very similar peak median earnings groups for a broad range of both white- and blue-collar occupations is indicative of an extensive overlap in "permanent income" among occupations.

Using data on 1965 and 1970 occupations from the 1970 PUS of all white males, I estimated what proportion of all men employed in a non-farm occupation at both dates were mobile and upwardly mobile, by age (Table 3.1). For the purpose of this table, I used a peak median-earnings classification that was more detailed than the condensed 18-group system used in the rest of the study. Occupational mobility was defined as moving from one to another of 33 peak median occupational groups between 1965 and 1970. Upward occupational mobility occurred if the change was from a lower to a higher peak median earnings group, regardless of the major occupational group involved.

Table 3.1 supports other occupational and job mobility data in showing a very strong negative relationship with age. Mobility declined from 50% of males who were 25–29 in 1970 to 24% for males in the 50–64 age group. Moreover, most of the decline in the proportions mobile between 1965 and 1970 had occurred by the 35–39 age group. Upward occupational mobility, as defined here, was also strongly related to age and the proportion who were upwardly mobile was much less than the proportion who were mobile at all. For example, for men who were 35–39 in 1970, although 32% had changed

I. Age–Earnings Profiles of Men by Occupation

TABLE 3.1
Occupational Mobility of White Males between 1965 and 1970, by Age in 1970 (Males Employed in Both 1970 and 1965)[a]

Mobility status	Age							
	25–29	30–34	35–39	40–44	45–49	50–54	55–59	60–64
Percentage of total who were mobile[b,c]	50	40	32	28	27	24	24	24
Percentage of total who were upwardly mobile[c,d]	30	23	18	16	14	13	11	11

Source: 1970 Public Use Sample of White Males.

[a]The peak median occupational classification system used in this table included 33 peak median occupational groups rather than the less detailed 18-category variable used throughout the rest of this study. See Appendix A for a description of the classification system.

[b]Shortly before going to press a final check of the occupational coding system revealed an error in the 1965 salesworker occupational categories. A number of salesworkers were classified into the lowest peak median sales category instead of the higher earnings sales groups. This will lead to some overstatement of 1965–1970 mobility in general and of upward mobility in particular.

[c]*Occupational mobility* was defined as moving from one to another of the 33 peak median occupation groups between 1965 and 1970.

[d]*Upward occupational mobility* was defined as moving from a lower to a higher peak median earnings group, regardless of the major occupational group involved.

from one peak median occupation group to another, only 18% had moved into an occupation group with higher peak median earnings.

In short, occupational mobility declines markedly with age and a considerable amount of what mobility occurs does not seem to involve movement into occupations with higher average earnings. Hence, once again, mobility should not be a major factor invalidating inferences drawn from interage comparisons of earnings within peak median occupational groups.

Relative Position of the Young

In general, both the 1960 and 1970 data show that no matter how their economic fates subsequently diverged, relatively low earnings were characteristic of most young men, whatever their occupational group (Tables 3.2 and 3.3). For all occupations combined, 18–24-year-olds had the lowest median earnings—usually less than half of any other age group. This is also true for each of the occupational groups for which we have data in 1960 and 1970. In fact, occupational differentials in earnings are just about at a minimum among young men, as the figures on the range in medians indicate.

TABLE 3.2
Median 1959 Earnings of White Males, 18–64 Years Old, by Occupation and Age (in 1969 Dollars)[a]

Occupation	Total	18–24	25–34	35–44	44–54	55–64
Total	6,440	2,976	6,559	7,358	6,877	6,189
Professionals						
I	10,864	3,852	8,963	12,750	13,330	11,479
II	8,509	3,427	7,992	9,503	9,710	9,219
III	6,662	2,780	6,406	8,166	7,657	7,593
Managers						
I	10,601	[c]	8,662	11,274	11,951	11,682
II	9,217	4,438	8,008	9,731	9,743	9,933
III	7,289	4,507	7,266	7,715	7,608	6,814
Sales						
II	8,281	4,292	7,952	8,792	8,782	8,903
III	5,870	2,237	6,308	7,234	6,313	5,424
Clerical						
III	6,425	3,155	6,387	7,187	6,905	6,529
IV	5,358	2,935	5,543	6,172	6,043	5,832
Craft						
II	8,943	[c]	7,548	9,244	9,360	9,000
III	6,979	4,136	7,018	7,583	7,139	6,656
IV	5,441	3,105	6,040	6,391	5,543	4,566
Operatives						
III	6,111	3,745	6,126	6,647	6,529	6,014
IV	5,289	2,925	5,599	6,144	5,760	5,052
Service						
III	6,781	[c]	6,713	7,197	6,470	6,379
IV	4,150	1,228	4,446	4,950	4,792	4,222
Laborers						
IV	4,071	1,857	4,951	5,193	4,656	4,296
Range	6,793	3,210	4,517	7,800	8,674	7,460

Sources: 1960 Public Use Sample of White Males; U.S. Bureau of Labor Statistics 1971c: 105; 1974b: 95.

[a] The medians for 1959 were inflated to 1969 dollars using the 25.8% increase in the Consumer Price Index in the 1959–1969 period.

[b] The age group at which the highest medians occurred is underlined.

[c] Sample size was too small to justify computation of a median.

Moreover, the particularly low earnings of occupations that frequently provide part-time temporary jobs for youths not fully in the labor market, such as the Sales III, Service IV, and Laborers IV groups, accounted for a lot of the variation in the range in medians.

I. Age–Earnings Profiles of Men by Occupation

TABLE 3.3
Median 1969 Earnings of White Males, 18–64 Years Old, by Occupation and Age

Occupation	Total	18–24	25–34	35–44	45–54	55–64
				Age[a]		
Total	8,120	3,385	8,359	<u>9,676</u>	9,273	8,047
Professionals						
I	13,729	4,391	11,265	15,684	<u>16,726</u>	15,823
II	10,650	4,922	10,110	12,517	<u>12,689</u>	11,593
III	8,781	3,372	8,454	10,494	<u>10,905</u>	10,207
Managers						
I	12,900	6,071	10,540	13,959	<u>15,534</u>	15,171
II	10,951	5,576	10,014	<u>12,368</u>	12,257	10,952
III	9,444	4,962	9,037	10,285	<u>10,374</u>	8,898
Sales						
II	10,772	5,380	9,842	12,469	<u>12,534</u>	11,083
III	7,749	2,650	8,241	<u>9,609</u>	9,434	7,798
Clerical						
III	7,961	3,592	8,044	<u>8,968</u>	8,791	8,372
IV	6,441	3,120	7,000	<u>7,860</u>	7,822	6,921
Craft						
II	10,734	7,222	10,078	11,160	<u>11,245</u>	10,569
III	8,595	5,118	8,624	<u>9,550</u>	9,208	8,441
IV	7,033	3,989	7,482	<u>7,857</u>	7,678	6,683
Operatives						
III	7,566	4,739	7,778	<u>8,282</u>	8,246	7,640
IV	6,541	3,206	7,135	<u>7,831</u>	7,495	6,658
Service						
III	9,005	6,175	8,831	<u>9,754</u>	9,691	8,531
IV	5,074	1,609	5,633	<u>6,731</u>	6,074	5,676
Laborers						
IV	4,817	1,966	6,219	<u>6,602</u>	6,578	5,621
Range	8,912	5,613	5,632	9,082	10,652	10,202

Source: 1970 Public Use Sample of White Males.
[a]The age group at which the highest medians occurred is underlined.

As the median earnings of young men are rather uniformly low, youthful earnings are not very highly correlated with the peak median level of their occupations. Earnings increased rapidly between age groups 18–24 and 25–34 at both census dates, but, even so, the differences among occupation groups were still well below those for older age groups. All this suggests, somewhat ironically, that the economic deprivation of young men, either already in Group I and II occupations or preparing to enter them, *relative* to older men in these occupations, is much greater than that experienced by youths with less favorable career trajectories.

Group I and II Occupations

Although low earnings are generally characteristic of the young, regardless of occupation, marked occupational differentials in earnings rapidly appear when we turn to progressively older men. This is already apparent in the median earnings of men 25–34 years old, but the differences become most pronounced for men past 35. Two major patterns seem to stand out: one primarily characteristic of higher peak-earnings groups (those in Group I and Group II occupations) and the other characteristic of lower-income groups (those in Group III and IV occupations).

In the case of the higher-income groups, although average earnings are low for the young, they rapidly rise from age group to age group, finally peaking at a rather late age. Such occupations roughly correspond to what Thompson Avery, and Carlson (1968) have called occupations with "late ceilings." For example, with but one exception in 1970, peak 1959 and 1969 median earnings occurred at age groups 45–54 or older for all Group I and II occupations. In 1959 the peak was not even achieved until age 55–64 in two occupational groups (Managers II and Sales II).

How much of an advantage in average earnings the peak medians represent is well illustrated by a comparison of the ratios of peak median earnings to median earnings at a younger age (Tables 3.4 and 3.5). For Professionals I, for example, the peak 1959 and 1969 median earnings were almost 50% higher than the median earnings at ages 25–34 and about 250% higher than the median earnings at ages 18–24. However, differentials between peak medians and those of men aged 35–44 were small. For the other Group I and II occupations, the interage improvements were not quite as big, but they were substantial nonetheless. Furthermore, differentials between peak and youthful median earnings were greater for Group I than Group II occupations in both 1959 and 1969. Of course, young men already in Group I and II occupations will not be representative of all men ultimately working in such occupations. At ages 18–24 most of these men will either still be in training (with very poor incomes) or working at jobs in lower-paid occupations. As a result the very high ratio of peak median earnings to median earnings at ages 18–24 will, if anything, probably understate the improvement in income men in high peak-earnings occupations will experience compared to the incomes of men in early adulthood.

How much average earnings "deteriorate" after the peak is also revealed by Tables 3.4 and 3.5. A major advantage men in the high income

I. Age–Earnings Profiles of Men by Occupation

TABLE 3.4
Ratio of Peak Median Earnings to Those at Different Ages for White Males 18–64 Years Old, by Occupation: 1959

Occupation	18–24	25–34	35–44	45–54	55–64
Total	2.47	1.12	1.00	1.07	1.19
Professionals					
I	3.46	1.49	1.04	1.00	1.16
II	2.83	1.22	1.02	1.00	1.05
III	2.94	1.27	1.00	1.07	1.08
Managers					
I	[a]	1.38	1.06	1.00	1.02
II	2.24	1.24	1.02	1.02	1.00
III	1.71	1.06	1.00	1.01	1.13
Sales					
II	2.07	1.12	1.01	1.01	1.00
III	3.23	1.15	1.00	1.14	1.33
Clerical					
III	2.28	1.12	1.00	1.04	1.10
IV	2.10	1.11	1.00	1.02	1.06
Craft					
II	[a]	1.24	1.01	1.00	1.04
III	1.83	1.08	1.00	1.06	1.14
IV	2.06	1.06	1.00	1.15	1.40
Operatives					
III	1.77	1.08	1.00	1.02	1.10
IV	2.10	1.10	1.00	1.07	1.22
Service					
III	[a]	1.07	1.00	1.11	1.13
IV	4.03	1.11	1.00	1.03	1.17
Laborers					
IV	2.80	1.05	1.00	1.12	1.21

Source: Table 3.2.
[a] Sample size was too small to justify computation of a median.

occupations have is that the career-cycle factor alone will probably lead to increases in earnings over much of their lives with only a falling off after age 55, if then. Partly because of this late age at peaking, the median earnings for men aged 55–64 compared quite favorable to the peak median earnings. In 1959 the ratio of peak median earnings to those of men 55–64 in Group I or II occupations only varied from 1.00 to 1.16 and in 1969 the range of variation was from 1.02 to 1.13.

TABLE 3.5
Ratio of Peak Median Earnings to Those at Different Ages for White Males 18–64 Years Old, by Occupation: 1969

Occupation	18–24	25–34	35–44	45–54	55–64
Total	2.86	1.16	1.00	1.04	1.20
Professionals					
I	3.81	1.48	1.07	1.00	1.06
II	2.58	1.26	1.01	1.00	1.09
III	3.23	1.29	1.04	1.00	1.07
Managers					
I	2.56	1.47	1.11	1.00	1.02
II	2.22	1.24	1.00	1.01	1.13
III	2.09	1.15	1.01	1.00	1.16
Sales					
II	2.33	1.27	1.00	1.00	1.13
III	3.63	1.16	1.00	1.02	1.23
Clerical					
III	2.50	1.11	1.00	1.02	1.07
IV	2.52	1.12	1.00	1.00	1.14
Craft					
II	1.56	1.12	1.01	1.00	1.06
III	1.86	1.11	1.00	1.04	1.13
IV	1.97	1.05	1.00	1.02	1.18
Operatives					
III	1.75	1.06	1.00	1.00	1.08
IV	2.44	1.10	1.00	1.04	1.18
Service					
III	1.58	1.10	1.00	1.01	1.14
IV	4.18	1.19	1.00	1.11	1.18
Laborers					
IV	3.36	1.06	1.00	1.00	1.17

Source: Table 3.3.

Group III and IV Occupations

The situation in the lower-paid Group III and IV occupations is in marked contrast to the pattern for high-income occupations. First of all, in Group III and IV occupations peak median earnings tended to occur at a young age—generally ages 35–44 (Tables 3.2 and 3.3). These are typically occupations which have "early ceilings" (Thompson *et al*. 1968). In 1959 the peaks were at ages 35–44 for all Group III and IV occupations and in 1969 only 2 occupation groups (out of a total of 12 in the III and IV category) had later peaks—Professionals III and Managers III had peak 1969 median earnings at ages 45–54.

A second feature of Group III and IV occupations is that although the peaks achieved were substantially larger than the median earnings at younger ages, as one might expect, they did not represent anywhere near the increase in earnings which were characteristic of the better-paid occupations (Tables 3.4 and 3.5). This was particularly true of the Blue Collar and Service III and IV groups. The major exceptions to this pattern of much more substantial improvements in youthful earnings for higher-level occupations are the Group III and IV occupations that are most likely to provide part-time employment—Sales III, Service IV, and Laborers IV where the ratio of peak/18–24 medians was substantial at both censuses.

What is probably more significant than a comparison of the peak/18–24 median earnings is the ratio of peak earnings to those achieved by men in the 25–34 age group, as this indicates the extent to which the increased advantage of greater experience tends to peter out rather early in life. Although the peak/25–34 ratios are still substantial for high-income occupations, they are (with the exception of Professionals III in both 1959 and 1969) very modest indeed for most of the occupations in the Group III and IV categories.

In sum, for the most of the Group III and IV occupations, the ratio of peak median earnings to those of younger men is only fairly high for the peak/18–24 comparison. If we can interpret this finding in terms of the career-cycle effect, this suggests that, after a sizable jump in earnings during early adulthood, increased work experience in many lower-level occupations yields relatively few economic advantages over younger men. This is certainly in sharp constrast to the picture presented by Group I and II occupations. All this, of course, is quite consistent with the hypothesized role of human capital investments in earnings differentials.

In comparing the earnings position of men who are older than those in the peak-median age group, once again the position of those in the lower-paid occupations appears relatively unfavorable. And since the peak is achieved at a younger age in the lower-income occupations, more men operate at the relative economic disadvantage of being in the "post-peak" group than is the case in the better paid occupations. This was particularly the case in 1959. The relative income position of 55–64-year-old men improved by 1969.[3] More significantly, perhaps, in 9 out of the 12 Group III and IV occupations, the 1959 and 1969 median earnings of men aged 55–64 were even lower than the medians of men aged 25–34.

---

[3] However, the more favorable cyclical conditions in 1969 may have contributed to the improvement for older men in blue-collar occupations.

In sum, if occupations do form rough reference groups defining relatively common or minimum appropriate life-styles, then these data imply that, at any one point in time, men at different stages of the career cycle are not equally capable of achieving such life-styles on the basis of their annual earnings alone. In particular, unless the economic aspirations of the young are really minimal, this age group is likely to perceive an acute sense of relative deprivation whatever the occupation but particularly for those going into Group I and II occupations. Second, the ability of older men to achieve similar or more elaborate life-styles compared to those of somewhat younger men seems to be much more feasible for those in Group I and II than in Group III and IV occupations.

II. THE LOWER WHITE-COLLAR SQUEEZE

Occupational Differences in Educational Attainment

A comparison of the educational attainment of men in different peak median occupations should provide a preliminary indication of structural sources of relative deprivation. For one thing, the educational experience is itself a socialization process that influences life-style aspirations. Moreover, if there is some positive relationship between educational attainment and the cost of these aspirations, then occupational differences in educational attainment will be indicative of systematic differences in the cost of achieving aspirations among occupations. More important, perhaps, the educational level of the man should be indicative of his and his wife's normatively based educational aspirations for their children—the idea being that social status considerations, as well as other cultural factors, would lead many parents to feel obligated to provide their children with at least an equal, if not higher, educational attainment than they themselves received (Turchi 1975a: Chapter 2; Freedman 1963). Finally, a comparison of educational levels of men in occupations at different earnings levels should indicate whether families of men in some occupations might be in an economically stressful position—at least at some points during the family cycle. For example, if men in certain occupations exhibit much higher educational attainments but similar or lower earnings than men in other occupations, an economic squeeze situation may exist.

Table 3.6 shows various measures of educational attainment for white

II. The Lower White-Collar Squeeze

males by peak median occupation.[4] As expected, within major occupational groups, educational attainment tends to be directly related to peak median earnings level. One important exception to this is found in the professions where the median school years completed of Professional III males was higher than for Professional II males at both census dates. This largely reflects a much greater propensity of Professional III males to have four or more years of college (55% versus 45% for Professional II men in 1970) and is probably due to the fact that the Professional III category includes elementary and secondary school teachers.[5] If life-style aspirations of Professional III men are related to their educational level—especially their educational aspirations for their children—then they may often experience some economic stress since their earnings levels are relatively low compared to all Group I and II occupations but their educational attainment is high compared to these very same occupational groups with the one exception of the Professional I group.

There is also evidence that economic stress is a structural characteristic of other Group III white-collar groups as well. Although their educational attainment is always below that of Group I and II white-collar occupations, it is nevertheless well above that for Group III blue-collar occupational groups. For example, in 1970, 74% of Sales III males and 81% of Clerical III males had completed 12 or more years of schooling as compared to 54% and 45% respectively for Craft and Operative III males. In fact, a substantial proportion of the Sales and Clerical III males had one or more years of college in 1970 (36 and 38% respectively) compared to very few of the Craft and Operative III males (12 and 9% respectively).[6]

In sum, a comparison of Group III white-collar occupations with Group I and II white-collar occupations, on the one hand, and with Group III blue-collar groups, on the other, suggests that men in Group III white-collar occupations frequently find themselves in an economic squeeze situation. As

---

[4]The sample base in this chapter varies slightly for the different tables. Tables 3.6 and 3.12 included all males in the 18-category peak median occupation variable (34,100 in 1960 and 124,809 in 1970). Tables 3.2 to 3.5 and 3.7 to 3.9, which deal with earnings data, are restricted to the slightly smaller subset of males with net positive earnings (32,811 in 1960 and 119,816 in 1970). Table 3.1 includes only those in the 25–64 age groups who were employed and gave an occupation in both 1965 and 1970. Tables 3.10 to 3.11 and 3.13 to 3.15 do not refer to the PUS data used in this study.

[5]Elementary and secondary school teachers constituted 30% of the Professional III group in 1960 and 34% in 1970.

[6]The relatively higher educational attainment of Group III white-collar males was characteristic of all age groups and not just of the young who might expect to be upwardly mobile out of such occupations.

TABLE 3.6
Educational Attainment of White Males 18–64 Years Old, by Peak Median Occupation: 1960 and 1970

		1960				1970		
		Percentage with				Percentage with		
Occupation	Median	12+ years	13+ years	16+ years	Median	12+ years	13+ years	16+ years
Total	12.0	50.3	23.4	11.5	12.4	63.1	29.9	15.2
Professionals								
I	17+	95.7	86.4	74.7	17.3	97.4	88.1	75.3
II	15.3	90.3	71.3	43.2	15.4	94.0	71.7	45.1
III	15.7	87.7	68.6	47.6	16.2	92.1	73.1	54.6
Managers								
I	13.7	80.3	55.3	31.6	14.6	89.2	61.7	39.9
II	12.5	63.2	34.5	16.0	12.8	76.9	42.0	20.5
III	12.3	59.4	27.7	10.5	12.6	71.2	33.0	13.9
Sales								
II	12.9	77.5	46.5	22.7	13.8	87.3	57.2	30.5
III	12.4	62.2	29.0	9.1	12.6	73.6	35.9	11.8
Clerical								
III	12.5	71.6	30.8	9.2	12.7	80.9	38.1	12.8
IV	11.8	48.4	11.6	2.4	12.3	60.8	19.6	3.0
Craft								
II	11.9	49.0	14.7	4.9	12.3	62.4	19.3	6.6
III	10.9	43.9	12.4	2.4	12.1	54.1	11.7	2.1
IV	9.7	30.4	6.3	0.8	11.2	43.0	9.0	1.5
Operatives								
III	10.0	33.0	5.9	0.8	11.4	45.0	8.6	1.0
IV	9.6	28.4	5.5	0.7	11.1	41.8	9.4	1.3
Service								
III	12.2	57.8	15.8	3.0	12.5	77.3	23.2	3.7
IV	9.5	30.5	10.8	2.2	11.3	44.6	15.4	2.5
Laborers								
IV	9.1	26.9	7.4	1.1	11.2	43.1	13.3	1.7

Source: 1960 and 1970 Public Use Samples of White Males.

indicated by their white-collar status and their educational level, consumption aspirations and obligations are likely to be high among these men and their families but they are in the same earnings group as males in many blue-collar occupations.

Occupational Differences in Earnings

Although the occupational classification system was set up according to a measure of earnings—peak median earnings in 1959—it is still useful to compare the median earnings of men in Group III white-collar occupations to those of men in various other occupations, especially the blue-collar groups. One reason is that the peak median groups were based on class intervals and there are systematic variations in median earnings among occupations within the same peak median earnings groups. In addition, 1970 data reflect changes in earnings over time as the same occupations were classified in the same way at both census dates, regardless of 1969 earnings.

As Table 3.7 indicates, a number of Group III white-collar occupations seemed to have been experiencing a lower-white-collar squeeze in both 1959 and 1969. Clerical workers and those in Sales III occupations were in an especially disadvantageous position in both periods, exhibiting lower median earnings than Craft III men in practically every age group. The relative disadvantage of 18–24-year-olds was particularly marked in 1959 and deteriorated even further by 1969. This probably reflects the use of these occupations as a source of part-time temporary jobs by many young men who were heading in other occupational directions.

Managers III males consistently had higher earnings than Craft and Operative III males—in both 1959 and 1969 although the differential between their earnings and those of Craft III males was often not very substantial. However, their relative position improved between 1959 and 1969.[7] The Managers III group was unique among Group III white-collar occupations in that it did not exhibit as depressed median earnings among the young—perhaps because of a high proportion of young men going into family businesses since all self-employed managers in retail trade fall into the Group III category. However, a very small proportion of Manager III males were in the 18–24 age group—only 6.5% in 1970—so this relatively favorable position is not of much general significance.

The overall economic position of Professional III relative to Craft III men was surprisingly poor, though it improved considerably during the decade (Table 3.7). However, the poor showing of those lower-level professionals was primarily a result of the relatively low earnings of men 18–24 and 25–34 years old. Thus, the ratio of the 1969 median earnings of Professional III males 18–24 to those of Craft and Operative III males was only 66 and 71% respectively. The relative earnings position of 25–34 year old Professional

---

[7]Their overall earnings relative to men in the Managers II group also improved—the median earnings ratio rose from 79 to 86% of the median for Managers II males.

TABLE 3.7
Median Earnings of Men in White-Collar III and IV Occupations as a Percentage of the Median for Men in Craft and Operative III Occupations, by Age: 1959 and 1969

Occupations	Total	18–24	25–34	35–44	45–54	55–64
	\multicolumn{6}{c}{Ratio of median to that for males in the Craft III group}					
Professionals III						
1959	95.4	67.2	91.3	107.7	107.2	114.1
1969	102.2	65.9	98.0	109.9	118.4	120.9
Managers III						
1959	104.4	109.0	103.5	101.7	106.6	102.4
1969	109.9	97.0	104.8	107.7	112.7	105.4
Sales III						
1959	84.1	54.1	89.9	95.4	88.4	81.4
1969	90.2	51.8	95.6	100.6	102.4	92.4
Clerical III						
1959	92.1	76.3	91.0	94.7	96.7	98.1
1969	92.6	70.2	93.3	93.9	95.5	99.2
Clerical IV						
1950	76.8	71.0	79.0	81.4	84.6	87.6
1969	74.9	61.0	81.2	82.3	84.9	82.0
	\multicolumn{6}{c}{Ratio of median to that for males in the Operatives III group}					
Professionals III						
1959	109.0	74.2	104.6	122.8	117.3	126.2
1969	116.0	71.2	108.7	126.7	132.2	133.6
Managers III						
1959	119.3	120.3	118.6	116.1	116.5	113.3
1969	124.8	104.7	116.2	124.2	125.8	116.5
Sales III						
1959	96.1	59.7	103.0	108.8	96.7	90.2
1969	102.4	55.9	106.0	116.0	114.4	102.1
Clerical III						
1959	105.1	84.2	104.3	108.1	105.8	108.6
1969	105.2	75.8	103.4	108.3	106.6	109.6
Clerical IV						
1959	87.7	78.4	90.5	92.8	92.6	97.0
1969	85.1	65.8	90.0	94.9	94.8	90.6

Sources: Tables 3.2 and 3.3.

III men improved considerably but was still below that of Craft III 25–34-year-olds—especially in 1959. However, the relative position of older Professional III males was much better.

II. The Lower White-Collar Squeeze

In general, the age pattern of earnings of Professional III men increasingly resembles that of Group I or II occupations. Like the higher-level occupations, Professional III occupations start out with low youthful earnings but exhibit substantial increases in median earnings between both the 18–24/25–34 and the 25–34/35–44 age groups. Furthermore, although peak median earnings were in the 35–44 age group for Professionals III in 1959, by 1969 the peak had moved to age 45–54. Finally, there was relatively little drop in earnings for men in the 55–64 age group. As a consequence, the median earnings of 55–64-year-old Professionals III far outstrip the earnings of the second highest Group III earners. Nevertheless, considering the much greater educational attainment of Professional III males, it is somewhat surprising that their earnings position is not even better when compared to blue-collar groups such as the Craft III workers. This is probably indicative of the fact that differences in job-related human capital investments are overstated by using the educational data. Systematic occupational differences occur in how and where human capital investments are made—in educational institutions by professionals and on the job by craft workers. However, if formal education—especially at the college level—is a socialization process itself, then it will probably expose those who will be Professional III workers to the cultural and socioeconomic characteristics of people from higher socioeconomic groups. Presumably this will have some effect on the aspirational levels—an effect that is different from that experienced by blue-collar workers undergoing on-the-job training in a largely blue-collar milieu.

In summary, the evidence shows that the earnings position of Group III white-collar males relative to Group III blue-collar occupations—particularly the Craft III group—is rather poor given the nonmanual status of these males plus their relatively high educational attainment. To the extent the consumption *obligations* of these white-collar groups (particularly their obligations to extensively educate their children), as well as their consumption *aspirations* are higher than those of blue-collar groups, the evidence is indicative of a lower-white-collar economic squeeze.[8] Later on, we shall consider whether the data further support this conclusion by showing elevated work rates for the wives of such men compared to the wives of men in Group III blue-collar occupations.

---

[8]Some years ago, Hamilton argued that the economic position of lower-middle-class males was not below that of skilled manual workers and, using his method of classification, he found rough equality in income (Hamilton 1964, 1966). However, the income similarities were partly achieved by including some higher-level occupations in the lower-middle-class group and eliminating other higher-paying groups from the skilled-worker category as well as cutting out some lower-income groups from the lower-middle-class category.

III. 1959–1969 CHANGES IN AGE AND OCCUPATIONAL PATTERNS OF EARNINGS: A DESCRIPTION

So far we have been focusing on the similarities between 1959 and 1969 earnings patterns by age. However, as the reader has undoubtedly noticed, earnings patterns by age did *not* remain the same during this period. Some age groups have improved their position and some seem to have lost ground over the decade and it is to this question we now turn.

Since I am focusing here particularly on age patterns of earnings and 1959–1969 differences or changes in these patterns, these changes will be described in terms of differential increases among the various age groups. Tables 3.8 and 3.9 give us somewhat different views of how the five age groups fared over the decade. Table 3.8 shows the percentage increase in median earnings for each age group by occupation and permits a very detailed comparison of changes in the age–earnings profile among the 18 occupational groups. It is computed from the medians presented in Tables 3.2 and 3.3. However, because of this extreme detail it is sometimes difficult to get an overall idea of the changes that have occurred and whether the experience of any one age group vis-à-vis other age groups was typical of most occupations. Thus one risks the danger of not being able to see the woods for the trees. However, there is a way to achieve a general idea of how much changes in certain age patterns were characteristic of many occupations. For each age group in a given occupation the percentage increase in median earnings can be compared to that of every other age group in the occupation. We can then do this for all occupational groups. These comparisons are then classified according to three possible alternatives: (a) the age group had a smaller increase in earnings compared to a different age group in the occupation; (b) it had approximately the same rate of increase in median earnings; and (c) it had a higher rate of increase. For each age group, then, we can look at a distribution of the comparisons according to the number of times among the 18 occupations the age group did better, worse, or the same as other age groups in the occupation. (Table 3.9).[9]

Two major questions arise in this analysis of age differentials in the percentage increase in 1959–1969 median earnings. First, did certain age groups do particularly well or particularly poorly relative to other age groups? Second, if this is the case (as it is) was this especially true for certain

---

[9] It would be possible to compare the increase for each age–occupation group to every other age–occupation group. However, the desire was to keep the occupation as a basic unit of analysis. My interest was whether, on the whole, for each occupation group a given age group did better or worse than other age groups—not whether Professional III 18–24-year-olds improved their earnings more than Clerical III 35–44-year-olds. The ultimate goal was describing changes in age patterns of earnings within occupations.

TABLE 3.8
1959–1969 Percentage Increase in Median Earnings, by Age and Occupation

		Age				
Occupation	Total	18–24	25–34	35–44	45–54	55–64
Total	26.1	13.7	27.4	31.5	34.8	30.0
Professionals						
I	26.4	14.0	25.7	23.0	25.5	37.8
II	25.2	43.6	26.5	31.7	30.7	25.6
III	31.8	21.3	32.0	28.5	42.4	34.4
Managers						
I	21.7	[a]	21.7	23.8	30.0	29.9
II	18.8	25.6	25.0	27.1	25.8	10.2
III	29.6	10.1	24.4	33.3	36.4	30.6
Sales						
II	30.1	25.3	23.8	41.8	42.7	24.5
III	32.0	18.5	30.6	32.8	49.4	43.8
Clerical						
III	23.9	13.8	25.9	24.9	27.3	28.2
IV	20.2	6.3	26.3	27.3	29.4	18.7
Craft						
II	20.0	[a]	33.5	20.7	20.1	17.4
III	23.2	23.7	22.9	25.9	29.0	26.8
IV	29.2	28.5	23.9	22.9	38.5	46.4
Operatives						
III	23.8	26.5	27.0	24.6	26.3	27.0
IV	23.7	9.6	27.4	27.4	30.1	31.8
Service						
III	32.8	[a]	31.6	35.5	49.8	33.7
IV	22.3	31.0	26.7	36.0	26.8	34.4
Laborers						
IV	18.3	5.9	25.6	27.1	41.3	30.8

Sources: Tables 3.2 and 3.3.
[a] Medians were not computed for 1959 because of small sample size.

occupations? As we saw earlier, compared to men in the peak-earnings group, the relative economic position of 18–24-year-old males was quite poor in both 1959 and 1969. In addition, however, Tables 3.8 and 3.9 reveal that their earnings position deteriorated even further over the decade. For men in all occupational groups combined, the percentage increases in median earnings for 18–24-year-olds was less than half that of men in every older age group (Table 3.8). Moreover, as Table 3.9 shows, in as many as 63% of the interage comparisons among occupations, 18–24-year-olds had lower

TABLE 3.9
Interage Differences in 1959–1969 Percentage Increases in Median Earnings

	Age and distribution of comparisons									
Standing of age group compared to other age groups in occupation[a]	18–24		25–34		35–44		45–54		55–64	
	N	%	N	%	N	%	N	%	N	%
Total	60	100	69	100	69	100	69	100	69	100
Lower percentage increase	38	63	21	30	14	20	6	9	15	22
Similar percentage increase	16	27	35	51	37	54	27	39	30	43
Greater percentage increase	6	10	13	19	18	26	36	52	24	35

Source: Table 3.8.

[a]This is the percentage of the time, for all occupations, that a given age group had approximately the same, a greater, or a lower percentage increase in median earnings compared to every other age group in the same occupation. The difference in the percentage change had to be at least five or more percentage points to count as a greater or lesser change. Four comparisons are theoretically possible for each occupation—72 comparisons in all for the 18 occupational groups. The number of actual comparisons is less because it is was not possible to compute medians for all occupations in the 18–24 age group.

increases than older age groups in their occupation—the highest proportion for any age group. As we go to older age groups, the proportion of comparisons in which the age group did worse than other age groups declines considerably, reaching a minimum of 9% for 45–54-year-old men.

The proportion of the time in which 18–24-year-olds did *better* as opposed to *worse* than other age groups was, as one might anticipate, very low. In only six cases, 10% of the comparisons, did the relative increase in earnings of 18–24-year-olds exceed those of an older age group. However, the proportion of comparisons in which a particular age group did better than other age groups in the same occupation rises as age goes up, reaching a maximum for men 45–54 years old. Again, 55–64-year-olds had a poorer showing compared to 45–54-year-olds but not compared to any other age group.

In sum, Table 3.9 indicates that, first of all, 18–24-year-olds fared quite poorly compared to the other age groups in 1959–1969 increases in median earnings. Men who were 25–34 years old did somewhat better but also lagged behind older age groups. Men who were 35–44 did better still but it was 45–54-year-old men who were both most likely to have improved their position compared to other age groups in an occupation and least likely to have achieved lower increases than other age groups (in fact, in only 9% of the comparisons). Finally, 55–64-year-old men did better than men 18–34 years old in the sense that in a smaller proportion of the comparisons did 55–

III. 1959–1969 Changes in Age and Occupational Patterns of Earnings

64-year-olds do worse than younger men in an occupation and in a higher proportion of cases they did better. Not even in the comparison of the improvement for 55–64-year-old men with 35–44-year-olds, did the older men come off too poorly.

The decrease in the relative economic status of young men seems quite consistent, of course, with Easterlin's argument that a decline has occurred in the economic position of such men relative to that of males in the parental age group (Easterlin 1968, 1973, 1978). However, the possible significance of father–son comparisons raises certain problems when, what we are doing is comparing older and younger men within the same occupation group. Even aside from the fact that we cannot actually match up fathers and sons, our inferences may be invalidated by unmeasured patterns of intergenerational mobility. This is so in two respects. First, father–son inferences are difficult when data are organized into occupational groups because of the unknown effect of intergenerational occupational mobility. Where such mobility has occurred, the characteristics of older men in an occupation will be an imperfect indicator of the characteristics of the fathers of younger men in that occupation.[10] Second, even if no father–son inferences are attempted, intergenerational occupational mobility and the possible salience of the parental household as a reference group raises the possibility that just the simple interage comparisons I have been making within occupational groups may be invalid. For example, an upwardly mobile young man may not really be comparing himself to older men in the same occupation (and hence would not be likely to feel as relatively deprived as our data imply) but rather to his adolescent experience in the household of a father who was at a lower-level occupation than the son. If the son is making *that* comparison, he might not feel deprived after all.

With regard to the validity of rough father–son inferences for the various occupational groups, intergenerational mobility probably does not raise a serious practical problem. The interoccupational differentials in median earnings for young men are so small that even when mobility has occurred, it will probably not affect inferences regarding the decline in the relative position of the young in most occupations. Inferences regarding the extent of the decline in the relative earnings status of sons compared to fathers may be very shaky but that a decline has occurred, on average, seems unquestionable.

Another problem concerns which reference groups individuals identify with and when transitions in reference group identifications occur. Presumably most people do not go through their lives using the parental

---

[10] It is actually, of course, the lagged characteristic that Easterlin discusses.

household of their teens as their major reference group.[11] At some point they begin to compare themselves with more temporally relevant groups such as others in the same occupation or in certain different occupations. To the extent that young people start to make the transition from childhood and adolescent reference groups to adult groups, comparisons with *these* groups become more salient.[12] Hence we might expect that for adults past 25, for example, adolescent reference groups are of less significance than more temporally proximate groups. However, given the state of our knowledge, it is difficult even to hypothesize—much less show empirically—which reference groups are the more salient for young adults. I am inclined to surmise that, once occupational commitments have developed, occupational reference groups become more relevant but this undoubtedly varies among socioeconomic groups and the closeness of kin ties. In short, to the extent that contemporaneous adult reference groups start to have more influence on young people than intergenerational comparisons, the kinds of cross-sectional comparisons I have been making are appropriate. Certainly they seem appropriate for older age groups. Furthermore, the low relationship between the median earnings of 18–24-year-olds and peak median occupation group indicates that little "excess" relative deprivation will be imputed to the young men in various occupations groups.

Turning back to Table 3.8 we can consider in greater detail the occupations in which the position of various age groups changed. Comparing 18–24-year-olds to men in the 35–54 age groups—the age groups where most of the peak medians occurred in 1969—we see that the percentage increase for 18–24-year-olds was less than for 35–54-year-olds in nine occupations (Professional I and III, Managers III, Sales II and III, Clerical III and IV, Operatives IV, and Laborers IV). These occupations accounted for 58% of the 18–24-year-olds in 1970 who had net positive earnings in 1969.[13]

A noteworthy feature of the occupational pattern of the declining relative economic position of 18–24-year-olds is that white-collar occupations

---

[11] Easterlin himself suggests this to be the case. "One reaches family-building age with preferences already molded by this heritage [childhood and adolescent experiences, etc.], but these preferences are subsequently modified by ongoing occupational, income, and family building experiences, among others [1969: 135]."

[12] In general, Easterlin seems to ignore the influence of peer groups among adolescents and young adults. Yet peers may be extremely influential at this point in the life-cycle and some attention might be paid to how they modify or reinforce the influence of the parental household.

[13] Professional II males formed a major exception to this trend as the increase for 18–24-year-olds was extremely high compared to that for other occupational groups. However, this rapid growth in the earnings for young Professional II men may be because of a rapid expansion of relatively well paid workers in this occupational category—particularly the growth in the number of computer programmers and related technical occupations.

III. 1959–1969 Changes in Age and Occupational Patterns of Earnings

comprised seven of the nine occupations in which the increase in the median earnings of this age group was consistently below that of men aged 35–54, accounting for 76% of white-collar 18–24-year-olds with net positive earnings in 1969. The other two occupations in which the increase in the median earnings of 18–24-year-olds was below that of men 35–54 were low-level blue-collar occupations that could least afford such low rates of increase—Operatives IV (the largest operative category) and Laborers IV. Furthermore, just these two blue-collar occupations accounted for 49% of all blue-collar 18–24-year-olds and 69% of Group IV blue-collar 18–24-year-olds.

As a consequence, of the relatively greater improvement in earnings for older men, the position of 45–54-year-olds in Group III and IV occupations improved relative to those in the peak-earnings group, typically the 35–44 age group. In fact, the median earnings of 45–54-year-old Professional III men rose so much (by 42%) that the peak median age group shifted from the 35–44-year-olds in 1960 to the 45–54-year-olds in 1970. The one major exception to this improvement of earnings for 45–54-year-old men was Service IV males whose relative earnings position actually deteriorated over the decade.

As we have already seen, 55–64-year-old men also often improve their median earnings more than younger men—particularly men in the 18–34 age range. As a result, the maximum differential between peak and 55–64 medians declined considerably—from 40% more in 1959 (for the Craft IV group) to 23% more in 1969 (for the Sales III Group) (Tables 3.4 and 3.5). However, older men did lose some ground in three occupations: Managers II, Sales II, and Clerical IV.

In sum, our analysis of the changes in the age pattern of earnings reveals that the relatively disadvantaged position of younger men in 1960 deteriorated even further over the decade while the relative economic position of older men, especially men 45–54 improved. If occupational groups form important life-style reference groups (whether positive or negative) then, other things being equal, younger men became even less able to achieve a life-style that was comparable to that of older men in the same occupational group. But, the ability of those past the peak median earnings years to maintain as expensive a life-style had, on the surface, improved rather than deteriorated. Alternatively, if we think in terms of Easterlin's father–son comparisons, the overall changes in the position of younger compared to older men indicates that, on the basis of their earnings alone, sons may have experienced a decrease in the ability to achieve the style of life their fathers' income made possible during the formative adolescent years. However, just how accurate this initial assessment is of the financial ability of the different age groups (or generations) to achieve similar standards of living will be shown by the analysis in Chapters 4 and 5 of variations in the extent of family responsibilies over the life-cycle.

IV. EXPLAINING CHANGES IN THE AGE PATTERNS OF EARNINGS

Our description of the 1959–1969 differences in earnings patterns by age provides a general idea of changes in age-related sources of relative deprivation during this period. However, a much more meaningful interpretation of these changes would be achieved if it were possible to disentangle the age, period, and cohort effects. For example, are the observed 1959–1969 differences in age patterns of earnings partly due to period effects of various sorts and, if so, might these be having a permanent or transitory impact on the age pattern of earnings? Or, alternatively, are cohort effects the major factor in the observed changes—producing perturbations that will gradually pass away, only to be replaced by other cohort effects? Obviously, if we could obtain some rough answers to these questions, it would greatly enhance our understanding of what kinds of changes are actually occurring— both during the 1959–1969 period and afterwards. Changes that are of cohort nature or which constitute *permanent* modifications in age patterns are of continuing significance, as opposed to differences that might be traced primarily to transitory factors. Hence, we now turn to the task of considering the role of age, period, and cohort effects in the different 1959 age patterns of earnings.

Cohort Effects

The discussion of the reasons for the observed 1959–1969 differences in age patterns of earnings will primarily be in terms of period and cohort effects with some evaluation of the implications of these for possible *permanent* shifts in the age pattern. As the reader will remember, 1959–1969 period changes in earnings cannot have affected the age pattern of earnings, *unless* period effects interacted with age. Hence, it is only necessary to consider the influence of those period effects that did interact with age. Cohort effects are another matter, however, and should provide a more significant influence on the 1959–1969 changes.

How did cohort effects influence the age differentials in the increase in earnings? First it is important to remember that the 1959–1969 median earnings for any particular age group always involves two cohorts. For example, the two cohorts involved in the percentage change in the earnings of

IV. Explaining Changes in the Age Patterns of Earnings

25–34-year-olds are the cohort of 1926–1935 which was 25–34 in 1960 and the cohort of 1936–1945 which was 25–34 in 1970. Theoretically, if there were no cohort effect and the period effect (growth in real earnings) did not interact with age, then the percentage increase in median earnings would be the same for every group. Taking the two cohorts involved in the increase for any one age group, my purpose is to consider whether any hypothesized cohort effects will offset or enhance the earnings increase due to period effects alone. For example, if we have reason to believe that the cohort that was 18–24 in 1960 was more favored economically than the cohort that was 18–24 in 1970, then we would be moving from the consideration of a *more* to a *less* favored cohort and this should depress the increase in earnings for the 18–24 age group. But if we are moving from a consideration of a less favored cohort of a given age in 1960 to a *more* favored cohort of the same age in 1970, this will tend to accentuate the period increase in earnings for this age group. In short, cohort effects will be viewed as modifiers of the overall, though unknown, period effect. Sometimes they will counteract the positive period influence and other times they will enhance it.

COHORT SIZE AND THE ECONOMIC CLIMATE
EARLY IN THE CAREER CYCLE

Which cohorts are likely to be in an especially favorable economic position and which in a particularly poor position? To make it easier to follow the discussion, Table 3.10 shows the ages of the relevant cohorts at every census date from when the oldest was 15–24 to the 1970 census. If, as a number of demographers have argued, a cohort's size is an important factor affecting its life-long economic position, then two of the cohorts under consideration would have been especially positively affected and one particularly negatively affected by relative size. One can, of course, look at the relative size of a cohort at many points in its life-cycle. However, since the early working years are presumed to be particularly important in affecting a

TABLE 3.10
Ages of Various Birth Cohorts at Different Census Dates: 1920–1970 (15–64 Age Range)

Birth cohort	Age in					
	1970	1960	1950	1940	1930	1920
1946–1955	15–24	—	—	—	—	—
1936–1945	25–34	15–24	—	—	—	—
1926–1935	35–44	25–34	15–24	—	—	—
1916–1925	45–54	35–44	25–34	15–24	—	—
1906–1915	55–65	45–54	35–44	25–34	15–24	—
1896–1905	—	55–64	45–54	35–44	25–34	15–24

cohort's life-long economic position, as well as its marriage and fertility behavior, I have used the ratio of the number in the cohort when it was 15–24 to the number of men in the prime working years at that time. Since men in the prime working years have strong attachments to the labor force, their labor-force status should not be measurably affected by the number of potential new workers reaching working age. Therefore, variations in the ratio of young males to those older males should provide a reliable indicator of variations over time in the demographic demands being made on the economy to assimilate new workers.[14]

As Table 3.11 reveals, the cohorts of 1926–1935 and 1936–1945 were relatively small, as both groups include those born during the Great Depression. The number of men who were 15–24 in 1940 amounted to 43% of the 25–54 age group in that year. However, this ratio dropped to 35% for the cohort of 1926–1935 when it was 15–24 in 1950. It was approximately the same for the cohort of 1936–1945. If relatively small size does confer an economic advantage, the cohorts of 1926–1935 and 1936–1945 would have had such an advantage over the other cohorts considered here. But, the large baby-boom cohorts of the 1946–1955 period presumably operate at a relative *disadvantage,* as Easterlin and others have argued. The cohort of 1946–1955 was 15–24 in 1970 and at that time their numbers constituted 51% of men 25–54, a ratio that was up from 36% for the previous 10-year cohort of 1936–1945 when it was 15–24 in 1960. Hence, the large relative size of these baby-boom cohorts is particularly outstanding because they followed immediately after the small depression cohorts. However, even comparing their relative size to that of the pre-depression cohorts (those 15–24 in 1920 and 1930) the number of 15–24-year-old baby-boom males in 1970 relative to older males of working age was quite impressive.

Although relative cohort size should have operated to the advantage of the 1926–1935 and 1936–1945 cohorts but to the disadvantage of the 1946–1955 cohorts, the economic climate of the early working years was also probably important, as the discussion of Chapter 2 suggested. Two cohorts

---

[14]Two alternatives were used to define the group: "males in the prime working years." First there were men who were 25–64 years old. However, 55–64-year-old men are a group whose labor-force attachment is starting to weaken. In fact, the labor-force rates of this age group have been declining steadily over the years. Such men may sometimes even find themselves at a competitive disadvantage with young males. The 55–64 age group usually has much less formal schooling and the skills obtained in on-the-job training may become obsolete. All this can make the greater cost of employing them, compared to new labor entrants, less appealing to employers. Thus the size of the 55–64 population group of males may be a variable indicator of the number of workers in the age group—a variability that may be affected by the number of young males reaching working age. Hence, the ratio of males 15–24 to those 25–54 was also used to measure demographically induced variations over time in the economy's need to absorb new workers.

IV. Explaining Changes in the Age Patterns of Earnings

TABLE 3.11
Relative Size of Male Cohorts at Age 15–24 Compared to Older Males

Cohort	Census year in which aged 15–24	Number 15–24 as a percentage of those aged: 25–54	Number 15–24 as a percentage of those aged: 25–64
1896–1905	1920	42.4	36.6
1906–1915	1930	44.3	37.7
1916–1925	1940	42.9	35.9
1926–1935	1950	35.4	29.1
1936–1945	1960	36.0	29.3
1946–1955	1970	50.7	40.4

Source: U.S. Bureau of the Census 1975a: 15.

included males in the 15–24 age group during the Great Depression. One was the cohort of 1906–1915 which was 15–24 in 1930 and the other was the cohort of 1916–1925 which was 15–24 in 1940. However, as hypothesized in Chapter 2, these cohorts probably experienced the depression somewhat differently with the most serious permanent career damage being experienced by those who were exposed to it for a longer period of time. If this is the case, then men in the cohort that was 15–24 in 1930 were more likely to have experienced a permanent handicap to their career prospects than those in the cohort that was 15–24 in 1940. Although some of the men in the older cohort reached working age during the prosperous 1920s, their early working years were then disrupted by the long Great Depression. Hence, during the period when stable job commitments are usually made and much upward mobility may occur these men were living in a period of great economic distress. The general unemployment rate went up from 3.2% in 1929 to 8.7% in 1930 and then continued up, reaching a peak of 24.9% in 1933. It then gradually declined but was still 14.6% in 1940 when the cohort was 25–34 (U.S. Bureau of the Census 1975a: 135). However, although a certain proportion of the cohort aged 15–24 in 1940 reached working age during the depression, the low unemployment of the World War II and post-war period rapidly followed. Hence, in contrast to the cohorts of 1905–1914, the economic instability experienced by this cohort was primarily during the very early working years when job and labor-force attachments are uncertain even in the best of times.

Another important factor that will undoubtedly produce cohort effects on earnings is cohort changes in educational attainment. Although some of these changes may simply reflect shifts in the locus of human capital investments, a considerable amount of change is undoubtedly "real." However, to simplify the discussion, I would first like to consider the effect on earnings patterns by age of the cohort factors already discussed—namely cohort size and business-cycle fluctuations. Then we can see what modifications might be warranted by the additional consideration of cohort difference in educational attainment.

The small earnings increases we have observed for 18–24-year-olds is quite consistent with the proposed effect of cohort size. The cohort that was 18–24 in *1960* (the 1936–1945 cohort) was a small cohort and hence was likely to be economically favored. But the cohort that was 18–24 in 1970 (the cohort of 1946–1955) was a large baby-boom cohort. Hence, when comparing the earnings of 18–24-year-olds in 1960 with those in the same age group (but from a different cohort) in 1970, we are comparing a presumably more economically favored cohort with a less favored one. As a consequence, the cohort-size factor should have *offset* improvement in earnings due to the general period effect.

The situation for 25–34-year-olds, is not as clear-cut. The cohorts that were 25–34 in 1960 and 1970 respectively were both partly small depression cohorts (the cohorts of 1926–1935 and 1936–1945) and both experienced their early working years in times of prosperity. Hence there does not seem so far to be any indication of a strong cohort effect that might offset or enhance the general period effect on earnings and, in fact, the percentage increase in median earnings for 25–34-year-olds, as a whole, most closely approximates the growth in median earnings for all age groups combined—a 27.4 versus a 26.1% growth respectively for the 25–34 age group and all age groups combined (Table 3.8).

A consideration of the cohorts who were 35–44 in 1960 and 1970 respectively indicates that differences in both cohort size and business-cycle conditions during the early working years should have produced a cohort effect that *enhanced* the earnings growth of this age group. On the one hand, the cohort that was 35–44 in 1960 was not a particularly small cohort. When it was 15–24 in 1940, its numbers amounted to 43% of men 25–54-years-old in 1940. Second, some members of this cohort did start their working years during a period of high unemployment, though the economy took a rapid turn for the better in the early 1940s. On the other hand, the cohort that was 35–44 in 1970 (the cohort of 1926–1935) was partly a small depression cohort whose relative size at age 15–24 in 1950 was quite small. In addition, the cohort was entering the economy during a period of prosperity. In short, theoretically the cohort that was 35–44 in 1970 should have been more economically favored than the cohort that was 35–44 in 1960. As a consequence, this would accentuate the overall period growth in earnings for this age group. In fact, the next to highest growth rates were achieved by 35–44-year-olds.

For all occupational groups combined, the 45–54 age group experienced

IV. Explaining Changes in the Age Patterns of Earnings 95

the greatest improvement in median earnings. Do our hypothesized cohort effect provide any support for such disproportionate increases for this age group? Once again, the answer is yes. How cohort size affects a cohort is not revealed by comparing these two cohorts. At the time each was 15–24, the ratios of their numbers to men in the prime working years were virtually identical. The big difference occurs in the economic conditions in effect during the early working years. The cohort that was 45–54 in 1960 (the cohort of 1906–1915) was 15–24 in 1930. Hence, this cohort lived out most of its early working years in the depths of the Great Depression. The cohort that was 45–54 in *1970* (the cohort of 1916–1925) was 15–24 in 1940. Although some of these men entered the labor force at the end of the depression, economic conditions soon improved substantially. In short, once again, when comparing the two contiguous cohorts who were 45–54 in 1960 and 1970 respectively, we are comparing an economically less favored earlier cohort to an economically more advantaged later cohort. Whether this can entirely account for the fact that this age group experienced the greatest earnings increases is difficult to determine from these data, however.

Finally, the cohorts that were 55–64 in 1960 and 1970 respectively (the cohorts of 1896–1905 and 1906–1915), did surprisingly well in the decade changes. Their earnings increase was, to be sure, below that of the 45–54-year-old age group but almost identical to that of males 35–44 and above that of the younger age groups. Can the cohort effects discussed so far help provide some explanation for the good showing of the oldest age group? By and large, they can not. Relative cohort size at age 15–24 is not very different for the two cohorts. However, the economic climate encountered by these two cohorts when they were 15–24 was very different. The cohort that was 55–64 in 1960 was 15–24 in 1920. Although there was severe unemployment in 1921 (11.7%), the early period of their labor-force participation appears to have been relatively prosperous (U.S. Bureau of the Census 1975a: 135). But the cohort that was 55–64 in 1970 was 15–24 in 1930. This then was, once again, the cohort that experienced most of its early working years during the Great Depression. Hence, theoretically, we are comparing a more favored cohort in 1960 to a *less* favored one in 1970. This should have depressed the earnings growth of this age group. Yet, they experienced a substantial rise in earnings. One reason for this may be the selective early retirement of very economically marginal men. Another might be that the effects of experiencing the Great Depression may have disappeared by this age. However, there are other cohort effects that might have a bearing on the issue to which we shall turn to presently. To sum up first, however, the presumed cohort effects hypothesized here do seem to support the observed differences in the 1959–1969 increases in median earnings of all age groups except for those 55–64.

COHORT DIFFERENCES IN EDUCATIONAL ATTAINMENT

Changing educational attainment is an important factor affecting earnings because it presumably indicates increases in human capital investments, the returns from which are enjoyed in the form of greater earnings. For each age group, Table 3.12 shows the 1960 and 1970 median school years attained as well as the proportion of males that completed 12 or more years of schooling. It provides impressive evidence that in either census year the educational attainment of older cohorts was far inferior to that of younger cohorts. For example, in 1960 only 28% of the cohort that was 55-64 had attained 12 or more years of schooling, but 66% of those aged 18-24 had attained this educational level. Furthermore, this understates the true cohort differences in educational attainment because not all males in the 18-24 group had finished their schooling. That this selective factor is significant is indicated by the change in the educational level of this cohort between 1960 and 1970—from 66 to 75% with 12 or more years of schooling.[15]

Because of the really enormous increases in education attainment as we move from earlier to later cohorts, there were, of course, large 1960-1970 increases in the attainment levels of various age groups as more extensively educated younger cohorts moved into the older ages. However, it is worth noting that the improvement in school years attained is not similar across age groups. The age group that exhibited the greatest improvement in educational attainment was the 55-64 age group, followed closely by the 45-54 age group. For example, in 1960 only 28% of 55-64-year-olds had attained 12 or more years of schooling, but in 1970 42% had. In the case of 45-54-year-olds, 40% had achieved at least a high-school education in 1960 but this rose to 57% in 1970. However, the increases in the proportions with 12 or more years of schooling were much less impressive for the younger age groups. For 18-24 year olds it was only 11%. Of course, the higher the proportion who have completed 12 or more years of schooling, the smaller can be the relative change in that proportion. However, the pattern is not just an artifact of this ceiling effect but is also observable for changes in median school years achieved.

In short, changes in the educational attainment of different cohorts led to particularly dramatic improvements for older men. This provides us with an additional reason for seeing a positive cohort effect on the earnings of males 45-54 in 1970. Furthermore, it helps explain the substantial improvements

---

[15] I am not, of course, exactly matching the cohort that was 25-34 in 1970 with the appropriate age group in 1960 since I excluded the males who were 15-17 in 1960. Cohort educational attainments do not always match entirely between the two census dates for older cohorts as well. This is probably because of improving educational attainment of some men plus selective factors that seem to reduce the labor-force participation of the less educated.

IV. Explaining Changes in the Age Patterns of Earnings

TABLE 3.12
Selected Educational Attainments of White Males, by Age: 1960–1970

	Those with 12 or more years of schooling			Median school years completed		
	Percentage		Percentage			Percentage
Age	1960	1970	change	1960	1970	change
All ages	50.3	63.1	25.4	12.0	12.4	3.3
18–24	65.8	72.8	10.6	12.4	12.6	1.6
25–34	61.1	74.8	22.4	12.4	12.6	1.6
35–44	54.1	64.5	19.2	12.1	12.4	2.5
45–54	40.2	57.0	41.8	10.6	12.2	15.1
55–64	28.5	42.5	49.1	9.5	10.9	14.7

Source: 1960 and 1970 Public Use Samples of White Males.

in the earnings of 55–64-year-olds—improvements that would not have been predicted on the basis of the other cohort effects considered so far.

Interactive Period Effects

HUMAN CAPITAL INVESTMENTS AND THE
EARNINGS POSITION OF THE YOUNG

Although intercohort differences in educational attainment have been partly examined as a cohort effect, it is also possible to consider how increasing school attainment, operating as a period effect, is probably interacting with age to change the overall age effect on earnings. The 18–24 age group is a particularly interesting one to focus on since it is approaching a ceiling in the earning improvements that can be achieved by increases in educational attainment or other human capital investments. As the proportion of males in successive cohorts who have completed high school nears 100%, little or no additional improvement can be made at the lower end of the educational attainment scale, that is, at educational levels that are typically achieved by age 18 or 19.[16] Hence any additional increases in educational attainment will have to be accomplished by cohorts *after* they are 18—particularly when they are in the 18–24 period in their life-cycle and sometimes even later. As a consequence, further improvements in

---

[16] For example, 85% of white males 20–24 in 1977 had completed 4 or more years of high school compared to 83% in 1970 and 75% in 1964 (U.S. Bureau of the Census 1965a: Table 1; 1970a: Table 1; 1977c: Table 1).

educational attainment by cohorts would probably serve to depress their earnings when they are 18–24 since some will be in school full time and not working at all while others still in school may be working but only part-time or part-year and at temporary low-paid stopgap types of jobs. All this will result in smaller proportions having made a permanent full-time commitment to the labor-force in the 18–24 age interval and many of those who have made such a commitment will be fairly new workers with few on-the-job human capital investments yet achieved. For these men too it will be a career-cycle period of substantial "foregone" earnings. Moreover, where firm-specific human capital investments are common, employers will be more willing to lay off younger workers in whom their human capital investments are less extensive (Becker 1975: 32–35). In short, *further* improvements in educational attainment are likely to change the age pattern of earnings rather than to simply produce a cohort effect that passes, wavelike, through the age structure. This change will reduce the relative economic status of young males.

In sum, other things being equal, a relatively low economic status among young adults seems intrinsic to the existence of a highly trained labor force and the more extensive the training, the *older* the young adults will be who are so affected. Furthermore, it is hard to see how any *further* increases in the level of human capital investments of cohorts can do anything but change the age effect on earnings to the detriment of younger people. This is regardless of how beneficial such investments may prove to the same cohorts at an older age. Only if the ages at which the bulk of human capital investments are made were to change greatly would this not be the case. Yet, as Becker has pointed out, extensive investments in human capital late in life are less likely since the total returns on such investments will be less than on those made earlier in life.

THE BUSINESS CYCLE

In addition to changes in human capital investments, there are other ways in which period effects will interact with age to affect the age pattern of earnings, even if only temporarily. As we saw in Chapter 2, cyclical downswings in unemployment had their greatest absolute effect on males under age 25. Males 55–64 did not appear to be especially sensitive to the business cycle in terms of unemployment rates. However, since men in this age group may respond to unemployment by earlier retirement, shifts in the unemployment rate could be an imperfect indicator of sensitivity to cyclical conditions. If that is so, then downswings in the business cycle may reduce the earnings of men 55–64 because of lower proportion of them will have worked year-round full-time, whether because of increased unemployment or

IV. Explaining Changes in the Age Patterns of Earnings

decreased labor-force activity. However, upswings will increase earnings because they may forestall a premature retirement (Sheppard 1976: 298–300).

Since 1969 was a year with generally lower levels of unemployment than 1959, this interactive factor should have helped improve the earnings of 18–24- and 55–64-year-olds in 1970. Considering young men first, it is obvious that the relatively low increases in their earnings occurred *in spite of* generally favorable cyclical conditions. This suggests that the relative economic status of young baby-boom males could deteriorate still further with downswings in the economy. This did, in fact, happen between 1970 and 1975 when the ratio of the median income of white males 20–24 to that of males 45–54 declined from 44% to 42% (U.S. Bureau of the Census 1977a; 1971a). In sum, the low 1959–1969 increases in the median earnings of 18–24-year-olds does not seem to be a result of cyclical economic conditions. Turning to older males, 55–64-year-olds, the more favorable cyclical conditions in 1969 were probably another reason why the improvements for this age group were so impressive, despite certain cohort factors operating to their disadvantage. However, if favorable cyclical conditions were an important factor in the high increases for 55–64-year-olds, then these improvements may have been partly transitory in nature and need not indicate a permanent improvement in the relative earnings position of older men.

INSTITUTIONAL CHANGES

Another period effect that interacts with age, as well as race and sex, are the changing institutional factors involving employment practices. Just a cursory view of the problem suggests that the impact of institutional factors is likely to be substantial. Some of these institutional factors are presumably characteristic of how internal labor markets operate. Others, such as recent laws and governmental rulings, may not only increase the institutionalized job rights of workers within stable internal labor markets but also, in effect, extend these rights to other workers.

There are a number of reasons why institutional factors affecting employment practices will tend to promote higher incomes for older workers. The perquisites of seniority are one major example. For one thing, they offer greater job security for older workers since layoffs are typically based on seniority (U.S. Bureau of Labor Statistics 1975d: 66; 1976a:26–28).[17] Hence, young males are more likely than older males to be laid off in

---

[17]To some extent this reinforces behavior dictated by the presumed nature of firm-specific human capital investments. Workers with more seniority have had the opportunity to acquire more firm-specific training and the employer's investment in them is greater, giving them more job security.

cyclical downswings as unemployment rates by age amply demonstrate. Since the amount of time worked in a year is a major factor in annual earnings, differences in job security can lead to important differences in earnings. Second, seniority is often an important factor in qualifying certain workers for promotions (U.S. Bureau of Labor Statistics 1970a:3–11; 1976a:29). It may not be the only factor that is taken into consideration, but it may be an important one—tipping the scales in the case of roughly equally qualified applicants with different amounts of seniority. Third, in many organizations, additional years of seniority almost automatically lead to institutionalized wage increases over and above any across-the-board cost-of-living increases enjoyed by all workers (U.S. Bureau of Labor Statistics 1975d: 33). In short, seniority in a stable internal labor market should provide considerable protection to the income of older workers as compared to younger workers or older men operating in secondary-type labor markets. This observed effect in a sample of economically active men would be accentuated by any tendency of older males not so protected to retire early.

In sum, at any single point in time, the institutionalization of job rights based on seniority will tend to favor older males. If, in addition, there is an increase in such institutionalized practices, or an increase in the proportion of males covered by institutional arrangements, it will promote disproportionate increases in earnings over time among older workers, that is, a further deterioration in the relative position of younger workers should occur. This is because a higher proportion of successive cohorts who move into the older age groups will have come under the protective umbrella of institutionalized job rights while the position of young males would not be measurably improved.

Whether an *increase* in internal labor markets favoring seniority provisions has occurred is not easy to document in an unambiguous fashion. One indication that this has happened is the considerable increase in employment in the public sector where seniority is given considerable weight. The proportion of all employed males who were government workers rose from 10.6% in 1950 to 15.7% in 1975 (U.S. Bureau of the Census 1963d: 236; 1977b: 349). As a consequence, the earnings position of somewhat older workers has been improved.[18]

---

[18] By and large, government workers seem to be very well sheltered from the vagaries of the business cycle. For example, in the severe 1974–1975 recession, government employment actually rose by 2.7% between September 1974 and April 1975 while it declined by 3.0% for all nonagricultural employment. In manufacturing industries the decline during this period was 9.7% (Bednarzik 1975b: 4)! Whether government workers will be equally well sheltered from the consequences of tax reductions and tax reforms such as those possibly involved in such actions as the 1978 Proposition 13 in California remains to be seen. To the extent the growth in government employment is reduced, however, this may largely result in fewer hirings of young people rather than layoffs. During such a transition process from higher to lower (or no) growth, one source of stable labor-market employment will be reduced for younger cohorts.

IV. Explaining Changes in the Age Patterns of Earnings

Another force for promoting institutionalized job rights based on seniority is the extent to which workers are unionized. Union contracts tend to emphasize the importance of seniority in promotions and especially layoffs (U.S. Bureau of Labor Statistics 1970a; 1976a). The trend here is in some ways ambiguous. Since 1940 the proportion of employed workers in nonagricultural industries who were union members first rose but then fell somewhat, going from 26.9% in 1940, to a high of 35.5% in 1945, down to 27.4% in 1970 (U.S. Bureau of the Census 1975a: 176–178). However, this decline in the proportion of workers who are union members has to be interpreted against changes in the occupational distribution of males during this period. For example, the proportion of nonfarm employed males who were in white-collar occupations (not including any service occupations) rose from 37% in 1950 to 42% in 1970 with the largest increase for professional workers—9 to 15% (U.S. Bureau of the Census 1953: Table 125; 1963c: Table 202; 1973a: Table 223). The decline in the proportion in manual occupations was entirely in the lower-paid laborer and operative categories. While the proportion of union members who are white-collar workers had also risen (from 14% in 1955 to 16% in 1970), white-collar union members were still very much in the minority (U.S. Bureau of the Census 1977b: 418). Hence, the proportion of manual workers covered by unions probably did not decline during this period, if one takes into account the accompanying shift out of manual occupations. Furthermore, the increasing proportion in white-collar occupations have been in those occupations where employment security and wages for workers in their thirties and older have been most favorable—namely professional and technical occupations. The proportion in clerical and sales occupations changed little in this period.

A number of recent laws and governmental rulings have also operated to benefit workers other than young white males, though the impact of these regulations will largely postdate the period actually covered by this study. There is, for example, the 1967 Age Discrimination in Employment Act. Until 1978, when it was amended to extend to 70-year-olds, the Act covered workers from 40 to 65 years old. It "prohibits discrimination because of age in hiring, job retention, compensation, and other terms, conditions, or privileges of employment [U.S. Department of Labor 1978: 5]." Amendment of the Act in 1978 extended coverage to those 70 years of age. This, in effect, extends the mandatory retirement age minimum to age 70. Originally, the Act covered something over one-half of the civilian labor force in the 40–65 age groups but, as of 1974, amendments expanded the coverage to 70% of the labor force in that age range (U.S. Department of Labor 1978: 5). One effect of the Act will probably be to increase the number of firms that lay off younger workers when reductions in the labor force are desired. Firms that lay off according to the principle of seniority will be little affected by the Act—there is, after all, no law against discriminating against the young and inexperienced. But firms that in the past disproportionately laid off older workers will no longer be able to do so (at least, not as easily). The impact of such a law, then, will depend in part on how many firms used to disproportionately lay off workers over 40. The competitive position of older workers relative to younger ones in hiring should also improve, especially in view of declining age differentials in formal schooling.

A second recent law that may strengthen the position of more senior, usually older, workers in a firm is the 1974 pension reform law. Prior to this law there were often few vesting provisions in pension plans.[19] The 1974 law requires that all plans provide minimum vested benefits and provide several options. However, whatever option is chosen, a minimum vesting of 50% of accrued benefits after 10 years of service and a maximum vesting of 100% is achieved (Schulz 1976: 117–118). Since employers make most of the contribution to private pension plans (92% in 1975), this indicates that discharging or permanently laying off a vested employee is not without costs to firms offering such plans (Yohalem 1977: 26). Hence, vesting should operate to reinforce or institute the practice of laying off workers according to seniority, that is, the more senior are the last to be laid off and the first to be rehired.

Finally, there is the possible impact that affirmative action programs are likely to have on age differentials in earnings among white males, assuming they achieve a certain measure of success. Such programs are not, of course, oriented towards any particular age group. However, given the importance of seniority in many, if not most, work organizations, the expansion of job opportunities to minorities and women in occupations that had previously been monopolized by white males will tend to have its major hiring impact at entry-level positions at least during the transition period to a more integrated occupational structure. As a consequence, other things being equal, the increased competition for such jobs occasioned by opening up the field may have a negative impact on young white males. Unless seniority provisions go by the board, older white males will be more sheltered from competition than younger white males.[20]

---

[19] "Vesting refers to the provisions in pension plans that guarantees that those covered by the plan will receive all or part of the benefit that they have earned (i.e., that has accrued), whether or not they are working under the plan at the time of retirement. Through vesting, the pension rights of otherwise qualified workers are protected whether they are discharged, furloughed, or quit voluntarily [Schulz 1976: 117]."

[20] There is some evidence that strict seniority provisions cannot always hold up to the push of affirmative action programs (see Leshin 1976, 1978). However, seniority, as an institutional principle affecting layoffs, promotions, etc., is so much to the advantage of a high proportion of workers, that once those on the "outside" gain much access to the advantages of such a system, opposition will diminish. Of course, much depends on the state of the economy.

In sum, there are a number of institutional factors that, in effect, favor older white male workers over young white males. Moreover, it seems likely that these institutional factors have been having a growing impact on age differentials in earnings. The importance of seniority appears to be increasing rather than declining. Furthermore, recent legislation and government rulings can be expected, ceteris paribus, to lead to an increase in the more favorable labor market position of older rather than younger white males. Of course, other things never are equal, and the impact of such institutional practices on the economic position of young white males depends heavily on the state of the labor market. When employment is rapidly expanding, institutionalized protection of the employment position of *older* workers need have little impact on the labor market position of *younger* workers. However, with a looser labor market, one might expect an adverse impact on the employment position of workers who are not specifically protected by such institutional practices and government laws and rulings. The unprotected, however, are increasingly the young.

V. PROSPECTS FOR THE 1980s

The argument that the relative economic status of young men will probably remain rather low, in spite of the favorable influence of future changes in relative cohort size, is considerably at variance with the position of Easterlin and Wachter (Easterlin 1978; Wachter 1977; Easterlin, Wachter, and Wachter 1978). They see the relative size of cohorts during the early working years as crucial to the relative economic position of the young and their ensuing reproductive behavior. More specifically, Easterlin has argued that the relatively small size of the depression cohort during its early working years greatly improved its labor market position. As a consequence, "when young males' income is high relative to older males', it means that they more easily support the aspirations that they and their potential spouses formed in their families of origin. Young people will then feel freer to marry and have children [Easterlin 1978: 403]." This is just what Easterlin maintains happened to the small depression cohorts when they entered the labor market in the 1950s. However, the relatively large size of the baby-boom cohorts is presumably having a negative effect on the relative economic position of young men from these cohorts (see also Welch 1979; Smith and Welch 1981). The consequence of this is marriage and birth postponements and the increasing labor-force participation of young women (Easterlin 1968, 1973, 1978). Wachter takes a similar position, arguing that "the timing of the decline in relative income for young workers coincides with the entrance of the baby bulge into the labor market in the late 1950s [Wachter 1977: 558]."

If cohort size is the major factor in the severity of the first life-cycle squeeze, then its difficulties should be greatly diminished with the entry of the baby-bust cohorts into the labor market. Indeed, Easterlin argues that just this will happen and that, as a result, there will be an upturn in fertility, "a return to the pattern of larger increases in participation rates for older than for younger women" and "a resumption of the rise in college enrollment rates," as well as numerous other effects such as a decline in cohort divorce rates, male suicide rates, and so on (Easterlin 1978: 416–417; see also Wachter 1977).

Although relative cohort size probably is an extremely important variable in the labor-market position of young males, the analysis in this chapter has indicated that other factors will also have a major impact. However, their impact would have a secular rather than a "swing" effect on the relative economic position of the young. The two factors that were explored at length here are changes in the skill level, or occupational composition, of the labor force and the trend toward institutionalization of labor markets. Both of these trends tend to favor workers in the middle and older age groups rather than younger workers. Hence, for these reasons alone, it seems unlikely that the 1980s will bring about a return to the conditions of the 1950s.[21] In short, we have a situation of two conflicting pictures of the probable relative economic position of young males in the 1980s.

The next question is whether there is any empirical evidence that can help us choose between these contrasting scenarios, short of waiting until the 1980s are over. One thing to be done is to examine educational attainment in greater detail since the earlier discussion was limited to the 1960 and 1970 PUS. The question is whether trends in educational attainment indicate that history will repeat itself just because the proportion of males in the younger age groups will sharply decline. Table 3.13 shows various educational attainments of young white males from 1940 to 1979. It reveals quite dramatically how much of an increase has occurred, until the 1970s at least, in the proportion of young white men finishing high school and going on to college. In 1950 when the small depression cohorts were starting to enter the labor force only 52% of 20–24-year-olds had finished high school and only

---

[21]There are other reasons as well. One major one is the much higher level of labor-force participation of young married women in the 1970s than in the 1950s. For example, in 1976, 55.3 and 51.0% of married women 20–24 and 25–29 respectively, with husband present, were in the labor force (U.S. Bureau of Labor Statistics 1977a: A-12). As late as 1960, only 30.0% of comparable women 20–24 and 26.8% of those 25–29 were in the labor force (U.S. Bureau of Labor Statistics 1961b: A-8). Even if women's labor-force rates were not to rise still more, the present level of their participation seems incompatible with any major upswing in fertility. Yet Easterlin and Wachter do not suggest that young women's labor-force rates will actually decline—only that the rate will level off (Easterlin 1978; Wachter 1977). See Chapter 8 for a further discussion of this issue.

TABLE 3.13
Percentage of White Males, Aged 20–24 Years Old, with at Least Four Years of High School and One or More Years of College: U.S. 1940–1977

	Percentage with	
Year	At least 4 years high school	One or more years of college
1940	44.8	14.2
1950	52.2	21.8
1960[a]	61.9	26.1
1970	80.7	43.0
1979	86.2	42.9

Source: U.S. Bureau of the Census 1953, 1963c, 1973a, 1980a.
[a] Includes nonwhites.

22% had one or more years of college. Thus the great majority of 20–24-year-olds had already completed their schooling before age 20. They had presumably already entered the labor force, had already or were soon to make serious occupational attachments, were undergoing on-the-job training and some, at least, had begun to build up seniority. In short, their careers had already been launched. However, by 1979, 86% of 20–24-year-olds had finished high school and 43% had finished one or more years of college. It is hard to imagine that such an enormous change does not signal a later average entry into the labor force—at least in the sense of obtaining or experimenting with serious job commitments rather than earning just enough money at various odd jobs to get through school. If that is the case, then this delayed attachment will also mean a delay in on-the-job training and lower seniority for more recent cohorts than those at the same ages in 1950, with the resulting negative effect on the relative earnings of young males. Unless educational attainment drops for the baby-bust children, it is unlikely that they will seriously embark on their work careers at an earlier age than the baby-boom cohorts. In fact, however, Easterlin argues that college enrollments (which have been declining recently) will rise for the baby-bust cohorts (Easterlin 1978: 417). However, if they do, it will signify further delays in the full-fledged entry of these young men into the occupational world.[22] Thus it is essential to distinguish between the cohort and age effects of trends in human capital attainment. High educational attainments may not

---

[22] A 1978 Current Population Report indicates, however, that recent declines in the college enrollment of young males is, in large part, artifactual (U.S. Bureau of the Census 1978a: 1–4). After adjusting the population base for variations in armed forces participation, it was found that there was hardly any decline in the enrollment rates of 21–22-year-old males.

completely offset the advantage conferred by small cohort size for the baby-bust males, of course. Nevertheless, the situation of the *1950s*, at least, does not appear repeatable because educational attainment levels—and the occupational composition—of recent cohorts have changed so considerably since that early postwar period.

A second approach to take in considering the possibilities for the 1980s is to ask whether, to date, the relative economic position of young males actually did exhibit a rough inverse relationship to the postwar fluctuations in the age structure. If it did, then this certainly supports Easterlin and Wachter's position. But if there is evidence of a secular decline in their relative economic position, even *before* the baby-boom cohorts reached working age, then relative cohort size is probably not the only important influence. Evidence of this nature would be indirect support for the view that factors such as long-run trends in human capital attainment and labor-market institutionalization might also be playing an important role in the relative economic status of young males.

The PUS data are not much help in providing a detailed description of trends in relative economic status since they only refer to two census dates and the early one is 1960, very near to the period when the early wave of baby-boom cohorts was starting to enter the labor market. However, CPS data—the same data Easterlin and Wachter have been using—can be utilized instead. Since the issue is whether variations in the relative economic status of young men is negatively related to their relative cohort size, two questions need to be investigated. One, of course, deals with changes over time in the income of young men relative to that of older males. What exactly has been the trend since 1947 when the CPS series starts? Is there evidence of declines in the relative income position of the young, even before the baby-boom cohorts began to reach working age? However, since the timing of possible declines in their relative income position is at issue and these declines are possibly a function of relative cohort size, a second important question is the timing of the entry of baby-boom cohorts into the working ages and when the impact of their large numbers started to be felt the most. Given the considerable importance Easterlin and Wachter attach to cohort size, let us start with this issue first.

Relative Cohort Size

Easterlin and Wachter have used a variety of measures of changes in cohort size, both absolute and relative. A feature common to all is the utilization of rather large age groups for the young. For example, in one article Wachter uses the proportion of persons aged 16–34 relative to the total civilian population aged 16 and older (Wachter 1977: 551). In this respect Wachter argues that "the members of the baby boom begin to enter the labor force in the late 1950s and early 1960s and the drop in relative earnings of young workers and families is dramatic [Wachter 1977: 556]." However, trend data on his measure of relative cohort size are not presented in the paper, although the variable is used in a regression analysis. Easterlin and the Wachters use a variant of this measure in other papers—the number of males aged 15–29, total and as a ratio of males 30–64 (Easterlin 1978; Easterlin *et al.* 1978). The trend is examined in terms of decennial data to 1950 and then quinquenially to 1975 (Easterlin 1978: 388; Easterlin *et al.* 1978: 9). The conclusion drawn is that "since the late 1950s, the United States has been experiencing a major upsurge in 15–29-year-olds, both absolutely and relative to those aged 30–64 [Easterlin, Wachter, and Wachter 1978: 8–9]."

One problem with these measures is that a grouping of 16–34-year-olds or 15–29-year-olds includes a very broad age range and hence is not particularly sensitive to the timing of the entry of baby-boom cohorts into the labor market. The measures of relative cohort size are also not symmetrical with the measures of relative economic status that Easterlin and Wachter use. The latter typically refer to the income position of more restricted age groups. Wachter measures changes in the relative personal income position of males by 5-year age groups among younger men (Wachter 1977: 556). Easterlin measures the relative income of *families* whose heads were 14–24 (Easterlin 1973: 185; 1978).[23] In short, measuring changes in relative cohort size by using broad age groups such as 15–29- or 16–34-year-olds does not permit us to examine when narrow age groups within this broad category were beginning to be affected by the large size of the baby-boom cohorts. It is thus difficult to assess whether changes in relative economic position actually do coincide with changes in relative cohort size.

A major question to consider in assessing the impact of changes in relative cohort size is just who is affected by the advent of baby-boom cohorts to the working ages. One possibility is that, initially at least, their large numbers affect just the age groups into which they are moving. For example, even though the numbers of 16–17- or 18–19-year-olds were increasing rapidly, this might still not have an impact on the labor-market position of 20–24 year olds. In that case, it is only when the number of 20–24-year-olds is climbing steeply that we will observe the start of the presumed negative impact of the

---

[23]This typically refers to a narrower age group than might appear since a relatively small proportion of families will have heads, particularly *male* heads, under age 18 or 19. For example, in 1977, only 2.9% of all families with a head in the 14–29 age group were families with a head aged 14–19-years-old (U.S. Bureau of the Census 1978c: 153).

baby boom on this age group. But another somewhat broader view is that the number in any one young age group will affect other age groups as well. In this case, when the number of 16–17-year-olds rapidly expands, the labor market position of 20–24-year-olds, as well as that of 18–19-year-olds, would deteriorate. This assumes that all young men are competitive with each other. Such an interpretation would allow the impact of the baby boom to occur earlier than if less interage competition were assumed possible because, of course, the baby boom arrived first at the younger ages. Easterlin does, in fact, take this position. For one thing, he dichotomizes the labor supply into two groups—the "career entry" group of young workers and older more experienced and skilled workers (Easterlin 1978: 400–401). Second, he classifies jobs in a somewhat parallel fashion:

> There are three classes of jobs: (a) "career jobs," involving considerable experience and skill, that are typically filled by older males because of their continuing labor force attachment and accumulated experience; (b) "career-entry jobs," that are typically held by younger males; and (c) "noncareer jobs," typically held by women. As a result, there is only limited substitution possible between younger and older males and between women and men, but a high degree of substitution between older and younger women [Easterlin 1978: 403].

While there is undoubtedly some competition among men in the under-25 age group, it seems unlikely that males in their mid teens are really operating in exactly the same labor market as men in their early twenties, much less those in their mid or late twenties, Thus the age limit of 16 or 15 is probably too low to obtain a good measure of the effect of cohort size on the economic position of young workers and especially young families. Easterlin argues that both the 15–29 and 30–64 age groups "are fully in the labor force; that is, their labor force participation rates are close to 100 percent [1978: 401]." However, this is really not true for most of the age groups in the 15–29 category. For example, in the 1947–1977 CPS series, the proportion of 16–17-year-old males in the labor force never rose above 55% and usually was below 50%. For 18–19-year-olds, it typically was below 80% and for 20–24-year-olds it was usually below 90%. Only for 25–34-year-olds is the percentage in the labor force usually over 95% (U.S. Bureau of Labor Statistics 1975b: 29; 1977a: 24; 1978a: A-6).

In short, groupings of 15–29-year-olds or 16–34-year-olds include very young people, many of whom have yet to work and others who have, at best, only a very marginal labor force attachment, probably while they are finishing school. It is hard to see such young men—especially the 16–17-year-olds—as really started on their work careers. A high proportion of even those who are working at any one point in times are probably in stopgap temporary and/or part-time jobs rather than in entry-level positions on a job

V. Prospects for the 1980s

ladder. In this respect, Easterlin's division of jobs into three classes—career jobs (typically filled by older males), career-entry jobs (typically held by younger males), and noncareer jobs (typically held by women)—seems to be something of an oversimplification. It is probably true that there are, in addition, a number of noncareer jobs that are not female jobs but are typically male and provide stopgap job opportunities for a wide variety of men, particularly young men who have not really launched into their adult occupational careers. These are jobs that do not usually lead anywhere but are interim arrangements.[24]

If many teenage males are involved in secondary labor-market jobs, it is questionable whether an increase in the number of teenagers—especially 16–17-year-olds—is a good indicator of demographic pressures on the job market of lower-level *ladder*-position occupations. Hence, the arrival of baby-boom males at ages 16–17, and even 18–19, to some extent, may not have an impact on the labor market position of males aged 20–24 who were still from small cohorts. Thus, using a lower age limit tends to make the apparent impact of the baby-boom cohorts appear earlier in time than actually occurred. All in all, then, a more sensitive measure of changes in relative cohort size would be achieved by examining the trends for narrower age groups than those used by Easterlin and Wachter. It would also be a good idea to look at annual changes in relative and absolute cohort size. For the postwar period Easterlin and his coworkers use quinquennial comparisons, starting with 1950. However, this too is a less sensitive indicator of the timing of the arrival of baby-boom males at various ages.

Figures 3.1 and 3.2 and Table 3.14 focus on the absolute and relative size of male cohorts in the 18–19, 20–24 and 25–34 age groups as the most important age groups to consider in assessing the trends in relative cohort size. The age group 25–34 was employed rather than the probably preferable 25–29-year-olds because CPS data on income for the period are available only for the 10-year age group. The ratio of younger to older men was computed with the 25–64 age group in the denominator.

By and large, the baby-boom did not really start to achieve significance until the 1960s. Starting with 18–19 year olds, the number in this age group was on the decline until 1953. It then gradually increased during the next few years but did not experience a sizable jump in numbers until 1961. It was not until 1958 that the number of 18–19-year-olds even exceeded the number in this age group in 1947. From about 1959 to 1966 the number increased at a considerable rate and then leveled off. In terms of the *relative* importance of 18–19-year-olds, this also declined and remained at a low level from 1947–

---

[24]See Chapter 4 for a further analysis of the attachment of young men to secondary labor-market types of jobs.

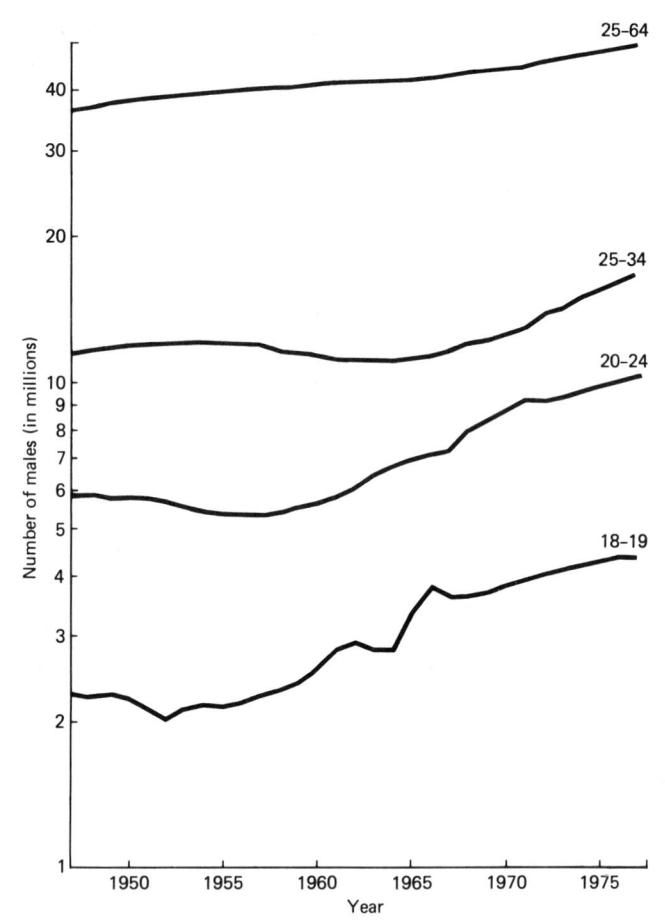

Figure 3.1. Total number of males in selected age groups: United States 1947–1977 (in millions). (*Source*: Appendix Table B.1 of this volume.)

1960. The ratio then increased considerably until 1966, after which point it has stabilized.

In sum, the baby boom did not begin to have an impact on the 18–19-year-old age group until 1960 or 1961. As a consequence, the impact of the baby boom on somewhat older age groups occurred even later in time. In the case of 20–24-year-olds, the absolute numbers of males in this age group were on the decline until 1960. Although the rate of increase in the number in this age group was considerable in the 1960s, 20–24-year-olds did not even achieve their 1947 numbers until 1962. Hence, it seems unlikely that the baby boom could have had a major deleterious effect on this age group until the beginning

V. Prospects for the 1980s

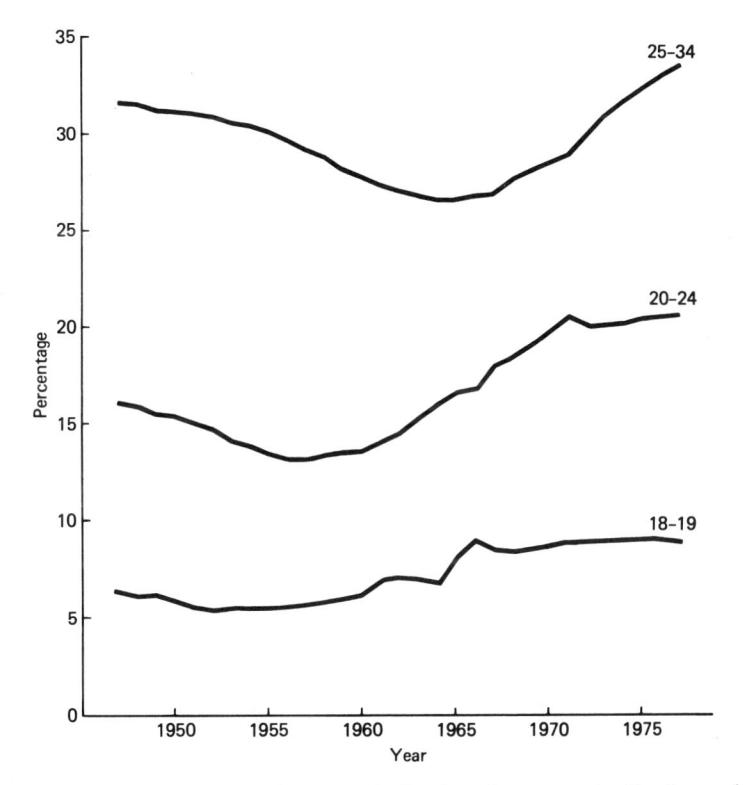

Figure 3.2. Ratio of the number of young males in selected age groups to all males aged 25–64: United States 1947–1977. (*Source*: Table 3.14 of this volume.)

of the 1960s at the earliest and possibly the mid-to-late 1960s if there is a necessary accumulation of large numbers of young workers before there is a significant impact on their collective labor-market position. This would especially be the case in view of the trend of rising school enrollments which would operate to offset the rise in the number of young people seeking a relatively permanent foothold in the occupational world. The ratio of 20–24-year-old males to those 25–64 years old declined, of course, for many years after 1947 until 1957, in fact, and did not start its upward climb again until 1961. It did not achieve its 1947 level until 1964 and did not really start a steep upward climb until 1967.

There is thus little evidence that the baby boom had any impact on the 20–24 age group until 1960. Its first effect was to return this age group to the absolute and relative size it enjoyed in the early postwar period and there is no evidence of an expansion of this age group beyond its very early post-war size until the mid- or late-1960s. If relative cohort size is the crucial factor,

TABLE 3.14
Males Aged 18–19, 20–24, and 25–34 as a Percentage of Those Aged 25–64 Years Old: United States, 1947–1977

Year	18–19	20–24	25–34
1947	6.3	16.0	31.5
1948	6.1	15.8	31.4
1949	6.1	15.5	31.2
1950	5.8	15.3	31.1
1951	5.5	15.0	31.0
1952	5.3	14.6	30.8
1953	5.4	14.1	30.6
1954	5.4	13.7	30.4
1955	5.4	13.4	30.1
1956	5.5	13.2	29.7
1957	5.6	13.1	29.2
1958	5.7	13.3	28.7
1959	5.8	13.5	28.1
1960	6.2	13.6	27.7
1961	6.8	14.0	27.3
1962	7.0	14.5	27.0
1963	6.8	15.3	26.8
1964	6.7	15.9	26.6
1965	7.9	16.5	26.6
1966	8.8	16.7	26.7
1967	8.4	18.0	26.9
1968	8.3	18.4	27.6
1969	8.4	19.1	28.1
1970	8.6	19.7	28.5
1971	8.8	20.5	28.9
1972	8.8	20.0	30.0
1973	8.8	20.1	30.9
1974	8.9	20.2	31.7
1975	8.9	20.4	32.4
1976	9.0	20.5	33.1
1977	8.8	20.6	33.6

Source: Appendix Table B.1.

these findings suggest that it is not until the late *1960s*, rather than the late *1950s*, that the relative income position of this age group would have deteriorated below that of the same age group in the late 1940s.

In the case of 25–34-year-olds, the impact of the baby boom was later still, of course. The relative size of this age group declined from 1947 to 1964 and did not return to its 1947 ratio until 1975. It was still, as of 1977, not much higher than its 1947 level. The absolute number in this age group did not exceed its 1954 level (which was somewhat greater than the number in the age group in 1947) until 1969.

V. Prospects for the 1980s

All in all, the data indicate that it is something of an exaggeration to say that the baby boom started to have a major impact on the labor-market position of young males in the late 1950s. The impact could not really have begun until the 1960s and probably did not have a major effect until the mid- to-late 1960s. Even then, the effect of the increased cohort size may have been blunted by the fact that fairly large numbers of young males were serving in the armed forces during the Vietnam conflict and hence not competing in the civilian labor market. The impact of rising school enrollments is also a factor to consider although it is true that this is not entirely an exogenous factor.

Changing Relative Income Position of Young Men

If the impact of the baby boom did not start until the 1960s, do the income data indicate that the deterioration in young men's relative economic position also started about that time or is there evidence that the decline started somewhat earlier? Table 3.15 and Figures 3.3(a), 3.3(b), and 3.3(c) show that although there is a certain amount of annual fluctuation in the relative economic position of young men, it has been declining for some time. Moreover the declines predated entry of the baby-boom cohorts into the age groups under consideration. The table and figures show the ratios of the median annual income of males aged 14–19, 20–24, and 25–34 to those 45–54 years old. The age groups in the numerator of these ratios are dictated by the age groups for which data were available in the CPS. The age group in the denominator is the same one used by Easterlin and Wachter in their analyses of changes in the relative economic status of the young over time.

Virtually all of the decline for 14–19-year-olds occurred by 1960–1961 and no trend is particularly noticeable since then. Hence, the deterioration in the relative income position of this age group cannot be related to the negative effect of large cohort size since it mainly involved depression cohorts. The influence of continued schooling seems like a much more reasonable explanation. In the cases of males 20–24 years old, annual fluctuations aside, the decline in their relative economic position also predates the numerical impact of the baby-boom cohorts. Thus, between 1950 and 1960, the median earnings of 20–24-year-olds declined from 63 to 48% of the median for 45–54-year-olds—a decrease of 15 percentage points or a 24% decline in the ratio. Between 1960 and 1970 the ratio declined from 48 to 44%—a decline of only 4 percentage points or an 8% decline in ratio. Between 1970 and 1977 a clear trend is not discernable. Moreover, although the relative *cohort size* of 20–24-year-olds was virtually identical in both 1964 and 1948, the relative *income* position of this age group had declined

TABLE 3.15
Young Men's Median Income as a Percentage of the Median for Males 45–54 Years Old: 1947–1977

	Percentage for males:		
Year	14–19	20–24	25–34
1947	21.4	58.5	91.3
1948	17.9	65.7	96.5
1949	16.1	62.9	100.1
1950	13.6	62.8	95.5
1951	14.3	68.8	100.3
1952	13.3	61.0	100.2
1953	12.9	53.1	97.1
1954	12.7	53.8	96.3
1955	10.3	53.7	94.1
1956	9.6	58.4	97.7
1957	9.1	52.9	97.3
1958	8.5	53.2	99.1
1959	8.5	53.8	97.8
1960	8.0	48.5	94.7
1961	7.5	49.9	94.8
1962	7.1	47.2	92.7
1963	7.0	45.2	93.9
1964	7.0	49.0	94.4
1965	7.2	50.1	94.4
1966	7.2	48.1	94.1
1967	7.3	45.7	92.2
1968	7.8	46.5	94.0
1969	7.7	43.7	92.5
1970	7.5	43.7	90.0
1971	7.1	42.8	88.7
1972	7.6	42.8	85.6
1973	7.8	44.2	86.4
1974	7.8	43.2	86.1
1975	7.4	41.5	83.6
1976	7.3	41.4	83.1
1977	7.4	41.0	80.6

Source: U.S. Bureau of the Census 1965c, 1967a, 1967b, 1969a, 1969b, 1971a, 1972d, 1973c, 1975d, 1976a, 1977d, 1978b.

from 66 to 49% of the median income of 45–54-year-old males. In short, the declining relative economic position of males 20–24 years old has been occurring for a long time—regardless of whether small or large cohorts were entering the labor market.

It is also worthwhile to consider the changing relative economic position of 25–34-year-old males to test still further the extent to which the relative economic position of the "older" young worker has been changing. By and large, the relative position of 25–34-year-olds did not start to change much until 1960. Since then, the ratio of their median earnings compared to those of men 45–54 years old declined from 95 to 81% in 1977. Nor can this decline be entirely blamed on the large cohort size of the postwar baby boom since, as we have seen, it is not until the 1970s that the baby-boom cohorts started to have much of an impact on this age group.

In sum, the declining economic position of young males relative to older males seems to be a long-standing trend in our society. Cohort size may, depending on the circumstances, offset or reinforce this trend but it does not appear to be the only factor affecting the relative economic position of the young. In fact, the changes in the relative income position of young men does not even appear to follow very closely the trend in the relative size of the young age groups under consideration.

Because the CPS series starts in 1947, it is not possible to study changes in the relative income position of young males prior to that time. However, Easterlin attempts a measure of their relative economic status by comparing total unemployment rates in different years. To do this he subtracts the 8-year average of the total percentage unemployed ending in a given year from the 20-year average ending 3 years earlier. Thus he subtracts the 8-year average unemployment rate ending in 1929 from the 20-year average ending in 1926, the 8-year average ending in 1930 from the 20-year average ending in 1927, and so on. The 8-year average unemployment rate is to be interpreted as roughly measuring the average employment conditions when sons were 18–25 and the lagged 20-year average as representative of the employment conditions when their fathers were 32–52 years old—and the sons were in 3–22-year age period and presumably living at home (Easterlin 1973: 192ff).

Such a measure has considerable problems as an indicator of the relative economic position of sons versus fathers or of younger men versus older men. For one thing, the unemployment rates used are the total unemployment rates rather than age-specific rates because there is no long-term series on age-specific rates. Hence, the measure is a comparison of *general* employment conditions in different periods rather than a comparison of the employment experience of younger versus older men. Regardless of this problem, however, these comparisons are extremely poor indicators of relative economic status differences related to cohort size because the relative unemployment indicator largely reflects shifts in cyclical economic conditions. This is partly because of the lagged nature of the measure and the unequal intervals used. As a result, period and cohort effects are hopelessly confounded. For example, in this relative economic status series, there is exhibited an increase in the relative economic positions of sons in the 1950s, that is, the 8-year unemployment average ending in 1960 is slightly *smaller* than the 20-year average ending in 1957 but the 8-year average ending in 1939 was much *larger* than the 20-year average ending in 1936. However, this shift is primarily because the 8-year average and lagged 20-year averages will differently reflect the Great Depression experience. For example, the 8-year averages ending in 1939 shows the unemployment rate of 1932 to 1939—all depression years with very high unemployment rates. However, the 20-year average ending in 1936 includes only 7 years of high unemployment and 13 years with typically much lower unemployment rates before the 1930s. Hence, this will reduce the 20-year average unemployment rate to well below that of the 8-year average ending in 1939. Then as we follow the series over time the 8-year series increasingly reflects the low unemployment conditions of the 1940s and 1950s. For example, the 8-year average declines from a rate of 19.7% for the 8 years ending in 1939 to rates in the neighborhood of 4–4.9% for the averages ending in the 1948–1960 period. However, the full brunt of the Great Depression starts to push up the 20-year average as we shift from a period where the average is for the 20 years ending in 1936—an average unemployment rate of 9.5%—to 1941 when the 20-year average goes up to 12.1% and remains in the neighborhood of 11–12% until 1951.

Given the enormous impact of movement into and out of the depression years on comparisons of these employment averages (which are both of different lengths in years and lagged as well), it is difficult to see how the measure can be reliably used to indicate the impact of changes in relative cohort size on the relative economic status of young males (Easterlin 1978: 402). In short, just as the later series of relative income measures indicates that changes in the relative economic position of the young do not closely follow shifts in relative cohort size, comparisons of general unemployment conditions for an earlier period also fail to make a strong case for the prime importance of relative cohort size in relative economic status.

Figures 3.3(a) to 3.3(c) not only show the ratio of income of young men in various age groups to that of males aged 45–54 but also the unemployment rates for the various age groups under consideration. These figures suggest that for some age groups at least, particularly the 20–24-year-olds, cyclical unemployment is a major factor in the fluctuations of the income ratios. Because the unemployment rate of 20–24-year-olds varies much more sharply than for 45–54-year-olds, there is an obvious tendency for the income ratio to move in the opposite direction. Hence, unemployment fluctuations will have a greater effect on the income of younger men. This phenomenon is less pronounced for 25–34-year-olds. However, the annual unemployment rate will probably not capture the full extent of the greater vulnerability to the business cycle of younger men because it does not tell us

V. Prospects for the 1980s

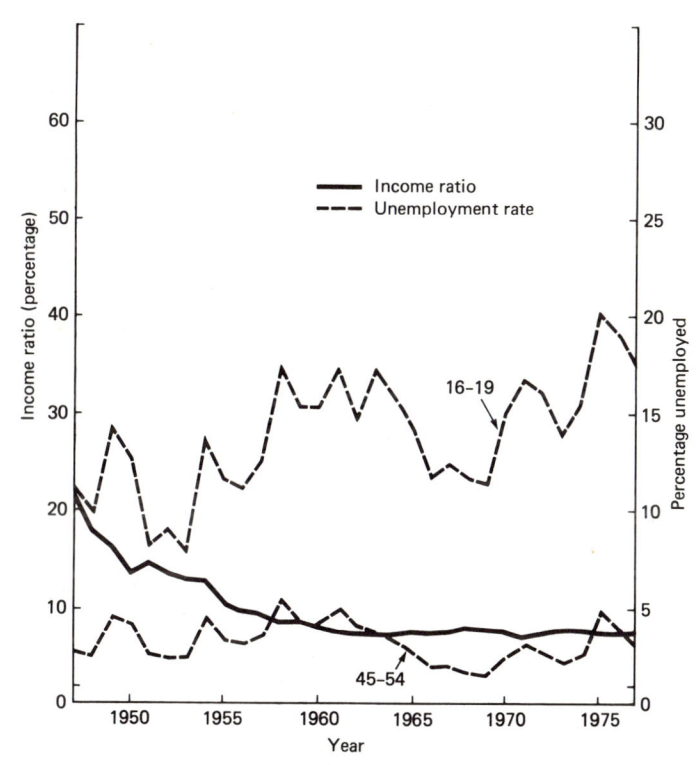

Figure 3.3(a). Median income of males, aged 14–19 as a percentage of the median for males, aged 45–54 and unemployment rates: United States, 1947–1977. (*Sources*: Table 3.15 of this volume; U.S. Bureau of Labor Statistics 1975b:148; 1977a:110; 1978a:A-6.)

about probable differences in the length of unemployment that would have a considerble impact on annual income. In any event, the fluctuations in the income ratio are not as pronounced for 25–35-year-olds as for 20–24-year-olds. With regard to 14–19-year-olds, the income ratio has varied little in recent years despite the much greater fluctuations in the unemployment rate of such men. Why this is so is not clear, however, except that it is probably related in some way to the much lower attachment of this age group to the labor force.

In sum, the short-term fluctuations in the income ratios of males aged 25–34, and especially those 20–24, seem to be largely a result of business-cycle fluctuations in unemployment—fluctuations that have a much greater effect on younger men than on older men. That this should be the case is, of course, quite consistent with human capital theories and internal labor-market theories. In spite of these fluctuations, however, the long-run trend is that of a decline in the relative income position of young men—a trend that is just as

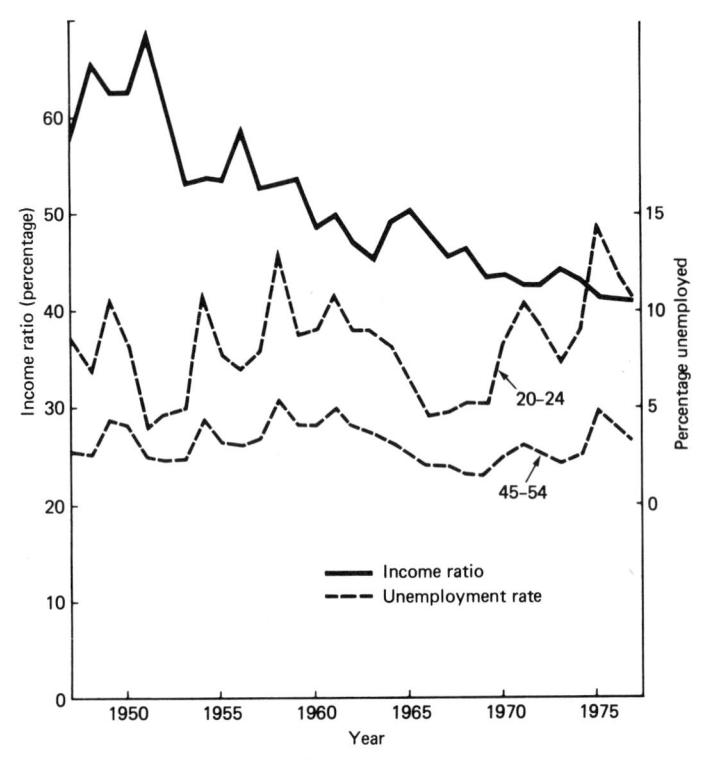

Figure 3.3(b). Median income of males aged 20–24 as a percentage of the median for males aged 45–54 and unemployment rates: United States, 1947–1977. (*Sources*: Table 3.15 of this volume; U.S. Bureau of Labor Statistics 1975b:148; 1977a:110; 1978a:A-6.)

characteristic of the period when depression cohorts were entering the labor force as when baby-boom cohorts were.

Why are these findings of a long-term decline in the relative income position of young men apparently so at odds with the relative income measures of Easterlin and Wachter, even though the common data source is the CPS? Starting with Wachter's findings, there are a number of reasons why our conclusions differ. For one thing, in looking at the trend in individual male income by age, Wachter only computes his ratios starting in 1955, although he computes ratios of *family* income for those with young heads dating back to 1947 (Wachter 1977: 556–557). Hence, that the decline in the relative income position of young males dated from the late 1940s is not as readily apparent from his table. This is particularly true since not the complete series but only selected dates are presented. Nevertheless, a 1955–1960 decline in the income ratio for 14–19- and 20–24-year-olds does show up in his calculations, as well as in mine, although his table only refers to the

V. Prospects for the 1980s

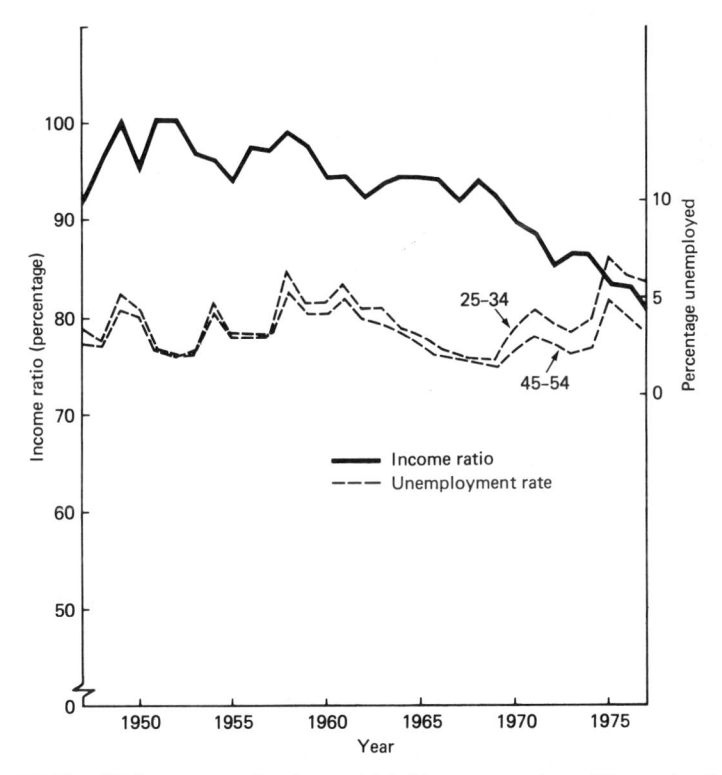

Figure 3.3(c). Median income of males aged 25–34 as a percentage of the median for males aged 45–54 and unemployment rates: United States, 1947–1977. (*Sources*: Table 3.15 of this volume, U.S. Bureau of Labor Statistics 1975b:148; 1977a:110; 1978a:A-6.)

income of year-round, full-time workers. In short, the apparent contradiction in our findings seem to stem primarily from two sources. First, the series Wachter presented starts later than the series presented here and, second, he placed the beginning of the effect of the baby boom in the late 1950s. If this were the case, it might presumably have accounted for the 1955–1960 decline in the income ratios, though not the earlier decline. However, as we have seen, a closer examination of the data indicates that the effect of the baby boom was really rather negligible in the 1955–1960 period, especially for 20–24-year-olds.

The contradictions with Easterlin's figures on changes in the relative income position stem largely from measurement differences. Although Easterlin repeatedly talks in terms of the relative income position of young *males*, what he really uses as his indicator of relative economic status is a ratio of the family income of families with younger heads as opposed to older heads (Easterlin 1975: 185; 1978: Table A-2).[25] Hence his measure is "contaminated" by other sources of family income—most notably the wife's. Since whether a wife works, and thus has an income, is partly a function of her husband's income, this seems like a particularly unfortunate way of measuring the husband's income position. Using family income will also provide a biased estimate of all males' income as it will reflect the selective factors that lead some young men to marry, a topic we will explore in Chapter 4. In addition, the series will reflect the growing numerical importance of female-headed families. Between 1963 and 1977, the proportion of families that were female headed rose from 8.1 to 15.2% (U.S. Bureau of the Census 1965b: 21; 1978c: 153). However, the income of female-headed families is much less than that of male-headed families. For example, in 1976 the median income of female-headed families was only 45% that of male-headed families. For families headed by a 14–24 year old, the ratio was only 33% (U.S. Bureau of the Census 1978b: Table 20). Hence, one reason for the decline in the relative economic status of young families is the increasing relative importance of low-income female-headed families.

All these considerations make it difficult to interpret the ratio as an indicator of changes in young males' income relative to older males'. The situation is further complicated by the fact that Easterlin's relative income ratios are quite complex constructs. The numerator consists of the averages of 5 years of income for families with heads 14–24 years old and the denominator is a 7-year average of income for families with heads 45–54 years old. In addition, the ratio is lagged. The numerator refers to a period starting 3 years after that of the denominator. For example, the 1950–1954 average for young families is divided by the 1947–1953 average for older families. In short, Easterlin's relative income measure is by no means a simple straightforward index of the relative income position of younger versus older males. This is partly because it was originally designed to measure the income position of young families compared to that of the parental household several years earlier. Hence it is not surprising that such a ratio variable is a rather imperfect indicator of changes over time in the current competitive labor market position of younger compared to older males.

[25]For example, "the relative income of young men may be taken as a rough index of the primary breadwinner's ability to support a young household's material aspirations." Another is, "when young males' income is high relative to older males', it means that they may more easily support the aspirations that they and their potential spouses formed in their families of origin [Easterlin 1978: 8]." The table and figure presenting the ratio of *family* incomes actually refers to them as "the relative income experience of young adult males" in the case of the table and "young men's income as percentage of that in family of orientation" in the chart (Easterlin 1978: Figure 2 and Table A-2; Easterlin 1973: 185).

All in all, the CPS data analyzed here indicate that there is a long-run trend in our society that favors the relative economic position of male workers in the middle years. The other side of this coin, however, is that the relative economic position of the young has deteriorated. This certainly seems consistent with long-run trends in educational attainment, occupational composition, and the growth of institutionalized employment practices. If this is true, then it would be unwise to predict the relative economic status of young males in the 1980s solely on the basis of changes in cohort size. Certainly, the small size of the baby-bust cohorts should operate to their economic advantage over their *lifetime* and will undoubtedly also help ameliorate the economic disadvantages of being young. Nevertheless, it seems risky to predict swings back to the conditions of the 1950s, given the long-run secular trends in other important variables. Relative cohort size may swing back to that of the 1950s but a host of other socioeconomic factors will not.

VI. CONCLUSION

There are several major findings in this chapter. First, a comparison of earnings and educational characteristics among occupational groups lends considerable credence to the notion that there is a built-in lower white-collar squeeze in our society. Second, age–earnings profiles, and their variation by occupation, provide evidence of other structural sources of relative economic deprivation. The income position of young men was relatively poor, regardless of occupation and, moreover, deteriorated between 1959 and 1969. However, the low relative earnings position of the young was particularly characteristic of those going into Group I and II occupations because of the steepness of these occupations' age–earnings profiles and the late age at peaking. Among Group III and IV occupations, the earnings data suggest that relative deprivation among older men may also be an important phenomenon, especially among blue-collar workers, as earnings peak at a younger age group in these occupations and there is a sharper drop-off in median earnings among older men than is the case for those in Group I and II occupations. However, the relative earnings position of older men in most occupations improved in the 1959–1969 period. In fact, the sharp rise in earnings for men in their forties and older was a major factor in the decline in the relative economic position of the young.

By and large, I have argued that both theoretical and empirical considerations provide compelling reasons for believing that a variety of factors, rather than just one, were instrumental in the decline in the relative earnings position of young men. Change in relative cohort size certainly seems to be an important variable promoting cyclical changes in the relative economic status of the young. This would lead, in turn, according to Easterlin's argument, to cyclical shifts in demographic behavior. In addition, however, certain secular period changes have been altering the nature of the age effect on earnings. These are, first of all, increases in educational attainment involving a later age at relatively permanent occupational commitments and shifts towards occupations with a steeper age–earnings profile combined with more job security in the later years. Second, the growing institutionalization of labor markets has improved the economic position of older men while having a neutral or negative impact on the earnings position of younger white men. Hence, given these secular shifts, it appears unlikely that the fluctuations in the relative economic position of the young will match the fluctuations in relative cohort size, as Easterlin and the Wachters have maintained.

In conclusion, we must remember that the discussion of this whole chapter has been based on at least one very simplistic notion—that observed differentials in earnings provide an adequate indicator of differences in relative economic affluence or deprivation. The situation is, of course, much more complex than this. A major complication arises out of differences among men in economic aspirations and the cost of achieving these aspirations due to differences in family-cycle stage. Two men in the same occupation group and with the same income but with very different family compositions will probably not really be operating at equivalent economic levels. The complication raised by family-cycle stage and its interaction with career-cycle stage and other sources of earnings variations is one of the major concerns of the next two chapters.

4

The First Life-Cycle Squeeze

Although there seems little doubt that there has been a secular decline in the relative income position of young males, there is still the question of whether relative *income* (or *earnings*) is really an adequate proxy for relative economic *status*. This is an important issue because income alone is so frequently used to measure the level of economic well-being. For example, Easterlin's assessment of the changing relative economic status of young people is done entirely in terms of the income position of young families relative to older families (Easterlin 1968, 1973, 1978). Similarly, income distribution studies have frequently not tackled the problem of assessing the influence of household size and composition on the evaluation of the extensiveness of and trends in economic inequality.[1] However, the potential problems associated with using income alone as a measure of economic well-being have necessarily been recognized by a number of investigators, especially those concerned with the question of defining poverty levels. For example, quite early on it was recognized that no single income level could equitably demarcate the poor from the nonpoor because the size and composition of the family affected the drain on the income resources

---

[1]However, recent investigators are increasingly addressing themselves to this problem. For example, see Kuznets (1974, 1976) and Treas and Walther (1978).

available (see, for example, David 1959; Orshansky 1965; Watts 1967). Similarly, the Bureau of Labor Statistics (BLS) ran into difficulties when setting up model budgets for families at different living levels because these budgets were based on a standard family of four persons with a 35-to-54-year-old husband, a nonworking wife, and two children (a girl aged 8 and a boy aged 13). Obviously, such budgets were of limited utility for other family types (Bureau of Labor Statistics 1968a, 1968b, 1969).

This study's emphasis on economic squeezes is also at variance with too complete a reliance on income alone to measure equivalent, or different, levels of economic well-being. Given how squeezes are defined (see Chapter 1) the husband's income level is only one component; others are aspirational levels and the *cost* of achieving and maintaining such aspirational levels. As a consequence, how these components *balance out* will better indicate whether or not relative deprivation is being experienced, than will just the value of any *single* component. Using this conceptionalization of the problem, I have hypothesized that two life-cycle squeezes are likely to be a chronic feature of modern American society. The first occurs when young people are attempting to set themselves up as independent adults—as individuals or as couples setting up separate households. The assumption is that launching oneself as an adult in our society is an expensive proposition. Furthermore, it occurs at a point in the life-cycle when young men's earnings are relatively low. I have reasoned that the second squeeze occurs when a family has adolescents in the home because the direct cost of children is likely to be at a maximum during this period. In part, the existence of this squeeze rests heavily on the cost factor. Men's earnings are certainly not at a relatively *low* point at this stage of their career cycle. Nevertheless, as we shall see, the age–earnings profile also plays a role in the severity of the second squeeze—especially for some occupational groups.

The major goal of this chapter and the next is to investigate these two life-cycle squeezes. The overall strategy is to examine the cost component of the squeezes and how, at any one point in time, this is likely to balance out against the earnings levels of husbands at various stages of their career cycle. Of importance also is how the severity of these squeezes may be changing over time.

I. THE COST OF SETTING UP A HOUSEHOLD

Household expenditure or cost estimates that are based on differences in household composition are useful, albeit crude, tools in the investigation of economic squeeze situations arising out of the number and ages of chidren present in the home. They are thus particularly relevant to the analysis of the second life-cycle squeeze. However, such data are of little use in documenting or measuring the severity of the first life-cycle squeeze. The presence of large numbers of "expensive" children is hardly a problem at this stage of the life-cycle. Rather, the notion of the first squeeze is based on the tension between the desire and the ability of young couples to invest in the heavy consumer durables that are an important part of launching into and living up to the standard of a "normal" adult life in our society—cars, a separate household (preferably owned), home furnishings, etc.[2]

Intuitively, it seems obvious that setting oneself up as an independent adult is expensive—especially in a society such as our own with its strong emphasis on material possessions. However, in order to investigate whether the cost component of the first squeeze has been changing over time, it is essential to obtain somewhat "harder" evidence than just our intuitive feelings. Fortunately, the Current Population Survey (CPS) has some data on consumer buying that is relevant to this problem. I have approached the issue from the perspective of considering measures of purchases or ownership of certain consumption items as indicative of the *desire* to own these goods. Hence, we form a preliminary notion of consumption aspirations by just seeing what people in various age groups actually own or what the age pattern of certain purchases is. Presumably, if the great majority of American households own a car, this is a high priority (though expensive) consumption item in our society. However, people may desire to own certain consumer durables but not have the means to do so. Thus many young adults may aspire to own a home but they lack sufficient capital for a down payment. Hence, using ownership or purchase of an item as a measure may underestimate consumption aspirations for that item. However, the rapidity with which changes in the proportion of people owning a type of item occurs as we move from younger to older age groups can be taken as a rough indicator of consumption goals that are shared by both younger and older families. The difference in behavior is then mainly due to the economic ability to carry out these purchases rather than due to differences in tastes between older and younger families. For example, given our knowledge of the age pattern of earnings, if the extent of home ownership rises more rapidly with age among younger families and levels off among older families, economic rather than taste factors are probably the major reason for the lower levels of home ownership among young adult families.[3]

---

[2] For an analysis of just this problem in nineteenth-century England, see Banks (1954). See also the discussion in Chapter 9.

[3] Cohort factors may enter in here but we cannot really consider them. However, it seems unlikely that more recent cohorts have a lower desire to own their own home than older cohorts.

Tables 4.1, 4.2, and 4.3 give three different perspectives on the consumption of various consumer durables that appear most relevant to a family setting itself up as an independent adult household. All three tables present data in terms of the age of the head of the household.[4] Table 4.1 shows the proportion of households owning various consumer durables in 1971. It reveals the ubiquity of ownership for some goods and gives us an idea of the age pattern of accumulation of other items. Table 4.2 shows the average expenditures per household in the 1968–1972 period on various consumer durables and thus provides a picture of the age pattern of consumption expenditures. Table 4.3 gives a somewhat different perspective, showing the number of durables per 100 households purchased in the 1968–1972 period. This provides additional information on the extent to which an item has a high priority in people's consumption behavior.

Age patterns in the ownership of and expenditure on cars is a particularly interesting consumer durable to focus on. One reason is that a car is such an expensive consumption item and hence constitutes a major budgetary outlay. Another is that, as Table 4.1 indicates, there is really very little relationship between the age of the household head and car ownership. The proportion of households with the head under 25 who had at least one car in 1971 was 83%, whereas the proportion only rose slightly to 88% for all the groups in the 25–54 age range, declining to 81% for those with a head 55–64 years old. Such a high degree of uniformity in car ownership certainly seems to indicate that the automobile is considered an essential investment by the great majority of American households, whatever their family-cycle stage.[5]

Although the great majority of households *owned* cars in 1971, regardless of the age of the head, CPS data indicate that *expenditures* on cars *are*

---

[4]The households studied in this survey consist of: "all the persons who occupy a house, an apartment, or other group of rooms, or a room, which constitutes a housing unit. A group of rooms or a single room is regarded as a housing unit when it is occupied as separate living quarters; that is, when occupants do not live and eat with any other persons in the structure, and when there is either (1) direct access from the outside or through a common hall, or (2) a kitchen or cooking equipment for the exclusive use of the occupants. The count of households excludes persons living in group quarters, such as rooming houses, military barracks, and institutions [U.S. Bureau of the Census 1972e:4–5]." Thus these households seem to include single-person households, households consisting of young people of one sex rooming together, female-headed households, etc. These data will, therefore, present only a very crude approximation of how consumption patterns of husband–wife families vary by age.

[5]The findings are doubly impressive if we take into account that in a number of American cities, car ownership is not particularly an advantage (New York, for example) and the smaller car-owning population in such areas is included in the denominator of these statistics. Furthermore, there is every reason to believe that car ownership among the PUS samples analyzed in this study is even more prevalent than the data in Table 4.1 indicate. Nonwhite and Spanish-speaking (hence lower-income) families are excluded from my public use samples, as are white female-headed (also poorer) families.

I. The Cost of Setting Up a Household

TABLE 4.1
Percentage of Households Owning Various Consumer Durables, by Age of Head: July 1971

	Age of head					
Consumer durable	Under 25	25–29	30–34	35–44	45–54	55–64
Home	21.1	40.1	59.7	69.2	74.9	73.1
Cars, one or more	83.1	87.6	87.5	88.1	87.9	81.4
Cars, two or more	20.3	26.6	31.7	42.2	43.2	28.6
Television sets, one or more	89.8	94.7	97.2	96.9	97.0	95.9
Washing machine[a]	45.4	69.3	81.4	83.6	82.4	74.7
Clothes dryer[a]	28.1	47.8	60.9	63.2	56.8	42.3
Freezer[a]	10.6	22.6	33.4	43.1	42.3	34.7
Dishwasher[a]	10.0	17.2	29.7	32.8	28.5	18.1
Room air conditioners, one or more[a]	30.6	34.1	34.4	30.1	33.0	30.7

Source: U.S. Bureau of the Census 1972e: Tables 1, 5, 6, and 9.

[a] Includes available items that were not owned. Items were considered available to a household if they were located in the housing unit. Washers and dryers located in the basement of an apartment building or anywhere else outside the actual housing unit were not considered available.

related to age. For example, average expenditures per household on cars over the 1968–1972 period were quite high for households with a head under 25 years old—$3,896. These expenditures were actually somewhat less for households with heads 25–29 and 30–34 years old with the 45–54-year-olds only slightly exceeding the level of expenditure of those under 25 ($3,957 versus $3,896). In sum, expenditures on cars were high for younger

TABLE 4.2
Average Expenditures per Household on Cars and Selected New Household Durables, by Age of Household Heads, Five-Year Periods: 1968–1972 (Dollars)

	Age of head					
Expenditure category	Under 25	25–29	30–34	35–44	45–54	55–64
Sum of all items	5,826	5,555	4,988	5,325	5,289	3,475
Cars	3,896	3,583	3,250	3,700	3,957	2,554
Selected Appliances[a]	521	602	514	495	418	309
Home entertainment items[b]	556	468	385	389	346	231
Home furnishings[c]	853	902	839	741	577	381

Source: U.S. Bureau of the Census 1974 a: Table B.

[a] Washing machines, clothes dryers, kitchen ranges, refrigerators and freezers, dishwashers, room air conditioners, and miscellaneous appliances.

[b] Television sets, radios, phonographs, and hi-fi equipment.

[c] Furniture, carpets, rugs, and other floor coverings.

TABLE 4.3
Number of Cars and Selected Other Durables Purchased per 100 Households, by Age of Household Head, Five-Year Total: 1968–1972

Expenditure item	Age of head					
	Under 25	25–29	30–34	35–44	45–54	55–64
Cars, total	281.7	219.8	194.2	212.4	203.6	124.7
New	78.2	74.1	63.8	70.7	84.5	57.7
Used	203.5	145.7	130.4	141.7	119.1	67.0
Washing machines	45.7	44.9	36.6	34.3	26.5	21.7
Clothes dryers	30.8	37.7	27.8	24.0	17.8	13.3
Kitchen ranges	24.3	25.7	19.3	19.1	20.7	13.6
Refrigerators and freezers	44.4	46.6	39.4	39.0	31.7	27.0
Dishwashers	6.4	15.4	18.8	16.0	11.1	6.3
Room air conditioners	21.7	24.0	17.9	16.4	16.8	13.1
Televisions	112.8	86.4	78.6	75.4	69.1	48.9

Source: U.S. Bureau of the Census 1974a: Table 7.

households, even though men's earnings are particularly low for these age groups. Another interesting finding is that within the 5-year period between 1968 and 1972, American households tended to buy more than one car and this pattern was also related to age (Table 4.3). For every 100 households with a head under 25 years of age, 282 cars were purchased. This figure declined to 220 cars for those with heads 25–29 and 194 for households with heads 30–34. There is then some increase for 35–44-year-olds but a decline thereafter. This pattern partly indicates, of course, that many households own more than one car. It also undoubtedly indicates that relatively frequent car replacement is a common phenomenon. This might be surprising in the case of younger, generally less affluent, households, who purchased the most cars during this period. However, a plausible explanation is that the first and even the second cars of young households are probably older, used models that the family needs or desires to replace, as finances permit, with more recent models. This suggests, however, that obtaining a reliable and satisfactory automobile is a series of approximations rather than a one-shot investment that sets the family up for a number of years. However, such an approximation process may be more expensive in the long run, and a particular drain on the finances of young families whose husbands are still at a low earning point in the career cycle. Evidence for this interpretation of the age pattern of the number of cars purchased is found in Table 4.1, which shows that the proportion of families with two or more cars rises sharply with

I. The Cost of Setting Up a Household   129

age, indicating that multiple car ownership (though not frequent car purchases) is much less common in young households.

In sum, an analysis of car ownership and purchases seems to have important implications for the first life-cycle squeeze. Cars are very expensive consumer durables—the most expensive of commonly purchased durables outside of homes. Nevertheless, regardless of the age of the head, most American households own at least one car, indicating that this is (or has been) considered an essential consumption item by the majority of Americans. To the extent this is true, aspirations for car ownership should provide one important component of the first life-cycle squeeze.

Turning to home ownership, the data in Table 4.1 suggest that the desire to own one's own home is common to a high proportion of Americans, though economic factors may prevent the realization of this important consumption goal. The proportion of households that owned their own home in 1971 rises rapidly as we progress from younger to older age groups, with the greatest increases between the younger age groups. Thus only 21% of households with a head under 25 years of age owned their own home in 1971 but this jumped to 40% of households headed by those aged 25–29. The proportions went up to 60 and 69% for households with heads 30–34 and 35–44, respectively. There is a small increase thereafter but the proportions seem to level off. Given the age pattern of earnings, this age pattern of home ownership strongly suggests that the aspirations of young couples to own a home is high but that economic contraints necessitate postponements of such a large purchase. This is yet another indication of the existence of an economic squeeze in young adulthood since the age at purchase does not adequately reflect the number of years that have gone into saving up for such a purchase.

Finally, let us briefly consider the case of other consumer durables—washing machines, television sets, dryers, home furnishings, etc. Table 4.2 indicates that expenditures on most of these items tend to be higher for younger households. For example, average expenditures per household for the 1968–1972 period on home furnishings was $853 and $902 for households with a head under 25 and 25–29 respectively compared to $577 and $381 for households with heads 45–54 and 55–64 years old respectively. Expenditures on appliances and home entertainment items such as televisions, radios, or stereos were also greater among the young in this period.[6]

In general, then, and not surprisingly, there is an observed tendency for younger households to be major purchasers of the kinds of consumer durables

---

[6]Expenditures were greater even though the credit position of young people was probably rather poor.

associated with setting up a separate household and preparing to start a family, even though the relative earnings position of young males was far from favorable in this period. This suggests that these goods do form important and valid components of potential economic squeeze situations. To the extent they do, however, how have trends in the costs of such items affected the first life-cycle squeeze over time? Earnings data for 1959 were, of course, inflated into 1969 dollars. Hence changes in the overall cost of living have presumably been taken into account in the earlier analysis of changes in the relative earnings position of young males. However, the question at issue here is whether there was a disproportionate rise in the cost of those consumer items that are a major component of the first squeeze.

Changes in the Cost Component of the First Squeeze

Table 4.4 shows, by 5-year periods, the percentage change in the Consumer Price Index (CPI) for a number of the types of consumption items we have just been discussing. Changes in the cost of medical care was added to the list because of its possible relevance to the timing of births—especially first births—and pediatric care. Sharply rising medical costs might presumably affect the first life-cycle squeeze by very visibly raising the cost of starting a family.[7]

The overall index, as well as most of the items listed in the table, shows a fairly substantial rise in the 1947–1952 period compared to the rest of the 1950s and early 1960s. This is probably due, however, to the adjustments following the lifting of price controls after the war and the shortages that occurred while the economy was shifting to the production of civilian goods and services. Particularly interesting is how low inflation was for many of these items in the 1952–1967 period. Rents rose fairly rapidly in the 1947–1957 period along with the costs of other items. However, the relative rise in the index for rents was quite low for the 1957–1967 period. A rise in home ownership costs (only measurable since 1953) was quite modest in the 1953–1962 period. The cost of owning a new car rose even more slowly than housing after the initial postwar jump—the increase being lower than the CPI as a whole in the 1952–1957 and 1957–1962 period. The cost actually declined in the 1962–1967 period. The cost of owning a used car declined between 1952 and 1957, though it rose rapidly in the next 5-year period. It was still low in the 1962–1967 period. House furnishings showed an even more favorable picture. Prices declined in the two 5-year periods between

---

[7]For a consideration of this issue, see Reed and McIntosh (1972).

TABLE 4.4
Percentage Change in the Consumer Price Index for Selected Items: 1947–1977

Item	1947–1952	1952–1957	1957–1962	1962–1967	1967–1972	1972–1977	1949–1959	1959–1969
All items[a]	18.8	6.0	7.5	10.4	25.3	44.8	22.3	25.8
Housing: rent	24.7	14.8	7.4	6.4	19.2	28.8	32.9	16.9
Home ownership costs[d]	—[b]	8.9[c]	7.6	13.8	40.1	46.2	—[b]	37.4
House furnishings	11.5	−3.6	−1.6	1.9	16.2	34.7	4.3	9.2
Appliances	0.3	−14.6	−7.5	−10.4	5.8	32.4	−15.8	−13.7
Autos: New	37.1	3.7	5.8	−3.9	11.0	28.7	27.9	−1.4
Used	—[b]	−13.2[c]	22.5	5.5	10.5	65.4	—[b]	20.8
Medical care	23.3	17.9	26.6	13.0	32.5	52.8	45.0	48.4

Sources: U.S. Bureau of Labor Statistics 1975b: Tables 124 and 128; 1977c: Table 23; 1978c: Table 23.
[a]Includes all items in the Consumer Price Index and not just those included in this table.
[b]Not available.
[c]Refers to 1953–1957. Data not available before 1953.
[d]Includes mortgage interests rates, property taxes, property insurance premiums, maintenance, and repairs.

1952 and 1962 and hardly increased at all (by only 2%) between 1962 and 1967.

In short, except for some sharp rises in the immediate postwar period, the cost of purchasing some of the major consumer durables associated with establishing an independent household rose rather modestly and often declined in the 1952–1967 period. It is interesting to note, however, that medical costs increased relatively rapidly (compared to the overall CPI) throughout most of this period.

Since 1967 an entirely different picture emerges.[8] The cost of home ownership had already started to escalate between 1962 and 1967 (rising by 14% compared to an 8% rise between 1957 and 1962). But this is a minor change compared to the 40% jump between 1967 and 1972 and the 46% increase from 1972 to 1977. Rental costs have risen much less, relatively speaking, but they too have shown signs of escalating in the 10 years between 1967 and 1977. The cost of furnishing a house also jumped after 1967. Although it had only risen by 2% between 1962 and 1967, the cost of house furnishings rose by 16% between 1967 and 1972 and by 35% between 1972 and 1977. Car ownership had also started to rise—especially after 1972. It is particularly interesting how much the cost of *used* cars rose in the 1972–1977 period—by 65%. Since used cars are likely to be the only kind many young households can afford, this signifies a considerable jump in cost for what we have seen to be a major consumer durable for all households, regardless of age.[9] Finally, although the cost of medical care was rising considerably faster than the overall CPI throughout the postwar period, an escalation of costs has really occurred since 1967—an increase of 32% in the CPI for medical care between 1967 and 1972 and of 53% between 1972 and 1977. In sum, the data suggest that the burdens of the first squeeze have been increasing considerably since the mid-to-late 1960s.

While it is true that the pace of inflation has stepped up enormously in recent years, a major question here is the rate of inflation between 1959 and 1969, the period to which our income data on couples in the 1960 and 1970 PUS refer. Here, the picture is not so clear-cut. The overall rate of inflation was not much higher between 1959 and 1969 than between 1949 and 1959— 26 versus 22% respectively. Rental housing increased in cost at a lower rate (a 17% rise) than the overall CPI between 1959 and 1969 and at a

---

[8] For recent discussions of how accurately the CPI measures inflation, particularly with regard to housing and automobiles, see Mitchell (1980) and Triplett (1980).

[9] However, one reason for the rapid increase in the price of used cars—as well as in many other consumer durables—may be the advent of the large postwar cohorts to adulthood and the consequent rapid rise in demand for these consumer durables.

I. The Cost of Setting Up a Household 133

considerably lower rate than between 1949 and 1959. The increase in the CPI for home furnishings was very modest (9%) between 1959 and 1969 and the cost of new cars actually declined. True, the cost of used cars went up by 21%, but this was still less than the overall increasse in the CPI. The two items listed in the table that exhibited a higher 1959–1969 increase in price than the overall CPI were home ownership (a 37% increase in the decade) and medical care (a 48% increase). In short, although subsequent inflationary trends indicate that the cost component of the first life-cycle squeeze has intensified enormously since the late 1960s, this was not as uniformly true between 1959 and 1969.

Considering the case of home ownership costs in more detail, a disproportionate share of the decade increase in the CPI for this item occurred near the very end of the decade (Table 4.5). For example, of the total 31.6% change in the cost of home ownership between 1959 and 1969, 33% of this increase occurred between 1968 and 1969 alone, 51% between 1967 and 1969, and 62% between 1966 and 1969. Just under 75% of the total decade change occurred in the 4 years between 1965 and 1969. The rise in the cost of medical care showed a somewhat similar, though more uneven pattern. This 1959–1969 inflationary pattern indicates that the cost component of the first life-cycle squeeze did not change dramatically during this period. Moreover, if all large increases happened only late in the decade, it seems unlikely that they could have had much effect on marriage, fertility, and wives' labor-force participation by 1970. Presumably there would have to be some lag before adaptive modifications of behavior started to occur. Hence, the 1959–1969 increases in the severity of the first squeeze that did arise were probably due more to the declining relative economic position of young males than to rapidly rising inflation.[10] The role of inflation in the squeeze did not appear to start until near the end of the decade. There seems little doubt that since then, however, the accelerating rate of inflation has been intensifying the first squeeze enormously.

If part of the long-term decline in the relative economic status of the young is due to rising investments in human capital and the age pattern of earnings this tends to produce, then presumably their low relative economic position might be viewed as temporary. Transitory economic difficulties might have a different effect on marriage and family formation and wives' labor-force participation if young people have "great expectations." However, if part of the relatively disadvantaged position of young males is a result of their poor labor-market position due to such factors as large cohort size and a slowing

---

[10]This does not, of course, take into account the possible role of rising aspirations in the 1959–1969 period.

TABLE 4.5
Annual Contributions to the Decade Changes in the Cost of Home Ownership and Medical Care: 1959–1969

Year	Percentage of 1959–1969 change in cost of home ownership — Occurring in each year	Cumulative	Percentage of 1959–1969 change in cost of medical care — Occurring in each year	Cumulative
Total 1959–1969 Percentage point change in index	(31.6)		(37.0)	
	100.0		100.0	
1968–1969	32.6	32.6	19.7	19.7
1967–1968	18.0	50.6	16.5	36.2
1966–1967	11.7	62.3	17.8	54.0
1965–1966	11.4	73.7	10.5	64.5
1964–1965	6.0	79.7	5.9	70.4
1963–1964	5.7	85.4	4.6	75.0
1962–1963	3.5	88.9	− 7.8	67.2
1961–1962	3.2	92.1	19.2	86.4
1960–1961	1.9	94.0	6.2	92.6
1959–1960	6.0	100.0	7.3	99.9

Source: U.S. Bureau of Labor Statistics 1975b: Table 128.

down in economic growth, then future expectations may not be so grand after all. Hence, in the case of cohorts reaching adulthood in the early postwar period at least, not only their *current* relative economic position but also their *expectations* regarding the future may have affected the marriage, fertility, and labor-force behavior of young people. Hence the bright *future* prospects possibly perceived by these small depression cohorts may have encouraged them to marry early and start childbearing early, even though the economic position of young males relative to older males was declining fairly rapidly during the early postwar period. This decline in the relative economic position of the young could actually then be interpreted by them in a very positive light if it is considered indicative of improved income prospects later in life. Relatively stable prices—especially for the necessities of setting up a household—might have encouraged them in this behavior pattern.

However, in recent years the large baby-boom cohorts reaching adulthood have been faced with a sluggish labor market and with much more uncertain prospects for the future. In addition, the cost of living—including the consumer items important to setting up an independent adult household—has been sky rocketing. There is, furthermore, as of this writing, no assurance that the rate of increase in the CPI will go down significantly in the near future. All in all, currently not only has the severity of the first life-cycle squeeze intensified considerably since the late 1960s but there seems little reason for cohorts recently in the first squeeze period to expect a big improvement in the near future. Hence, for these cohorts, behavior that might be oriented to the anticipation of *future* conditions will not be very different from behavior based on their *current* economic situation.[11] In fact, it might be hypothesized that strong inflationary conditions cannot help but encourage child postponement and increased wives' labor-force participation. If, as the data indicate, setting up a household involves heavy expenditures on consumer durables, and the price of these durables is rising rapidly, then the economically rational thing for individual households to do is to try to purchase such items as soon as possible—before their cost becomes prohibitive. There is already evidence that young people (as well as many other groups) are being priced out of the housing market—at least in some parts of the country. In addition, because of the resale value of homes in a rising market, there should be a continued push to own a home as a form of investment. In short, the well known fact that inflation tends to fuel itself puts a premium on behavior modifications that might discourage postponements of expenditures on some consumer durables, but at the expense of currently engaging in other activities—marriage, childbearing, or the cessation of work by young mothers.

II. MARRIAGE AND THE FIRST SQUEEZE

The Overall Picture

So far I have relied on age patterns of earnings as a rough measure of career-cycle stage. These clearly indicate that young men are, on average, at the early stages of their careers, regardless of occupation. However, the census also provides other variables that more fully describe the nature of men's work and occupational attachments—school enrollment and weeks worked, for example. As we shall see, they all suggest that the work and occupational attachments of young males are relatively unstable. This

---

[11]There is also the question, to be considered later in this study, that changes in behaviors that are an adjustment to the first squeeze—such as the employment of the wife in the early years of marriage, can themselves have feedback effect. The result is that people no longer respond to repetitions of the same conditions as they did in the past.

instability, combined with the high cost of setting up a separate household, should lead to a strong relationship between marital status and career-cycle stage. This is for reasons which are, unfortunately, confounded in cross-sectional data. One is that the responsibilities of marriage will encourage young married men to have a more stable labor-force attachment. In this case, marriage affects work behavior. But the reverse causal direction is even more likely as voluntary or involuntary marriage postponement is one traditional way of dealing with the potential difficulties of the first squeeze.[12]

The rest of this chapter will be largely devoted to a comparison of characteristics of men in the white couples samples of the PUS with those of the all white males samples and the never-married segments of the white male samples. The objective is twofold. First, since most of the remaining data analysis in the study is on the married couples samples, it is important to get some understanding of the different socioeconomic characteristics of married men living with their wives compared to those of men in the all males samples which provided the data source for Chapter 3. At the same time, a comparison of the socioeconomic characteristics of males in different age and marital status groups will present a clearer picture of the nature of the marital selection process by career-cycle stage. All this should provide some indication of how marriage formation is affected by career stage.

MARITAL STATUS BY AGE

Is there evidence of much marriage postponements among young men? Moreover, given their declining relative economic position, was there an increase in marriage postponement in the 1960 to 1970 decade? Table 4.6 reveals that the majority of 18–24-year-old males were still single while most 25–34-year-olds had married. Furthermore, there was little change between 1960 and 1970. Annual data from the CPS provided a similar picture (Table 4.7). Relatively few 18–19-year-old males are married at any date. However, in the case of the 20–24-year-olds, there is little evidence of a trend in the proportions single between 1950 and 1970. However, since 1970 it has risen

---

[12]Another reason why married males will probably be farther along in their career cycle stems from the size of the age intervals used. Since marriage and career-cycle stage are both related to age, older men are more likely to be married and to be at a later stage of their career cycle. Hence, within the same age grouping of young people—the 18–24 age group, for example—the married are more likely to be nearer the upper limit of the age category whereas the single will tend to be concentrated near the younger limit of the category. In other words, the age intervals used probably do not sufficiently hold age constant, given the rapid marital and work-related changes occurring in early adulthood.

TABLE 4.6
Percentage of White Males Who Were Never Married, by Age: 1960 and 1970

Age	1960	1970
Total	14.6	15.9
18–24	59.8	58.5
25–34	13.4	12.9
35–44	6.1	6.1
45–54	5.2	4.7
55–64	5.5	4.9

Source: 1960 and 1970 Public Use Samples of White Males.

TABLE 4.7
Percentage of White Males Who Were Never Married, by Age: 1960–1979

Year	18–19	20–24	25–29
1960	91.0	54.7	23.0
1961	92.7	55.1	22.3
1962	90.7	52.4	21.4
1963	93.7	53.6	21.3
1964	93.1	55.9	19.2
1965	92.4	52.9	17.2
1966	92.0	51.8	16.7
1967	93.5	53.8	15.2
1968	91.9	55.1	20.8
1969	91.9	54.6	18.0
1970	92.5	55.2	19.7
1971	92.3	56.0	22.1
1972	91.9	56.9	19.3
1973	90.4	57.1	21.2
1974	91.6	57.0	22.6
1975	93.1	59.9	22.3
1976	91.9	62.1	24.9
1977	93.9	63.7	26.1
1978	94.4	65.8	27.8
1979	94.9	67.4	30.2

Sources: U.S. Bureau of the Census 1961, 1962, 1963e, 1965d, 1965e, 1967c, 1968, 1969c, 1970c, 1971b, 1971c, 1972f, 1973d, 1974b, 1975c, 1977e, 1978d, 1979a, 1980b.

considerably—from 55% in 1970 to 67% in 1979. In the case of 25–29-year-olds, the proportion single has also risen substantially since 1970.[13]

The recency of this trend to postone marriage suggests that perhaps the similarly recent acceleration in the rate of inflation has played an important role in marriage behavior. However, it is unclear why the male age at marriage remained so low throughout this period, even though the relative economic status of young men was declining. One reason may be that the increased labor-force participation of young wives has served as a functional substitute for rising earnings of young males, thus permitting males to continue to marry at a young age despite declines in their relative earnings position (Table 4.8).[14,15]

CAREER-CYCLE STAGE AND MARITAL STATUS

The census offers a variety of variables which, with age, are indicative of career-cycle stage. Along with earnings, there are weeks worked in the year, hours worked during the census reference week, and occupation.[16] We will take up the question of occupation after dealing with the other indicators of career-cycle stage.

To obtain a more concrete picture of the relationship of age to career-cycle stage the procedure we will follow is first to compare men aged 18–24 with older men, particularly those aged 25–34, on such characteristics as weeks or hours worked. Second, we will see if such age differences in weeks or hours

---

[13] Possible increases in the proportion of young men who were single may be understated during the Vietnam period when there was a considerable rise in the number and proportion of young males in the armed services. This is because the CPS marital status data do not take into account members of the armed forces living in the United States in barracks or stationed overseas (U.S. Bureau of the Census 1971b:1). The whole role of "marriage squeezes" on changes in the proportions of young men who are married has not been taken into account either. These would have operated to favor young men's marriage chances during the 1960s but this advantage was declining in the 1970s. See, for example, Akers 1967.

[14] The considerable increases in the labor-force participation of young wives during the 1940–1960 period is often overlooked because of the much greater relative increases for older wives. For example, between 1940 and 1950, the proportion of wives who were in the labor force rose by 107% for 45–54-year-old women as compared to the 50% increase for 20–24-year-olds (Oppenheimer 1970:11). Nevertheless, as Table 4.8 documents, substantial rises in the labor-force participation of young wives has been occurring throughout the postwar period.

[15] Such sources of income as the G.I. Bill and veteran home loans may have also played a role in encouraging early marriage in the postwar period.

[16] Since these samples are composed of males who reported a non-farm occupation within the previous 10 years—whether or not they were currently working—there will be variations in the work status of males. Not all were in the labor force at the time of the censuses and some, though very few, had not even worked in the year before the census.

TABLE 4.8
Labor-Force Participation Rates of Married Women Aged 18–19 and 20–24 with Husband Present: United States, 1940–1976

	Wife aged 18–19		Wife aged 20–24	
Year	Percentage in labor force	Percentage change in rate	Percentage in labor force	Percentage change in rate
1940[a]	10.3	—	17.3	—
1950[a]	21.7	110.7	26.0	50.3
1960[a]	29.2	34.6	31.1	19.6
1960[b]	29.4	n.a.	30.0	n.a.
1970[b]	39.1	33.0	47.4	58.0
1979[b]	52.9	35.3	61.2	29.1

Sources: U.S. Bureau of the Census 1963f: Table 6; U.S. Bureau of Labor Statistics 1961b: Table B; 1971d: Table B; and 1981a: Table B.
[a] Decennial census data.
[b] Current Population Survey Data.

worked, labor-force status, etc., are less among married males, as would be the case if the married 18–24-year-olds are farther on in their career cycle and hence more closely resemble older men. This should indicate the extent to which marital status is related to career-cycle stage. Comparing marital status groups within the same age category will also have a bearing on this issue.

As Tables 4.9 through 4.11 show, there is substantial evidence that marital status is highly related to a variety of factors indicative of career cycle stage.[17] All the variables represented in these tables show a strong relationship with age and hence appear to be useful indicators of career-cycle stage. Thus, 18–24-year-olds were much *more* likely than 25–34-year-old males to be in school and much *less* likely to have worked 35 hours or more during the reference week or 50–52 weeks in the year. Moreover, this age pattern was particularly characteristic of single men and, within age groups, it was more characteristic of the single, indicating that they had less stable work attachments and were therefore at an earlier stage in their careers despite similarities in age. For example, in 1970, 32% of the males aged 18–24 in

---

[17] The data for Tables 4.9 through 4.21 for the single males and males of all marital statuses combined come from the PUS on all white males. The data for the married men come from the white couples sample. The men in the white couples samples will not always be identical to the married males, wives present, in the all white males samples since in 1970 couples where the wife was not white were eliminated and so were those where the husband was not the household head.

TABLE 4.9
Percentage of Males under Age 35 Who Were Enrolled in School, by Age and Marital Status: 1960 and 1970

	1960			1970[a]		
Age	Total males	Single males	Married males	Total males	Single males	Married males
Total under age 25	14.8	32.2	7.1	17.0	35.7	8.5
18–24	29.0	40.0	12.1	31.8	43.6	15.9
25–34	6.7	12.6	5.8	6.5	10.2	6.1

Sources: The data for all males and single males are from the 1960 and 1970 Public Use Samples of All White Males. The data for married males are from the 1960 and 1970 Public Use Samples of White Couples.
[a] Data for 1970 are for those attending school.

TABLE 4.10
Hours and Weeks Worked by Males, by Marital Status and Age: 1960 and 1970[a]

	1960			1970		
Age	Total males	Single males	Married males	Total males	Single males	Married males
Percentage of Males Who Worked 35 or More Hours during the Census Reference Week						
Total	92	81	94	90	74	92
18–24	81	73	90	75	64	87
25–34	94	91	95	92	86	92
35–44	95	90	96	93	87	94
45–54	94	89	94	93	87	93
55–64	91	84	92	90	84	90
Percentage of Males Who Worked 50–52 Weeks in 1959 and 1969						
Total	70	42	75	73	43	80
18–24	41	28	60	42	28	65
25–34	73	57	77	78	63	82
35–44	77	61	79	82	71	84
45–54	74	62	76	81	70	82
55–64	70	56	72	75	62	76

Sources: The data for all males and single males are from the 1960 and 1970 Public Use Samples of All White Males. The data for married males are from the 1960 and 1970 Public Use Samples of White Couples.
[a] Those who did not work at all in 1959 or 1969 were excluded from the base.

II. Marriage and the First Squeeze

TABLE 4.11
Median 1959 and 1969 Earnings of Males, by Marital Status and Age (1969 Dollars)

	\multicolumn{5}{c}{Age of man}
	18–24	25–34	35–44	45–54	55–64
Median earnings					
All males					
1959	2,976	6,559	7,358	6,877	6,189
1969	3,385	8,359	9,676	9,273	8,047
Percentage change	12.2	26.9	30.9	34.2	29.2
Single Males					
1959	1,869	5,107	5,467	4,990	4,641
1969	2,026	6,531	7,519	6,651	6,004
Percentage change	8.4	27.9	37.5	33.3	29.4
Married males[a]					
1959	4,751	6,817	7,522	7,098	6,443
1969	5,820	8,756	10,074	9,656	8,338
Percentage change	22.5	28.4	33.9	36.0	29.4
Ratio of medians					
Single males/husbands					
1959	39.3	74.9	72.7	70.3	72.0
1969	34.8	74.6	74.6	68.9	72.0
All males/husbands					
1959	62.6	96.2	97.8	96.9	96.1
1969	58.2	95.5	96.0	96.0	96.5

Sources: The data for all males and single males are from the 1960 and 1970 Public Use Samples of All White Males. The data for married males are from the 1960 and 1970 Public Use Samples of White Couples.
[a] Earnings refer only to those males who were heads of husband–wife families.

the all white males sample were in school compared to only 6% for 25–34-year-olds (Table 4.9). Among the single, however, 44% of 18–24-year-olds were in school compared to only 10% of 25–34-year-olds. The weeks-and-hours-worked data also support the notion that the married state strongly selects those with a full-time permanent attachment to the labor force—that is, those who were more fully launched into their work careers (Table 4.10). And, as one would expect, the earnings data similarly bear this out (Table 4.11). The median earnings of single males were well below those of married men with the discrepancy being the greatest for 18–24-year-olds. In 1959, for example, median earnings of single males aged 18–24 were only 39% of that of married men in this age group. One consequence of this was that the relative earnings position of young husbands compared to older husbands was by no means as poor as the earnings position of young single males, or all young males, compared to older single males, or older males of all marital statuses combined (Table 4.12).

There is also some evidence that the relationship between marital status and earnings had increased over time. There was a much greater rise in median earnings for the married than for the single 18–24-year-olds—a 22 versus an 8% increase over the decade. As a result, the ratio of the median earnings of single to married males aged 18–24 declined from 40 to 35%. All this suggests that lower-income males were less likely to be married in 1970 than in 1960, and higher-income males were more likely to marry.

In sum, subject to the limitation of the age intervals used, the analysis of the various economic characteristics of young males suggests that there are strong selective factors determining who marries and who stays married. All the data indicate that young males aged 18–24 were at an earlier stage of their career cycle than 25–34-year-old males. Moreover, this was particularly characteristic of younger single men who tended to have a less permanent and less stable labor-force attachment and lower earnings than married men. In short, marriage postponement remained one important device for dealing with the potential economic difficulties of the first life-cycle squeeze, though it is no longer the only means at the disposal of young people.

Occupations and the Timing of Marriage

STOPGAP JOBS

Young men's occupational attachments will undoubtedly reflect the frequently stopgap or marginal nature of their employment experience. Some jobs may more easily lend themselves to part-year or part-time employment while the young man is completing his schooling or until he has "settled down" to a permanent labor-force attachment. Some of these jobs, of course, may just be the lowest rungs on the recognized career ladder. Hence, it is difficult to use occupation alone to distinguish those who have from those who have not, yet, made a relatively permanent commitment to work. Nevertheless, a number of the occupational groups used in this study seem particularly likely to provide stopgap job opportunities. These are the Sales III and the two clerical groups in the white-collar category and the Operative, Service, and Laborer IV occupations in the blue-collar group. Craft IV

TABLE 4.12
The Ratio of Peak Median Earnings to Those at Different Ages, by Marital Status

	Age of man				
Ratio of medians	18–24	25–34	35–44	45–54	55–64
1959					
All males	2.47	1.12	1.00	1.07	1.19
Single males	2.92	1.07	1.00	1.10	1.18
Married males[a]	1.58	1.10	1.00	1.06	1.17
1969					
All males	2.86	1.16	1.00	1.04	1.20
Single males	3.71	1.15	1.00	1.13	1.25
Married males[a]	1.73	1.15	1.00	1.04	1.21

Sources: The data for all males and single males are from the 1960 and 1970 Public Use Samples of All White Males. The data for married males are from the 1960 and 1970 Public Use Samples of White Couples.
[a] Earnings refer only to those males who were heads of husband–wife families.

occupations are less likely to fit into this category because their craft nature implies that some job-specific skills are required and this would presumably tend to discourage the employment of young men seeking temporary work.

Two types of data provide evidence that these occupational groups offer temporary job opportunities for young men. One is the occupational composition of men by age and the other is the 1965–1970 occupational mobility data from the 1970 Census. As far as occupational composition is concerned, Table 4.13 indicates that at both census dates a much higher proportion of 18–24- than 25–34-year-old males were in these six hypothesized "stopgap" occupational groups, both separately and combined. For example, in the case of individual occupations, as high as 14% of males aged 18–24 were in the Laborers IV group in 1970 compared to only 5% of those aged 25–34 years old. Looking at these six occupational groups combined, the cumulative effect of the greater concentration of younger males in such low-level occupations is considerable. In 1970 57% of 18–24 year-olds were in these occupations compared to just 33% for 25–34-year-olds. Furthermore, these 25–34-year-olds were 15–24 in 1960. However, at that time as high as 60% of 18–24-year-olds were in the six stopgap types of occupational groups. Hence it is obvious that among this cohort, a substantial amount of out-mobility from these occupational groups occurred during the decade.

The 1965–1970 occupational mobility data from the 1970 Census provide further evidence that the stopgap occupational groups experienced a disproportionate amount of out-mobility by young men.[18] Since my interest is in the function of these occupations for the young, the analysis will be limited to the 1965–1970 occupational mobility of just those males who were 25–29 years old in 1970.[19] Table 4.14 shows what proportion of males, aged 25–29 in 1970 were in the same occupational group in 1970 as in 1965. The occupations are arranged in ascending order, from those where the least mobility to those where the most mobility was observed. It indicates that these six hypothesized stopgap occupations, and the Managers II group, had the highest outward occupational mobility in the 1965–1970 period. The mobility out of these occupations is not only quite different from that exhibited by men in many higher-level occupations, such as the professions, but from more ordinary Group III occupations that might be thought of as providing "career" jobs. For example, only 36% of men who were in the Laborers IV group and 38% of men in the Sales III group, in 1965 remained in their groups, but 77% of Service III males, and 68% of Craft III workers stayed in the same occupational group.

In sum, the six occupations in question do seem to conform to the stopgap label insofar as mobility out of them by young men was higher than that out of virtually all of the other occupational groups. However, it is still possible that such occupations provide entry-level jobs—that is, jobs on the lowest rung of an institutionalized career ladder. As such, they would not constitute "stopgap" occupations in the sense used here which corresponds more closely to the notion of jobs in secondary types of labor markets—that is, jobs that do not lead anywhere (Doeringer and Piore 1971: Chapter 8). But if they are dead-end jobs, they can still be used as stopgap employment by young men who will be moving on to "bigger and better things" as they mature. The issue is whether the mobility data show that a disproportionate number of men in these low-level stopgap occupations in 1965 actually moved on to fairly high-level occupations by 1970. This is an extremely troublesome question because of the difficulty of establishing what might constitute

---

[18]The mobility data are undoubtedly plagued with serious problems of recall. This is, unfortunately, especially likely to be the case for the stopgap types of occupations under discussion here. Ephemeral or casual employment may, almost by definition, be forgettable. Moreover, some men did not report on their occupation in 1965—either because they did not have one or, if they did, did not remember what it was. Thus, 8.5% of employed males who were 25–29 years old in 1970 did not report an occupation in 1965. Despite such recall problems, however, the occupational mobility data should provide some evidence relevant to the hypothesized stopgap nature of the six occupational groups in question.

[19]However, it is certainly possible that these occupations also provide stopgap job opportunities for older men whose stable occupational career pattern has been temporarily disrupted. Still others may find themselves trapped in occupations that may have begun as only temporary jobs. Finally, these occupational groups may include a number of occupations—low-paying though they may be—that do provide relatively stable occupational careers.

II. Marriage and the First Squeeze

TABLE 4.13
Occupational Composition of Males Aged 18–24 and 25–34: 1960 and 1970

	Total males			
	1960		1970	
Occupation	18–24	25–34	18–24	25–34
Total	100.0	100.0	100.0	100.0
Professionals				
I	1.4	5.1	1.9	6.6
II	4.2	6.0	4.7	8.0
III	4.8	5.3	5.5	6.9
Managers				
I	.4	2.5	.8	2.9
II	1.3	3.5	1.6	4.0
III	1.3	3.9	1.5	3.1
Sales				
II	1.3	3.2	1.2	3.0
III	7.2	4.8	5.7	4.5
Clerical				
III	8.9	6.7	6.7	5.3
IV	3.4	1.3	3.1	1.5
Craft				
II	.3	1.1	.3	1.2
III	10.6	16.0	11.5	16.5
IV	5.6	6.0	5.8	5.9
Operatives				
III	8.9	8.2	7.8	7.3
IV	20.9	16.2	18.5	12.7
Service				
III	.5	1.6	.7	1.9
IV	5.7	3.0	8.8	3.6
Laborers				
IV	13.4	5.8	14.1	5.1
Stop-gap occupations[a]	59.5	37.8	56.9	32.7

Sources: 1960 and 1970 Public Use Samples of All White Males.

[a] Stopgap occupations include the following groups: Sales III, Clerical III and IV, Service IV, Operatives IV, and Laborers IV.

"disproportionate" upward mobility. However, Table 4.15 is a crude effort to tackle this problem. The table examines two types of mobility. One shows data on the proportion of men in the different occupations in 1965 who were in Group I and II white-collar occupations in 1970, to see how the high upward mobility of men in the stopgap occupations compares to men in

TABLE 4.14
Percentage of Employed Males Aged 25–29 in 1970 Who Were in the Same Occupation in 1970 as in 1965, by Occupation in 1965[a]

Occupation in 1965	Percentage in same occupation in 1970
Service III	77
Professional I	74
Professional II	72
Craft III	68
Craft IV	63
Professional III	61
Managers I	57
Craft II	55
Managers III	54
Sales II[b]	50
Operatives III	49
* Operatives IV[c]	48
Managers II	46
* Service IV	45
* Clerical III	40
* Sales III[b]	38
* Laborers IV	36
* Clerical IV	30

Source: 1970 Public Use Sample of All White Males.

[a]Excluded from the table are 830 males who did not report an occupation in 1965—8.4% of employed males aged 25–29 in 1970.

[b]Shortly before going to press a final check of the occupational coding system revealed an error in the 1965 salesworker occupational categories. A number of salesworkers were classified into the lowest peak median sales category instead of higher earnings sales groups. This will lead to some overstatements of 1965–1970 mobility out of the Sales III group. The impact on mobility out of the Sales II group is much less.

*Asterisks precede stopgap occupations.

various presumably more career-ladder types of occupations. And, in fact, men in at least five out of the six stopgap occupations seem to have moved disproportionately into high-level occupations, the exception being those in the Operative IV category. For example, 28% of males in the Sales III group and 27% of those in the Clerical III group had moved into Group I and II white-collar occupations in 1970. This compares to a mobility into the I and II groups of only 22% for Professional III males and 14% for Manager III males. When we turn to blue-collar and service occupations, we also find that, given the low level of these occupations, a rather surprising proportion of men moved all the way up to the Group I and II white-collar occupations. Thus 9% of men who were Service IV males in 1965 and 7% of those who were in the Laborer IV category had moved into the Group I or II occupations. This compares very well to the upward mobility of such higher level occupations as the Service III or Craft III groups.

Occupational comparisons of the mobility into Group I and II white-collar occupations is useful, especially for white-collar occupations, as it permits a fairly wide range of comparisons of hypothesized stopgap occupations with other Group III occupations. However, it only includes mobility into very high occupational levels. This is a particular drawback in evaluating the mobility out of the blue-collar and service stopgap occupations since they have to achieve more long-distance mobility than Sales III or Clerical III males for it to count. Hence, the second column in Table 4.15 adds the Managerial and Professional III groups to the higher-level occupations as 1970 destinations.[20]

Fairly substantial numbers of young men did move into these mediums and higher-level white-collar occupations. It is most characteristic of the Sales III and Clerical III males, of course—32% of the Clerical III males and 39% of the Sales III men in 1965 had made this transition. However, disproportionate mobilities were noted for the stopgap blue-collar and service occupations as well. For example, 16% of males who were in the Service IV group and 12% of those in the Laborer IV group in 1965 had moved into these relatively high-level occupations by 1970. This compares to 10% for Craft III males and 8% for Craft IV men. The partial exception to this pattern are men in the Operatives IV group. A slightly higher proportion of these than of Craft IV males but less than those in Craft III had moved into these higher-level occupation groups.

OCCUPATIONS AND MARITAL STATUS

Turning now to the role of occupation in the relationship of marital status to career-cycle stage, is there any indication that occupation is related to the timing of marriage? Are young men in the presumed stopgap types of occupations, and hence at an earlier stage of their work careers, less likely to be married? Are men in such occupations also more likely to exhibit other evidence of a less stable work attachment—higher rates of school enrollment, for example, or a lower tendency to work full time? Moreover, if this is the case, is it more characteristic of single males, indicating that a considerable amount of marital selection is occurring?

[20]It will be remembered, moreover, that the age–earnings profile of the Professional III group has a closer resemblance to that of Group I and II occupations than to that of most other Group III occupations. This was especially the case in 1969.

TABLE 4.15
Selected Upward Mobilities of Employed Males Aged 25–29 in 1970, by Their 1965 Occupational Group

Occupation in 1965	Percentage who moved into or remained in white-collar I or II occupations	Percentage who moved into or remained in sales II, professional, or managerial occupations
Total	20.2	29.5
Professionals		
I	88.4	92.1
II	85.8	89.3
III	21.8	84.3
Managers		
I	74.7	77.8
II	62.1	68.4
III	13.9	70.6
Sales[a]		
II	68.6	73.6
*III	28.4	39.2
Clerical		
*III	27.1	32.4
*IV	11.8	16.8
Craft		
II	15.0	18.0
III	6.7	9.7
IV	4.9	7.9
Operatives		
III	6.6	8.9
*IV	5.6	8.9
Service		
III	3.9	8.6
*IV	9.2	15.9
Laborers		
*IV	7.3	12.4
Not reported	18.4	26.7

Source: 1970 Public Use Sample of White Males.

[a] Shortly before going to press a final check of the occupational coding system revealed an error in the 1965 salesworker occupational categories. A number of salesworkers were classified into the lowest peak median sales category instead of high earnings sales groups. This will lead to some overstatement of 1965–1970 mobility in general and particularly mobility out of the Sales III group.

*Asterisks precede stopgap occupations.

Age at Marriage

Occupational differences in the age-earnings profile—the "age effect" on earnings—suggest that occupational differences in age at marriage would be a rational response to these earnings patterns. As a consequence, the proportion who are still single in the younger age groups should vary considerably, depending on the occupation. For men whose career trajectory will fall entirely within the middle-to-lower level occupations—most Group III and IV occupations—a fairly early age at marriage seems the more economically rational strategy. This is because the greatest age-related improvements in earnings seem to occur between the 18–24 and 25–34 age groups. Hence marriage postponement—as well as birth postponements—would only delay the expensive adolescent period of childbearing until late in the career cycle when the major factors operating to increase income are the less predictable trends in the growth of real earnings or the similarly less predictable improvements due to occupational mobility.[21] However, men whose career trajectory falls into the higher-level occupations—Group I and II white-collar occupations—would be more likely to delay marriage. This is because the age–earnings profile reveals much lower relative earnings for the young and substantial age-related increases continue until much later in life. Hence, a later age at marriage would be an economically rational way of postponing both the first and second life-cycle squeezes until relatively much more affluent periods in the man's career cycle.

While this argument regarding the relationship of marriage timing to occupation is certainly reasonable, it is also a serious oversimplification of the issue since it fails to take occupational mobility into account. Of particular concern are mobilities related to career-cycle stage (see also U.S. Bureau of Labor Statistics 1967, 1975e, 1979b). As we have just seen, a fairly sizable proportion of young men are only temporarily in certain low-level jobs with rather flat age-earnings profiles (see also Spilerman 1977). As a consequence, a significant (though unknown) proportion of young men in

---

[21]CPS data on mobility within a 1-year period indicate sharp declines in occupational mobility with age. For example, of males who were employed in both January of 1966 and 1965, 32% of 18–19-year-olds and 28% of 20–24-year-olds had changed occupations during the year. However, the proportions changing occupations only varied between 4 and 8% for men in the 35–64 age groups (Saben 1967:34). A similar study covering mobility in 1972 showed the same pattern. If anything, there was a slight decline in mobility for the 35–64-year-olds (Byrne 1975:55). Furthermore, changing occupations was highly associated with changing employers. Approximately 75% of the men in the 35–64 age group who changed occupations between January 1965 and January 1966 also changed jobs (Saben 1967: Table K). Whether this worked entirely to their advantage is unclear since, although the job and occupational shifts may have led to higher hourly earnings, they also would have resulted in a loss of seniority and hence of job security. See also the discussion of occupational mobility in Chapter 3 and the discussion of marriage strategies in Chapter 9.

such occupations are men whose *life-time* career trajectory will resemble that of men in occupations with a relatively steep, rather than flat, age–earnings profile. Hence, for these males, a pattern of later, rather than earlier, marriage is the more rational response to their expected life-time earnings patterns. Moreover, upward mobility *out* of these low-level occupations may, in part, depend on the postponement of the early assumption of heavy economic responsibilities—permitting, for example, further investments in human capital though at the price of deferred earnings.

An additional complication is that there is probably some economic threshold effect operating, even for men whose career trajectory is in a lower-level occupation. Men operating below this threshold may tend to postpone (or forego) marriage until they can be assured of a relatively stable—even if low-paying—work career. Here again, the lowest-paid occupations should include a disproportionate number of such males.

Additional problems arise in trying to work from information on current occupation when the relevant variable is really anticipated career trajectories. Young males already in Group I and II occupations may be very atypical in a number of ways. Most of the men who will spend much of their working lives in such high-level occupations will not be working in them during their young adult years—either because they are still in training (e.g., in professional schools) or are in lower-level occupations. Hence, the marriage behavior of those 18–24-year-olds currently in Group I and II white-collar occupations will probably not be representative of the marriage behavior of men from the same cohort who will ultimately enter such occupations.

In sum, we should observe some evidence of marriage postponement among men in the stopgap occupations and in Group I and II occupations, although 18–24-year-olds already in high-level occupations are likely to be atypical in a number of respects, including marital behavior. However, a high proportion of males already in other Group III occupations that provide fairly stable career patterns will probably marry at a young age—simply because a high proportion are already launched into the types of occupations that will carry them through much of their working lives. Furthermore, these are early-peaking occupations where an early rather than a late marriage age might be more advantageous.

Table 4.16 shows the proportion of 18–24-year-old men who were single in 1960 and 1970, arranging the data according to the occupation with the lowest proportion single to the highest. As expected, a relatively high proportion of 18–24-year-old males in the stopgap occupations were single, with the possible exception of Operative IV 18–24-year-olds. Although 58% of all 18–24-year-old males in 1970 were single, the proportion of single Service IV males was 77% and for Laborers IV it was 73%. Young men in

II. Marriage and the First Squeeze

TABLE 4.16
Ranking of Occupations, by the Percentage of Males Aged 18–24 Who Had Never Married: 1960 and 1970

	1960[a]			1970	
	Occupation	Percentage single		Occupation	Percentage single
1.	Managers III	29	1.	Craft II	23
2.	Managers II	43	2.	Managers I	34
3.	Sales II	45	3.	Service III	36
4.	Craft III	50	4.	Managers II	41
5.	Operatives III	51	5.	Managers III	42
6.	Craft IV	52	6.	Sales II	45
7.	Professionals I	55	7.	Craft III	45
8.	Professionals II	55	8.	Operatives III	48
*9.	Operatives IV	58	9.	Craft IV	48
	Total	60	10.	Professionals I	48
10.	Professionals III	64	11.	Professionals II	50
*11.	Clerical III	67	12.	Professionals III	57
*12.	Sales III	68	*13.	Operatives IV	58
*13.	Clerical IV	70		Total	58
*14.	Laborers IV	70	*14.	Clerical III	63
*15.	Service IV	80	*15.	Sales III	66
			*16.	Clerical IV	69
			*17.	Laborers IV	73
			*18.	Service IV	77

Sources: 1960 and 1970 Public Use Samples of White Males.
[a]In three occupations sample sizes for 18–24-year-old males were too small to compute percentages.
*Asterisks precede stopgap occupations.

the Clerical III and IV and Sales III groups were also more likely to be single than all 18–24-year-olds. This pattern was observed for 1960 as well. Only the proportion of single Operative IV males was not particularly high.

Table 4.17 suggests that mobility effects were indeed operating for these low-level occupations. For example, although a relatively high proportion of males in the Sales III and both clerical groups were single in 1960 and 1970, the age at marriage for somewhat older men in these same occupations is not particularly high.[22] Thus the median age at marriage for married Sales III

---

[22]I did not think it advisable to try to estimate 1960–1970 changes in the median age at first marriage. This median was computed by the Census Bureau on the 1970 PUS but was less accurately estimated by this researcher for the 1960 PUS, using age at last birthday in years and year of marriage. This estimating procedure seems to have led to a systematic bias toward *under*stating the age at marriage. Hence it did not appear wise to make intercensal comparisons. Nor is it useful to make intercohort comparisons within any given census year to estimate cohort differences in the median age at marriage, especially given the broad age intervals used. This is because older cohorts of the married typically include more late marriers than younger cohorts.

men aged 25–34 was 22.2 in 1970, just about the same as that of all males aged 25–34. Clerical IV males also almost match the overall median age at marriage. Hence the youngest age group in these occupations was inflated by many later marrying males who were destined to have left the occupation by their late twenties or early thirties. This also appears to have been the case for Service IV males, who showed the highest proportion of 18–24-year-olds who were single—80% in 1960. Yet the median age at marriage for 25–34-year-olds was the same as for all males combined by 1970. The Laborer IV groups shows a similar pattern. Even Operative IV males do not prove to be the exception Table 4.16 seems to indicate. Although the proportion of Operative IV 18–24-year-olds who were single was about average for both 1960 and 1970, the median age at marriage for older Operative IV males was well *below* average. For example, while, in 1970, the median age at marriage was 22.3 for all 25–34-year-old married men, it was 21.7 for Operative IV males—the second lowest age at marriage. This implies that for this occupational group, as well, the 18–24 age group included a significant proportion of males who were transitory occupants and who exhibited a more delayed marriage pattern. Some of these may have been destined for upward mobility and some for downward, keeping them below the threshold of ready marriageability.[23]

With regard to the Group III occupations that may provide career opportunities within their confines—the three craft occupations, and the Operative III and Service III groups—the findings are also consistent with our expectations of a fairly early age at marriage. All had relatively low proportions of their 18–24-year-olds still single in 1970—and in 1960, where sample sizes permit a comparison. Low median ages at marriage for 25–34- and 35–44-year-olds were also characteristic of men in these occupations. (Table 4.17).

Group I and II occupations show that relatively low proportions of men aged 18–24 were single—in most cases less than the proportion of all males in this age group (Table 4.16). However, these data do not reflect the late entry of males into these occupations and hence are biased by the probably atypical character of males already working in them at such a young age. Evidence of this is found in the relatively small proportion of 18–24-year-olds in these occupations (Table 4.13) and by the high median age at marriage for 25–34- and 35–44-year-olds (Table 4.17). This is certainly the case for men in the professions, Sales II, and Manager I groups.

In sum, despite the methodological difficulties raised by high occupational mobility during the early working years, the data suggest that age at marriage

---

[23]However, given the young age structure of the very low level occupations, it seems unlikely that there is a great deal of mobility *into* them by prime working-age males.

TABLE 4.17
Ranking of Occupations, by the Median Age at Marriage for Married Males Aged 25–34 and 35–44: 1960 and 1970[a]

	25–34				35–44			
	1960		1970		1960		1970	
	Occupation	Median	Occupation	Median	Occupation	Median	Occupation	Median
	Service III	21.5	Craft IV	21.5	Craft II	22.2	Craft II	22.4
	*Operative IV	21.7	*Operative IV	21.7	*Operative IV	23.0	Craft IV	22.6
	Operative III	21.7	Craft II	21.8	Craft IV	23.0	*Operative IV	22.7
	Craft II	21.7	Craft III	21.8	Service III	23.5	Service III	22.7
	*Laborers IV	21.8	Operative III	21.9	Craft III	23.5	Craft III	22.7
	Craft III	22.0	Service III	22.0	*Clerical IV	23.5	*Sales III	22.7
	Managers III	22.0	Managers III	22.0	Managers III	23.5	*Clerical IV	22.8
	Managers II	22.0	*Laborers IV	22.1	Managers I	23.6	Operatives III	22.8
	Craft IV	22.1	*Sales III	22.2	*Sales III	23.7	Managers II	22.9
	*Sales III	22.2	*Service IV	22.3	Sales II	23.7	Managers III	22.9
	Total	22.2	Managers II	22.3	Total	23.7	Total	23.1
	*Service IV	22.5	Total	22.3	*Laborers IV	23.8	*Laborers IV	23.1
	*Clerical III	22.6	*Clerical IV	22.4	Operative III	23.8	*Service IV	23.2
	Managers I	22.6	Managers I	22.5	Managers II	23.9	Sales II	23.5
	Sales II	22.8	*Clerical III	22.6	*Clerical III	24.3	*Clerical III	23.5
	*Clerical IV	22.8	Sales II	22.8	Managers I	24.4	Managers I	23.6
	Professionals III	23.0	Professional III	23.1	Professionals II	24.5	Professionals II	23.9
	Professionals I	23.0	Professionals II	23.1	Professionals I	24.7	Professionals III	24.1
	Professionals II	23.3	Professionals I	23.4	Professionals III	25.0	Professionals I	24.5

Sources: 1960 and 1970 Public Use Samples of White Couples.
[a]Household heads only.
*Asterisks precede stopgap occupations.

153

TABLE 4.18
Percentage of Males under Age 35 Who Were Enrolled in School, by Age, Occupation, and Marital Status: 1960 and 1970

	1960						1970					
	Total		Single		Married		Total		Single		Married	
Occupation	18–24	25–34	18–24	25–34	18–24	25–34	18–24	25–34	18–24	25–34	18–24	25–34
Professionals												
I	52	15	58	15	—[a]	15	44	14	50	16	40	14
II	44	13	53	16	36	13	34	12	38	12	29	12
III	44	20	52	31	26	18	38	16	45	19	29	17
Managers												
I	—[a]	4	—[a]	—[a]	—[a]	3	20	6	34	4	13	6
II	23	3	—[a]	—[a]	—[a]	2	22	5	34	5	14	5
III	12	6	—[a]	16	7	4	18	3	32	4	9	2
Sales												
II	13	7	—[a]	—[a]	—[a]	4	24	3	32	7	17	3
*III	43	7	55	12	16	6	46	6	59	12	23	6
Clerical												
*III	37	9	46	14	20	7	36	10	45	12	23	9
*IV	34	7	40	—[a]	20	6	33	4	42	6	15	4

Craft														
II	—[a]	2	—[a]	—[a]	—[a]	—[a]	2	8	3	—[a]	—[a]	—[a]	2
III	16	4	22	8	8	8	3	16	3	24	7	9	3
IV	19	4	29	12	7	7	2	19	2	31	3	8	2
Operatives														
III	15	5	24	4	4	4	5	16	2	27	5	7	2
*IV	21	3	30	7	8	8	3	28	3	40	7	10	2
Service														
III	—[a]	7	—[a]	—[a]	—[a]	—[a]	7	19	12	26	18	17	12
*IV	50	7	58	13	18	18	5	54	9	61	11	34	10
Laborers														
*IV	35	4	47	11	9	9	3	42	5	52	11	17	4

Source: The data for all males and single males are from the 1960 Public Use Samples of All White Males. The data for married males are from the 1960 and 1970 Public Use Samples of White Couples.

[a]Sample sizes were too small to compute percentages.

*Asterisks precede stopgap occupations.

is related to the type of career trajectory men will follow—or plan to follow. Those who will operate in or move into a type of occupation, or "family" of occupations with a steep age–earnings profile are more likely to delay marriage until a more propitious point in their career cycle. Indeed, the achievement of a toehold in relatively high-level occupations may sometimes be a result of deferring the economic responsibilities usually accompanying marriage—either by delaying marrying or having a working wife. On the other hand, the age of marriage will be younger for those men who will be working in the type of occupation(s) where the age–earnings profile is flatter and where peak earnings occur in the younger age groups. However, some men who are in very low-paying occupations may have a greater difficulty in reaching a threshold of economic security sufficient to form an early marriage. This suggests the kind of dilemma facing many such economically marginal males. Marriage postponement may be necessary or inevitable until a minimum level of economic security is achieved. Yet considerable marriage and family postponement is not the ideal strategy because the age effect on earnings favors the young over the middle aged. Hence, for some of these men, there is always the chance that life will pass them by. Before they have reached a minimum level of economic attainment, they may have passed their prime.[24]

School Enrollment

School enrollment data provide additional evidence regarding the nature of early occupational attachments and their relationship to marital status. If certain low-level white-collar and blue-collar occupations actually do offer temporary or part-time jobs for young men headed for better-paying occupations, then high levels of school enrollment should be characteristic among the young in these occupations. Table 4.18 indicates that this is indeed the case. Even though educational attainment is positively related to peak median earnings level within the major occupational groups, 18–24-year-old males in all the six lower-level stopgap occupations under discussion had high proportions currently in school. For example, in 1970, 54% of the Service IV 18–24-year-olds were attending school compared to 19% of the Service III 18–24-year-olds, even though 77% of Service III males of all ages combined had 12 or more years of schooling compared to only 45% of Service IV males (Table 3.6). Laborer IV males aged 18–24 had similarly high proportions enrolled in school (42%) that were only

---

[24]Furthermore, those marriages that are formed may be unstable.

II. Marriage and the First Squeeze

slightly lower than those of Professional I and Sales III males—44 and 46% respectively.

All this supports the notion that many of these low-level blue-collar and white-collar occupations provide interim jobs rather than entry-level positions in an ordered occupational hierarchy. A high proportion of males still in school in the 18–24 age groups are probably in college rather than in high school. However, Operative, Service, and Laborer IV occupations do not seem likely prospects for career-entry jobs for men with one or more years of college. How true this is for Sales III and the clerical occupations is less certain, of course.

The data on school enrollment by marital status and occupation also show that the probability of being enrolled in school is consistently much more characteristic of single males than of the married. In all occupations, the differences between the single and the married in the proportions enrolled were considerable. In addition, some of the greatest differences by marital status were for the low-level occupations that seem to provide "temporary" types of jobs. For example, comparing the 18–24-year-olds in 1970, the difference in the proportions in school between the married and the single was 36 percentage points for Sales III males but only 15 percentage points for Sales II males. For Service IV males the difference was 27 percentage points compared to 9 percentage points for Service III males.

Amount of Time Worked and Earnings

As was the case for males in all occupational groups combined, and for both 1960 and 1970, 18–24-year-olds in the various occupations were less likely to have worked at least a 35-hour week or 50–52 weeks in the year before the census (Tables 4.19 and 4.20). This was particularly true for young single men, especially those in the stopgap occupations. For example, in 1970, the proportion of single males in the Service IV group who worked 35 or more hours during the reference week was only 43% compared to 76% for the married. Among Sales III workers, only 47% of the single 18–24-year-old males worked 35 or more hours compared to 85% for the married.

As one would anticipate, the earnings data reflect the age, marital, and occupational differentials in the amount of time worked during the year (Table 4.21). For example, in 1969, the earnings of single males aged 18–24 varied between only 33 and 35% of those for married for men in the Laborers IV, Service IV, Sales III, and Operative IV occupations. However, the ratios were considerably higher for men in more stable career occupations. Thus in 1969, the ratio was 56% for Professional I males and 66% for Service III males 18–24 years old.

TABLE 4.19
Percentage of Males Aged 18–24 and 25–34 Who Worked 35 or More Hours during the Census Reference Week, by Occupation and Marital Status: 1960 and 1970

	1960							1970						
	Total males		Single males		Married males		Total males		Single males		Married males	
Occupation	18–24	25–35	18–24	25–35	18–24	25–35	18–24	25–35	18–24	25–35	18–24	25–35
Professionals												
I	76	95	—[a]	95	—[a]	95	68	88	62	86	74	88
II	83	97	79	96	86	97	81	91	75	87	88	92
III	76	91	66	92	89	90	72	87	65	80	81	89
Managers												
I	—[a]	98	—[a]	—[a]	—[a]	98	92	96	84	93	95	97
II	93	97	—[a]	—[a]	—[a]	97	87	96	74	92	96	97
III	97	98	—[a]	—[a]	—[a]	98	89	98	80	97	95	98
Sales												
II	87	98	—[a]	—[a]	—[a]	98	84	94	77	90	88	95
*III	70	94	61	82	87	96	62	94	47	85	85	95

158

Clerical											
*III	83	95	78	93	90	95	76	91	68	87	85	92
*IV	88	95	82	—^{a}	—^{a}	94	77	93	68	92	94	94
Craft												
II	—^{a}	95	—^{a}	—^{a}	—^{a}	95	94	94	—^{a}	—^{a}	—^{a}	95
III	93	95	90	96	96	96	87	93	80	88	92	94
IV	79	91	73	—^{a}	84	94	82	91	72	88	88	92
Operatives												
III	87	93	80	94	92	93	84	90	78	90	89	90
*IV	83	92	75	85	91	94	78	91	68	84	88	92
Service												
III	—^{a}	100	—^{a}	—^{a}	—^{a}	100	94	98	86	—^{a}	97	98
*IV	54	93	46	—^{a}	—^{a}	98	52	87	43	77	76	90
Laborers												
*IV	72	89	61	88	86	90	63	86	54	82	81	87

Sources: The data for all males and single males are from the 1960 and 1970 Public Use Samples of All White Males. The data for married males are from the 1960 and 1970 Public Use Samples of White Couples.

^{a}Sample sizes were too small to compute percentages.

*Asterisks precede stopgap occupations.

159

TABLE 4.20
Percentage of Males Aged 18–24 and 25–34 Who Worked 50–52 Weeks in 1959 and 1969, by Occupation and Marital Status

	1959						1969					
	Total males		Single males		Married males		Total males		Single males		Married males	
Occupation	18–24	25–34	18–24	25–34	18–24	25–34	18–24	25–34	18–24	25–34	18–24	25–34
Professionals												
I	41	80	—[a]	67	—[a]	82	39	78	25	64	55	80
II	43	83	31	61	59	87	51	86	35	70	69	90
III	40	60	33	40	53	65	35	63	23	43	52	68
Managers												
I	—[a]	93	—[a]	—[a]	—[a]	96	60	90	41	78	68	91
II	67	86	—[a]	—[a]	—[a]	88	61	87	44	75	76	90
III	70	92	—[a]	—[a]	—[a]	93	62	90	41	82	77	91
Sales												
II	57	87	—[a]	—[a]	—[a]	90	56	85	34	64	73	88
*III	44	81	34	57	66	86	41	83	29	62	66	88
Clerical												
*III	46	83	33	73	72	86	47	83	36	69	67	87
*IV	46	74	37	—[a]	—[a]	76	40	78	28	72	68	80

Craft												
II	—[a]	90	—[a]	—[a]	—[a]	90	79	90	—[a]	—[a]	—[a]	91
III	52	73	38	59	66	75	56	81	40	67	71	84
IV	35	60	24	—[a]	49	64	44	71	27	53	63	74
Operatives												
III	44	70	36	58	53	71	51	78	34	69	70	81
*VI	37	66	24	49	55	70	41	74	26	58	65	78
Service												
III	—[a]	89	—[a]	—[a]	—[a]	90	64	91	44	77	74	93
*IV	25	65	18	43	—[a]	72	27	70	21	57	51	77
Laborers												
*IV	27	51	17	35	46	57	27	64	20	54	50	68

Sources: The data for all males and single males are from the 1960 and 1970 Public Use Samples of All White Males. The data for married males are from the 1960 and 1970 Public Use Samples of White Couples.

[a]Sample sizes were too small to compute percentages.

*Asterisks precede stopgap occupations.

TABLE 4.21
Ratio of the Median Earnings of Single Males to Married Male Heads of Household, by Occupation and Age (Percentage)

	Ratio of 1959 medians		Ratio of 1969 medians	
Occupation	18–24	25–34	18–24	25–34
Total	39.3	74.9	34.8	74.6
Professionals				
I	40.2	82.5	55.6	79.6
II	48.6	76.7	51.3	80.4
III	41.1	76.2	43.3	82.8
Managers				
I	—[a]	—[a]	57.1	77.4
II	64.7	—[a]	47.8	81.7
III	—[a]	64.5	46.5	85.3
Sales				
II	—[a]	70.2	47.6	77.6
III	26.6	78.2	33.6	69.7
Clerical				
*III	41.5	84.8	41.7	76.6
*IV	42.0	—[a]	43.2	72.2
Craft				
II	—[a]	—[a]	—[a]	—[a]
III	56.8	80.2	47.9	77.8
IV	43.8	64.3	40.0	67.7
Operatives				
III	49.1	85.0	48.2	75.7
*IV	40.4	70.2	35.4	70.4
Service				
III	—[a]	—[a]	66.2	86.6
*IV	30.5	57.8	33.7	57.5
Laborers				
*IV	31.1	60.3	32.8	68.6

Sources: The data for single males are from the 1960 and 1970 Public Use Samples of All White Males. The data for married males are from the 1960 and 1970 Public Use Samples of White Couples.
[a]Medians were not computed for sample sizes below 25.
*Asterisks precede stopgap occupations.

III. CONCLUSION

The goals of this chapter on the first life-cycle squeeze were twofold. First I wanted to obtain some concrete empirical documentation of the notion that early adulthood was a period when young couples aspire to invest in a variety of expensive consumer durables associated with setting up an independent

III. Conclusion

household in our society—especially one that is suitable for raising a family. This is despite the relatively low income characteristics of young men. As we saw from the actual expenditure patterns of young households compared to older ones, there was considerable support for the notion that the first years of marriage are a time of considerable investments in heavy consumer durables and, hence, it is a period of high consumption aspirations. With respect to changes in the setting-up costs of young couples, CPI data on changes in the cost of those consumer durables most involved in the first-squeeze period indicated little evidence of a disproportionate rise in the price of these items before the late 1960s. So, if the first squeeze did intensify between 1960 and 1970 it seems to have been largely a result of an apparent declines in the relative income position of young males. However, very sharp increases in the cost of such consumer durables have been characteristic of the period since the late 1960s, keeping pace with and often exceeding the generally sharp rise in the CPI in recent years. Hence, since the late 1960s the severity of the first squeeze seems to have intensified both because of inflation and declines in the relative income position of young men.

A second goal was to investigate one major response to the severity of the first squeeze—age at marriage. One would expect marriage formation to be closely related to whether young men are fully launched into their occupational careers. Furthermore, different career trajectories should vary in their compatibility with earlier or later marriage patterns. Finally, since the remainder of this volume deals with married couples, it was important to compare the socioeconomic characteristics of married males with all males in order to achieve some understanding of the selective factors operating to differentiate that subset of males who were married.

By and large, the data on the characteristics of single and married males provide strong support for the notion that marriage tends to select those young men who are further advanced in their career cycle. This was indicated first by the much greater tendency for young *single* rather than young *married* males to be enrolled in school, working part-time, achieving lower incomes, etc. Second, the young were more likely to be concentrated in occupational groups that seem to provide stopgap types of job opportunities rather than just low-level career-entry positions. This was indicated by the disproportionately high 1965–1970 mobility *out* of these occupations by young men into very different types of occupations—often at a much higher socioeconomic level, unlikely to simply belong to a higher rung in a single-career ladder. Furthermore, data on school enrollment by age and occupation, as well as the amount of time worked and other economic characteristics, support the notion that these occupational groups are important providers of stopgap types of jobs.

With regard to how different types of career trajectories may affect the age at marriage, I hypothesized that marriage postponement was a relatively adaptive strategy for men whose career trajectory would approximate a steep age–earnings profile; whereas there was little advantage in marriage postponement, once a minimum economic threshold had been achieved, for men following a flatter age–earning trajectory. Despite measurement difficulties, the data provided some support for this hypothesis. There was evidence of marriage postponement among young men in occupational groups providing stopgap job opportunities for the young, although age at marriage for older men in these occupations was not particularly high. Age at marriage for men in white-collar Group I and II occupations was relatively late whereas that for Group III blue-collar and service males was early.

In sum, the data in this chapter provide additional support for the view that the first life-cycle squeeze is a very real social phenomenon and that it has intensified in recent years. Furthermore, marriage postponement remains a common strategy among men for dealing with the first squeeze although its adaptive value varies among occupational groups, with age patterns of marriage varying accordingly.

5

The Second Life-Cycle Squeeze

Although the cost component of the first life-cycle squeeze is defined primarily in terms of the expense of setting up an independent household, the second squeeze focuses on the effect of variations in the direct cost of children as they mature. The concept of the second squeeze is actually rather complex. It involves the interaction of the peak child-dependency burden with the income of the husband during the same period. I have used husband's age as the means of linking these cost and income variables together. Variations in the direct cost of children by their age, and by the age of the husband when these costs peak, not only depend on the total number of children born but on variations in the age composition of dependent children, assuming that direct dollar costs vary with the age of the child. Since the age composition of children in a family depends on child spacing, variations in the total cost of children over the family cycle will partly be a function of spacing as well as family size. For example, if there are two families with four children, the family with their children *2* years apart is more likely to have higher peak costs in the second-squeeze period than the family with their children each *4* years apart. In fact, whatever the family-cycle stage, annual costs are likely to vary between these two spacing patterns because the age-mix of children will be continously affected by timing. The husband's age at the start of childbearing will affect his age during the period in which peak costs are occurring. In addition, of course, the severity of the second squeeze is a function of how this dependency burden interacts with men's earnings in the same time period. Any particular age–dependency profile will have different economic implications for families of men who are in occupations with late rather than early peaking age–income profiles.

The complexity of the dependency dimension of the second squeeze affects the interpretation of age patterns, as well as changes in them, in terms of age, period, and cohort effects. Age and cohort effects are likely to be dominant in the adolescent-dependency burden whereas period effects may be of less importance. For one thing, there seem to be intrinsic limits to the possible variation in the age at which the second squeeze can occur in our society since it cannot start to appear until about 12 or more years after the birth of the first child. So, it is very unlikely to be experienced by young men in their twenties. It is also unlikely to occur with any frequency to couples in thier mid-sixties or older. Thus, the biological rhythm of childbearing plus the basic definition of the second squeeze imposes a certain "age effect" on the squeeze variable.

By definition, couples in the second squeeze have already had their children. Hence, period effects are improbable explanations of 1960–1970 age similarities or differences in the family composition of such couples since these similarities or differences will primarily reflect events (i.e., births) that occurred many years previously. Period effects may show up, however, via changes in the age at leaving home or school and if remarriage complicates the picture of family composition that we get from the census. Occupational comparisons may also be affected by occupational mobility. However, by and large, age and cohort effects are probably the most important factors in the age composition of children of older couples.

For younger couples, childbearing is usually not over with yet, however. Hence, 1960–1970 differences could reflect period effects, thereby increasing the difficulty of interpreting 1960–1970 changes for young couples or interage comparisons involving young couples. Nevertheless, even if the changes observed cannot safely be attributed to completed fertility, they must indicate timing changes. However, timing changes will not be purely transitory in their effect on the second squeeze because the nature of this squeeze is itself partly a function of timing. Hence, when such timing changes are observed, they are actually cohort rather than pure period effects—that is they interact in a permanent way with age for a given cohort. Thus, although the *number* of children present may sometimes vary due to a period effect for young people, in the sense that postponed births can be made up, timing patterns are not as completely subject to modification. For example, if the evidence suggests that delayed childbearing is occurring for younger cohorts, then the second life-cycle squeeze will occur later in the husband's life-cycle than for earlier cohorts. How severe the squeeze will turn out to be, however, partly depends on completed fertility and the subsequent timing of births of the more recent cohorts—something we do not yet know. However, we do know that many have passed the point where early childbearing is still an option.

An important problem that arises in studying the second squeeze is the difficulty of developing a moderately satisfactory indicator of variations in the "cost" of children by their ages. This issue will be discussed later in this section and dealt with at length in Appendix C. For the moment, let us assume that usable estimates can be derived. If so, a number of questions can be explored regarding the second squeeze.

First, how do child-dependency burdens vary by the age of the husbands in our Public Use Samples? If 1960–1970 similarities in the timing of the peak dependency period are observed, we will interpret this as a rough indication of the family-cycle component of the second squeeze—that is, as an age effect. Even if we do not try to make interpretations that transcend the periods of our observations, age differences in the dependency burden indicate that in 1960 and 1970, at least, men in different age groups experienced different levels of economic responsibility for their children. If marked age differences among men in the cost of children occur but minor differences in men's income, this implies age differentials in economic status. In short, how does the additional consideration of child-care costs modify our picture, based on earnings alone, of the relative economic position of men in these different age groups at any single moment of time?

Second, what *changes* in the dependency burden were observed for different age groups? For example, did it become heavier for 35–44-year-olds in 1970 than in 1960, suggesting an intensification of the severity of the second squeeze? Furthermore, if changes in the nature of the dependency burden varied among age groups, then the economic position of particular age groups vis-à-vis others will also have changed. Most important, do the apparent improvements in the relative economic position of older men hold up once child dependency is taken into account?

Third, can our data tell us anything about how child dependency changed over the life-time of particular cohorts? We can only observe any cohort at two points in its life-course. Nevertheless, this provides some idea of temporal changes in the dependency burden over the family cycle. For example, how did the child-care costs change for cohorts who were 25–34 in 1960 but 35–44 in 1970? This was a transition that brought about considerable changes in the number and ages of childbearing in the home.

Finally, given our knowledge of occupational differentials in age–earnings profiles, as well as 1960–1970 changes in these, what occupational differences in family-cycle patterns are observed? What can these tell us about occupational variations in the timing and severity of the second squeeze and how these changed over time?

All these questions are important in assessing the relative economic status of different age groups at one point in time as well as age-group changes in relative economic status over time. As such, the analysis should provide a better understanding of the kinds of economic pressures that may have influenced wives' economic behavior during this period. However, such questions of relative economic status are also relevant to an empirical evaluation of another aspect of Easterlin's theories regarding fertility fluctuations in the postwar period. Easterlin has argued that the increases in the income position of young families relative to the families of men in the parental generation encouraged earlier marriage and higher fertility by depression cohorts in the postwar period. Similarily, *decreases* in the relative economic status of young baby-boom cohort families in the late 1960s and 1970s have had the reverse effect (Easterlin 1968, 1973, 1978). We have already seen that the relative income position of younger versus older *males* has, except for cyclical fluctuations, declined throughout the postwar period, whatever the changes in the lagged relative economic position of younger compared to older *families,* and despite sharp shifts in relative cohort size. An additional consideration, however, is the impact of changes in child-care costs on the relative economic position of young families. Easterlin's measures of relative economic status have been entirely in terms of relative *income* position, without taking into consideration factors that might offset income changes such as shifts in child-care costs. Thus, Easterlin emphasizes the importance of relative cohort size but only really considers its impact at that point in the life-cycle when young males are in the early working years. However, if cohort size is an important demographic factor at this point in the life-cycle, it seems arbitrary not to consider its possible significance at other life-cycle points as well. In particular, another potentially important period during which cohort size can have an impact is during adolescence and during the ages young people typically go to college. Here the economic impact is on the cohort's families of orientation and the presumed consumption levels these families have been able to achieve.

I. THE COST OF CHILDREN

Variations by Age

There is little doubt that assessing the "cost" of children is a complex task. Ideally, one would presumably have to specify the actual shopping list of consumption items implicit in a given standard of child "quality."[1] This is much too difficult a conceptual and measurement problem for the present study. However, as already suggested in Chapter 1, the actual shopping list implied by a given standard of child quality will be affected by the age of the child. To refer to an earlier example, the cost of particular types of items—blue jeans and hamburgers—will vary according to the size and amount consumed by the child. This, in turn, is highly related to how old the child is. Other sources of variation in child-care costs related to the age of the child are differences in the consumption items appropriate to different age groups living at the same standard of living. To the extent there are age-related differences in the appropriate market basket for children, however, the age of a child will be related to differences in the cost of children at a given standard.

In actual studies estimating the cost of children by age, what is observed is expenditures on children and how these vary by age rather than the cost of achieving certain standards of child quality. Assessing these age variations in cost has been approached in two related ways. One strategy is represented by estimates of the *relative* cost of children of different ages, the other, more controversial, approach has been to develop dollar estimates for each of the different age groups.

RELATIVE COSTS BY AGE

A number of scales have been developed over the years to measure either the relative cost of children at different ages or of families of different sizes and age composition. For convenience, only one such scale will be discussed here—the Revised Equivalence Scale of the Bureau of Labor Statistics (U.S. Bureau of Labor Statistics 1968b).[2] Some years ago, the BLS constructed

---

[1] There is also the problem of attributing costs to individuals of shared consumption items. For a discussion of this question see Lazear and Michael (1979).

[2] For a discussion of this and other scales, see Espenshade (1973: Chapter 1), U.S. Bureau of Labor Statistics (1968b), Lindert (1978). The BLS equivalence scale is being discussed because it is set up under the same basic assumptions as Espenshade's estimates of direct expenditures on children, used later in this chapter.

model family budgets for a "standard" family but, since most families do not conform to the standard, the budgets would have been of limited utility without some method of adjusting them for differences in family size and composition (U.S. Bureau of Labor Statistics 1970d, 1969, 1966b). To accomplish this, the BLS constructed a scale for estimating equivalent incomes by family type (Table 5.1). In the process, they have given us a rather useful—if rough—indicator of how the cost of living varies by family size and life-cycle stage.

TABLE 5.1
Revised Equivalence Scale for Urban Husband–Wife Families of Different Size, Age, and Composition (Four Person Family—Husband 35–54, Wife, Two Children, Older 6–15 = 100)[a]

	Age of head		
Size and type of family[b]	Under 35	35–54	55–64
No children	49	60	59
One-child families: average[c]	62	81	86
Child under 6	62	69	—
Child 6–15	62	82	88
Child 16–17	—	91	88
Child 18 or older	—	82	85
Two-children families: average[c]	74	99	109
Older under 6	72	80	—
Older 6–15	77	100	105
Older 16–17	—	113	125
Older 18 or older	—	96	110
Three-children families: average[c]	94	118	124
Oldest under 6	87	97	—
Oldest 6–15	96	116	120
Oldest 16–17	—	128	138
Oldest 18 or older	—	119	124
Four-children-or-more families: average[c]	111	138	143
Oldest under 6	101	—	—
Oldest 6–15	110	132	140
Oldest 16–17	—	146	—
Oldest 18 or older	—	149	—

Source: U.S. Bureau of Labor Statistics 1968b: Table 1.

[a] The scale values shown here are the percentages of the cost of goods and services for family consumption of the base family (four persons—husband age 35–54, wife, 2 children, older child 6–15) required to provide the same level of living for urban families of different size, age, and composition.

[b] Husband–wife families with their own children (including adopted and stepchildren) present, but with no other persons living with the family.

[c] Scale values for individual family types weighted by the number of families of each type in the universe. The averages include some types for which values were not shown separately because of the small number of such families in the sample.

I. The Cost of Children

The basic problem in constructing such scales is to obtain an objective means of identifying equivalent levels of consumption for families of varying composition. According to the BLS:

> The measure used to determine equivalent income was the proportion of income after taxes spent on food. It is based on the assumption that families spending an equal proportion of income on food have attained an equivalent level of total consumption. Formulation of the equations used for the ... equivalence scales was preceded by extensive research showing that essentially the same form of relationship between food expenditures and income was observed in eight major consumer expenditure surveys conducted by the BLS between 1888 and 1960 ... Similar research on the income elasticity of food expenditures was conducted with data from the Survey of Consumer Expenditures, 1960–61 [U.S. Bureau of Labor Statistics 1968b:1].

Table 5.1 shows that in order to maintain an "equivalent" level of well-being, income must increase as the number of children increases. Thus, relative to the base family type, the ratio increases from 49%, on the average, for a childless couple to 111% for a family of four or more children when the husband is under 35. When the head of the family is 35–44, the ratio rises from 60% to 138%. In addition to the effect of the *number* of children, their ages also make a considerable difference according to these estimates. Taking the case of families where the head is 35–54 and there are two children, the equivalence ratio goes up from 80% for families where the oldest child is under 6 to 113% where the oldest is 16–17. Looking at what might represent a more-or-less typical range over the family life-cycle for parents producing the baby-boom cohorts—a childless couple where the husband is under 35 compared to a three-child family where the oldest child is 16–17 and the husband is in the 35–54 age group—we see that the ratio varies from 49% to 128%. In other words, according to the BLS scale, the income of the three-child couple at the later stages of the family cycle would have to be more than 2.5 times as great as the younger childless couple to maintain an equivalent level of consumption.[3]

Useful though relative costs or cost ratios may be, they also have drawbacks. Since families will typically have children present in a number of different age groups, it is hard to obtain an overall picture of the child-cost burden from relative cost estimates. This impedes detailed comparisons among families—particularly, of the effect of 1960–1970 changes in family composition on the overall dependency burden of families in the second life-

---

[3] The scale also does not adequately reflect the "setting-up" costs of young couples. However, since I have used other data to indicate the timing and severity of the first squeeze, this limitation is not very serious.

cycle squeeze period. It is then impossible to get a clear idea of the 1959–1969 changes in the real income of husbands, net of changes in child-support costs. Thus, although any dollar estimates of direct child-care costs are difficult to derive and are bound to be controversial in a number of ways, the analytical utility of such estimates is enormous. Because of their high potential value, dollar estimates of direct child-care costs will therefore be made and utilized in part of the analysis of this chapter, although it is recognized that they are only rough approximations.

DIRECT DOLLAR COSTS

Estimating the direct cost of children is a topic of increasing concern to demographers—particularly economic demographers—and involves considerably complex issues.[4] Without going into these complexities here, rough estimates are presented of average annual expenditures on children in three different age groups—ages 0–5, 6–11, and 12–17. These estimates are based on a scaled-down version of 1960 expenditures on children under age 18, developed by Thomas Espenshade.[5] Espenshade's estimates, like the BLS equivalence scales, are based on the assumption that families spending the same proportion of family income on food have attained equivalent levels of living. For a detailed discussion of the estimates see Appendix C and Espenshade (1973).

Espenshade's expenditure estimates were for 1960 but the same estimates were used for 1970 as well. Holding constant age-specific expenditure estimates of children will make it possible to measure the impact of changes in the number and ages of children on the cost of children. In essence, then, the operating assumption is that families in 1969 wanted to spend at least the same amount on each child at each age as families did 10 years previously. The resulting standardized expenditures estimates might therefore be called *equivalent expenditures* and when the term cost is used in discussing them, it is in the sense of indicating the cost of maintaining the same level of expenditure per child of a given age in 1969 as in 1959. However, to

[4]For a discussion of these issues and various estimates see, for example, Espenshade (1973, 1977), Turchi (1975a), and Lindert (1978). However, much of the demographic interest in the cost of children stems from a desire to explain fertility decisions—particularly those in the early years of marriage—rather than from an interest in assessing the current dependency burden of couples. The relevant "costs" are not indentical for these two different research goals. Thus, the opportunity costs, in terms of the wife's time lost from the labor force for one or more children, is a much more potentially significant cost factor in fertility decisions than in the labor-force decisions made by women in their thirties or forties.

[5]I am extremely grateful to Thomas Espenshade for his comments and suggestions while I was reworking his cost-of-children estimates to conform with the aims of the present study. Of course, the responsibility for the revisions and any faults in them are mine alone.

facilitate 1960–1970 comparisons of child-care costs, the 1960 expenditure estimates were inflated into 1969 dollars. This makes it possible to estimate the impact of changes in equivalent expenditures on the 1959–1969 changes in the earnings of men since these too have been presented in 1969 dollars.[6]

Expenditure estimates for children of different ages under 18 are presented in Table 5.2. Estimates for families where the husband was 18–24 years old are a little different because the children in such families are more likely to be firstborns. The cost of firstborn children is estimated to be greater than that of higher birth order (Espenshade 1973). Consistent with the equivalence scales discussed earlier in this chapter, Table 5.2 indicates that the cost of children rises considerably with their age. Thus, expenditures on 6–11-year-olds are estimated to be about 50% higher than expenditures on a child under 6 and expenditures on 12–17-year-olds were 55% greater than on a child in the 6–11 age group. As a result, depending on the age composition of children in the household, total child-care expenditures should vary considerably.

II. THE OVERALL PICTURE

The Number and Ages of Children

Let us turn now to the problem of trying to ascertain the timing and severity of the second squeeze, as well as detecting any 1960–1970 changes. I will concentrate first on all occupational groups combined since measurement difficulties preclude a completely parallel analysis for the different occupational subgroups. Because dollar estimates of the cost of children of various ages are rather crude, and hence somewhat controversial, the problem of child-dependency burden will be dealt with first by examining patterns and trends in the number and ages of children in the households of men in different age groups.

One measure of child dependency is the average number of children ever born to the wife.[7] For older couples, this is indicative of intercohort

[6] Although expenditure estimates are in terms of 1969 dollars, the number and ages of children present refer to 1960 and 1970. Of necessity, it was assumed that the family composition for 1960 and 1970 is a relatively accurate estimate for the composition in 1959 and 1969 respectively.

[7] This is a somewhat crude measure since not all children of the husband will be counted and hence we may underestimate his economic responsibilities. However, this may be offset by uncounted income transfers for children born to the wife from a previous marriage. One could, of course, limit the analysis to couples still in their first marriage but this raises selectivity biases and would reduce the comparability of the analysis to other sections of the study.

TABLE 5.2
Estimated per Capita Annual Expenditures on Children under Age 18, by Age of Husband (1969 Dollars)

	Age of husband			
	18–24		25–64	
Age of child	Cost in dollars	Percentage change	Cost in dollars	Percentage change
0–5	1,273	—	1,036	—
6–11	1,903	49.4	1,549	49.5
12–17	2,943	54.6	2,397	54.7

Source: Appendix C.

differences in completed fertility and, hence, differences in the overall level of economic responsibilities of families for their children. For younger families, the mean number of children ever born provides some notion of timing changes, though not necessarily changes in the ultimate total dependency burden. However, by and large, the mean number of children ever born tells us little about variations in the dependency burden due to variations in the age-composition of children over the husband's life-cycle.

In order to obtain a better indicator of the timing of the second squeeze I have computed the mean number of children present in various age groups under age 25. These means will be used as a measure of how the presence of children at more compared to less expensive ages varies by the husband's age. They can also be put in relative terms to indicate family-cycle stage by computing the ratio of the mean number of children present in each of the age groups to the total mean number of children. I have used the mean number of children ever born to wives as the base for these ratios rather than the mean number present in order to permit more meaningful comparisons. Ignoring children no longer at home would lead to distorted measures of family-cycle stage because they are usually older than those present and subgroups vary in the age at which children leave home. The distribution of these means will be interpreted as the approximate proportion of the mean number ever born that are accounted for by the mean number present in these age groups. The difference between the total mean number of children under age 25 who are present and the total mean number ever born is interpreted as a crude measure of the mean number of children no longer in the home—primarily adults, though not necessarily economically independent ones. Also included in this residual category will be the mean number of children aged 25 or older who are still at home, also assumed to be economically independent. There will, of course, be some error in these procedures because some of the children in the home may not be born of the wife and

II. The Overall Picture 175

some children may not be living with their mothers. Still others will have died. Hopefully, these errors will tend to average themselves out in the group means. In any event, there does not seem to be any other way of roughly taking into account *all* the children born and not just those present.

This analysis of the relative age decomposition of the mean number of children ever born in 1960 and 1970 should indicate the timing of the second squeeze and intergroup differences in its timing and severity. However, as a *relative* measure it has some drawbacks. Absolute intercohort differences in the child-dependency burden can occur without being revealed in such a measure. For example, the mean number of children ever born was greater for the cohorts who were 45–54 in 1970 than for those of the same age in 1960. Given such a rise in fertility, even if there were no change in the *ratio* of the mean number of children aged 12–17 to the total mean number ever born, the mean number of 12–17-year-olds actually present in the home would probably have risen. Thus it is also important to look at the mean number of children present in each age group and the 1960–1970 percentage changes in this mean to get a more complete picture of the second squeeze.

LIFE-CYCLE VARIATIONS IN THE DEPENDENCY BURDEN

Table 5.3 shows the mean number of children present in each of five age groups for husbands of different ages and Table 5.4 presents these means as a percentage of the total mean number of children ever born to the wives of these men.

At either census date husbands under age 35 were, of course, in the early stages of the family cycle. For 25–34-year-old husbands, for example, the mean number of children under age 12 still accounted for over 90% of the mean number ever born to their wives. It is for the 35–44 age group that the dependency burden appears to be at a maximum. Compared to all other age groups, these men had the highest mean number of children present under age 25. Furthermore, although a high proportion of the mean number ever born to the wives of 35–44-year-olds was still in the age groups under 12, the mean number present over 12 had risen significantly. Thus in 1960, the ratio of the mean number aged 12–17 to the mean number ever born was 4% for 25–34-year-olds but 27% for 35–44-year-olds—an absolute difference of 0.6 of a child. There were also substantial differences in the means in the 18–24 category and the "other" category.

As a group, 45–54-year-old husbands were naturally even farther along in the family cycle. At both census dates, the mean number of children present under age 6 was no longer an important percentage of the total mean number ever born and the ratio of the mean number in the 6–11 age group had also dropped sharply. Children aged 18–24 years old were a relatively and absolutely more important segment and, in particular, the mean number of

TABLE 5.3
Mean Number of Children under Age 25 Who Were Present in the Household, by Age of Child and Age of Husband: 1960 and 1970[a]

Husband's age	Age of child				
	Total under 25	Under 6	6–11	12–17	18–24[b]
	1960				
18–24[c]	.99	.96	.03	—	—
25–34	2.04	1.32	.63	.09	—
35–44	2.34	.62	.94	.69	.09
45–54	1.42	.14	.36	.64	.28
55–64	.48	.02	.07	.22	.17
	1970				
18–24[c]	.76	.71	.04	.01	—
25–34	1.87	1.04	.71	.11	—
35–44	2.61	.44	1.02	1.00	.15
45–54	1.52	.08	.34	.72	.38
55–64	.46	.01	.05	.20	.20

Sources: 1960 and 1970 Public Use Samples of White Couples.
[a] Only families where the husband was the head of the household were included.
[b] The mean number of children aged 18–24 who were present in 1960 had to be estimated. See Appendix C for a description of the estimating procedure.
[c] It was assumed that men under age 35 had no children in the 18–24 age group.

children in the "other" category rose rapidly in numerical significance. The ratio in these two groups combined to the total mean number ever born rose from 12% for 35–44-year-olds in 1960 to 51% for husbands aged 45–54 years old. The comparable change in 1970 was from 15 to 58%.

Due to these age differences in family-cycle stage, the mean number of children under age 25 who were present in the home of husbands in the 45–54 age group was well below that for 35–44-year-old husbands—1.42 versus 2.34 in 1960 and 1.52 versus 2.61 in 1970 (Table 5.3). However, it is difficult to evaluate whether this indicates a really significant drop-off in the child-dependency burden. The major problem is our inability to determine the economic dependency of older children—both those within and especially those outside of the home. For example, published data show that the proportion of 18–19-year-olds enrolled in school was 57% in 1970, 21% of the 20–24-year-olds were in school (U.S. Bureau of the Census 1972g:Table 73). Furthermore, CPS data on the living arrangements of college students 14–24 years old indicate that most (e.g., 62% in 1971)

II. The Overall Picture

TABLE 5.4
Mean Number of Children in Each Age Group as a Percentage of the Mean Number Ever Born, by Age of Husband: 1960 and 1970

	Mean number in each age group as a percentage of mean number ever born					
Age of husband	Total ever born	Under 6	6–11	12–17	18–24	Other[a]
1960[b,c]						
18–24	(1.05)					
	100.0	91	3	—		6
25–34	(2.12)					
	100.0	62	30	4		4
35–44	(2.58)					
	100.0	24	36	27	3	9
45–54	(2.34)					
	100.0	6	15	27	12	39
55–64	(2.29)					
	100.0	—	3	10	7	79
1970						
18–24	(0.83)					
	100.0	86	5	1		8
25–34	(1.92)					
	100.0	54	37	6		3
35–44	(2.91)					
	100.0	15	35	34	5	10
45–54	(2.70)					
	100.0	3	13	27	14	44
55–64	(2.34)					
	100.0	—	2	8	8	80

Sources: 1960 and 1970 Public Use Samples of White Couples.
[a] *Other* was defined as the total mean number of children ever born minus the mean number under age 25 within the household.
[b] Only families where the husband was the head of the household were included.
[c] The mean number of children aged 18–24 who were present in 1960 had to be estimated. See Appendix C for a description of the estimating procedure.

were not living with their parents or other relatives (U.S. Bureau of the Census 1973e:Table 1). Hence, there was probably a significant proportion of young adult children not living at home who were still at least partially dependent on their parents. As a consequence, these data will understate the dependency burden of husbands in the 45–54 age group—and, probably, especially those in the 45–49 part of this age category.

Turning finally to the 55–64 age group of husbands, most of these families were well past the second-squeeze period. At both census dates, the mean number of children in the "other" category (not in the home or over age 25 if present) accounted for about 80% of the total mean number ever born.

In sum, these tables give us a preliminary indication that child-care costs are probably at or near their highest level for a substantial proportion of married men in the 35–54 age groups. This is not to say that the peak costs associated with the presence of adolescent or near-adolescent children last for 20 years but that the 35–54 age group is the 20-year period in which most men will experience these peak costs. For some men, this peak will occur earlier in the period, for others later, but for most it will tend to happen some time between their late thirties and early fifties with perhaps a peak in the 35–44 age group. Unfortunately, just how long the peak cost period does last for individual families is impossible to ascertain from these data. However, almost the same proportion of husbands from the cohort that was 35–44 in 1960 and 45–54 in 1970 had at least one 12–17-year-old in the home— about 48% (Table 5.5). In addition, 31% of this cohort had at least one 18–24-year-old present in 1970 as compared to 7% in 1960.

TABLE 5.5.
Percentage of Families with Children Present in Various Age Groups, by Age of Husband: 1960 and 1970[a,b]

Age of children and year	Age of husband				
	18–24	25–34	35–44	45–54	55–64
No children[c]					
1960	33.2	13.0	12.0	33.3	67.5
1970	45.4	17.2	9.1	29.3	65.4
Children under 6					
1960	66.2	75.2	42.0	10.6	1.7
1970	52.8	67.4	33.1	6.9	.9
Children 6–11					
1960	2.4	41.4	59.8	26.5	5.5
1970	3.2	42.7	61.7	24.7	4.3
Children 12–17					
1960	.5	7.4	49.3	45.9	16.2
1970	.9	8.1	59.7	48.3	15.0
Children 18–24					
1960	.1	.4	7.4	20.7	12.8
1970	.3	.4	13.2	31.4	17.0

Sources: 1960 and 1970 Public Use Samples of White Couples.
[a] Includes only those families where the husband was the head of the household.
[b] 1960 data refer only to single children.
[c] Includes those with no children of any age present.

II. The Overall Picture

1960–1970 CHANGES

Although 1960 and 1970 age patterns of the dependency burden showed strong similarities in the timing of peak child-care costs important changes are also observable. Postwar shifts in the number and timing of children have had a substantial impact on the severity of the second squeeze. For one thing, the large postwar rise in fertility increased the *overall* dependency burden (Table 5.6). The mean number of children ever born to wives of men who were 35–44 rose from 2.58 in 1960 to 2.91 in 1970. The comparable change for wives of 45–54-year-olds was from 2.34 to 2.70 children. However, increased child postponement, at the very least, was observed for younger cohorts. The mean number of children ever born to wives of 18–24-year-olds declined from 1.05 to 0.83; for 25–34-year-old husbands the decline was from 2.12 to 1.92 children. Given the low fertility of the 1970s this will probably not just represent shifts in the timing of children but in completed fertility as well.

Not only did completed fertility rise for some of the older cohorts but there is also evidence of the well-known postwar trend towards the earlier initiation and completion of childbearing, suggesting a closer spacing of children. This is best illustrated by Table 5.4 and is particularly noticeable for the cohorts who were 35–44 in 1970 (the cohort of 1926–1935) compared to those 35–44 in 1960 (the cohort of 1916–1925). The ratio of the mean number of children under 6 to the total ever born declined from 24% in 1960 to 15% in 1970 indicating a drop in the age at the birth of the *last* child despite rising fertility. Increases in the proportion of the mean number ever born who were in the older age groups indicate that a decrease in the age at the birth of the *first* child had occurred.

These postwar shifts in the number and timing of children should have increased the severity of the second squeeze considerably. The proportion of 35–44-year-old heads with at least one 12–17-year-old in the home rose from 49 to 60% during the decade (Table 5.5). Data not presented in tabular

TABLE 5.6
Mean Number of Children Ever Born to Wives, by Age of Husband: 1960 and 1970[a]

Mean number of children ever born	Age of husband				
	18–24	25–34	35–44	45–54	55–64
1960	1.05	2.12	2.58	2.34	2.29
1970	0.83	1.92	2.91	2.70	2.34
Percentage change	−21.0	− 9.4	+12.8	+15.4	+ 2.2

Sources: 1960 and 1970 Public Use Samples of White Couples
[a] Includes only those families where the husband was the head of the household.

form show that the proportion with *two* or more 12–17-year-olds rose from 16 to 30%. The proportions with 18–24-year-olds at home rose from 7 to 13% for 35–44-year-old heads from 21 to 31% for 45–54-year-olds. The rise in the dependency burden is also well illustrated by the mean number of children present (Table 5.3). The total mean number present for men under 35 years of age declined between 1960 and 1970 whereas it increased for men in both the 35–44 and 45–54 age groups. For 35–44-year-olds what is particularly impressive is the rise in the number of 12–17-year-olds—from a mean of 0.69 in 1960 to 1.00 in 1970. The mean number of 18–24-year-olds increased as well. However, the mean number under 6 declined. In short, not only was there an increase in the total number of children present in such households but it was almost entirely due to the rise in the number of older, more expensive children.

The number of children present rose for men aged 45–54 years old too, but not as much as for men aged 35–44. However, there was a pronounced shift towards older children with the mean number under 6 declining during the decade while the mean numbers aged 12–17 and 18–24 rose. Furthermore, as argued earlier, these data probably substantially understate the dependency burden of 45–54-year-old husbands. The lack of information on the economic dependency of older children no longer in the household not only distorts the dependency burden of these older husbands at any one census date but also our estimates of *changes* in the dependency burden, because of rising enrollments among college-age youth. Among those aged 18–19 (nonwhite as well as white), the proportion enrolled in school rose from 42% in 1960 to 57% in 1970. For those aged 20–24, the rise was from 15 to 21% (U.S. Bureau of the Census 1972g:Table 73).[8]

Dollar Estimates of the Dependency Burden

Using the data on the estimated costs of children by age in Table 5.2 and the mean number of children present in each age group (Table 5.3), I have constructed estimates of the average equivalent child-care costs for families of husbands at different stages of the family cycle in 1959 and 1969. Table 5.7 shows these estimates for children under age 18 for husbands aged 18–34 years old and for children under age 25 years for husbands aged 35–64—total and broken down by age of child. It was assumed that men under 35 had no children aged 18–24.

---

[8]The number of 18–24-year-olds in the home had to be estimated for the 1960 PUS. There is reason to believe these estimates were too high, thus leading to an understatement of the interdecade changes in the number present in this age group. See Appendix C for a discussion of the problem.

II. The Overall Picture

TABLE 5.7
Estimated Expenditures on Children Who Were Present in the Household, by Age of Husband and Age of Child: 1960 and 1970 (1969 Dollars)

Ages of husband and children	1959	1969	Change Absolute	Change Percentage
Husband 18–24[a]				
0–5	1,222	904	−318	−26
6–11	57	76	19	33
12–17	—	29	29	—[b]
Total cost	1,279	1,009	−270	−21
Husband 25–34[a]				
0–5	1,368	1,077	−291	−21
6–11	976	1,100	124	13
12–17	216	264	48	22
Total cost	2,560	2,441	−119	− 5
Husband 35–44				
0–5	642	456	−186	−29
6–11	1,456	1,580	124	8
12–17	1,654	2,397	743	45
18–24[c]	74	136	62	84
Total cost	3,826	4,569	743	19
Husband 45–54				
0–5	145	83	− 62	−43
6–11	558	527	− 31	− 6
12–17	1,534	1,726	192	12
18–24[c]	240	359	119	−50
Total cost	2,477	2,695	218	9
Husband 55–64				
0–5	21	10	− 11	−52
6–11	108	77	− 31	−29
12–17	527	479	− 48	− 9
18–24[c]	147	191	44	30
Total cost	803	757	− 46	− 6

Sources: 1960 and 1970 Public Use Samples of White Couples.
[a] It was assumed that men under 35 had no children in the 18–24 age group.
[b] It is not possible to compute a percentage change because the base was zero.
[c] Net of estimated income of offspring in this age group. Includes estimated costs for education of children in the home. See Appendix C for a description of how costs for this age were derived.

Using these expenditure estimates we will explore further the three questions raised earlier. First, how did the dollar cost of children vary among men in different age groups at both census dates? In particular, what does this tell us about the timing and severity of the second life-cycle squeeze? Second, compared to younger and older men at the same point in time, how did the severity of the second squeeze change between 1960 and 1970? What implications did this have for changes in the relative economic status of younger men? Finally, following particular cohorts from one census date to the other, what seemed to be the impact of their fertility behavior on the severity of their economic responsibilities for their children over this 10-year period in their life cycle?

1959 AND 1969 SIMILARITIES

Consistent with the data already presented, the peak estimated total cost of children occurred for men in the 35–44 age group, followed, though not closely, by men aged 45–54 (Table 5.7). For example, in 1969, the total estimated child-care costs for families of men 35–44-years-old was $4,569 compared to $2,695 for the families of men who were 45–54 years old and $2,441 for the families of husbands who were 25–34 years old. For husbands in the 25–34 age group, at both census dates the greatest estimated dollar costs were for children in the under-6 and 6–11 age groups. Families where the husband was 35–44 years old, however, had the highest costs for children in the 12–17 age group but they were also still in that stage of the family cycle where 6–11-year-olds were a frequent major economic responsibility. Thus, in 1969 the estimated expenditures on children aged 12–17 was $2,397 and for children aged 6–11 it was $1,580. Estimated expenditures on younger and older children were under $500.

The situation is rather different for families of men 45–54 years old. In both 1959 and 1969, estimated expenditures on preadolescent children had dropped way below that for families of men 35–44 years old. Expenditures on children in the 12–17 age group, however, were relatively high, though not greater than for men 35–44 years old. However, expenditures on 18–24-year-olds were higher for men aged 45–54 in 1969, for example. In short, at both census dates, 45–54-year-old husbands were at the stage in their family cycle when most of their children were 12–17 or 18 and older. However, husbands who were 35–44 years old had a significant number of children in the 6–11 as well as the 12–17 age groups but relatively few in the 18–24 age group. Hence, the inability to measure the economic contribution of parents of children over age 18 is likely to be particularly characteristic for the families of men 45–54 years old and probably leads to serious underestimates of the child-care costs for families at this stage of the family cycle.

In sum, these data suggest that if families with adolescents relied just on the husband's annual income, they might have a difficult time maintaining a life-style comparable to the one they were accustomed to when their children were younger or comparable to that of currently somewhat younger men in the same socioeconomic reference group but with younger, less expensive

II. The Overall Picture

children. The second life-cycle squeeze, as the first, seems to be a very real phenomenon. True, these cost estimates are very crude, but given the fact that both the age composition of dependent children and the income of the husband varies by *his* age, then, if the annual cost of children varies by *their* ages, some kind of economic-squeeze situation is implied by the data, unless savings patterns and credit purchases can successfully offset these life-cycle "rhythms" in expenditures and income.[9]

1959–1969 CHANGES IN EXPENDITURES FOR DIFFERENT COHORTS

The data discussed so far illustrate age differences in the dependency burden as of 1960 and 1970. I have also used 1960–1970 similarities in this age pattern to infer life-cycle differences in the dependency burden that would presumably transcend single moment-of-time comparisons. It would be even better if we could also measure how the annual child-dependency burden varied over the life-cycle of particular cohorts by actually following them over their life course. The 1960 and 1970 PUS provide us with the opportunity to do this in a very limited fashion by comparing the situation of the same cohort at two different periods in time.

Table 5.8 shows that a substantial increase occurred in the direct cost of children for the cohorts who were 25–34 in 1960—a decade rise of 78%. This was partly because of the aging of their children, of course, but also because not all the cohort's children had been born by 1960. The mean number born to the wives of this cohort rose from 2.12 in 1960 to 2.91 in 1970—a 37% increase (Table 5.6). Peak earnings are also achieved in the 35–44 age group but, as the reader may remember, the age effect on earnings, at least, is only rather modestly positive between these two age groups.

In the case of the cohort that was 35–44 in 1960, the direct annual cost of their children declined by about 30% over the decade due to the increase in the proportion of children who were no longer at home. For example, only 12% of the total mean number of children born to this cohort in 1960 were in the 18–24 or "other" categories combined whereas this proportion rose to 58% in 1970 when this cohort was aged 45–54 (Table 5.4). However, the

---

[9] I am not aware of studies that directly address this issue. However, some years ago, Juanita Kreps remarked that: "reapportionment of a family's lifetime income in accordance with its needs is accomplished in large measure through the use of consumer credit. Given a high rate of time preference for goods, however, the tendency for many families is to reallocate income quite generously to the present, giving much less attentionto the low-income retirement period [Kreps 1971: 94]." The question is whether this might not also typify the expenditure behavior vis-à-vis the second life-cycle squeeze. If so, this suggests that *current* income remains an important factor in the severity of that squeeze, if only because it may affect the total debt load the family can carry.

TABLE 5.8
1959–1969 Changes in Equivalent Expenditures on Children Present under Age 25 for Three Cohorts of Husbands (1969 Dollars)

	Cohorts and their age in 1960		
Total estimated equivalent expenditures on children	(1926–1935) 25–34	(1916–1925) 35–44	(1906–1915) 45–54
1959	2,560	3,826	2,477
1969	4,569	2,695	757
Percentage change	+78	−30	−69

Source: Table 5.7.

30% decrease in direct child-care costs of this cohort is probably greatly overestimated because of our inability to estimate the economic dependency of children no longer in the home. The decline of 69% in the direct child-care costs for cohorts who were 45–54 years old in 1960 is probably a much better picture of changes in the child-dependency burden because this life-cycle transition is completed. In sum, this minicohort analysis indicates, as do the data presented in other forms, that from a longitudinal as well as a cross-sectional point of view, direct child-care costs seem to reach a peak for men in the 35–44 age group—compared to men in other age groups at one point in time and compared to their own past and future experience.

1959–1969 CHANGES IN THE IMPACT OF CHILD-CARE EXPENDITURES

Since fertility has been going down for more recent cohorts, the total equivalent expenditures on children declined for husbands aged 18–34, especially for those who were in the 18–24 age group. But, for husbands aged 35–44, those experiencing the greatest increase in the number of adolescent children present, the total cost of children rose by $743, or 19%, mainly due to the rising number of 12–17-year-olds present in households (Table 5.7). The apparent increase in costs for husbands aged 45–54 was somewhat smaller, rising by only 9%. In short, the higher fertility of the cohorts that produced the postwar baby boom operated to increase the cost component of the second life-cycle squeeze between 1959 and 1969. However, the lower or more delayed fertility of younger cohorts led to a reduction in the economic burden of children between 1959 and 1969, thus offsetting the declining relative income position of young men—especially in the case of 18–24-year-olds.

Such changes in equivalent child-care costs should have an important bearing on Easterlin and Wachter's argument of declining relative economic status among young men. The question is the extent to which the increasing

II. The Overall Picture

severity of the cost component of the second life-cycle squeeze offsets the much greater relative increases in the median earnings of men in the 35–54 age groups. Table 5.9 addresses this question by relating the estimates of the change in the total equivalent expenditures on children (CCC) to the 1959–1969 change in income of particular age groups of husbands. Despite relatively low growth rates in income for husbands aged 18–24, the decrease in the cost of children led to an estimated increase in income, net of CCC, of $1,329 for this age group. Although the income increases of husbands aged

TABLE 5.9
Changes in Equivalent Expenditures on Children under 25 in Relation to the 1959–1969 Increases in Median Earnings and Income of Husbands, by Age of Husbands (1969 Dollars)[a]

	\multicolumn{5}{c}{Age of husband}
	18–24	25–34	35–44	45–54	55–64
Median earnings of husband					
1959	4,751	6,817	7,522	7,098	6,443
1969	5,820	8,756	10,074	9,656	8,338
Increase					
Absolute	1,069	1,939	2,552	2,558	1,895
Percentage	22	28	34	36	29
Median income of husband					
1959	4,787	6,905	7,673	7,197	6,484
1969	5,846	8,820	10,174	9,871	8,365
Increase					
Absolute	1,059	1,915	2,501	2,674	1,881
Percentage	22	28	33	37	29
Change in total cost of children	−270	−119	+743	+218	−46
Increase in median earnings of husband, net of change in total equivalent expenditures on children					
Total	1,339	2,058	1,809	2,340	1,941
As a percentage of 1959 earnings	28	30	24	33	30
Increase in median income of husband, net of change in total equivalent expenditures on children					
Total	1,329	2,034	1,758	2,456	1,927
As a percentage of 1959 income	28	30	23	34	30

Sources: Table 5.7 and 1960 and 1970 Public Use Samples of White Couples.
[a] Includes only those families where the husband was the head of the household.

35–44 were well above those of husbands aged 18–24, the rise in the older group's estimated equivalent expenditures on children reduced their net increase to $1,758, lowering the differential in income growth between the two age groups from $1,442 to $429. Relative to the husbands' median income in 1959, this represented a 28% increase in median income, net of CCC, for husbands aged 18–24 but only a 23% increase for those aged 35–44. Hence reduced fertility probably more than compensated for the smaller increases in the annual income of young husbands.

If, as Easterlin argues, the reduced fertility of 18–24-year-olds is a compensatory response to declines in their relative economic status, it would also be appropriate to compare the increase in median earnings, net of CCC, for husbands aged 35–44 to the *gross* increase in median earnings for 18–24-year-olds. In this way, we assume no change in fertility for the latter and hence no decrease in child-care expenditures. It is then only fertility changes for the *older* cohorts that would affect relative economic status. Even then, however, the increase in the income of husbands aged 18–24 was almost identical to those aged 35–44—a 22% rise compared to the 23% increase in median income, net of CCC, for the 35–44-year-olds.

In the case of husbands aged 45–54, the increase in income, net of CCC, still exceeds that for husbands aged 18–24 (assuming no change in child-care expenditures for the younger age group)—resulting in a 34% increase in median income for the older men compared to the 22% increase for the 18–24-year-olds. If the change in child-care expenditures for 18–24-year-old husbands is added, the percentage increases in median income are much closer for the two age groups—34% for husbands aged 45–54 and 28% for husbands 18–24 years old. Of course, if better estimates of child-care expenditures were available for husbands aged 45–54, the relative advantage of these older men might become rather small, if not entirely disappear.

Finally, we can also look at changes in the median income, net of CCC, for different cohorts (Table 5.10). Focusing first on husbands who were aged 25–34 in 1960, the median income (in 1969 dollars) of this cohort rose quite substantially during the decade—by 47%. However, the dependency burden of adolescent children also rose considerably, resulting in large increases in equivalent expenditures on children. If these increased costs of children are deducted from the increases in median income achieved by the cohort over the decade, the apparent increase in median income is drastically reduced—dropping from 47 to 18%.

The situation for the cohorts of husbands who were aged 35–44 and 45–54 in 1960 was quite different. The total increase in their median income was actually much less than for the younger cohorts—a 29 compared to a 47% rise. The increase for the cohort that was 45–54 in 1960 was even lower—only 16%. However, since child-related expenses eased up considerably for the cohorts aged 35–44 and 45–54 in 1960, husbands' median income, net of

TABLE 5.10
Gross and Net 1959–1969 Increases in Husband's Median Income for Three Cohorts of Husbands

Percentage change in median income of husband	Cohorts and their age in 1960		
	(1926–1935) 25–34	(1916–1925) 35–44	(1906–1915) 45–54
Gross	47	29	16
Net of changes in expenditures on children	18	43	40

Source: Table 5.8 and 5.9.

CCC, rose by 43% for the cohort of 1916–1925 and by 40% for the cohort of 1906–1915 (Table 5.10). Thus, it seems that the economic position of these older cohorts improved substantially over the decade as compared to the apparently sluggish improvements experienced by the families of the cohort of 1926–1935.

SUMMARY

In summary, these findings further modify the picture of the 1959–1969 changes in the relative economic position of young males obtained in Chapters 3 and 4. As we saw in Chapter 4, the decline in the relative income position of young *married* males was much less precipitous than that for males of all marital statuses combined. This is because of the continuing strong positive relationship between marriage and the economic position of young men. Second, the data presented in this chapter indicate that much, if not most, of the remaining greater increase in the earnings of older as opposed to younger *married* men was offset by increasing expenditures on children—occasioned not by a change in "tastes," or even prices, but simply by the rise in the number of adolescent and youthful dependents that occurred during this period.

If the economic burden of the baby-boom adolescents offsets the much greater increases in the income of older versus younger men, the reverse might also turn out to be true when the baby-bust cohorts start reaching adolescence and young adulthood. In other words, even if the small size of the baby bust cohorts is sufficient to produce a significant improvement in their labor-market position, as Easterlin and Wachter argue, if one also takes into account the lower economic burden these smaller cohorts make on parents than there may, in fact, be little real change in the relative economic position of young males. This is because the level of living in parental households without numerous progeny will be high, fostering, in turn, the development of more expensive tastes by the next generation. In sum, in the one case, the declining relative income position of young husbands may not be as bad as it first appears. In the other case, any improvement in the relative economic position of young males due to their small cohort size may also not turn out to be as great as it might first appear on surveys of males' income data alone. Hence, this is still another reason to make a rather conservative assessment of what economic and demographic consequences will follow from the passage of the current baby-bust cohorts through the age structure.

To the extent income is an important factor in economic stress situations, neither the severity of the first nor the second life-cycle squeeze depends on men's earnings alone, of course. In particular, the economic contribution of wives to family income is also an important factor to consider. Married women's labor-force participation has been increasing considerably throughout the postwar period. Furthermore, the most rapid increases in labor-force participation rates were first characteristic of older married women. A further question of importance, then, is how wives' changing labor-force participation, and the timing of these changes, may have affected the severity of the two squeezes and hence other types of responses families make to such situations of economic stress. This is a question we will consider at some length in Part III. There I will argue that wives' labor-force participation can have both direct and indirect effects on the life-cycle squeezes because it not only changes the income position of families but also their aspirational levels and child dependency burden as well. For the moment, however, the main point to be made here is that on the basis of the husband's income alone, any assessment of changes in the relative income position of younger compared to older families is likely to be affected by variations in the dependency burden of older families—that is, their past reproductive performance. This, in turn, has and will continue to offset the recent relative disadvantages of younger baby-boom males and any future advantage that may accrue to young baby-bust males due to their small cohort size.

III. OCCUPATIONAL DIFFERENTIALS

Unfortunately, it is not possible to replicate the above analysis of childcare costs on the different occupational subgroups. All the problems and uncertainties involved in making direct dollar estimates of child-care expenditures for the entire sample are magnified several fold when it comes to constructing such estimates for individual occupational groups. It does not seem reasonable to assume constant age-specific child-care expenditures across occupations since this is tantamount to arguing that child-care standards do not

III. Occupational Differentials

vary among occupational groups as divergent as the Professional I and Laborer IV groups. This seems extremely unlikely. Espenshade does attempt estimates for child-care expenditures for three different income levels (Espenshade 1973). However, it seemed inadvisable to try to adapt these to the 18 peak-median occupational groups used here. The problem of estimating interoccupational differences in the cost of young adult children was in itself enough to discourage such an undertaking, not to mention the difficulties associated with developing estimates for other age groups. Furthermore, income group alone is probably an inadequate indicator of lifestyle aspirations. For example, child-care *obligations*, if not *aspirations*, are probably rather different for white-collar and blue-collar occupational groups at similar peak median earnings levels. In short, it seemed unwise to attempt to make direct dollar estimates, useful as they certainly would have been.

Lacking dollar estimates of child-care expenditures, the analysis of interoccupational differences in the nature of the second squeeze rests entirely on the number and ages of children present in the household. My primary concern is to compare interage differences in dependency among the various occupational groups, as well as 1960–1970 changes in these. Once again, I will emphasize three types of measures to make these comparisons. One is a crude measure of the total child dependency burden over the family cycle— the mean number of children ever born to the wife. To get an idea of the timing of the second squeeze, holding family size constant, I will use the ratio of the mean number of children present in the four age groups to the total mean number ever born. Finally, for a still more detailed picture of the severity of the squeeze—one that is a combined function of birth timing and the number of births—we will look at the mean number of children present in the various age groups. All these measures will be examined for both 1960– 1970 similarities and differences. In this way, it should be possible to detect systematic occupational differences in the timing and severity of the second squeeze as well as the direction of any observed 1960–1970 changes. However, no attempt will be made to follow cohorts within occupations from one census to the other since occupational mobility makes such a procedure rather questionable. Finally, I will limit the discussion to the men most vulnerable to the second squeeze—those in the 35–54 age groups.

Males Aged 45–54 Years Old

THE TIMING AND SEVERITY OF THE SECOND SQUEEZE

At both census dates substantial occupational differences in the timing of the second squeeze existed for 45–54-year-old husbands. Despite their typically higher fertility, the families of men in blue-collar occupations were much more likely to be at a later stage of the family cycle than families of men in most white-collar groups (Table 5.11 and 5.12). The clearest indication of this is that within the blue-collar groups a much higher proportion of the mean number ever born could be accounted for by the mean number who were either not in the home or, if there, were over age 25 (Table 5.11). For example, in 1960 only 26% of the total mean number ever born fell into this category (the "other" category) for Professional I husbands, 30% for Clerical III males and 35% for Sales III husbands. This compares to 48% for Service IV males, 43% for the Craft and Operative III groups, and 42% for Operative IV husbands. A similar pattern was observed in 1970. There were also considerable occupational differences in the ratio of the mean number of children aged 12–17 to those ever born. In 1970, for example, the ratio varied between 32 and 35% for families of men in the three professional groups compared to a ratio in the neighborhood of 23–25% for all the operative and craft groups.

These occupational differences in the timing of the second squeeze have a number of interesting implications. In the case of blue-collar groups, the earlier timing of marriage and childbearing seems like a rational accommodation to the traditionally poor relative position of older males in these occupational groups. Too great a postponement of childbearing would have pushed the second squeeze period into a more economically precarious time in the husband's career cycle.[10] However, in the case of Group I and II white-collar occupations, the most economically vulnerable time seems to occur early in the man's career cycle. Hence delayed marriage and childbearing operates to greatly ameliorate the difficulties of the first squeeze. Moreover, since the relative earnings position of these men at older ages is quite favorable, such postponements should not intensify the difficulties of the second squeeze, as might be the case for those in manual occupations.

The situation of lower-paid white-collar workers suggests that they may be especially vulnerable to the second squeeze. On the one hand, the age–earnings profiles of these occupations tend to peak in the 35–44 age group, as is the case for men in blue-collar occupations, although Group III white-collar workers undoubtedly achieve a greater income *stability* in their later years because of a greater job security. Nevertheless, the Group III white-collar males, aged 45–54, were at an earlier stage of their family cycle in both 1960 and 1970, indicating that the second squeeze was not necessarily

[10]Increasing human capital investments, the declining importance of physical strength, safer working conditions, and the growth of institutionalized factors protecting the employment position of older males have been changing the relative economic position of these older age groups, of course. Hence this will probably modify the constraints under which the family-building behavior of such occupational groups must operate.

III. Occupational Differentials

occurring at an optimum point in the husband's career cycle. Moreover, there has undoubtedly been a greater emphasis on children attending college within these white-collar groups than among blue-collar families with a similar income, implying a greater economic dependency of children in their late teens and early twenties. Whether this is adequately offset by the somewhat lower fertility of Group III white-collar families compared to Group III and IV blue-collar families is unclear.

CHANGES IN THE SEVERITY OF THE SECOND SQUEEZE

The 1960–1970 15% rise in the number of children ever born for all occupational groups combined masks considerable occupational variations in the change in completed or almost completed fertility for this age group (Table 5.13). The increases for the white-collar occupations (including Service III males) were much greater than for blue-collar occupations. In 7 of the 11 white-collar occupations, the growth in the mean number of children ever born was over 30%, while the increases were much lower for the wives of blue-collar males (see also Rindfuss and Sweet 1977). Some of the biggest changes, furthermore, were for Group I and II occupations although the increases for Sales and Clerical III males were also substantial. However, this partly reflects the exceptionally low family sizes of men in these cohorts in 1960 (see also Kiser, Grabill, and Campbell 1968). Within the blue-collar group, the growth in family size was also positively related to peak median earnings level. The increase for Group IV occupations was actually minimal—only between 1 and 2% for the Craft and Laborers IV group and 6 and 7% respectively for the Operative and Service IV groups (see also Grabill, Kiser, and Whelpton 1958).

A major result of these considerable occupational differences in the growth of completed family size was a marked decrease in occupational differentials in fertility. All this suggests that child-related economic responsibilities increased more during this period for white-collar couples than for blue-collar couples, especially for several Group III white-collar occupations with earnings levels on a par with Craft III workers but with probably a "taste" for more expensive children.

Tables 5.11 and 5.12 also indicate that for most occupations the age at the start of childbearing decreased. Moreover, although there appears to have been a general shift towards earlier childbearing, the change was most marked for white-collar families. For example, the percentage of the mean number of children ever born who were in the 18–24 or "other" categories rose from 35 to 45% for Professional I families. Moreover, the growing tendancy to complete childbearing earlier was more characteristic of white-

TABLE 5.11
Percentage Distribution of Mean Number of Children Ever Born to the Wife, White Families with a Husband Aged 45–54, by Age of Children, Their Household Status, and Occupation of Husband: 1960 and 1970

	Mean number present in each age group as a percentage of mean number ever born										
	1960						1970				
Occupation	Total ever born	Under 12	12–17	18–24[a]	Other[b]		Total ever born	Under 12	12–17	18–24	Other[b]
Total	100	21	27	12	39		100	16	27	14	44
Professionals											
I	100	29	36	9	26		100	21	35	13	32
II	100	25	33	11	31		100	18	33	14	35
III	100	28	34	9	30		100	17	32	14	37
Managers											
I	100	22	30	13	35		100	15	31	15	39
II	100	21	32	14	33		100	14	28	14	44
III	100	24	28	11	37		100	16	26	15	43
Sales											
II	100	24	29	14	33		100	16	29	17	39
III	100	22	31	12	35		100	15	27	15	43

Clerical							
III	100	24	31	14	30	16	26	17	41
IV	100	16	25	15	44	15	23	17	46
Craft							
II	100	20	28	16	36	11	24	18	47
III	100	19	27	12	43	15	24	14	46
IV	100	20	25	11	43	16	25	13	46
Operatives							
III	100	18	25	14	43	13	25	14	48
IV	100	22	25	12	42	14	23	13	49
Service							
III	100	18	25	15	43	13	26	19	43
IV	100	20	21	11	48	16	22	13	49
Laborers							
IV	100	24	24	8	43	18	23	12	47

Sources: 1960 and 1970 Public Use Samples of White Couples.

[a]The mean number of chilren aged 18–24 had to be estimated for 1960. See Appendix C for a discussion of the procedure used.

[a]*Other* was defined as the total mean number of children born minus the mean number under age 25 within the household.

TABLE 5.12
Mean Number of Children Present, by Their Age and Household Status and by the Occupation of Husbands Aged 45–54: 1960 and 1970

	1960							1970						
	Mean number present by age							Mean number present by age						
Occupation	Under 6	6–11	12–17	18–24[a]	Total[b]	Other[c]		Under 6	6–11	12–17	18–24	Total[b]	Other[c]
Total	.14	.36	.64	.28	1.42	.92		.08	.34	.72	.38	1.52	1.18
Professionals													
I	.13	.46	.74	.19	1.52	.54		.12	.46	.96	.35	1.89	.87
II	.12	.34	.61	.21	1.28	.57		.08	.37	.84	.36	1.65	.88
III	.16	.42	.72	.18	1.48	.62		.08	.36	.83	.36	1.63	.97
Managers													
I	.07	.35	.58	.24	1.24	.66		.07	.34	.85	.41	1.67	1.05
II	.12	.33	.69	.31	1.45	.73		.06	.31	.73	.38	1.48	1.14
III	.15	.38	.63	.24	1.40	.83		.08	.32	.66	.37	1.43	1.10
Sales													
II	.13	.34	.57	.28	1.32	.65		.07	.35	.76	.44	1.62	1.02
III	.10	.32	.60	.22	1.24	.67		.08	.31	.69	.38	1.46	1.11

Clerical										
III	.11	.34	.58	.27	1.30	.57	.08	.32	.66	.42	1.48	1.01
IV	.08	.27	.53	.32	1.20	.94	.06	.37	.64	.47	1.54	1.29
Craft										
II	.10	.34	.63	.36	1.43	.81	.05	.25	.65	.48	1.43	1.27
III	.13	.33	.66	.29	1.41	1.05	.08	.34	.68	.39	1.49	1.28
IV	.20	.37	.70	.31	1.58	1.20	.08	.36	.71	.36	1.51	1.30
Operatives										
III	.15	.30	.61	.33	1.39	1.05	.07	.30	.70	.40	1.47	1.35
IV	.18	.41	.66	.31	1.56	1.12	.09	.32	.65	.38	1.44	1.39
Service										
III	.09	.30	.54	.32	1.25	.93	.07	.26	.67	.50	1.50	1.12
IV	.09	.40	.51	.26	1.26	1.15	.10	.30	.58	.34	1.32	1.26
Laborers										
IV	.23	.47	.71	.24	1.65	1.27	.12	.40	.68	.36	1.56	1.41

Sources: 1960 and 1970 Public Use Samples of White Couples.
[a]The mean number of children aged 18–24 had to be estimated for 1960. See Appendix C for a discussion of the procedure used.
[b]Mean total number present under age 25.
[c]*Other* was defined as the total mean number of children ever born minus the mean number under age 25 within the household.

TABLE 5.13
1960–1970 Changes in the Mean Number of Children Ever Born to Wives of Men Aged 35–44 and 45–54, by Husband's Occupation[a]

	Mean number of children ever born and husband's age						
	35–44			45–54		
Occupation	1960	1970	Percentage change	1960	1970	Percentage change
Total	2.58	2.91	13	2.34	2.70	15
Professionals						
I	2.54	2.79	10	2.06	2.76	34
II	2.35	2.77	18	1.85	2.53	37
III	2.35	2.73	16	2.10	2.60	24
Managers						
I	2.56	2.83	10	1.90	2.72	43
II	2.58	2.89	12	2.18	2.62	20
III	2.49	2.85	14	2.23	2.53	13
Sales						
II	2.56	2.75	7	1.97	2.64	34
III	2.37	2.75	16	1.91	2.57	34
Clerical						
III	2.34	2.72	16	1.87	2.49	33
IV	2.33	2.94	26	2.14	2.83	32
Craft						
II	2.50	2.88	15	2.24	2.70	20
III	2.55	2.94	15	2.46	2.77	13
IV	2.85	3.15	10	2.78	2.81	1
Operatives						
III	2.67	3.07	15	2.44	2.82	16
IV	2.80	3.08	10	2.68	2.83	6
Service						
III	2.48	2.92	18	2.18	2.62	20
IV	2.31	2.80	21	2.41	2.58	7
Laborers						
IV	2.88	3.16	10	2.92	2.97	2

Sources: 1960 and 1970 Public Use Samples of White Couples.
[a] Includes only those families where the husband was the head of the household.

collar than of blue-collar families. Whether closer spacing was also involved is more difficult to determine but is likely.[11]

These timing and fertility shifts should have disproportionately increased the severity of the second squeeze for white-collar families (Tables 5.12 and 5.14). The increase in the mean number of 12–17-year-olds present was greater for most white-collar groups than for blue-collar. For example, it was 46% for Manager I families compared to just 1% for Craft IV families. Data on the number of 18–24-year-olds at home also provide support for this view—that is, if we can interpret an increase in the mean number of 18–24-year-olds at home as a net cost to parents rather than a net source of additional income. This certainly seems like a fairly reasonable assumption for white-collar groups, given the rise in school enrollments and the probable greater attendance rate of middle-class as opposed to blue-collar children. By and large, the rise in the mean number of 18–24-year-olds present was greater—often much greater—for white-collar families than for blue-collar. For example, in 10 of the 12 white-collar groups, the increase was greater than 36%—the increase for all occupational groups combined—whereas this was true in only one of the seven blue-collar groups.

In short, to the extent 18–24-year-olds are financially dependent on their families this economic burden increased more for white-collar families than for blue-collar. This is partly due to the greater rise in the number of such children in white-collar homes but also because these children were more likely to be in school than were blue-collar children of the same age (Table 5.15). Of the families with at least one child aged 18–24 present, the mean number of children attending college in 1970 was considerably higher for most white-collar groups than for blue-collar groups with the one exception of the Craft II families. For example, for men 45–54 the mean was between .50 and .56 for the three professional groups and it varied from .42 to .56 for the manager groups. It was even high for the Sales and Clerical III groups— .44 and .42 respectively. These means contrast considerably with the .20–

---

[11]Data are not available on this issue for families by the occupation of the husband. However, CPS data on child spacing by the educational attainment of women at various parities indicate that closer spacing did occur as one progressed from the 1920–1924 to the 1935–1939 cohorts, especially for women with 4 years of high school or 1 or more years of college. For example, for wives with 1 or more years of college who had three or more children, the proportion who had their second child within 2 years of their first rose from 36% for the cohorts of 1920–1924 to 60% for the cohorts of 1935–1939. For women with less than 4 years of high school, the increase for the same cohorts was from 42 to 54%—a rise of only 12 percentage points compared to 24 points for the more educated cohorts. However, where the birth in question was the *last* birth, the change in timing was not nearly as marked. For example, for women with 1 or more years of college who had a completed family size of three children, the percentage having their third and last child within 4 years after their second only rose from 62% for the cohorts of 1920–1924 to 70% for the cohorts of 1935–1939 (U.S. Bureau of the Census 1978e: Tables 21 and 22).

TABLE 5.14
1960–1970 Percentage Change in the Mean Number of Children under 25 Who Were Present, by Age and Occupation of Husbands Aged 45–54

	Percentage change					
	Mean number present					
Occupation	Under 6	6–11	12–17	18–24	Total[a]	Other[b]
Total	−43	− 6	+12	+ 36	+ 7	+28
Professionals						
I	− 8	—	+30	+ 84	+24	+61
II	−33	+ 9	+38	+ 71	+29	+54
III	−50	−14	+15	+100	+10	+56
Managers						
I	—	− 3	+46	+ 71	+35	+59
II	−50	− 6	+ 6	+ 23	+ 2	+56
III	−47	−16	+ 5	+ 54	+ 2	+32
Sales						
II	−46	+ 3	+33	+ 57	+23	+57
III	−20	− 3	+15	+ 73	+18	+66
Clerical						
III	−27	− 6	+14	+ 56	+14	+77
IV	−25	+37	+21	+ 47	+28	+37
Craft						
II	−50	−26	+ 3	+ 33	—	+57
III	−38	+ 3	+ 3	+ 34	+ 6	+22
IV	−60	− 3	+ 1	+ 16	− 4	+ 8
Operatives						
III	−53	—	+15	+ 21	+ 6	+29
IV	−50	−22	− 2	+ 23	− 8	+24
Service						
III	−22	−13	+24	+ 56	+20	+20
IV	+11	−25	+13	+ 31	+ 5	+10
Laborers						
IV	−48	−15	− 4	+ 50	− 5	+11

Source: Table 5.12.
[a]Mean number present under age 25.
[b]*Other* was defined as the total mean number of children born minus the mean number under age 25 within the household.

III. Occupational Differentials

TABLE 5.15
Mean Number of Children, Attending College: Familes with at Least One Child 18–24, by Husband's Occupation and Age, 1970

	Husband's age	
Occupation	33–44	45–54
Total	.28	.35
Professionals		
I	.47	.56
II	.38	.53
III	.36	.50
Managers		
I	.43	.56
II	.38	.42
III	.32	.46
Sales		
II	.35	.50
III	.35	.44
Clerical		
III	.35	.42
IV	.17	.35
Craft		
II	.21	.37
III	.24	.26
IV	.27	.25
Operatives		
III	.19	.22
IV	.17	.20
Service		
III	.34	.41
IV	.23	.27
Laborers		
IV	.18	.22

Sources: 1960 and 1970 Public Use Samples of White Couples.

.27 range for all but one of the blue-collar groups. Since white-collar families were also undoubtedly more likely to have children *away* at college, all this suggests a greater rise in the severity of the second squeeze for white-collar than for blue-collar groups.

The mean number of children not at home or who were present but over the age of 25—the "other" category—also rose more steeply for the white-collar families (Table 5.14). For example, it rose by 50% or more for eight of the white-collar groups. However, the increase was less than 30% for all but one of the blue-collar groups. This change is hard to interpret in life-cycle-squeeze terms because we do not know what proportion of such children are still partially dependent on their parents. However, it is probably higher for white-collar families, once again indicating a greater rise in the dependency burden for these occupational groups.

These findings on occupational differences in the age pattern of child dependency suggest that a rough parallel exists between the timing of childbearing and the nature of the age–earnings profile of the husband's occupation. On the one hand, early childbearing was the rule, on average, for families of men in blue-collar early-peaking occupations. This seems like an economically rational adaptive strategy since delayed childbearing would result in heavy dependency burdens at a point in the husband's life-cycle when the age-effect on earnings might be neutral or even negative and hence when further increases in earnings over the life-course would depend on such factors as upward occupational mobility, secular increases in real hourly earnings, overtime, moonlighting, etc. On the other hand, there was a tendency for more delayed childbearing among men in the later peaking Group I and II white-collar occupations. This, too, seems like a rational strategy since the earnings of young men in most of these occupations were very depressed relative to that of older men and earnings peaked at a later age. And if the early career-cycle stage is the time of greatest vulnerability for such men, their marriage and fertility behavior should be particularly sensitive to changes in economic conditions. It was also true that a number of Group III white-collar occupations showed a pattern of delayed childbearing. Considering that these were usually early-peaking occupations then the timing of the second squeeze was later in the husband's life-cycle than for Group III and IV blue-collar occupations. This might have operated to the relative disadvantage of such lower-level white-collar occupations. Such a disadvantage would, of course, be offset by their lower fertility. However, since lower white-collar families may feel more obligated to have a "taste" for more expensive children than may blue-collar families, it is not clear how much their reduced fertility offsets the disadvantages of a later second squeeze.

Males Aged 35–44 Years Old

THE TIMING AND SEVERITY OF THE SECOND SQUEEZE

Occupational differences in family-cycle stage were not as noticeable for men aged 35–44 as for those aged 45–54 at the two census dates, probably

III. Occupational Differentials

because the wives of nonmanual 35–44-year-olds had not yet completed their childbearing. However, it may also partly reflect an occupational convergence in the timing of child-bearing as well as in completed fertility for the more recent cohorts in the second-squeeze period. Evidence supporting this possibility is the 1960–1970 convergence in apparent timing noted for husbands who were 45–54 years old. Men who were aged 45–54 in 1970 were, of course, 35–44 years old in 1960. Hence, if a convergence had taken place, it would also be observed for this cohort in 1960. This does not take into account, however, the possible distorting effect of occupational mobility.

Looking at the case of males who were aged 35–44 in some detail, at both census dates the ratio of the mean number of children in the "other" category tends to be somewhat higher for blue-collar than for white-collar families (Table 5.16) although most families did not have older children. This may be because the children of blue-collar workers leave home earlier than those of white-collar workers, although this seems rather unlikely. Nevertheless, if we think of the "other" and 18–24 categories as a single group, roughly representing older children, the ratio of these combined means to the mean number ever born was larger for blue-collar occupations than for most white-collar. For example, in 1970, the ratio was 7 and 10% for Professional I and III males respectively compared to 19 and 20% for Craft and Operative IV husbands respectively. Hence, for this age group, as well as for 45–54-year-olds, there is evidence that blue-collar couples started their families earlier in the husband's life cycle.

As for the timing of the last child, the findings must be extremely tentative for such a young age group of husbands. There was some indication that white-collar families were more likely to have children under age 12 than blue-collar, particularly professionals. For example, in 1960, the ratio of the mean number of children under age 12 to the mean number ever born was 75% for Professional I husbands whereas it was only 55% for Operative IV men. This pattern might be even more pronounced at a later age for these cohorts, as the data for the cohorts involved in the 45–54 age-group comparisons suggest.

The data for 35–44-year-olds also suggest that the timing of the squeeze roughly synchronizes with the age–earnings profile for Group I and II white-collar occupations and for Group III and IV blue-collar occupations. However, once again, the Group III white-collar families may find themselves in a more difficult squeeze situation. On the other hand, their pattern of childbearing more closely resembled that of Group I and II occupations. On the other hand, their age–earnings profile peaked in the 35–44 age group—somewhat similar to Blue Collar III and IV occupations.

TABLE 5.16
Percentage Distribution of the Mean Number of Children Ever Born to the Wife, White Families with a Husband Aged 35–44, by Age of Children, Their Household Status, and Occupation of Husband: 1960 and 1970

	\multicolumn{7}{c}{Mean number present in each age group as a percentage of mean number ever born}

	\multicolumn{7}{c}{1960}	\multicolumn{7}{c}{1970}

Occupation	Total ever born	Under 6	6–11	12–17	18–24[a]	Other[b]	Total ever born	Under 6	6–11	12–17	18–24	Other[b]
Total	100	24	36	27	3	9	100	15	35	34	5	10
Professionals												
I	100	33	42	20	1	4	100	20	43	31	4	3
II	100	31	42	22	2	3	100	17	39	34	4	5
III	100	31	38	24	3	4	100	18	41	32	4	6
Managers												
I	100	26	37	29	5	3	100	14	38	36	5	6
II	100	22	37	29	3	10	100	14	34	37	6	9
III	100	23	35	29	4	8	100	15	34	36	6	9
Sales												
II	100	23	41	27	3	6	100	16	37	36	5	6
III	100	25	39	26	4	6	100	15	36	36	5	7

Clerical									
III	100	28	39	23	3	8	100	15	35	34	6	10
IV	100	24	37	27	6	6	100	14	32	35	5	14
Craft									
II	100	21	30	32	4	14	100	14	34	36	6	10
III	100	22	37	28	3	9	100	14	34	36	5	10
IV	100	23	35	26	4	12	100	13	34	34	6	13
Operatives									
III	100	23	34	27	4	12	100	14	33	34	6	13
IV	100	21	34	28	4	13	100	15	31	34	6	14
Service									
III	100	25	35	29	5	6	100	17	36	35	6	6
IV	100	25	32	31	4	8	100	15	33	30	6	16
Laborers									
IV	100	23	33	28	3	12	100	15	33	31	5	16

Sources: 1960 and 1970 Public Use Samples of White Couples.
[a]The mean number of children aged 18–24 had to be estimated for 1960. See Appendix C for a discussion of the procedure used.
[b]*Other* was defined as the total mean number of children ever born minus the mean number under age 25 within the household.

203

Changes in the Severity of the Second Squeeze

In the case of 45–54-year-olds, the 1960–1970 15% increase in the mean number of children ever born masked quite pronounced occupational differences in intercohort increases in completed family size. Most of the white-collar occupational groups exhibited a much greater rise in completed fertility than blue-collar families. For Blue-Collar IV groups, the increase was really quite trivial. No such marked or systematic occupational differences in the 1960–1970 increases in family size were observed for the cohorts who were 35–44 years old in 1970 compared to their counterparts in 1960 (Table 5.13). However, this just may be because white-collar families were less likely than blue-collar families to have completed childbearing when the husband was still relatively young, making these data poor indicators of relative changes in completed fertility. But, if the data do reflect a real pattern, this lends support to the notion that white-collar groups and higher socioeconomic groups were more likely to modify their early fertility behavior in response to changing socioeconomic conditions than were blue-collar and lower-income groups. If so, the much greater fertility increase for white-collar than blue-collar cohorts of 1916–1925 over the 1906–1915 cohorts would be partly a function of the poor economic conditions experienced by the 1906–1915 cohorts in the first part of their career cycle and partly a result of the much more favorable conditions operating for the 1916–1925 cohorts at a comparable period in their life-cycle. Thus the cohort of 1906–1915 was 15–24 in 1930, the start of the Great Depression. For all occupational groups combined, when this cohort was 45–54, the mean number of children born to their wives was 2.34. However, the mean family size of many of the white-collar members of this cohort was much lower than this—often below 2.0. For example, it was 1.85 for Professional II families, 1.90 for Managers I wives, 1.91 for the Sales III group and 1.87 for Clerical III families. However, members of the cohort of 1916–1925—who was aged 45–54 in 1970—were 15–24 in 1940. Hence they experienced the more prosperous war years and postwar economic boom in the early part of their career cycle. To the extent their marriage and fertility behavior was sensitive to shifts in cyclical economic conditions and the previous low fertility was of necessity rather than choice, a substantial rise in their fertility was to be expected. This, of course, is just what occurred. However, in the case of the cohorts who were 35–44 in 1960 and 1970, we are comparing the cohort of 1926–1935 with that of 1916–1925. The latter were 15–24 in 1940 whereas the younger cohort was 15–24 in 1950. Although the economic conditions early in the career cycle of the younger cohort were undoubtedly better, the improvement was probably not nearly as great as the one that occurred when comparing the cohorts of 1916–1925 with those of 1906–1915. Hence one would not again expect such a disproportionate rise in white-collar fertility, sensitive though it might be to cyclical conditions. Furthermore, white-collar

III. Occupational Differentials

fertility had already risen so enormously that some sort of ceiling effect might have been operating to make comparable relative increases in fertility unlikely.[12]

Turning to the question of timing, Table 5.16 indicates that the age at starting and completing childbearing seemed to be getting younger in the intercohort comparisons involving 35–44-year-olds, as well as those involving 45–54-year-olds. In terms of starting childbearing, most occupations exhibited a slight increase in the ratio of the mean number of children either 18–24 or in the "other" category but there was little evidence of occupational differences in this change. However, one might not expect much of a pattern since 35–44-year-old males are a very young age group to have many older children, even if they did start their families at a relatively early age. A more relevant question is whether differences in the extent to which there was a rise in the ratio of the mean number aged 12–17 to the mean number ever born were related to occupation. By and large, there are not strong or systematic occupational differences in the change in this ratio either. However, the greatest shifts occurred for a number of white-collar occupations—Professionals I and II, Sales II and III, and Clerical III families. Moreover, the shifts were lower for several lower-level blue-collar occupations. For example, there was virtually no change for Service IV families and only a small one for the families of Laborers IV.

With regard to the age at ending childbearing, all occupational groups exhibited a rather sharp decline in the ratio of the mean number of children under age 6 who were present compared to the total number ever born. Strong occupational differences in the decline were not particularly noticeable, except that it seemed to be greater—sometimes much greater—for families of men in the professions and in the Clerical III group.

In terms of the mean numbers of children of various ages present in the home, and changes in these means, indications are that for most occupations there were substantial shifts towards higher means in the 12–17 and 18–24 age groups (Tables 5.17 and 5.18). This was as one would expect, of course, from the ratios presented in Table 5.16. However, there seem to be

---

[12]Data from the Current Population Survey also indicate that white-collar families are more responsive in their family behavior than blue-collar families to changing conditions. For example, although the difference between the proportion of white-collar and blue-collar wives who had their first birth by age 25 dropped slightly for the cohorts of the 1930s compared to the 1920–1929 cohorts, it has increased enormously since then. In the case of the 1945–1949 cohorts, for example, only 59.2% of the wives of white-collar workers had had their first child by age 25 (down from 74.7 for the 1935–1939 cohorts) compared to 80.4% for the blue-collar wives (only down from 82.0% for the 1935–1939 cohort). As a consequence, the white-collar–blue-collar difference in the proportion having their first child by age 25 went up from 7.3 percentage points for the 1935–1939 cohorts to 21.2 percentage points for the 1945–1949 cohorts (U.S. Bureau of the Census 1978e: Table 12). Unfortunately, it is not possible to separate out the role of marriage as opposed to birth postponements in this change.

TABLE 5.17
Mean Number of Children Present, by Their Age and Household Status and by the Occupation of Husbands Aged 35–44: 1960 and 1970

	1960						1970					
	Mean number present by age						Mean number present by age					
Occupation	Under 6	6–11	12–17	18–24[a]	Total[b]	Other[c]	Under 6	6–11	12–17	18–24	Total[b]	Other[c]
Total	.62	.94	.69	.09	2.34	.24	.44	1.02	1.00	.15	2.61	.30
Professionals												
I	.85	1.06	.51	.02	2.44	.10	.56	1.19	.86	.10	2.71	.08
II	.72	.99	.52	.04	2.27	.08	.48	1.08	.95	.11	2.62	.15
III	.72	.90	.57	.07	2.26	.09	.48	1.11	.88	.10	2.57	.16
Managers												
I	.66	.95	.74	.13	2.48	.08	.41	1.07	1.03	.14	2.65	.18
II	.57	.95	.74	.07	2.33	.25	.41	.98	1.06	.17	2.62	.27
III	.57	.88	.72	.11	2.28	.21	.42	.97	1.04	.16	2.59	.26
Sales												
II	.59	1.04	.70	.08	2.41	.15	.45	1.01	.99	.12	2.57	.18
III	.60	.92	.61	.09	2.22	.15	.42	1.00	.99	.15	2.56	.19

Clerical										
III	.65	.91	.53	.07	2.16	.18	.42	.96	.93	.15	2.46	.26
IV	.55	.86	.64	.13	2.18	.15	.41	.95	1.02	.15	2.53	.41
Craft										
II	.52	.75	.79	.10	2.16	.34	.41	.97	1.04	.17	2.59	.29
III	.57	.95	.72	.08	2.32	.23	.42	.99	1.07	.16	2.64	.30
IV	.66	.99	.74	.11	2.50	.35	.42	1.06	1.07	.18	2.73	.42
Operatives										
III	.61	.91	.71	.12	2.35	.32	.44	1.02	1.03	.17	2.66	.41
IV	.59	.95	.77	.12	2.43	.37	.45	.96	1.04	.19	2.64	.44
Service										
III	.63	.87	.72	.12	2.34	.14	.51	1.04	1.01	.17	2.73	.19
IV	.58	.73	.71	.10	2.12	.19	.43	.93	.84	.16	2.36	.44
Laborers										
IV	.66	.95	.81	.10	2.52	.36	.47	1.04	.98	.16	2.65	.51

Sources: 1960 and 1970 Public Use Samples of White Couples.

[a] The mean number of children aged 18–24 had to be estimated for 1960. See Appendix C for a discussion of the procedure used.
[b] Mean total number present under age 25.
[c] *Other* was defined as the total mean number of children ever born minus the mean number under age 25 within the household.

TABLE 5.18
1960–1970 Percentage Change in the Mean Number of Children under 25 Who Were Present, by Age and Occupation of Husbands Aged 35–44

Professionals	Percentage change Mean number present					
	Under 6	6–11	12–17	13–24	Total[a]	Other[b]
Total	−29	+ 8	+45	+ 67	+12	+ 25
Professionals						
I	−34	+12	+69	+400	+11	− 20
II	−33	+ 9	+83	+175	+15	+ 88
III	−33	+23	+54	+ 43	+14	+ 78
Managers						
I	−38	+13	+39	+ 8	+ 7	+125
II	−28	+ 3	+43	+143	+12	+ 8
III	−26	+10	+44	+ 45	+14	+ 24
Sales						
II	−24	− 3	+41	+ 50	+ 7	+ 20
III	−30	+ 9	+62	+ 67	+15	+ 27
Clerical						
III	−35	+ 5	+75	+114	+14	+ 44
IV	−25	+10	+59	+ 15	+16	+173
Craft						
II	−21	+29	+32	+ 70	+20	− 15
III	−26	+ 4	+49	+100	+14	+ 30
IV	−36	+ 7	+44	+ 64	+ 9	+ 20
Operatives						
III	−28	+12	+45	+ 42	+13	+ 28
IV	−24	+ 1	+35	+ 58	+ 9	+ 19
Service						
III	−19	+20	+40	+ 42	+17	+ 36
IV	−26	+27	+18	+ 60	+11	+132
Laborers						
IV	−29	+ 9	+21	+ 60	+ 5	+ 42

Source: Table 5.17.
[a] Mean number present under age 25.
[b] *Other* was defined as the total mean number of children born minus the mean number under age 25 within the household.

few systematic occupational differences in the change in means. Nevertheless, it is true that the rise in the mean number of 12–17-year-olds was particularly high for the Professional I and II groups, Sales III, and both clerical groups whereas it was lowest for the Craft II group and Operative, Service, and Laborers IV husbands.

In sum, in comparison with the cohorts who were aged 45–54 in 1960 and 1970, families of 35–44-year-old men shared certain occupational patterns in the nature of the family cycle. For both age groups, families of white-collar workers were typically at an earlier stage of the family cycle than those of blue-collar workers. However, these occupational differences were probably much more marked for the older age groups because the families of younger white-collar males were less likely to have neared the end of their childbearing period. Comparisons of the cohorts that were 35–44 at both census dates differed in other ways from those who were 45–54 years old. The 1960–1970 changes in the number and timing of children exhibited by the younger cohorts did not vary by occupation nearly as strongly as was the case for 45–54-year-olds. Once again, however, this may still have been too early a point in the family building process for such occupational differences to emerge. Nevertheless, on the face of it, intercohort changes in the number and timing of children ever born interacted more systematically with occupation for the cohort of 1916–1925 than of the cohort of 1906–1915.

IV. CONCLUSION

This exploration of the second life-cycle squeeze has come up with several significant findings. These can be summarized under two headings. One concerns 1960 and 1970 *similarities* in the age pattern of the second squeeze, including occupational variations in their timing and severity. The other involves *changes* in both the timing and severity of the squeeze and occupational differences in such changes.

With regard to 1960 and 1970 similarities in the timing of the second squeeze, peak dependency burdens (and hence direct dollar costs) occur sometime in the 35–54 age range, particularly for males who were aged 35–44 years old although the difficulty of estimating expenditures on children no longer in the home decreases our ability to estimate comparable child-care costs for 45–54-year-old husbands. Moreover, significant occupational differences in the timing of the second squeeze were observed. Such differences indicated that delayed marriage and/or childbearing was more characteristic of white-collar families than blue-collar families who appear to start and end their childbearing earlier.

A timing pattern of later childbearing for higher-level white-collar males and earlier childbearing for blue-collar males seems to represent a rational strategy given the historically less favorable economic position of older versus younger blue-collar males compared to older versus younger high-level white-collar males. There are two economic constraints blue-collar males seem to have traditionally faced: (*a*) that of trying to get sufficiently established in a job to permit marriage and family formation; and (*b*) the difficulties involved if too much postponement occurs and, as a result, child dependency is still high at a point in the husband's career cycle when the age-effect on earnings is neutral or even negative and where older cohorts may suffer an educational disadvantage compared to younger cohorts. Declining age differentials in educational attainment combined with the growing institutionalization of labor markets may be easing these constraints, however. But, this may be offset by trends in schooling—prolonging the child-dependency period. In the case of high-level white-collar males, postponement of childbearing helps mitigate the difficulties of the first life-cycle squeeze and does not entail as great a risk for the second squeeze since the economic circumstances of older males in Group I and II occupations, at least, are relatively favorable.

The 1960–1970 changes in the severity of the second squeeze are best documented for the cohorts who were aged 35–44 in 1970 as compared to 1960 since such men did not yet have a high proportion of their children living away from the parental household. For this age group, at least, the severity of the second squeeze increased significantly between 1960 and 1970. Using estimates of direct child-care costs, the greater increase in the income for 35–44-year-old men compared to younger males was entirely offset by rising equivalent child-care costs occasioned by increases in family size. This, in turn, indicates that the decline in the economic status of younger married males relative to older married men was not as important a phenomenon as Easterlin has argued. If that is true, however, then an explanation of the current baby bust primarily in terms of the relative income position of *married males* is open to question. There seems little doubt, however, that the income position of *all* young males declined relative to the income position of older men, even after changes in child-care costs are deducted for the older males (but not the younger).

The extent of the change in the situation of 45–54-year-olds is much less clear because of measurement problems. However, as of 1970, the change in their relative economic status compared to the younger men was probably favorable. However this does not mean that the cohorts who were 45–54 in 1970 did not experience an intensification of the second squeeze earlier in their life-cycle before the departure of so many of their children from the

IV. Conclusion

household. Unfortunately, without PUS data for 1950, it is impossible to investigate this issue.

Although the impact of changes in the second squeeze were most noticeable for cohorts who were *35–44* in 1970 versus 1960, occupational differences in changes in the dependency burden were best documented by a comparison of cohorts who were *45–54* in 1970 versus 1960. Such a comparison shows marked occupational differentials in the changes in the number and timing of children. Compared to the rather modest increases for blue-collar workers, white-collar families with a head aged 45–54 exhibited a sharp rise in fertility and a marked trend toward earlier childbearing. Furthermore, within both the white-collar and blue-collar groups, fertility increases were directly related to occupational level of peak median earnings. As a consequence, there was a considerable decline in occupational differentials in fertility patterns. This trend should have operated to intensify the second squeeze for white-collar groups more than for blue-collar and to place the squeeze earlier in the husband's life-cycle.

In short, the data presented in this chapter indicate first that child-care expenditures are likely to vary considerably among men at different stages of the family cycle and in ways that are often difficult to synchronize with age variations in earnings. Thus the second life-cycle squeeze seems to be a very real phenomenon. Second, the timing of the squeeze varies among occupational groups, occurring at later ages for white-collar husbands, especially those in Group I and II occupations, than for blue-collar men. This is to be expected, however, given the different ages at which the age–earnings profiles peak. Third, the data reveal that the intensity of the second squeeze increased because of the considerable rise in fertility of cohorts reaching adulthood in the 1940s and 1950s. Finally, changes in the severity of the *dependency* dimension of the second squeeze, at least, seemed especially characteristic of postwar white-collar families since their increases in fertility were more substantial than those exhibited by blue-collar families.

III

THE NATURE OF WIVES' SOCIOECONOMIC CONTRIBUTION TO THE FAMILY

6

The Effect of Socioeconomic Pressures and Deterrents on Wives' Labor-Force Participation

Two concerns have dominated the discussion so far. The first has been to specify and empirically investigate structural sources of economic stress and how these may have been changing over time. Here I have focused particularly on life-cycle squeezes and economic squeezes related to men's occupational attachments. A second concern has been some of the demographic responses to such built-in economic squeezes, focusing particularly on the age at marriage of men and the numbers of children and the timing of their births.

Part III of this volume now turns to a consideration of wives' work behavior as another type of response to economic squeezes. The present chapter considers whether wives' labor-force participation is indeed related to the hypothesized pressures for an additional income discussed in earlier chapters. Chapter 7 will examine the relationship of wives' labor-force participation to their potential socioeconomic contribution to the family. Finally, Chapter 8 will assess the relative socioeconomic impact of wives' employment on their families and its implications for women's changing socioeconomic roles.

This chapter employs an ordinary least-squares multiple regression analysis with the wife's labor-force status as the dichotomous dependent variable. The independent variables are a variety of dummy variables designed to measure different types of economic pressures for wives to work as well as the major deterrent to their labor-force participation—the presence of young children. A measure of the wife's potential socioeconomic contribution to the family is included in all regressions although the discussion of this variable is postponed until Chapter 7.

Two variants of the general earnings level of the husband's occupation were inserted in separate regression models. The peak median earnings level of the husband's occupation—Levels I through IV—was used first as a crude preliminary measure of the effect of variations in families' general economic level, regardless of the husband's particular occupation. Presumably, the lower the peak median earnings level of the husband's occupation, ceteris paribus, the greater the chronic economic pressures for the wife to work.

Although the peak median earnings of an occupation will provide a rough idea of the *general* economic levels of families, it is quite a crude measure because of the tremendous variability in the types of occupations included in many of these peak median groups (indicative of the lumping together of disparate reference groups), as well as some systematic income differences among occupations in the same earnings group. The outstanding example of both these problems is the Group III occupations which include occupations from all the major groups with the exception of Laborers. The full 18-category peak median occupational variable was therefore used to compare groups that are thought to have similar life-style aspirations but typically different incomes (e.g., white-collar occupations at different income levels) as well as occupational groups with presumably somewhat different aspirations but similar median earnings (e.g., blue- and white-collar groups at similar earnings levels). In this respect, the impact of the hypothesized lower white-collar squeeze has been one of the major issues to investigate.

Three other variables were also employed to measure types of income variation. One was the husband's age as an indicator of the career-cycle effect on earnings. A second was a ratio variable designed to measure the current economic status of the husband relative to others in the same general occupational reference group and at approximately the same stage of the career cycle. The interpretation of this ratio variable as purely a measure of *relative* economic status is somewhat controversial, however. The absolute level of *permanent* income was very roughly held constant in the regression analysis via the peak median occupation variable. However, the absolute level of *current* earnings was not incorporated into the original regression analyses—primarily to avoid multicollinearity problems since current earnings formed the numerator of the ratio variable. As a consequence, however, one could argue that the ratio variable may just be measuring the effect of *absolute* rather than *relative* earnings on wives' labor-force participation.[1] Since there is some reason to believe this may be true, the interpretation of the effect of this variable has been rather conservative.

Finally, in a somewhat belated effort to investigate this question of relative versus absolute income, a new correlation matrix was created in which the 1969 earnings variable (in dummy form) was included. However, because of the programming limitations of SPSS, the peak median occupation variable had to be dropped from the matrix. To the extent that *inter*group variations in earnings have a different effect from *intra*group variations, these distinctions cannot be observed when one major measure of intergoup earnings differences was eliminated. As a result, it has been difficult to resolve the question of whether intraoccupational relative economic status is an important factor.

Another situation in which economic pressures for the wife to work might arise is related to the marital history of husbands and wives. For example, a number of investigators have argued, that a previous marital disruption can lead to circumstances promoting the labor-force participation of wives in subsequent marriages. Both Cain and Sweet in their analyses found some support for this idea (Cain 1966; Sweet 1973). Since the 1970 Census obtained data on whether the first marriage ended with divorce, it provided an opportunity to investigate this issue in some detail.

Next we come to one of the most important factors among those designed to measure variations in relative economic deprivation and hence in economic pressures to work. This relates to life-cycle squeezes. To investigate this whole problem, a variable was created to indicate the family-cycle stage of the couple, including information on the number and ages of children present in the household.

The final variable included in the regression discussed in this chapter is the wife's potential relative socioeconomic contribution to the family as indicated by the joint educational attainment of the spouses. The measure is somewhat crude, of course. For example, it does not take into account differences in human capital investments that postdate the completion of formal schooling and especially sex differences in such investments. However, a number of other labor-force studies analyzing 1960 Census data have also used the wife's educational attainment as a measure of her potential socioeconomic level (Cain 1966; Bowen and Finegan 1969; Sweet 1973). Hence, there are certain advantages for comparative purposes in continuing to use education. However, the actual discussion of the impact of this variable will be postponed until the next chapter when wives' socioeconomic characteristics will be discussed in greater detail.

---

[1] For example, a simple correlation of the relative economic status variable with husband's earnings (in dummy form) resulted in an r^2 of .61.

TABLE 6.1
Regression Models for Total Sample; Dependent Variable Is Wife's Labor-Force Status

Independent variables[a]	I	II	III	IV	V	VI
Peak median earnings group of husband	X					
Peak median occupation group		X	X	X		
Husband's relative economic status in 1969	X	X	X	X	X	
Spouses' previous marital experience	X	X	X	X	X	X
Family-cycle stage	X	X		X	X	X
Wife's relative educational attainment	X	X	X		X	X
Wife's absolute educational attainment				X		
Husband's earnings					X	
Husband's age	X	X	X	X	X	X

[a] All variables were dummied.

All in all, six regression models were used to analyze wives' labor-force participation, not counting interaction analyses. Table 6.1 defines the models in question and Appendix D shows the dummy variable categories employed for each variable. Although six models were used, the main model under discussion is Model II.

Sample Used

The regression analyses reported in the present chapter were only performed on the 1970 Census data and not on the 1960 data. Since a number of the dummy variables involved complex recodes and sample sizes were purposely large to permit complicated dummy variable construction, resource constraints discouraged conducting the analysis on both census. Also, the two censuses did not obtain exactly the same information so that comparable regressions could not be run for both censuses without sacrificing valuable data obtained in 1970. For example, the 1970 PUS, but not the 1960, had data on whether the first marriage ended in divorce, as well as information on the number of children 18-24 present in the household. Therefore, the regression analysis was limited to the 1970 Public Use Sample.[2]

[2] In addition, given the exploratory nature of this study, it became clear during the course of the regresssion analysis on the 1970 data that some of the variables used had measurement problems and the techniques employed were not as sophisticated as might be desired. So, it did not seem particularly fruitful to try to exactly replicate the analysis on the 1960 data. It would be better at some future date to analyze the 1960 data and reanalyze the 1970 data at a more sophisticated level.

Methodology

A dummy-variable (MCA) analysis of the dichotomous dependent variable—wife's labor force status—was employed although there is growing evidence that this procedure involves a number of statistical problems (Goldberger 1964:250 ff; Goodman 1972, 1973). One is that the assumption of homoscedasticity is violated by such a variable. This casts some doubt on the validity of tests of significance. However, with a sample size of over 90,000 families, the utility of tests of significance is somewhat doubtful anyway since one rarely encounters statistically insignificant results. Second, although a dichotomous dependent variable is bounded between the limits of 0 and 1, it is still possible to obtain regression estimates ouside this range with the ordinary least-squares method. However, as Goodman has indicated, this problem is less serious when the probability of observing one value of the dichotomous dependent variable lies within the .25 to .75 range (Goodman 1973). Since this is typically the case for wives' labor-force participation in 1970, I did not attempt more sophisticated and less well-known statistical procedures, given the time delays these would have involved in a study that had already gone on for too long.

Following Bowen and Finegan's lead, the results of these regressions are presented as "adjusted labor-force participation rates." These adjusted rates are constructed from the net partial regression coefficients and are interpreted as the difference in participation associated with membership in the different categories of any particular set of dummy variables under consideration (e.g., age) after the effects of all other variables included in the regression equation are taken into account (Bowen and Finegan 1969: 42, 642–644; Melichar 1965).[3] The tables will also present "unadjusted participation rates" for the various sets of dummy variables: the percentage of women in the labor force for different categories of a given variable, without taking other variables into consideration. In addition, the F ratios for each of the variables are also shown.[4]

---

[3] For interested readers, the partial regression coefficients are also presented in Appendix D.

[4] The F test for the effect of the set of categories constituting a dummy variable was computed using the following formula:

$$F = \frac{\text{Incremental } SS \text{ due to } X_i}{SS_{\text{res}} / (N - k - 1)}$$

where the numerator is the difference between the sum of squares explained by the regression equation when all dummy variables are included and when the dummy variable X_i is excluded. SS_{res} is the residual (unexplained) sum of squares, k is the number of independent variables in the equation (the number of dummy variable categories, excluding the omitted categories), and N is the sample size.

I. THE ROLE OF INCOME AND OCCUPATION

Impact of Earnings

Whichever earnings measure is employed, the regression analyses indicate that the nature of the income effect is complex. Two general findings appear to emerge. One is that occupation does indeed make an important difference in wives' work propensities and, second, that the income effect is not linear.

The nonlinear nature of the impact of income is illustrated in the effect of both husband's current income and that of the crude proxy for his permanent income—his peak median earnings group. Table 6.2 shows the gross and net effects of occupational earnings level on wives' labor-force participation. Although both the unadjusted and adjusted rates show an inverse relationship to general economic level, there is an important anomaly: The work rates of wives of men in Group IV occupations (the lowest-paid occupations) were not much higher than those of the wives of men in Group III occupations. The unadjusted rates for Group IV wives are actually slightly lower than those of Group III wives and the adjusted rates are only very slightly higher. Furthermore, the Group IV families account for 28% of the sample and hence hardly constitute a trivial minority of cases. In short, the negative effect of the husband's general economic level (as measured by the peak median earnings level of his occupation) seems to peter out for the wives of men in the poorest paying occupations, even when all other variables are taken into account.

The regression model using husbands' 1969 earnings reveals a similar pattern (Table 6.3). Although wives' labor-force participation varies markedly with the earnings of the husband, this relationship is not very strong for families where the husband earned less than $9,000 in 1969. In fact, there were some reversals. Wives of men in the $5,000–6,999 earnings group were more likely to be working than wives of men earning $1–4,999. Furthermore, although earnings of $7,000–8,999 led to a work rate that was less than for the $5,000–6,999 earnings group, the difference was not marked. In sum, once again—this time using actual earnings—there does not appear to be a consistent and marked gradient of wives' labor-force participation for men in lower earnings groups. Nor do such men represent a small proportion of the total. Approximately half of the men earned less than $9,000 in 1969.

Previous researchers using measures of current income have observed a similar phenomenon—this time in the 1960 1/1,000 Public Use Sample. For example, Sweet found that nonblack wives' employment was lower if the 1959 family income (minus wife's earnings) was less than $2,000 than if it was $2,000–3,999 (Sweet 1973: 95). Furthermore, when using his measure

TABLE 6.2
Effect of Husband's Peak Median Earnings Group on Wife's Labor-Force Participation

Peak median earnings group of husband	1969 median earnings[b]	Distribution of sample Number	Distribution of sample Percentage	Labor-force participation rates[a] Unadjusted	Labor-force participation rates[a] Adjusted I[c]
Total		91,937	100.0	43.0	
I	14,030	8,649	9.4	34.6	32.8
II	11,345	15,346	16.7	40.5	39.1
III	8,839	41,844	45.5	44.9	44.7
IV	7,136	26,098	28.4	44.0	45.7
F					156.58[d]

Source: 1970 Public Use Sample of White Couples. The adjusted participation rates were derived from the partial regression coefficients in Regression Model I listed in Appendix D.
[a] Percentage in labor force.
[b] Excludes those with zero or negative earnings ($n = 2,573$; 2.8% of sample).
[c] Model I: Adjusted for the effects of husband's intraoccupational relative economic status, husband's age, family-cycle stage, previous marital experience of spouses, and wife's relative educational attainment.
[d] Significant at the .01 level.

TABLE 6.3
Effect of Husband's 1969 Earnings on Wife's Labor-Force Participation

| | Distribution of sample || Labor-force participation rates[a] ||
Husband's earnings	Number	Percentage	Unadjusted	Adjusted V[b]
Total	91,937	100.0	43.0	
0 or negative	2,573	2.8	41.2	41.7
1– 4,999	11,666	12.7	49.1	48.3
5,000– 6,999	14,082	15.3	50.4	50.5
7,000– 8,999	19,670	21.4	47.4	48.1
9,000–10,999	16,620	18.1	42.5	43.2
11,000–12,999	9,910	10.8	38.9	39.4
13,000–14,999	5,247	5.7	35.1	35.1
15,000–19,999	6,449	7.0	32.0	31.0
20,000+	5,720	6.2	25.4	22.6
F				81.7[c]

Source: 1970 Public Use Samples of White Couples. The adjusted participation rates were derived from the partial regression coefficients in Regression Model V listed in Appendix D.
[a] Percentage in labor force.
[b] Model V: Adjusted for the effects of husband's intraoccupational relative economic status, husband's age, family-cycle stage, previous marital experience of spouses, and wife's relative educational attainment.
[c] Significant at the .01 level.

of "income adequacy" (family income minus the wife's earnings as a ratio of a measure of the minimum income needs of the family based on its composition) Sweet's analysis showed that although wives were much more likely to be employed if the income adequacy ratio was 1.1 or less than if it was over this amount, there was little variation among the three income-adequacy categories within that low range (Sweet 1973: 48, 90; see also Bowen and Finegan 1969: 133).

In sum, whether we use a measure of men's current earnings, of general economic level (the peak median earnings level of the husband's occupation) or of actual current family income (minus wife's earnings) or a measure of income adequacy, the negative relationship between income and a wife's labor-force participation appears to weaken within the lower-income groups. On the face of it then, these results suggest that low earnings do have a positive impact on wives' work rates, but that increase in earnings do not have a large negative effect on wives' work rates until a certain threshold is reached. Furthermore, some factors must offset the positive labor-force impact of low earnings by the husband. For example, the lower adjusted rates for wives of men in the zero or negative earnings category compared to the wives of men in the $1–1,000 range suggests the possible importance of income transfers of one sort or another to the families of these nonearners.

Husband's Occupation

That husband's peak median occupation has an important impact on wives' work propensities is born out by the pattern of the adjusted rates for the occupation variable (Table 6.4). For all white-collar and service occupations there appears to be a substantial relationship between the earnings level of the husbands' occupations and wives' labor-force participation (Table 6.4). Furthermore, it is strongest for professional occupations. The adjusted work rates varied from 33% for the Professional I group to 49% for the Professional III group. But, for blue-collar occupations, the relationship between occupational earnings level and wives' work rates all but disappears. Taking Craft occupations, for example, the adjusted participation rate was 39% for Craft II occupations (the only Group II blue-collar occupation, consisting mainly of foremen and being relatively small numerically), and was 43% for both Craft III and Craft IV occupations. In the case of Operatives, the unadjusted rates for Group III and IV were identical and the adjusted rate was only .5 of a percentage point higher for the Operative IV group than the Operative III group. Finally, for Laborers—a Group IV occupation—the adjusted work rate was virtually indentical to the rates for Craft III and IV groups and was slightly *lower* than for Operatives III.

In sum, although for white-collar occupations, earnings level within occupation groups is strongly related to wives' labor-force participation, the relationship is very weak for blue-collar occupations. Since husbands in Craft IV, Operatives IV, and Laborer IV occupations accounted for about 80% of all Group IV husbands in 1970 and blue-collar Group III husbands accounted for 54% of all Group III occupations, the weak relationship between earnings level and wives' labor-force participation among families of men in blue-collar occupations seems to account for the small difference between the labor-force participation of wives of Group III as opposed to Group IV husbands.

Not only was the effect of peak median earnings groups small within the Craft IV, Operatives IV, and Laborer IV occupations accounted for about occupations usually exhibited lower adjusted work rates than those of men in higher earnings white-collar occupations.[5] For example, Professional III

---

[5]One reason may be the higher concentration of families of blue-collar men in areas where there were fewer job opportunities for women—for example, in metropolitan areas in which goods-producing as opposed to service-producing industries are more important. However, this pattern would not account for the puzzling finding that Group IV blue-collar wives were rarely more likely to be working than wives of higher-paid Group III blue-collar men.

TABLE 6.4
Effect of Husband's Peak Median Occupation Group on Wife's Labor-Force Participation: Earnings Levels within Occupation Groups

Peak median occupation group	1969 median earnings[b]	Distribution of sample		Labor-force participation rates[a]	
		Number	Percentage	Unadjusted	Adjusted II[c]
Total	8,926	91,937	100.0	43.0	—
Professionals					
I	14,489	5,329	5.8	33.8	32.7
II	11,431	5,626	6.1	41.9	40.2
III	9,627	4,508	4.9	51.3	48.6
Managers					
I	13,286	3,320	3.6	35.8	34.8
II	11,537	5,309	5.8	39.2	38.5
III	9,800	4,069	4.4	45.4	45.3
Sales					
II	11,372	2,828	3.1	40.8	40.2
III	8,772	4,415	4.8	47.9	46.9
Clerical					
III	8,609	4,778	5.2	47.3	45.7
IV	7,404	1,308	1.4	52.5	51.5

Craft				
II	10,838	1.7	39.6	38.8
III	8,989	17.2	42.1	42.6
IV	7,530	6.4	41.3	42.7
Operatives				
III	8,049	7.5	43.4	44.5
IV	7,425	11.8	43.4	45.0
Service				
III	9,234	1.5	44.3	44.7
IV	6,325	4.3	50.8	51.2
Laborers				
IV	6,475	4.4	40.4	42.5
F				30.0[d]

Source: of 1970 Public Use Sample White Couples. The adjusted participation rates were derived from the partial regression coefficients in Regression Model II listed in Appendix D.

[a] Percentage in labor force.
[b] Excludes those with zero or negative earnings.
[c] Model II: Adjusted for the effects of husband's intraoccupational relative economic status, husband's age, family-cycle stage, previous marital experience of spouses, and wife's relative educational attainment.
[d] Significant at the .01 level.

wives had the highest adjusted rate (49%) whereas Craft III wives had the lowest rate (43%). However, Professional III men had considerably higher median earnings than Craft III or Operatives III husbands in every age group in the 35–64-year-old range. For all age groups combined, the median 1969 earnings of Professional III males was $9,627 compared to $8,989 for Craft III husbands and $8,049 for men in the Operatives III Group (Table 6.4). Similarly, Sales III and Clerical III husbands generally had higher median earnings than Operatives III men but instead of the adjusted work rates for their wives being lower, the rates were higher. And Service III men consistently earned more than Operatives III but the wives were just about as likely to be in the labor force.[6]

The occupational pattern within the Group II and III levels also indicates that the main reason the adjusted rates were higher for Group III occupations as a whole compared to Group II occupations was because of the high work rates of the wives of men in Group III *white*-collar occupations. The adjusted rates for Group III blue-collar and Group II occupations were actually quite similar. Thus the adjusted work rate for Craft III wives was only about 2 percentage points above that of Professional and Sales II wives and the adjusted rate for Operatives III was only 4 percentage points higher. However the adjusted rate for Professional III wives was 8 percentage points above that for Professional II wives, and 10 percentage points above that for wives of men in the Managers II group.

A major exception to this pattern of unexpectedly low rates for blue-collar wives is the very high work rates of wives of Service IV men. Why their behavior is so different from other blue-collar wives is unclear. It is true that the median earnings of Service IV males are, age by age, considerably and consistently lower than those of every blue-collar group but Laborers. Even compared to Laborers, their median earnings are somewhat lower in three out of five age groups considered. But this does not seem enough to account for the fact that the wives of Service IV men had an adjusted work rate of 51% in the labor force whereas that of Laborers IV wives was only 42%. As a consequence, the high propensity of Service IV wives to work remains something of a mystery. (See also Bowen and Finegan 1969: 154–158.)

In sum, then these findings indicate that occupation is an important factor

---

[6]Service III occupations, the protective services, seem to be undergoing a transition into occupations of a more white-collar type. Earnings for Service III males rose rapidly between 1959 and 1969 and educational attainment has also been rising rapidly so that on these two variables Service III men in 1970 resembled other white-collar workers much more than they did in 1960. Therefore, I have tended to view them as white-collar occupations. However, since the socioeconomic position of these occupations has been rising rapidly, it is unclear whether the lower-white-collar squeeze would hold for these families in a way similar to that for those in more traditional white-collar occupations.

I. The Role of Income and Occupation

in the nature of the income effect on wives' work propensities. The hypothesis that lower white-collar squeeze exists and that higher rates of wives' employment is one adaptive response is strongly supported by the regression results. The adjusted work rates for White-Collar III wives were not only considerably higher than for the wives of men in the higher-paying White-Collar II occupations but they were even higher than the rates for the wives of men in *lower* paying blue-collar occupations with the one exception of the Service IV group.

Another significant finding, and one that was not anticipated, was that, except for Service IV families, blue-collar wives' adjusted work rates were unrelated to the earnings level of the husband's occupation and were sometimes even similar to the much higher paid White-Collar II adjusted rates. These results, combined with the findings in Chapter 5, suggest that there may be some important differences in white-collar and blue-collar family strategies. In spite of lower earnings of manual workers, their wives' employment seems to have provided a less important adaptive response to economic squeezes than among white-collar families.

An interaction analysis of relative economic status within the peak median occupation provides further support for the finding that the effect of income depends, in part, on occupational attachments (Table 6.5). Interoccupational comparisons within the same ratio categories make it possible to compare men in the same relative economic status position within their occupation and age groups but who differ in earnings since median earnings by age and occupational groups are known (Table 3.5). For example, we know that Operatives III males have lower median earnings than Professional III males for every age group above 18–24. Therefore, if we compare Operatives III and Professional III males in the same relative economic status category, we know that the Professional III males must, as a group, have higher actual earnings than the Operatives III men. If they did not, they could not be in the same ratio category. As a consequence, we can predict the ordering of actual earnings of men in certain different occupations groups but within the same relative economic status group. Also, a cross-tabulation of earnings by occupation and relative economic status permits us to compute the actual median earnings of men in each occupation and ratio category and thus get a more accurate view of absolute earnings differentials (Table 6.6).

Within any ratio category, there was a strong inverse relationship between peak median earnings level and wives' work propensities for white-collar wives, although the differences were often much less for the low-ratio categories. For example, among professionals, where the husband's income was 100–125% of the median for husbands in the same age and peak median occupational group, the adjusted work rates rose from 31.5% for Professional I wives to 49.0% for Professional III wives. However, once

TABLE 6.5
Effect of Husband's Intraoccupational Relative Economic Status on Wife's Labor-Force Participation in 1970 by Husband's Peak Median Occupation (Adjusted Labor-Force Rates)[a]

Peak median occupation	Less than .50	.50–.74	.75–.99	1.00–1.24	1.25–1.49	1.50–1.99	2.00+
Professionals							
I	40.6	46.4	37.7	31.5	26.5	25.3	17.3
II	51.9	50.8	45.6	39.8	32.8	29.9	26.7
III	52.4	58.0	57.5	49.0	46.4	40.7	32.4
Managers							
I	49.6	48.4	42.1	32.9	27.5	21.0	13.0
II	49.2	51.5	42.4	37.2	34.0	28.8	22.2
III	49.2	51.3	51.3	48.3	43.6	33.1	28.1
Sales							
II	48.3	55.4	46.6	39.5	29.7	29.2	19.0
III	51.0	56.5	54.3	47.7	40.7	39.1	28.9

Relative economic status ratios

Clerical							
III	47.1	52.6	54.7	46.7	41.9	30.6	26.7
IV	46.8	62.1	58.1	52.2	47.4	35.9	29.6
Craft							
II	29.0	54.1	46.7	37.2	28.0	27.7	20.4
III	46.1	50.3	46.3	40.7	34.4	28.0	24.5
IV	44.8	45.9	44.6	41.2	34.6	32.7	30.9
Operatives							
III	42.9	50.8	46.9	43.9	36.9	26.7	25.6
IV	42.4	52.6	46.4	43.1	37.6	35.6	28.6
Service							
III	47.2	54.1	48.2	41.9	35.8	36.3	19.3
IV	51.7	52.8	54.1	53.8	47.8	42.5	41.1
Laborers							
IV	38.3	38.9	44.6	44.7	38.0	33.8	26.7

Source: 1970 Public Use Sample of White Couples.
[a] Adjusted for the effects of husband's age, family-cycle stage, previous marital experience of spouses, and wife's absolute educational attainment.

again the adjusted rates for blue-collar wives were similar to or below that of families in other occupations at a higher earnings level. For example, the adjusted work rate for wives of Craft IV husbands was approximately equal to or below that of Craft III husbands at every relative economic status category until husbands were making 150% or more of the median for the reference group. This is despite the significantly lower earnings of Craft IV as compared to Craft III husbands (Table 6.6). Furthermore, except for the Service IV groups, the adjusted rates in both the Blue-Collar III and IV groups were typically similar to or, more usually, lower than White-Collar III groups at higher earnings levels. For example, although in each ratio category the median earnings for Craft IV husbands was well below that of the medians for every white-collar group, the adjusted work rates were practically always lower than those of White-Collar III wives, whatever the ratio category. Thus, if the husbands were making 75–99% of the median of their reference group, the adjusted rate for Craft IV wives was only 44.6%. This compared to an adjusted rate in this relative economic status category of 57.5, 51.3, 54.3, 54.7 and 48.2% for Professionals, Managers, Sales, Clerical, and Service III wives respectively.

In short, these data once again show that absolute income in itself does a poor job of predicting the labor-force participation of blue-collar wives when interoccupational comparisons are involved. However, if we compare differences in the adjusted rates within occupation groups, there is evidence of a negative relationship between earnings and wives' labor-force participation for blue-collar occupations as well as white-collar. This suggests that perhaps relative economic status *within* groups is an important factor in wives' labor-force participation.

In general, one of the most outstanding aspects of the regression results is that, in 1970 at least, blue-collar couples seem to have been much less likely than white-collar couples to utilize wives' market employment as a common method of maintaining an economic homeostasis in the family. Furthermore, with the exception of the Service IV group, this pattern was even more characteristic of lower-level blue-collar families, thus offsetting the upward pressure on wives' employment that presumably accompanies a lower income.

Information on the past work experience of wives shows that blue-collar wives were more likely *never* to have worked than white-collar wives (Table 6.7). Furthermore, Group IV blue-collar wives had the highest proportions who never worked—between 28 and 34% of Operative, Craft, and Laborer IV wives of the cohort of men in the 55–64 age group in 1960, for example. Moreover, intercohort comparisons show that the total lack of labor-market experience was much more characteristic of older cohorts of blue-collar wives so that a life devoted entirely to domestic employments is also becoming increasingly rare among blue-collar wives. It is true that these occupational and cohort differences will, in part, result from differences in school attainment (and hence employability), age at marriage, and age at the birth of the first child. However, even so this reflects, in part, a life-style that did not seem to anticipate that wives would make important market-income contributions to their families, not even early in marriage.

Husband's Age

Husband's age was originally included in the regression analysis because it is a direct, if rough, indicator of earning variations associated with career-cycle stage. However, age-related variations in husband's earnings alone do not determine whether economic pressures for the wife to work exist but how his earnings balance out against the income needs or aspirations of the family. These, in turn, are highly related to family-cycle stage and the couple's reproductive performance. Since family-cycle stage, like career-cycle stage, is also related to age, I anticipated that the family-cycle variable, being a more direct measure, would be a much more sensitive indicator of life-cycle squeeze pressures and the time-demands made by children than husband's age alone. Hence, the family-cycle variable would be dominant in measuring age effects on wives' work propensities. However, the husband's age can also be interpreted as a cohort measure, assuming age affects have been largely controlled for by the family–cycle variable.

Table 6.8 shows the influence of husband's age on wife's labor-force participation—alone and in conjunction with several other variables. When we consider just the unadjusted work rates for the effect of age, the pattern resembles the traditional one for female age-specific work rates during this period—high participation rates for young women, followed by a sharp decline for age groups where young children are most likely to be in the home, then increasing rates, until they start to fall again for older women. Furthermore, when all the other variables are taken into account *except* the family-cycle variable, the pattern is not greatly changed (Adjusted Rates III). However, when the family-cycle variable is also included, the effect of age, net of the other variables, changes radically (Adjusted Rates II). At that point, age has a pronounced *negative* effect on whether the wife works—the older the husband (and wife by inference), the less likely she is to be in the labor force (Model II).

All this is certainly suggestive of a cohort effect. However, to say that age is functioning partly as a cohort effect in this regression model is, to some extent, simply restating the problem. The deeper question concerns the

TABLE 6.6
Median 1969 Earnings of Husband by Occupation and Intraoccupational Relative Economic Status (Dollars)

Peak median occupation	Relative economic status ratios							
	Less than .50	.50–.74	.75–.99	1.00–1.24	1.25–1.49	1.50–1.99	2.00+
Professionals							
I	3,991	10,188	13,337	17,056	20,676	25,899	43,960
II	2,753	7,766	10,537	13,297	15,960	20,314	30,750
III	2,333	6,419	8,819	11,068	13,838	16,894	25,667
Managers							
I	5,221	9,504	12,200	16,058	20,067	25,008	37,889
II	4,052	7,506	10,234	12,951	16,464	20,263	31,757
III	3,171	6,365	8,424	10,687	13,590	17,217	25,954
Sales							
II	3,361	7,530	10,287	13,027	16,371	20,375	32,650
III	2,755	5,693	7,914	10,349	12,301	15,398	24,206

Clerical							
III	2,022	5,630	7,741	9,765	11,852	14,731	21,750
IV	2,433	5,043	6,602	8,277	10,223	12,024	17,667
Craft							
II	4,000	7,100	9,585	12,114	14,781	17,845	25,300
III	2,818	5,827	8,025	10,276	12,428	15,158	21,795
IV	2,226	4,866	6,756	8,632	10,573	12,586	17,750
Operatives							
III	2,366	5,037	7,157	9,086	11,273	13,302	19,333
IV	2,300	4,899	6,700	8,556	10,254	12,354	18,250
Service							
III	2,938	6,098	8,183	10,424	12,369	15,750	20,750
IV	1,635	4,076	5,644	7,210	8,504	10,902	15,100
Laborers							
IV	1,746	3,793	5,732	7,712	9,108	10,704	14,870

Source: 1970 Public Use Sample of White Couples.

TABLE 6.7
Percentage of Wives Who Have Never Worked, by Husband's Age and Occupation: 1960 and 1970

Husband's occupation	1960					1970				
	18–24	25–34	35–44	45–54	55–64	18–24	25–34	35–44	45–54	55–64
Professionals										
I	—[a]	5.0	6.0	11.4	18.6	3.2	3.0	4.6	4.5	9.4
II	3.7	4.5	4.2	6.8	13.0	3.9	3.7	3.0	4.0	9.0
III	7.8	5.0	6.0	10.1	12.3	4.3	4.3	4.3	5.8	8.8
Managers										
I	—[a]	6.2	7.4	10.3	16.7	5.2	4.1	5.5	7.0	11.9
II	—[a]	7.5	8.4	17.0	21.8	11.3	6.3	7.0	8.0	13.0
III	—[a]	8.8	9.4	12.3	17.0	5.6	7.6	8.6	8.2	12.7
Sales										
II	—[a]	6.8	8.0	12.1	17.1	6.1	4.1	7.0	7.5	8.9
III	11.9	5.0	4.9	11.7	14.8	8.7	5.6	6.7	7.7	10.5

Clerical										
III	7.1	5.4	4.2	8.4	15.2	4.6	5.3	6.3	5.9	9.1
IV	—[a]	10.8	9.3	12.5	18.3	8.3	6.5	6.1	10.1	11.4
Craft										
II	—[a]	5.9	9.4	11.0	27.4	—[a]	4.3	7.7	11.4	14.9
III	17.5	12.6	12.4	17.1	22.9	12.4	9.9	9.0	10.3	16.5
IV	28.4	13.9	13.9	22.0	30.0	11.0	12.8	10.4	11.5	20.9
Operatives										
III	23.1	14.7	13.8	19.8	29.3	14.1	11.7	10.2	12.5	17.2
IV	20.5	16.4	16.4	18.8	27.7	16.2	12.7	11.8	13.0	17.9
Service										
III	—[a]	5.8	9.4	14.0	—[a]	12.2	6.5	7.9	7.5	17.0
IV	—[a]	15.8	10.8	14.2	20.4	10.7	11.4	8.4	8.8	12.9
Laborers										
IV	27.8	21.9	23.9	21.4	33.6	14.7	14.4	14.6	15.2	21.2

Sources: 1960 and 1970 Public Use Samples of White Couples.
[a] Percentages not computed because of small sample size.

TABLE 6.8
Effect of Husband's Age on Wife's Labor-Force Participation

	Distribution of sample		Labor-force participation rates[a]		
				Adjusted	
Husband's age	Number	Percentage	Unadjusted	III[b]	II[c]
Total	91,937	100.0	43.0		
18–24	6,975	7.6	48.7	48.1	51.0
25–34	21,886	23.8	38.1	37.1	49.8
35–44	22,457	24.4	42.2	42.5	45.4
45–54	23,221	25.3	47.7	48.1	40.5
55–64	17,398	18.9	41.4	42.0	31.4
F				166.9[d]	182.2[d]

Source: 1970 Sample of White Couples. The adjusted participation rates were derived from the partial regression coefficients in Regressions II and III listed in Appendix D.
[a] Percentage in labor force.
[b] Model III: Adjusted for husband's peak median occupation group, husband's intraoccupational relative economic status, previous marital experience of spouses, and wife's relative educational attainment.
[c] Model II: Adjusted for the same variables as in Model III but with the addition of family-cycle stage.
[d] Significant at the .01 level.

nature of this cohort effect. It undoubtedly has several components, some of which we might try to specify.

To the extent norms and preferences as well as realistic expectations regarding married women's employment have been changing over the past 35 years, older cohorts will have matured and lived at least some of their adult family life in a different normative and "perceptual" environment than younger cohorts. Thus work outside the home would have been somewhat less acceptable or desirable for these older cohorts, at least during certain periods of their lives. Hence, a smaller proportion of them worked at various points in their life-cycle, particularly as they got older and some of the life-cycle economic pressures eased (see Durand 1968: 123ff.).

A variety of other factors, often interrelated, are important in the cohort effect on women's labor-force participation. For examply, older cohorts probably have had less initial investment in human capital because of lower levels of schooling. If for this and other reasons (e.g., normative constraints) they worked less throughout their lives, then some of the human capital they entered adult life with was likely to deteriorate and certainly less likely to have been added to as a consequence of accumulated work experience (see Mincer and Polachek 1974). As a consequence, a given level of schooling will not signify the same level of "current" human capital for older as it will for younger cohorts, and this will lead to differentials in employment prospects. In addition, however, in recent years older women have probably started to operate at an increasing competitive disadvantage with younger, better educated women. Since these younger women are from the numerous baby-boom cohorts, their combination of large supply, higher educational attainment, plus high work motivation may be having an adverse effect on the market position of older women—particularly in view of the fact that labor demand in the more desirable traditionally female occupations is not rising as fast in recent years as in the immediate postwar period (Oppenheimer 1972).

There is yet another way in which the current labor-force participation rates of older women are partially dependent on their labor-force participation in the past. Women have often tended to work on and off throughout their lives rather than continuously from young adulthood to retirement age. One increasingly common pattern in the postwar period has been for women to enter—or more likely reenter—the labor force in large numbers as their youngest child nears or reaches school age. However, the longer a woman delays reentry into the labor force, the more difficult it becomes to do so at a later age, if only for reasons of human capital depreciation. Hence, the work rates of older women would depend to some extent on the past labor-force behavior of these same cohorts. If a woman in her fifties had not reentered the labor-force sometime in her late thirties or early forties, the likelihood that she could now satisfactorily do so is considerably reduced. In addition, however, since reentry into the labor-force for women in their late thirties or forties has been on the rise in the postwar period, this means that older cohorts in 1970, for example, will be less likely to have rentered the labor force when they were in their thirties than women *currently* in their thirties. Thus a higher proportion of these older cohorts will have postponed or foregone reentry to the point when the decision not to work became irreversible. Hence, there will be a cohort effect reducing the work participation of older women due to their work behavior 10 or 20 years previously and this is not very adequately represented by the current work rates of women in their thirties and early forties.

A second—and undoubtedly complementary—explanation for the negative net effect of age on wives' labor-force participation is that some life-cycle effects are persisting despite the family-cycle variable. Here, all the factors that might lead to somewhat depressed rates among older *men* (depreciation of human capital with age, supplementary sources of income, ill-health, social security eligibility, etc.) would also affect older women's work rates. However, although the net negative effect of age is stronger the older the woman is, being the most pronounced for the 55–64 age group, it is not limited to older women alone. For example, the adjusted participation rate was 40% for wives of 45–54-year-old men compared to 45% for the 35–44-year-old group, and 50% for the wives of 25–34-year-olds (Model II). As a consequence, since most of the life-cycle effects, except those connected with approaching old age, should have been taken into account by the family-cycle variable, the cohort effect is probably dominant—especially for women under 55 years old.

Since husband's age is related to family-cycle stage, there is the question of whether problems of multicollinearity may jeopardize the cohort interpretation of the age effect when family-cycle stage is also included in the regression equation. In a simple regression of husband's age (in single years) on family cycle stage a relatively high r^2 is certainly observed—70% of the variation in age was explained by the family-cycle variable. However, I do not believe this seriously threatens the cohort interpretation of the age effect, net of other variables. First of all, from a theoretical point of view, at any one point in time age is an indicator of two different phenomena—life-cycle stage and cohort (Schaie 1967; Mason et al. 1973) As a consequence, age will, of course, be correlated with any other measure of either of these two variables. Hence the observed correlation between husband's age and family-cycle state is certainly not surprising. However, when a separate measure of this family-cycle variable is introduced into the regression equation, the age variable should then, by and large, turn into a measure of the cohort effect. From an empirical point of view, it does not seem likely that this interpretation of the situation is unwarranted. Although there is multicollinearity, it is below the extreme level. Moreover, the sample size is very large, reducing the seriousness of multicollinearity problems. Finally, the F ratio for the effect of age on wife's labor-force participation in the main regression model was also very large—182.2 (Table 6.8)—quite a bit higher than for many other variables in the same equation (see Tables 6.4 and 6.9) though well below the F ratio for the family cycle variable (Table 6.11). Hence, there is little evidence that the regression coefficients for age are unstable. If not, then the intercorrelation between family-cycle state and age should not create any serious problems for the analysis of a model including both these variables.

II. PAST MARITAL INSTABILITY AS A FACTOR IN WIVES' LABOR-FORCE PARTICIPATION

Previous studies have observed higher rates of labor-force participation among women who had experienced a marital disruption (Cain 1966; Sweet 1973). Cain argued that having been divorced would increase wives' labor-force participation—partly as a kind of insurance policy against the possibility of a future divorce and partly because wives are more likely to experience the major burden of child support in the event of a divorce (Cain

II. Past Marital Instability as a Factor

1966: 82–83, 95, 106, 109).[7] Furthermore, he found some support for his hypothesis in the 1960 1/1,000 sample from the Census. Whether the wife had been remarried had a modest but positive effect on her labor-force status (Cain 1966: 106, 109). Picking up on Cain's findings, Sweet also investigated the effect of the previous marriage experience of spouses on wives' employment probabilities (Sweet 1973: 105–107). However, instead of just considering the past marriage experience of wives, Sweet looked into that of husands as well. His findings for nonblack women were that the highest employment probabilities were for couples where both spouses had been previously married. More interesting, perhaps, was his finding that if only one spouse (husband or wife) had been previously married, the wife's employment probabilities were higher than for couples where both were in their first marriage (Sweet 1973: 106).

Both Sweet and Cain were somewhat hampered by deficiencies in the 1960 Census which only obtained information on whether spouses had been previously *married*, not whether they had been previously divorced. Since the previously widowed might behave somewhat differently from the previously divorced, the effect of marital instability can be distorted by using such data. In 1970, however, the Census Bureau determined whether first marriages no longer in existence had ended by widowhood or divorce.[8] Now that it is possible to separate the widowed from the divorced, we should be able to explore the effect of past marital instability on wives' labor-force behavior a little more rigorously, in addition to bringing more recent data to bear on the issue.

As Table 6.9 indicates, a previous divorce did increase the likelihood that wives would be in the labor force in 1970 but the magnitude of the effect depended partly on who had been divorced. If just the wife had experienced a divorce but the husband was in his first marriage, wives' adjusted labor-force participation rates were somewhat higher than for wives in first marriages for both spouses but the difference was not very impressive—only 1.6 percentage points. But, when the wife was in her first marriage and her husband had been previously divorced, the adjusted work rates were significantly higher—48% as opposed to the adjusted rate of 42% for couples

---

[7]Cain developed this rationale for the effect of past marital instability in his discussion of *black* wives and though he tested it on white wives as well, it is unclear whether he thought the same argument held for whites as well as blacks.

[8]Data on whether a person's first marriage ended in divorce were obtained indirectly: "persons ever married who reported they had been married more than once were asked if their first marriage ended because of death of spouse. This information is used in conjunction with current *marital status* to classify the entire ever married population by *marital history* [U.S. Bureau of Census 1972a:147]."

where both were in their first marriage. And when *both* spouses had been previously divorced, the likelihood that the wife was in the labor force rose somewhat higher still—to 49%.

The range in variation in the adjusted rates is not extremely large, though it is statistically significant, and hence the previous marital experience of spouses does not appear to have a major effect on wives' labor-force participation—at least compared to other variables such as family-cycle stage. However, one reason a past divorce may affect a remarried woman's labor-force status is because of economic pressures that are sometimes a consequence of divorce. For example, compared to wives in their first marriage, wives who have been divorced in the past are more likely to have economic obligations in the form of children from the previous marriage. However, not all previously divorced wives will have such economic obligations. In other words, these economic responsibilities which sometimes, but not always, are a consequence of divorce operate as an unmeasured intervening variable between a previous divorce and a remarried woman's labor-force status. Therefore, the previous marital experience variable may not fully reveal the exact nature of the effect of divorce on wives' subsequent economic behavior.

A second interesting aspect of the findings is that the relationship between the variable and wives' 1970 labor-force status is not entirely consistent with Cain's explanation of the reasons a previous divorce should have an impact on work behavior in a current marriage. According to Cain, the two major propelling factors in the situation are, first, the knowledge that a previous divorce increases the likelihood that a second marriage might also end in divorce and, second, that a previous divorce often puts special economic burdens on wives. If these were the only important factors operating, then the wife in a first marriage (to a previously divorced husband) would not have higher work rates than a previously divorced wife (married to a man in his first marriage). A wife in her first marriage is less likely to have children of her own to support from a former union than a previously divorced wife. Also, it is not clear why the effect of divorce on wives' perception of the fragility of marriage (and hence of the need for economic self-sufficiency) would be stronger when the husband rather than the wife has been previously divorced. In sum, Cain's hypothesis regarding the effect of past marital instability on wives' labor-force participation does not seem to provide an adequate account of the differentials in wives' labor-force participation between couples where just the husband and those where just the wife had been previously divorced.

An explanation for these apparently anomalous results may be found in the selective mating patterns of remarriers. Young childless divorcées are probably operating in approximately the same marriage market as single (i.e.,

II. Past Marital Instability as a Factor

never-married) women and, hence, will have a relatively good chance of finding a young single male who would be a desirable marriage partner. If so, then such marriages will usually have few or no economic encumbrances from a previous marriage. As a consequence, the subsequent labor-force behavior of these wives will closely resemble that of wives in unions where both partners are in their first marriage. And this, of course, is what was observed. The adjusted work rates of such wives were only 1.6 percentage points higher than the rates of wives in unions where both partners were in their first marriage.

However, the marriage market position of the older divorcée, often with children, is quite different. The availability—and desirability—of young single men would be considerably more limited. Hence, these women will probably find their most attractive opportunities among divorced men. In such marriages, however, there will often be economic obligations (usually in the form of children) resulting from *two* previous marriages plus the desire to maintain a certain level of living in the new marriage. Hence, economic pressures on the wife to work will be the greatest of all the marital history groups considered. In addition, if the wife had been divorced for any length of time before remarriage, she may have developed relatively strong and rewarding occupational attachments that make work a relatively permanent part of her life-style and, in fact, increase her attractiveness as a marriage partner. And, of course, the highest work rates were observed for wives in such unions.

In the case of divorced men, it seems likely that their remarriage chances include a broader range of choices than is the case for divorced women. Norms regarding the appropriate age differences between husbands and wives and the relationship of physical attractiveness to age both favor somewhat older men marrying younger women more than the reverse mating pattern. The result of this, however, is that the unions of divorced men and single women are less likely to be free of economic responsibilities incurred during a first marriage than the unions of divorced women and single men. As a consequence, the economic pressures on these married-once wives of divorced men are likely to be greater, resulting in higher work rates. Again, this is just what has been observed. Moreover, it is interesting to note that the adjusted work rates for previously single wives of divorced men was only 1.6 percentage points below that of wives in marriage where both spouses had been previously divorced.

In sum, the labor-market behavior of these wives is consistent with hypotheses about how the selective factors affecting remarriage combine with the economic pressures resulting from multiple marriages. Moreover, NCHS data on the median ages of brides and grooms by their previous marital status provide some evidence—if rather indirect—that these hypothesized

TABLE 6.9
Effect of Spouses' Previous Marital Experiences on Wives' Labor-Force Participation

Spouses' previous marital experience	Distribution of sample		Labor-force participation rates[a]	
	Number	Percentage	Unadjusted	Adjusted II[b]
Total	91,937	100.0	43.0	
Both in first marriage	74,732	81.3	42.2	42.3
Husband in first marriage—wife previously divorced	4,450	4.8	44.2	43.9
Husband previously divorced—wife in first marriage	4,519	4.9	47.6	47.7
Both previously divorced	4,567	5.0	49.7	49.3
Husband previously divorced—wife previously widowed	961	1.0	45.6	43.3
Husband previously widowed—wife previously divorced	534	0.6	47.8	48.1
Either or both previously widowed—neither previously divorced	2,174	2.4	41.0	39.7
F				27.1[c]

Source: 1970 Public Use Sample of White Couples. The adjusted participation rates were derived from the partial regression coefficients in Model II listed in Appendix D.

[a] Percentage in labor force.

[b] Model II: Adjusted for the effect of husband's peak median occupation group, husband's age, husband's relative economic status, family-cycle stage, and wife's relative educational attainment.

[c] Significant at the .01 level.

selective remarriage patterns actually occur. This is because the relative ages of men and women at marriage should be different, depending on their previous marital status and the marriage market selectivities just outlined. Brides and grooms alike should be young when both are entering their first marriage. Divorced brides marrying single grooms should be young women reentering the marriage market of the single—though perhaps the somewhat older segment of that marriage market. Hence, they will be marrying relatively young males. Third, the greater ease with which divorce males—both with and without children—can marry younger women should lead to a greater age gap when they marry single women than when divorced females

II. Past Marital Instability as a Factor

marry single males. Finally, if divorced women who are older or who have children are less likely to marry younger males but are more likely to find their greatest remarriage prospects among older divorced males, then the ages of brides and grooms should be older when both have been previously divorced. Table 6.10 shows 1969 data on the median ages of brides and grooms by their previous marital status and supports all these predictions.

In sum, the influence of marital instability on wives' labor-force participation is probably a rather complicated affair. It will, to be sure, probably affect women's motivations to work because past instability sensitizes them to the possiblity of a future instability and all its attendant economic hardships. In addition, however, what has received less consideration is that, given certain social norms defining the characteristics of desirable mates, separation and divorce probably release people into rather different marriage markets depending on their sex, age, and family responsibilities. This, in turn, leads to certain selective remarriage patterns which will affect the economic load placed on the subsequent marriage(s). As the data suggest, this not only affects previously divorced women but the previously single wives of divorced men.

Only a small proportion of the couples had one or both partners previously divorced in 1970. However, the proportion that will fall into these higher work propensity categories will rise significantly over time, given our rapidly rising divorce rate. After an early postwar peak in 1945–1947, the divorce rate declined and for a number of years remained rather stable at a level of about 15–17 divorces annually per 1,000 married women 14–44 years old. Since the early 1960s, however, the rate has risen considerably—from 17 in 1963–1965 to 32 per 1,000 in 1972–1974 (Norton and Glick 1976). The significance of these trends can be better appreciated by considering the proportion of people in successive cohorts who are likely to have their first marriage, at least, end in divorce. In an article published in 1973, Glick and Norton estimated that although 19% of the women in the cohort born in the 1920–1924 period would have their first marriages end in divorce, the proportion would probably go up to 29% for the cohort born in 1940–1944 (Glick and Norton 1973: 309). However, the rise in divorce has been so rapid that more recent estimates are that, instead of 29%, 34% of this latter cohort of women will have their first marriages end in divorce and so will 38% of the next younger cohort—those born in 1945–1949 (U.S. Bureau of the Census 1976b: 6; see also Preston and McDonald, 1979). In sum, divorce is becoming an increasingly common cause of marital dissolution in our society. One consequence of this will undoubtedly be a long-term positive impact on wives' labor-force participation, affecting some women in their first marriages as well as remarried divorcées.

TABLE 6.10
Median Age at Marriage of Bride and Groom by Previous Marital Status of Each Partner: Marriage Registration Area, 1969[a]

Marital status of each partner	Median age
Both single	
Bride	20.4
Groom	22.2
Bride divorced, groom single	
Bride	26.3
Groom	26.6
Bride single, groom divorced	
Bride	23.3
Groom	29.2
Both divorced	
Bride	33.1
Groom	37.3
Bride divorced, groom widowed	
Bride	45.0
Groom	53.0
Bride widowed, groom divorced	
Bride	46.4
Groom	47.7
Bride widowed, groom widowed	
Bride	58.3
Groom	63.8

Source: U.S. National Center for Health Statistics 1973: Table 5.
[a] The Marriage Registration Area includes 39 states plus the District of Columbia. This table, however, excludes data from Michigan and Ohio.

III. FAMILY-CYCLE STAGE

Two features of the family cycle should particularly affect wives' labor-market behavior. One is the time demands children make on their mothers, an aspect of the family cycle that has received by far the most attention in previous research. The other dimension is the direct money cost of children, which has been particularly stressed in this study (see also Smith 1977). Of necessity, both these aspects of the family cycle are measured by the number and ages of children present and their joint consideration forms the basis of the family cycle variable I have contructed (see Table 6.11). This variable represents an effort to make a rough distinction between typical chronological stages of the family cycle as characterized by differences in the ages and number of children. At the same time, it tries to vary time demands and costs of children so that in some cases they work together to raise or

III. Family-Cycle Stage

lower wives' work rates whereas in other cases their separate effects work in opposite directions.[9] The reason for this is to attempt to verify that both factors—time demands and child-care costs—instead of just one, actually affect wives' labor-force participation. We will discuss this aspect of the problem in greater detail somewhat later in this section. The family-cycle variable was created partially to achieve an aproximate representation of typical chronological stages of the family cycle. However, since couples vary in their completed family size and in child spacing, they will not all pass through every stage distinguished. But most couples who have children will be represented by several of the stages shown. Take, for example, the case of a family with a completed fertility of two children. Assuming their children are only 2 or 3 years apart and the first child was born before the husband reached age 30, this couple will progressively pass through the following numbered stages represented in the family-cycle variable:[10]

1. No children present, husband under 30
2. One child under 6
3. All children under 6, two or more present
4. One child under 6 and one 6–11
9. All children 6–11, two or more present
10. One child 6–11 and one 12–17
15. All children 12–17, two or more present
16. One child 12–17 and one 18–24
19. All children 18–24, two or more present
18. One child 18–24 present
20. No children under 25 present, husband 30 or older

Depending on family size and spacing, the set of stages any particular couple will progress through varies and there are a variety of "typical" stages that could be created from all the possibilities distinguished. Hence, to

---

[9] I did not use the child expenditure estimates developed "earlier" in the study for a number of reasons. One important one was that the present regressions were already planned and being set up before I had developed the expenditure estimates. Second, since children are both cost and time intensive, utilizing the expenditure estimates would have tapped only one dimension of the effect of children. Trying to introduce another variable which would have then measured the time demand aspect of children might have resulted in serious problems of collinearity. Besides, I think the expenditure estimates tend to understate the costs to young couples incurred by trying to set up a household suitable for children. Of course, whether any particular young couple are or are not trying to set up such a household, we cannot tell. In sum, it seemed simpler just to construct a family-cycle variable that distinguished families by the number and ages of children directly, and in this way try to get at both time and expenditure demands on parents.

[10] Due to the large number of categories in this dummy variable, it was not possible to distinguish couples by too many family sizes. This was particularly impractical since, even in this large sample, the number of families with, for example, three or four children aged 6–11 was very small, due to the spacing constraints such an age span imposes.

simplify the discussion and presentation of results, the family-cycle variable was organized according to the age of the youngest child, in order to roughly but systematically distinguish periods where time demands vary.

First there is the stage where the couple is young and no children have yet been born, which is characterized by minimal home demands being made on the wife's time (Category 1 of the family-cycle variable). However, the economic difficulties of the first life-cycle squeeze will be especially severe at this point. The result should be high work rates by such wives and this is indeed the case. Both their unadjusted and adjusted work rates were the highest of the 20 family-cycle categories under consideration. Second, there is the stage when children are present and at least one is under 6 years of age (Categories 2 through 7 of the variable). This group includes families who were just starting childbearing as well as those who had recently completed it. Some of the couples with only young children may still have been in the first squeeze or just emerging from it but they were also generally in the position of having the maximum time demands made on the mother. Hence, as other researchers have found, the adjusted work rates of these wives were very low—by far the lowest among the 20 family-cycle categories. For example, for those with two or more children under 6, the adjusted participation rate was only 14% compared to the high of 61% for young wives without children present. In sum, the presence of young children still had a very strong negative impact on wives' labor-force participation in 1970 despite the rapid incease in work rates for young mothers during the preceding decade.

In the third general stage distinguished the youngest child is in the 6–11 age group and, presumably, a high proportion of couples will have completed their childbearing (Categories 8 through 11). This group includes all couples with young school-age children present, but there will be variations in the extent to which there are older school children as well. Time demands made on the mother will be easing off but the direct cost of children will be increasing. The result is the higher work rates of these mothers. For example, the adjusted work rates for wives with children under 6 varied from 14 to 35% in the labor force whereas for those with their youngest aged 6–11, the adjusted participation rates varied from 39% for those with two or more children aged 6–11 to 45% for those with a 6–11- and a 12–17-year-old.

Fourth, there is the stage when the youngest child is in the 12–24 age group (Categories 14 through 19). All couples in this group had at least one adolescent or young adult child but varied in the number of such children and in the presence of older—college- or working age—children present. In addition, for many families a certain (but unknown) number of children were away at college and not enumerated in the household but still adding to the family's child-care expenses. In short, couples in this group were well into the second life-cycle squeeze but, unlike mothers of 6–11-year-olds, had fewer time-intensive child-care responsibilities. As a consequence, we observe, as

III. Family-Cycle Stage

expected, much higher work rates than for mothers whose youngest was in the 6–11 age group. The difference varied, of course, by the number of children present and the ages of the other children, but were consistent with our expectations regarding the effect of such factors on mothers' labor-force participation. For example, if the family had two or more children aged 6–11, the adjusted rate was 39% in the labor force whereas if there were two or more children 12–17, the adjusted rate rose to 53%. Or, if there were two children in the family, one aged 6–11 and the other 12–17, the adjusted rate was 45% in the labor force whereas in the case of the two-child family where one was aged 12–17 and the other 18–24, the adjusted rate was higher still—56% in the labor force.

In sum, then, the joint effects of greater child-care expenses combined with the reduced time demands of older children resulted in higher work rates among mothers of older children though the differences between their work rates and those of mothers whose youngest child was 6–11 are not as great as the differences between the latter mothers and those with children under 6.

Finally, there are the older wives with no children present in the household (the husband was 30 or older). If the lack of children present is a good indicator of freedom from financial responsibility for children, then such wives had passed the second life-cycle squeeze and hence were under less pressure to work. Our measurement will be somewhat faulty in this respect, however, as there is no way of detecting economic responsibilities for children no longer in the home—those away at college, for example. Furthermore, some of these couples may be preparing for a third life-cycle squeeze—the economic difficulties often experienced by retired couples. With no children in the home, the time demands made on them are greatly reduced, facilitating a more extensive labor-force envolvement. But these women were older, on the average, and life-cycle and cohort effects on willingness to work plus human capital depreciation may have reduced their likelihood of working. In sum, a number of factors tend to offset each other for women in this family-cycle stage and it is hard to make a priori prediction about what their net effects would be. As it turns out, these wives were about as likely to be in the labor-force as wives with their youngest child in the 12–24 age group. These results might indicate that without the propelling effect of expensive adolescent children in the home, the lack of time demands from children is not in itself sufficient to greatly elevate the work rates of such women.

Time Demands versus Child-Care Expenses

So far, we have just considered how the operation of life-cycle squeezes and the time demands of children jointly affect wives' labor-force participation. The question is whether we can ever separate these two dimension of family-cycle stage. I am not sure that, in actuality, it *will* be possible to measure the separate effects of these two factors on wives' labor-force participation. However, it should at least be possible to determine whether both or only one is affecting the propensity of wives to work. First, let us review the conceptualization of the problem.

We begin with the premise that the ages of children are related to two factors that will affect the propensity of wives to work. First, the younger the children are, the more time intensive they are and, as a result, the harder it has been for their mothers to work. Conversely, the older children become, the fewer time demands they make and, given other motivations to work, the less the deterrent effect of children on wives' labor-force participation. Certainly there is ample evidence that the time demands of children are highly related to their ages (Morgan *et al.,* 1966: Chapter 8; Hill and Stafford 1974; Turchi 1975: Chapter 3).

Second, as we have seen in considerable detail, the age of children is very much related to their cost and here the relationship is direct rather than inverse, as is the case with time demands. Older children (up to a point, of course) are more expensive than younger children and, because of this, encourage wives' labor-force participation. Thus, these two factors operate jointly. Since older children are less time intensive (promoting a greater labor-force participation) but more goods intensive (also promoting labor-force participation) it becomes impossible to disentangle the influence of each of these factors when both are being measured by the age of a child. However, we ought to be able to ascertain whether these factors together have a causal role in wives' labor-force participation, although it will be impossible to measure their separate effects. This can be done by considering the *number* of children present in the household, as well as their ages.

The number of children present affects both the time demands made on mothers (usually the one who has had principal responsibility for children) and the economic pressures to work. More children are more work but they are also more expensive.[11] By considering the number of children present, as well as their age, it should be possible to construct stituations where both the cost of children *and* their time demands increase. When we consider age alone the time demands typically *de*crease as expense *in*creases and thus the two factors tend to reinforce each other. However, by holding age of children roughly constant and varying the number of children present, the time demand effect should offset the expense effect (more children take more time and are more expensive), thus permitting a test of whether one or both factors are operative. If the time demand factor were dominant then, where both time demands and costs are greater (two children 12–17 years old as opposed to

---

[11] See Appendix E for an extended comment on the time demands of children.

III. Family-Cycle Stage

one), wives' labor-force participation should be less, as it is when younger versus older children are present. However, if the expense factor were dominant than the opposite would be the case—wives' labor-force participation would be greater, as it is when older versus younger children are present. However, if *both* factors are operating (the time demand factor to decrease participation and the cost factor to increase it) then the effect of the two variables would be to offset each other (i.e., cancel out). An important exception to this would be the case where the additional children are quite young. This is because young children—preschoolers and young schoolagers—are at the most time-consuming but least expensive ages.[12] Hence, where comparisons involve increases in the number of *young* children, the time demand effects will probably outweigh expenditure effects. As a result, the work rates of such wives should be less.

In sum, by considering the number of children, as well as their ages, it ought to be possible to determine whether both the time demand and child-care cost factors are operating or only one is operating. However, it does not seem possible to measure the separate effects of these two variables with the data at hand.

Let us consider, first, comparisons where the increased number of children is likely to involve more young children in the home so that we would expect the work rates of wives so affected to be depressed. There are four comparisons where this is likely to be the case.

1. All children are under 6 years of age.
2. Children are in both the under-6 and 6–11 age groups.
3. Children under age 6 as well as children 12–24 years old are present.
4. All children are in the 6–11 age group.

In the case where all children are in the 6–11 age group, although they are presumably of school age, the presence of two or more in the 6–11 group indicates that, in a certain proportion of families at least, the youngest will be nearer 6 than 11 and, hence, this is a borderline situation of high time demands.

In all four comparisons the mothers of larger families had substantially depressed adjusted and unadjusted labor-force rates (Table 6.11). For example, in the case where all children are under 6, the adjusted rate was 25% for mothers of one child under 6 but 14% for mothers of two or more children under 6. Where children were in the under-6 and 6–11 age groups, the adjusted rate for mothers of two children was 25% but where 3 or more children were present it was 18% in the labor force. And where all children

---

[12]Except that having children at all tends to commit couples to certain types of capital investments they might not otherwise make.

TABLE 6.11
Effect of Family-Cycle Stage on Wives' Labor-Force Participation

Family-cycle stage	Distribution of sample Number	Distribution of sample Percentage	Labor-force participation rates[a] Unadjusted	Labor-force participation rates[a] Adjusted II[b]
Total	91,937	100.0	43.0	
No children under 25 present, husband under 30	5,862	6.4	72.8	61.4
Children under 6 present				
All under 6: 1	7,158	8.2	32.7	24.8
All under 6: 2+	6,084	6.6	20.6	14.3
Under 6 and 6–11: 2	3,178	3.5	30.4	25.2
Under 6 and 6–11: 3+	5,498	6.0	21.7	17.6
Widespread–A[c]	678	0.7	35.5	35.3
Widespread–B[d]	4,702	5.1	27.5	26.8
Youngest 6–11				
All 6–11: 1	2,499	2.7	46.6	44.3
All 6–11: 2+	3,336	3.6	42.2	38.7
6–11 and 12–17: 2	2,922	3.2	45.4	45.4
6–11 and 12–17: 3+	5,753	6.3	43.7	43.3
6–11 and 18–24: 2+	705	0.8	45.7	48.8
6–11, 12–17, and 18–24: 3+	2,064	2.2	44.8	47.4
Youngest 12 or over				
All 12–17: 1	5,225	5.7	50.2	53.8
All 12–17: 2+	3,616	3.9	51.9	53.4
12–17 and 18–24: 2	2,494	2.7	51.8	56.0
12–17 and 18–24: 3+	1,837	2.0	50.3	54.5
All 18–24: 1	4,348	4.7	50.7	57.1
All 18–24: 2+	941	1.0	50.1	55.2
No children under 25 present, husband over 30	22,677	24.7	47.5	53.8
F				326.9[e]

Source: 1970 Public Use Sample of White Couples. The adjusted participation rates were derived from the partial regression coefficients in Regression II in Appendix D.

[a] Percentage in labor force.
[b] Model II: Adjusted for husband's peak median occupation, husband's intraoccupational relative economic status, previous marital experience of spouses, wife's relative educational attainment, and husband's age.
[c] All under 6 and 12 or older.
[d] Under 6, 6–11, and 12–17; 18–24 years, if present, are included as well.
[e] Significant at the .01 level.

III. Family-Cycle Stage

were aged 6–11 the adjusted work rate for mothers of one child was 44% as opposed to 39% for mothers of two or more children. In sum, when comparisons involve greater or lesser numbers of young children, the time demand factor certainly seems to dominate the effect of family-cycle stage on wives' labor-force participation.

In the case of comparisons involving older children, however, the situation changes. There are five comparisons possible here.

1. The children are in the 6–11 and 12–17 age groups.
2. Children aged 6–11 and 18–24 are present.
3. All children are aged 12–17
4. The children are in the 12–17 and 18–24 age groups.
5. All children are in the 18–24 age group.

In all cases involving these five sets of comparisons, the differences in work rates are trivial—on the order of 2 percentage points or less. For example, where all children were in the 6–11 and 12–17 age groups, the adjusted rate was 45% in the labor force if two children only were present and 43% if three or more children were present. If all children were 12–17, the adjusted rate was 54% if there was only one child present and 53% if there were two or more. If all children present were in the 12–17 and 18–24 age groups, the adjusted rate was 56% if there were two present and 54% if there were three of more present.

In general, then, when the increased number of children present involves *older* and, hence, more expensive but less time-consuming children, the differences between the work rates become trivial. This indicates, I think, that in such situations, the time demand and expense factors tend to cancel each other out. However, when comparisons involve families with more versus fewer very *young* children, as we might expect, the time demand factor seems to outweigh the expense factor, resulting in a substantial reduction in wives' labor-force participation.

These findings may seem at odds with Bowen and Finegan who dismiss the higher cost of older children as a factor in wives' labor-force participation (Bowen and Finegan 1969: 97–100). They do this on the basis of their finding that the adjusted participation rates of wives in households with children in both the 6–13 and 14–17 age groups were virtually identical to the adjusted rate for wives with only 6–13-year-olds in the home. Thus, they argue that the *added* presence of older, more costly 14–17-year-olds did not seem to lead to higher adjusted work rates (Bowen and Finegan 1969: 100). However, they neglected to consider the numbers of children, as well as their ages. The category that included only children 6–13 years old consisted of families with fewer children, on the average, than the category that included families with children in both the 6–13 and 14–17 age groups. A family must have had at least two children to have been included in the latter category but only one was necessary for membership in the 6–13 age group. Besides, the wider interval of the 6–13 and 14–17 age group categories increases the likelihood that three or more children were present. Although I used slightly different age intervals in my analysis of the 1960 PUS data, my data are more than sufficient to indicate that important differences in family size existed between these two types of families. For example, 55% of the white couples in my 1960 PUS who had children just in the 6–11 age group had only one child. Only 9% had three or more children. But 50% of the couples with children in both the 6–11 and 12–17 age groups had three or more children. More children make more time demands on the mother, counteracting their greater cost. They may, in part, even represent a premeditated trade-off between work and fertility. So, it is not surprising to find that Bowen and Finegan's 1960 adjusted work rates were no higher for mothers of children in the 6–13 and 14–17 age groups. My own multiple-regression findings for the 1970 PUS, for example, indicate that for families with children in both the 6–11 and 12–17 age groups, the adjusted participation rates were slightly less if there were three or more present than if only two children were present (Table 6.11).

Summary

As other investigators have found, the regression analyses just discussed indicate that there is a positive relationship between the age of children and the wife's propensity to work. This is consistent with the hypothesis that younger children are less expensive (after the initial first life-cycle squeeze) but more demanding of the mother's time whereas older children are less time intensive but more goods intensive. Also, a closer examination of the family-cycle variable indicates that when we hold age of children roughly constant, but vary the number of children present, the resulting adjusted work rates provide further (if somewhat indirect) support for this thesis.

IV. CONCLUSION

This chapter has focused on the impact of socioeconomic pressures on wives' 1970 labor-force status, using dummy-variable regression analysis as the statistical tool. A number of measurement and methodological difficulties have precluded a thoroughly rigorous analysis of the problem. Nevertheless, several of the findings appear to be highly significant and often rather surprising.

IV. Conclusion

One important finding has been that the hypothesis of the lower white-collar squeeze seems to receive considerable support. Even controlling for such possibly important confounding factors as the number and ages of children, as well as the wife's educational attainment, the work propensities of Group III *white*-collar wives were not only higher than those of Group I and II white-collar wives, but, in addition, were usually above those of Group III or IV *blue*-collar wives. This was even true in cases where the median earnings of the white-collar husband were higher than those of the blue-collar husbands, and, hence, the presumed income effect should have led to *lower* work rates for such white-collar wives. In consequence, these finding certainly seem to suggest that lower-level white-collar families are under particular economic stress with one common solution to this problem being the employment of the wife. Another important result was that the negative relationship between the husband's economic status (however measured) and wives' work propensities was weak among the lower-level income groups. Furthermore, this seems to have been partly because while there was a strong inverse relationship between the peak median occupational group of the husband and wives' work rates within white-collar major occupational groups, such was not generally the case between different peak median manual occupations. This, in large part, may be the major factor in the weak relationship between husband's income (or peak median income group) and wife's labor-force status which was observed for the lower end of the income distribution. Hence, wives' employment seems to have been a less frequent strategy for maintaining an economic homeostasis within blue-collar than in white-collar families—at least as of the 1970 Census.

Other variables in the regression analysis also provide evidence that economic pressures increased wives' labor-force participation. Of particular importance, given the emphasis of this study on the role of the second life-cycle squeeze, has been the impact of adolescent and young adult children in the home. Although the separate impact of money and time costs of children on wives' labor-market behavior are almost imposible to completely disentangle, the evidence supports the idea that money cost of children is an important factor in wives' labor-force participation. In other words, the second squeeze was a major factor in the labor-force participation of older wives during the period covered by these PUS data.

In general, then, the analysis of this chapter indicates that economic motivations were an important factor in wives' labor-force participation, whatever the impact of other factors, many of which are impossible to measure with these data (e.g., changing sex-role ideologies). The next question which we will tackle in Chapter 7 is the impact of wives' potential and actual socioeconomic contribution on their labor-force participation.

7

Wives' Potential Socioeconomic Contribution and Their Labor-Force Status

I. THE SOCIOLOGY OF WOMEN'S ECONOMIC ROLE IN THE FAMILY

This chapter will investigate how wives' potential socioeconomic contributions to the family affect their labor-force participation. However, before becoming immersed in the empirical analysis, let us first undertake a more general theoretical consideration of the nature of wives' socioeconomic role in the family.

Neoclassical economics has relatively well developed theories regarding the effect of wives' potential economic contribution on their actual work behavior. However, economic theory has concerned itself primarily with the impact of the wife's potential *wage* rather than with more sociological factors such as the possible effect the of wife's potential occupational *status* on her working. Of course, if income and status were perfectly correlated, then one might possibly ignore the potential status impact of wives' working. However, this is not the case, as students of social stratification are well aware. Moreover, most studies of the "achieved" status of women indicate that, however occupational status is measured, it does not appear to lead to the same economic returns for women as for men (Featherman and Hauser

1976; Treiman and Terrell 1975). Hence, conceivably, status and economic factors could sometimes conflict in the direction of their influence on wives' economic behavior. As a consequence, my major concern, as a sociologist, is to investigate the influence of both these factors together on women's economic role and in a way that is compatible with the relativistic model on which this study is based. Given that goal, are there any existing sociological theories dealing with both social status and economic factors which can help guide the empirical analysis?

Status issues have, of course, been traditionally of considerable interest to sociologists. Furthermore, theories do exist that are relevant to the whole question of the *relative* socioeconomic impact of wives working. However, such theories were developed in what almost amounts to a different era in American society and hence require some modifications to make them relevant tools for the analysis of recent patterns and changes in wives' economic role.

In the 1960s and early 1970s, sociologists were faced with the uncomfortable situation that women's actual economic behavior was rapidly diverging from traditional sociological theory regarding women's economic role in the family. Since the 1940s married women's labor-force participation had risen enormously. This was readily apparent by the 1950 Census and since then the changes have been even more dramatic. Although these changes started sometime in the 1940s, they largely went unnoticed by most sociologists until well into the 1960s. Why this is so is a matter of some speculation, of course. However, I think one of the reasons is that many sociologists at that time were not used to dealing with census-type data and hence behavioral changes that could have been readily detected by this means were easily overlooked. Indeed, it was primarily among demographers and economists that women's changing behavior first came under close research scrutiny. Also, sociological theory had traditionally argued that women's socioeconomic role in the family is negligible. Hence this theoretical bias also probably delayed sociologists' perception of the considerable changes that were actually occurring.

The traditional assumption that women's economic role in the family is unimportant was particularly characteristic of stratification research which had typically concerned itself with measuring and studying the socioeconomic status of males alone. This approach was based on the long-accepted theory that an adult female's socioeconomic status is determined by her husband because a woman's major role is that of wife and mother whereas it is only her husband who has an important occupational role. Occupation, in turn, has been generally considered the major source of socioeconomic status in our society. Hence, by ascertaining the occupational status of a man one could, at the same time, determine the socioeconomic status of his wife and, incidentally, of his minor children as well (Parsons 1943; Centers 1949; Turner 1964; Warner et al. 1941).[1] Thus as long as wives' economic role in the family could be considered negligible the conceptualization and measurement of socioeconomic status—whether of individuals or of family units—had considerable theoretical simplicity.

In recent years, however, there has been a rapidly blossoming interest among stratification researchers in measuring the socioeconomic status and social mobility of women. This is partly because of a resurgence of interest in marriage as a status-attainment process and partly because of a growing recognition of the status implications of the enormous increases in married women's labor-force participation. One group of researchers has been primarily interested in mobility, following very much in the footsteps of such classic studies as Blau and Ducan's *The American Occupational Structure* (1967). However, instead of just analyzing samples of males, they have increasingly focused on women as well (Sewall, Hauser, and Wolf 1980; Featherman and Hauser 1976; McClendon 1976; Chase 1975; Glenn, Ross, and Tully 1974; Dejong, Brawer, and Robin 1971; Treiman and Terrell 1975; Tyree and Treas 1974). Their concern has been primarily to measure intergenerational mobility of women, typically taking father's occupation as the origin point. For the destination status, two alternatives have generally been chosen. One is the woman's (usually a wife's) own occupation to get at a measure of social mobility via occupational achievement. The alternative destination status often selected is the socioeconomic status of the woman's husband, the goal here being to study marital mobility.

Unfortunately, by opting for only one of these alternatives, such studies present a unidimensional view of socioeconomic status. They look at either the wife's own occupational status *or* her status as derived from her husband but not both simultaneously.[2] Hence, to the extent a wife's (or husband's, for that matter) *overall* socioeconomic status is partly a function of her (his) labor-force and occupational status and partly a function of her husband's (his wife's) occupational status, these approaches cannot give us an overall measure of the socioeconomic status of wives, their husbands, or the family as a unit. Nor can they enlighten us on the relationship between the occupational statuses of husbands and wives. They fail in this because, in effect, the rules of the game have changed. Measuring the occupational status of one individual in a family now frequently provides nothing more than a partal indicator of either the *family's* socioeconomic status or that of the

---

[1] For a critical discussion of these traditional views of women's socioeconomic role, see Day (1961), Watson and Barth (1964), Ackers (1973), Haug (1973), Ritter and Hargens (1975).

[2] Tyree and Treas consider both, but not simultaneously, looking on them as alternate routes to status attainment.

individual in question because socioeconomic status will be influenced by the occupational achievements of other members of the family as well—most notably by the spouse for adult married people. This is not to say that these studies necessarily claim that they are measuring overall socioeconomic status and that they have failed to live up to this claim but that, whether or not they have tried to construct an overall measure, they have not succeeded in doing so. Hence, mobility research is no longer the source of measures of general status position it was in those simpler days when the unchallenged assumption prevailed that only the husband's socioeconomic characteristics counted. What we have instead is a rather fragmented view of the socioeconomic status of both individuals and families.

Although current mobility investigators have not attempted to create a composite measure of socioeconomic status for either individuals or family units, a number of other investigators have dealt more explicitly with this problem—arguing that the wife's as well as the husband's occupational status should be jointly considered in determining the socioeconomic status of an individual or family (see Day 1961; Barth and Watson 1967; Ritter and Hargens 1975; Haug 1973; Rossi, Sampson, Bose, Jasso, and Passel 1974; Sampson and Rossi 1975; and van Velsor and Beeghley 1979). However, despite the valuable contributions made by such studies in social stratification, there is still much to be done. For one thing, these investigators were primarily concerned with the issue of whether wives, as well as husbands, have an impact on the wife's or family's socioeconomic status. They were not overly interested, however, in the *relationship* between the husband's socioeconomic characteristics and his wife's economic role in the family, including the socioeconomic implications of her working. But this is precisely the problem of major concern here. We have, for example, already considered in depth how the husband's socioeconomic characteristics may be one factor in the growth of economic pressures for wives to work. In addition, however, the husband's socioeconomic characteristics may not only influence his wife's labor-market behavior because of their role in the creation of economic pressures but because of their influence on her *response* to such pressures or on her propensity to work for other reasons as well. And the effect of the husband's socioeconomic characteristics may not only be limited to influencing the wife's propensity to work but, via this, it will influence the socioeconomic level of her occupation as well. This will occur if the potential socioeconomic effect of any particular occupational attachment on the part of the wife influences her work behavior. For example, the wife's socioeconomic status, as derived from her husband, may sometimes discourage her employment unless occupational opportunities the family defines as "socially acceptable" are available.

In sum, the problem we face is whether we shall be limited to a purely empirical analysis of the effect of the husband's socioeconomic characteristics on his wife's economic role in the family or to an analysis guided only by economic theories. Or is there not a third alternative—the development of a sociologically oriented theoretical perspective? I think such a perspective can be achieved by taking as a point of departure certain traditional sociological theories regarding sex roles. Subjecting them to critical analysis we can then modify them to achieve a theoretical approach that is sociological in nature but is, at the same time, more in keeping with the emerging realities of men's and women's socioeconomic behavior and characteristics.

Although a number of sociologists have discussed the nature of women's socioeconomic role in the family, one of the most important theories dealing with this issue is found in the writings of Talcott Parsons.[3] Partly because Parsons's work has been so influential over the years, and also because it constitutes one of the more carefully elaborated statements on the topic, I will limit my discussion of sociologically "traditional" views of women's economic and family roles to a critical examination of some aspects of Parsons's approach. In addition, Parsons's work is of particular interest here because his theory about women's economic role in the family is mainly developed in terms of certain hypotheses regarding the causal relationship between husbands' and wives' occupational behavior.[4]

Parsons's discussion of the nature and determinants of women's socioeconomic role in the family has a number of facets. Particularly important is his argument that sex-role segregation is a functional necessity for marital stability in our society. As a consequence, Parsons argues, most women must be relatively excluded from the occupational system, "at least in a status-determinant sense [Parsons 1949:195]." This is so, Parsons maintains, because the marriage relationship is structurally unsupported in an urban industrial society and, as such, is fragile and easily disrupted without protective mechanisms. The major mechanism preventing disruptive competition between husband and wife is a sex-role segregation where the dominant male role is the occupational role and the dominant female role is that of housewife and mother (Parsons 1949:193). Marital stability also requires sex-role segregation, according to Parsons, because conjugal soli-

---

[3]Parsons's theories regarding the relationship of the family and occupational systems in our society seem to have been first formulated in the early 1940s as many of his articles on the topic date from this period (Parsons 1942, 1943, 1949, 1955). My discussion of the theories is primarily based on his 1949 article in Anshen's reader as this seems to me the most complete statement of his position.

[4]For an earlier and in some ways more extensive version of this argument see Oppenheimer 1977.

darity is incompatible with drawing class distinctions among members of the nuclear family. Since the major source of socioeconomic status is an occupation in our society, if a married woman works this raises the possibility of disruptive competition between the spouses. Again, if marital stability is to be maintained, married women must either avoid work or if they do work it must be at an occupation that is not status competitive—for example, it must be at a "job" rather than a "career" and "ordinarily does not produce a comparable proportion of the family income [Parsons 1949:193ff]."

Parsons's primary interest was in the conditions of marital stability rather than in the nature of the wife's socioeconomic impact on the family. Therefore the exact meaning of his statements regarding the nature of wives' work involvement is somewhat ambiguous when our major interest shifts to the extent and nature of the wife's socioeconomic contribution to the family. Nevertheless, although the main thrust of his argument is that if a wife works her lower-status occupation prevents disruptive competition, an additional implication of his position seems to be that the wife's nonthreatening type of job will make an insignificant impact on the family's socioeconomic status. Thus he argues: "the separation of the sex roles in our society is such as, for the most part, to remove women from the kind of occupational status which is important for the determination of the status of a family [Parsons 1954a: 80]."

In general, then, Parsons's theory supports and elaborates on the traditional assumptions of stratification research. He argues that women's socioeconomic role in the family had to be minor to avoid the disruptive competition that would arise if the wife as well as the husband were working. Competition was also a danger, he maintains, because of the frequent status discrepancies that were likely to arise if both spouses had occupational attachments.

In undertaking a critical assessment of the relevance of Parsons's theory to women's socioeconomic role in the family I shall scrutinize quite carefully his emphasis on the importance of status consistency within the family. I will argue, with Parsons, that status consistency—or at least a liberalized version of the concept which I shall call *status compatibility*—is important in maintaining family solidarity. However, the reasons I think status compatibility is important are very different from those posited by Parsons. His reasons have to do with the deleterious effects of competition whereas the argument presented here emphasizes the role of status maintenance and status enhancement as the crucial factor. The desire for status maintenance or enhancement is seen as encouraging the employment of wives under certain conditions and discouraging it under others. Furthermore, if wives do work, it will influence the nature of their socioeconomic contribution.

Status Compatibility and the Problems of Status Maintenance

One reason that Parsons gives for the necessity of sex-role segregation is that conjugal solidarity is inconsistent with drawing class distinctions between husband and wife. If such distinctions did arise, he argues, disruptive competition would occur. Whether or not disruptive competition will necessarily occur, it is clear that Parsons' position is based mainly on his assessment of how the internal dynamics of the conjugal family operate.[5] However, the problem might be more profitably approached from a somewhat broader perspective—that is, by focusing, in addition, on the family as a basic unit in the stratification system. If we view families within the context of the larger stratification system and hence in competition with other families for status then it is clear that one problem families face, as "solidary" units, involves status maintenance or improvement. This perspective on the family is, moreover, thoroughly consistent with Parsons's own views. He emphasizes the universalistic and achievement orientation (i.e., competitive nature) of our occupational system as well as seeing the family as a basic unit of stratification that is inevitably concerned with its status position relative to other families in the society (Parsons 1954a:77ff, 88ff, 1954b:422ff).

However, Parsons did not really follow through on this picture of the family in analyzing the determinants of women's economic role. Looking at the family as a solidary unit concerned with status maintenance and enhancement should help us see how these larger status concerns can promote rather than minimize wives' economic role while, at the same time, structuring the nature of that role.

To begin with, by focusing on the family's concern for status maintenance, it is clear that a working wife could be a considerable socioeconomic asset. To some extent Parsons recognized the importance of economic pressures promoting wives' labor-force participation in his assessment of the more important economic role of women among the "low ranges of occupational and income status" although he thought a high price was paid for this in marital instability (Parsons 1949:194). However, as we have already seen in considerable detail in this study, economic pressures for the wife to work are not just limited to lower-class families but are operating throughout society and are probably increasing over time. Moreover, opportunities for wives to

---

[5]For a discussion of whether competition is as important a problem in the two-worker family as Parsons maintains, see Oppenheimer 1977. By and large, I argue that Parsons overestimated the competitive difficulties inherent in such a situation and failed to consider a number of factors that could prevent or neutralize the competive conflicts he saw as inevitable.

work rose rapidly in the postwar period, encouraging this response to a desire for a higher family income (Oppenheimer 1970, 1973).

An emphasis on the importance of the family as a unit in a larger stratification system leads to a somewhat different interpretation from that of Parsons of the role of status consistency. Thus Parsons argues that it is essential to have status consistency within the family because status discrepancies would lead to disruptive competition. I would argue, with Parsons, that status consistency is important but I think there are more compelling reasons for its importance than the possibility of disruptive competition. Consistency is significant not so much because highly divergent statuses would lead to competition but because they would threaten the status position of the family as a whole as well as the statuses of individual members of the family. Parsons does not take this possibility into consideration because, first, he neglects to keep in mind the status-maintenance problems of the family and, second, he develops only a one-sided view of the negative consequences of status inconsistency. Thus Parsons's theory implies that the only labor-force involvement of wives compatible with family stability is one where the wife has a lower-level job than her husband—a job which, as a consequence, somehow does not count. Presumably, if she should have a job at a higher socioeconomic level, such a discrepancy would "put an intolerable strain on the imperative of class equality" and hence on the marriage (Parsons 1949:195). However, one might just as well argue that if there are negative effects stemming from a wife having a *higher* occupational status than her husband, there will also be negative effects if she has a much *lower* status. Thus Parsons is not consistent in the development of his basic argument—the importance of status homogeneity within the family. What his theory comes perilously close to being is an argument for the functional necessity *not* of equivalent evaluation within the family but of male superiority.

It is possible to start with Parsons's original idea—the importance of status homogeneity—and develop it in a more relaxed and evenhanded fashion, without any recourse to functional imperatives. First of all, I think it is reasonable to assume that the social statuses of closely associated individuals tend to rub off on each other. Because status liabilities, as well as benefits, tend to be shared among intimates, there is a strain towards status consistency within social groups such as the family. This is so because when one or more of the statuses of one member of the family is much lower than the statuses of the other members it reflects poorly on the others. In addition, the individual with the much lower status is at a disadvantage vis-à-vis the others and perhaps at a disadvantage relative to the other statuses in his or her own status set. As far as the internal social system of the family is concerned, this may result in a loss of prestige, power, or affection. Hence, a strain toward status consistency is often to the advantage of all concerned. As a consequence, where a publicly known status of one member of the family group is much below that of other members, we might expect certain social mechanisms to come into play to deal with the disadvantages resulting from such a marked status inconsistency. Without attempting to set up an exhaustive classification of those mechanisms there are several that readily come to mind.

1. The offending status is given up, if possible, or if only contemplated its attainment is not pursued.
2. The negative effect of the highly discrepant status is somehow neutralized. This is most likely to be the case where there are some benefits as well as potential liabilities to be derived from the status. One way neutralization may be achieved is by a consensus on the temporary nature of the status. For example, the status may be considered appropriate for one stage of the individual's life cycle but not for another.
3. The relationship with the family member who had the much lower status is broken off. Thus, at one time, young women who became premaritally pregnant and with no wedding in sight so compromised their own status and that of their families that many ran the risk of being disowned.
4. The family opts out of the usual evaluative system. With respect to the social stratification system, for example, they may decide to recognize no hierarchy of occupational statuses at all and hence the highly discrepant status is definitionally eliminated. This is perhaps an alternative currently open to radical left groups in this society but it does not seem to be an subjectively feasible alternative to most people as yet. Besides, as long as any evaluative systems are in force the dilemma remains.

How are such mechanisms likely to operate in marriages where both spouses are not only working or contemplating employment but where the possibility of highly divergent occupational statuses also arises? In such cases, the operation of these mechanisms has been strongly influenced, I think, by the relatively long-standing norm in our society that the man be the major provider and status determiner. When such a norm is flourishing, it will affect which mechanisms come into play because a different meaning will necessarily be attached to the status inconsistency depending on whether the wife's or husband's status is the much lower one.

Take first the case where the wife has achieved a much higher occupational status than her husband. Because the normative expectation is that the husband should be the major status-determiner for the family, this limits the kinds of mechanisms that will deal with this type of status inconsistency. He does not, for example, have the social option of eliminating the status discrepancy by quitting work. While the negative effects of the discrepancy may be neutralized for a time by interpreting his much lower status as temporary for some socially acceptable reason, unless he can soon achieve considerable upward mobility he remains at a disadvantage. On the wife's part, she does have the social option of eliminating the status discrepancy by quitting work and this may be one resolution of the conflict but probably at considerable psychic cost to her, not to mention the economic costs. However, she may change husbands—or at least do without the lower-status husband—rather than relinquish a relatively rewarding occupational career for a socioeconomic status that is lower than she could achieve herself. Of course, what happens in any particular case will depend on other aspects of the marriage as well. However, given traditional family norms, this type of status discrepancy tends to create severe strains in the marriage relationship thereby increasing the probability of separation and divorce as the means of dealing with the problem.

But what about the situation where the wife's occupation—if she has one—is of much lower socioeconomic status than her husband's? Most married women in our society have had a ready-made socioeconomic status set for them by their husbands. According to my general reasoning regarding the "contagious" nature of social statuses, in the case where the husband's occupational status is much higher than the wife could realistically achieve on her own (given her current occupational qualifications and current labor-market conditions) her working at a low-status job would reflect poorly on the family's standing in the community. However, a socially acceptable solution to this problem for the wife, but not the husband, is to quit work. In sum, whether or not a wife works will depend importantly on whether her occupation enhances or detracts from the family's socioeconomic position. Because many wives, unlike most husbands, have traditionally had the option *not* to work they have had the option—and perhaps even the obligation—not to have an occupation that would reflect poorly on their own or their family's position. If this is true, the higher a women's derived socioeconomic position, the higher her occupation must be if she is to have a serious work commitment. Furthermore, it will be to the advantage of both the wife and her family if she can optimize her occupational status provided it does not cause too many inconveniences.

Just as giving up a much lower occupational status is more feasible normatively for the wife than the husband, so is the neutralization of the possibly negative consequences of a considerably lower status. Thus a common type of labor-force attachment of wives is temporary. Many women will not mind holding jobs that would not be commensurate with their present or expected future status as long as these jobs are considered short-term rather than providing a regular self-identifying adult role—working as a secretary, for example, while the husband is a medical intern or working to send the children to college. Other types of jobs that might form exceptions are those that can blend into avocations such as artist, musician, or even actress, and in general, jobs that are considered chic—though not necessarily remunerative. Of course, the social distance between a women's occupational status and her derived social status cannot be too great.

In sum, I am arguing first that the status maintenance or enhancement concerns of the family produce pressures on the wife to work. Second, however, the same status considerations influence how serious and long-term her work commitment will be, if she does work, as well as her occupational level. The view presented here is that, for reasons of status maintenance, status *compatibility* among family members is important although status *equality* is not as essential. In terms of the wife's socioeconomic role in the family this means that she is more likely to work if her potential occupational status—and its economic rewards—would serve to *enhance* the family's socioeconomic status. However, if her relative economic contribution to the family were to be negligible and her occupational status much below that of her husband's, she would be less likely to work because there would be little net socioeconomic advantage to her and the family for her to do so. Hence, arguing from the standpoint of the external status maintenance problems of the family rather than the internal complications raised by competition *within* the family, we arrive at quite different conclusions about wives' socioeconomic role than those of Parsons. However, this approach is certainly more consistent with recent economic and demographic research which has both predicted and found a positive relationship between wives' potential absolute and relative economic contribution and their labor force status (Cain 1966; Bowen and Finegan 1969; Oppenheimer 1972; Sweet 1973; Leibowitz 1975; Willis 1974). The present study also provides considerable empirical support for this view and it is to this question we now turn.

II. THE LABOR-FORCE IMPACT OF THE POTENTIAL SOCIOECONOMIC ADVANTAGE OF WIVES WORKING

Education as a Measure of the Wife's Potential Socioeconomic Contribution to the Family

Since the major focus here is on the general socioeconomic advantages of a wife working and not simply on the "wage effect" variable so important in the research of economists, it would not be appropriate to measure a woman's possible contribution only in terms of her potential wages. More suitable would be some measure of potential occupation because this could not only give us a rough idea of potential earnings but also of the general status and social advantages (or disadvantages) of working. However, it is methodologically very difficult to obtain a direct measure of potential occupation. Many women were not working in 1970 and our information on their past occupations is very limited. Another approach is to use the wife's educational attainment which, as we shall see, is a fairly good indicator both of the type of occupations wives could work at if they entered the labor force and of the income they could then expect to earn. Furthermore, this measure has been frequently employed by researchers in female labor-force participation (Cain 1966; Bowen and Finegan 1969; Sweet 1973). Hence, wife's education will be used in the regressions in this chapter as a proxy for the potential socioeconomic desirability of her employment—for herself and her family. The joint educational attainment of husbands and wives will, in turn, be used to measure the effect of wives' potential *relative* socioeconomic contribution. An additional interaction analysis will investigate the effect of wives' educational attainment on their work rates for each peak median occupational group of the husband.

Just how good an indicator is a women's educational level of her potential socioeconomic contribution to the family? The answer to this question depends on whether a given educational attainment seems to affect the occupational level of a working woman. If there is a strong relationship between educational attainment and occupational type, then this should provide a rough measure of the kinds of occupations in which women at different educational levels are likely to find employment. For example, if relatively few economically active women with only a high-school degree are found in professional occupations, then it seems reasonably safe to conclude that less educated women will have difficulty finding work in a profession. If such a woman is married to a high-level professional, then her potential socioeconomic contribution to the family via *paid* employment may be rather low, if not negative. We can further pin down the potential *economic* contribution the wife can make by investigating how women's earnings vary according to their occupation. If women in professional occupations earn considerably more than women in clerical occupations, for example, and a college education is an important prerequisite for employment in a professional occupation, then a college education can be taken as a crude indicator of the potential economic contribution the wife can make. In short, we will investigate whether educational level is a good indicator of potential occupational types. Occupation, in turn, will be used as a dual indicator—

first as a crude measure of the social status and work desirability of the potential job and, second, as a proxy for the woman's potential income.[6]

EDUCATIONAL ATTAINMENT AND OCCUPATION

Tables 7.1 and 7.2 show the peak median occupational distribution of employed wives in the 1960 and 1970 PUS. By and large, the pattern is similar at both census dates and indicates a very strong relationship between these women's educational level and their occupation. Women with 8 years of schooling or less were concentrated in blue-collar occupations—primarily in the low-level Group IV operative and service occupations. Hardly any were to be found in craft jobs or even in the Operative III group. Thus the occupational opportunities available to women at these two low educational attainment levels seem to be very poor indeed. However, the achievement of at least some high-school experience led to a considerable increase in the proportion of women in white-collar occupations, even if they did not graduate from high school. This shift was largely accomplished through a sharp rise in the proportion in clerical occupations (from 13 to 33% in 1970) combined with declines in the proportions in Operative IV and Service IV occupations. There was no evidence of much change in the proportion of wives in Craft III or Operative III occupations.[7] However, such women were still well underrepresented in white-collar occupations compared to all educational groups combined.

Graduating from high school signified an enormous difference in the occupational distribution of wives at both census dates. In 1970, for example, the proportion of those with 4 years of high school who were in white-collar occupations was 74% as compared to the 51% for women with only 1–3 years of high school. Once again, this is almost entirely because of the very large increase in the proportion in clerical jobs, accompanied by a sharp drop in the proportions in operative and service occupations. In sum, graduating from high school seemed to mark a major transition to a situation where most working wives were disproportionately concentrated in white-collar occupations, albeit in the somewhat lower level white-collar jobs.

---

[6] Although this reasoning refers to the general relationship for women between education and occupational type and between occupational type and earnings, rather than to the nature of the relationship specific to *married* women, I will use the white couples PUS data of this study to illustrate these relationships. The reason for this is to facilitate comparisons involving the peak median occupational classification system used so extensively in this investigation. As far as major occupational groups are concerned, the results are very similar to those obtained using published census data for all white women in non-farm occupations (see Oppenheimer 1972).

[7] This is undoubtedly due to the nature of the sex labeling of blue-collar occupations.

TABLE 7.1
Peak Median Occupational Distribution of Employed White Wives, by Their Educational Attainment: 1960 (Percentage)[a]

Occupation of wife[b]	Total	Less than 8	8	9–11	12	13–15	16	17+
Total	(9,246) 100	(690) 100	(1,090) 100	(2,024) 100	(3,613) 100	(1,101) 100	(524) 100	(204) 100
Professionals	14	1	1	3	8	34	72	88
I	—	—	—	—	—	—	2	12
II	2	—	—	1	2	2	4	7
III	12	1	1	2	6	32	66	69
Managers	4	4	2	3	5	4	3	1
I	1	—	—	—	1	1	1	—
II	1	1	1	1	2	1	1	1
III	2	3	1	2	2	2	1	—
Sales	10	7	11	14	10	9	3	2
II	1	—	1	1	1	2	1	—
III	9	7	10	13	9	7	2	2
Clerical	36	7	14	28	53	44	21	6
III	32	4	11	22	49	41	20	6
IV	4	3	3	6	4	3	1	—
Craft	1	3	2	2	1	1	—	1
Operatives	19	49	38	28	12	3	1	—
III	4	7	6	7	3	—	—	—
IV	15	42	32	21	9	3	1	—
Service	16	29	30	21	12	5	3	1
IV	14	23	26	19	11	4	2	1
Private household	2	6	4	2	1	1	1	—
Laborers	—	1	1	1	—	—	—	—

Source: 1960 Public Use Sample of White Couples.
[a]Includes some families where the husband was not the head.
[b]Non-farm occupations only.

TABLE 7.2
Peak Median Occupational Distribution of Employed White Wives, by Their Educational Attainment: 1970 (Percentage)

Occupation of wife[a]	Total	Less than 8	8	9–11	12	13–15	16	17	18+
Total	(37,946)	(1,592)	(2,213)	(9,441)	(15,178)	(5,442)	(2,554)	(881)	(645)
	100	100	100	100	100	100	100	100	100
Professionals	18	2	3	5	8	31	77	89	89
I	1	—	—	—	—	1	2	7	18
II	3	1	1	1	2	6	7	5	5
III	14	1	2	4	6	24	68	77	66
Managers	4	2	3	3	5	5	2	1	1
I	1	—	—	—	1	1	—	—	—
II	1	1	1	1	2	2	1	—	—
III	2	1	2	2	2	2	1	—	—
Sales	8	7	9	10	9	6	3	1	2
II	1	—	—	1	1	1	1	—	1
III	7	7	9	9	8	5	2	1	1
Clerical	38	9	13	33	52	48	15	6	5
III	33	6	9	27	46	44	13	5	5
IV	5	3	4	6	6	4	2	1	—
Craft	2	3	3	2	2	1	—	—	—
Operatives	15	46	38	25	11	2	—	—	—
III	4	10	10	7	3	1	—	—	—
IV	11	36	28	18	8	1	—	—	—
Service	15	28	31	20	14	6	1	1	1
IV	14	24	28	19	13	6	1	1	1
Private household	1	4	3	1	1	—	—	—	—
Laborers	1	2	2	1	1	—	—	—	—

Source: 1970 Public Use Samples of White Couples.
[a]Non-farm occupations only.

Achieving some college training marks the beginning of another transition. The proportion of such working wives who were in white-collar employment again rose sharply—to about 90% for both 1960 and 1970. But this did not happen because of any further increases in employment in clerical occupations. Actually, in both 1960 and 1970 the proportion in clerical jobs was *higher* for those with four years of high school than for those with 1–3 years of college. The upward shift in the proportion of white-collar employment was entirely due to a sharp increase in the proportion in Professional III occupations, combined with continued declines in the proportions in operative and service jobs. There was no positive effect on their entry into Sales II or managerial occupations. This transition into professional employment was carried much further by women who had attained 4 or 5 years of college-level training. Thus for these wives—97% of whom were in white-collar occupations in 1970—there was a sharp decline in the proportion in clerical occupations—from 48% in 1970 for those with 1–3 years of college to only 15% for those with 4 years of college and on down to only 6% for those with 5 years. However, the proportion in the professions rose dramatically. In 1970, it increased from 31% for women with 1–3 years of college to 77% for those with 4 years of college and up to 89% for 5 years women. These shifts were, however, primarily because of the considerable increases in the proportion in the lower-level Professional III jobs. Thus, if they worked, completing 4 or 5 years of college seemed to have virtually ensured the location of these women in a professional job—though in the lower level and probably predominantly female professions.

Turning finally to women with an educational attainment of 6 or more years at the college level, the only data on this high an attainment category are for 1970. Although there was little difference in the proportions in different major occupational groups, there was a distinct change *within* the professional category. For this highest educational attainment group there occurred a considerable rise in the proportion in Professional I occupations—up from 7% for women with 5 years at the college level to 18% for women with 6 or more years in 1970. Accompanying this was a decline in the proportion in the Professional III group. There was no change observable in the proportion in the Professional II group.

In short, increasing educational attainment makes a considerable difference in the occupational distribution of working women. If the type occupation a women is likely to qualify for affects her decision to enter the labor market, then these data suggest that, ceteris paribus, her educational attainment will be a fairly good indicator of her potential occupational position and, hence, of the potential relative socioeconomic impact of her work on the family. All this is quite consistent, of course, with the research of investigators in social stratification. These studies have found tht educational attainment was the most important variable in explaining the occupational status of working women (see, for example, Featherman and Hauser 1976; Treimen and Terrell 1975). However, a given educational level may be a *necessary* but not a *sufficient* condition for current employability in any particular type of occupation. Other types of training will undoubtedly be important too, as well as past work experience and the structure of labor demand. Hence the use of educational attainment as an indicator of a women's potential current occupational level must be treated with considerable caution.

Occupation and Wives' Earnings

Earnings data for employed women indicate considerable differences among occupational groups. Table 7.3 presents the median earnings, by occupation, for all employed wives and for employed wives who worked "full-time" (defined here as those women who worked 35 or more hours during the reference week and 40–52 weeks in the year preceding the census).

In general, women in white-collar occupations had higher median earnings than women in blue-collar or service occupations. Exceptions on the white-collar side were the extremely low earnings of Sales III women, even if presumably working full-time. However, in both 1959 and 1969, Clerical III women had higher median earnings than Operative III wives, although the differences were not very large—always less than $400. Hence, the economic advantage of many clerical jobs over Operative III jobs was not marked although the status advantages and the possibly better working conditions may have made the clerical occupations far more attractive. However, job opportunities for women in operative occupations seemed to be much greater in the Operative IV than the Operative III group. In 1970, 11% of all employed wives were Operative IV workers but only 4% were in the Operative III group (Table 7.2). There was little doubt, furthermore, that the earnings of Operative IV women compared quite poorly to those of Clerical III women. As for other numerically important manual occupations, women in the Service IV group made very low earnings—a 1969 median of only $3,690 for full-time working Service IV wives compared to $5,125 for full-time working Clerical III wives. In short, white-collar jobs of numerical importance for women tended to pay considerably better than numerically important blue-collar and service jobs. Hence, to the extent a higher educational attainment was a prerequisite for a white-collar job, education paid off in better-paying jobs.

Within the white-collar group as a whole, there was little doubt that

TABLE 7.3
Median 1959 and 1969 Earnings of Employed Wives, by Own Occupation and Work Experience (1969 Dollars)

	Median earnings			
	1959[a]		1969	
Wife's occupation	All employed wives	Wives employed full time[b]	All employed wives	Wives employed full time[b]
Total	3,139	3,797	3,898	4,938
Professionals				
I	—[c]	—[c]	7,173	8,789
II	4,676	5,382	5,571	6,597
III	4,199	4,960	5,866	7,226
Managers				
I	4,753	4,788	6,054	6,393
II	3,685	4,268	5,191	5,723
III	3,849	4,306	4,508	5,060
Sales				
II	2,564	3,145	4,266	5,812
III	2,004	2,682	2,477	3,613
Clerical				
III	3,916	4,336	4,437	5,125
IV	2,937	3,407	3,120	4,583
Craft				
II	—[c]	—[c]	5,610	c
III	3,486	3,848	4,541	5,150
IV	—[c]	—[c]	3,109	3,857
Operatives				
III	3,749	4,222	4,149	4,785
IV	2,905	3,334	3,623	4,175
Service[d]				
IV	1,776	2,375	2,405	3,690
Private household	876	1,191	843	1,479
Laborers	—[c]	—[c]	3,179	3,963

Sources: 1960 and 1970 Public Use Samples of White Couples.

[a] Includes some families where the husband was not the head.

[b] *Wives employed full time* refers to those women who worked 40–52 weeks in the year preceding the census and 35 or more hours during the census reference week.

[c] Medians not computed where sample size was less than 40.

[d] Service III women were omitted because there were too few of them to warrant calculating medians in either 1959 or 1969.

working at a professional or technical occupation conferred a considerable income advantage on wives in 1969. The situation for 1959 is a little less clear, at least in comparison to Clerical III jobs. There was only about a $300 advantage to Professional III work over Clerical III work in 1959. The earnings dfferential was much larger in 1969 for all employed wives and for full-time working wives as well.

In sum, higher educational attainments seemed to increase the opportunities and probably the desire to work in white-collar occupations, with college training being especially important as an *entrée* into professional and technical occupations. Employment in white-collar occupations, with the exception of Sales III and Clerical IV jobs led, in turn, to higher earnings than women workers achieved in most manual occupations. Finally, working in the professions paid off with substantially improved earnings, especially compared to the Clerical III group—the single largest white-collar group for women. Hence, differences in educational attainment do seem to signify important differences in women's potential economic contribution to their families.

Effect of Wife's Educational Attainment on Her Labor-Force Status

EFFECT OF ABSOLUTE EDUCATIONAL ATTAINMENT

Table 7.4 shows the effect of wife's education on her labor-force status. One interesting finding is that although both Sweet's study and that of Bowen and Finegan show a very weak *gross* effect of education in 1960,[8] but a strong positive *net* effect, the 1970 data indicate that a relatively strong positive relationship exists even on the gross level. The relationship was enhanced, as in previous studies, when all other variables were included. Particularly noteworthy was the sharp jump in the positive effect of schooling at the seventeenth year—an increase from a work rate of 53% for those with 16 years to 66% for those with 17 years of schooling. Bowen and Finegan also found this to be the case in their analysis of the 1960 1/1,000 sample (Bowen and Finegan 1969:116).

In general, then, the net relationship of wives' labor-force participation to their educational level is consistent with past findings and with economic theories regarding the wife's wage effect. It also supports the notion that a higher potential occupational position for the wife is more likely to be considered a family asset rather than a liability by couples and, as such, leads to an increased probability that the wife will enter the labor force.

[8]This was due to the positive relationship of education to income and the negative relationship of income to wife's labor-force participation.

TABLE 7.4
Effect of Wife's Educational Attainment on Her Labor-Force Participation: 1970

Number of school years completed by wife	Distribution of sample		Labor-force participation rates[a]	
	Number	Percentage	Unadjusted	Adjusted IV[b]
Total	91,937	100.0	43.0	
Less than 8	5,131	5.6	33.1	27.7
8	6,312	6.9	37.5	33.2
9–11	24,276	26.4	41.2	39.5
12	36,150	39.3	43.6	44.2
13–15	12,201	13.3	45.7	48.2
16	5,486	6.0	46.8	52.9
17	1,396	1.5	62.9	66.4
18+	985	1.1	65.5	71.8
F				235.9*

Source: 1970 Public Use Sample of White Couples. The adjusted participation rates were derived from the partial regression coefficients in Regression IV listed in Appendix D.
[a] Percentage in labor force.
[b] Adjusted for husband's peak median occupation, husband's intraoccupational relative economic status, previous marital experience of spouses, family-cycle stage, and husband's age.
*Significant at the .01 level.

THE EFFECT OF THE WIFE'S EDUCATIONAL LEVEL RELATIVE TO HER HUSBAND'S

If the potential *relative* socioeconomic impact of a wife working on her family's, including her own, socioeconomic position will affect her labor-force behavior, then this should be detectable in a regression analysis of wives' labor-force participation and the joint education attainment of the two spouses. However, the interpretation of such a regression analysis is not entirely straightforward. Suppose, for example, one looks at the effect of variations in the wife's educational attainment for each education level of the husband, and finds a positive relationship between the wife's education and her probability of being in the labor force in each case. In itself, this pattern can simply be attributed to the wife's absolute wage effect—that is, it can be interpreted as a measure of her potential *absolute* rather than her *relative* socioeconomic contribution. It may also be indicative of a rising taste for work if education is partly a proxy for "taste of employment" or for "psychic income" (Waite 1976; Cain 1966; Bowen and Finegan 1969; and others). Similarly, if we look at the variations in the effect of husband's educational attainment for each educational level of the wife and find an inverse relationship, this can simply be interpreted as evidence for the "income interaction effect that we can hope to detect whether the wife's *relative*

II. Labor Force Impact of Advantage of Wives Working

socioeconomic impact is a factor in her labor-force participation. And this interaction effect is one which involves various thresholds.

In order to explain what type of threshold effects are at issue, I will backtrack a bit and refer to the theoretical discussions at the beginning of the chapter to provide a foundation for my argument. Consistent with the line of reasoning developed earlier, it is possible to think of roughly four types of potential occupational situations for wives relative to their husband's socioeconomic position. Two involve occupations that are status compatible and two involve the kinds of occupations that tend to be incompatible with a woman's derived socioeconomic position. However, to which of the four categories a particular occupation may be appropriately assigned will vary, depending on the husband's socioeconomic position. It is rarely an inherent feature of any occupation.

At the low end of this typology, there are occupations for the wife that might be considered status demeaning by the family and which, in addition, yield little or no relative economic advantage. For example, many families of men in white-collar occupations might feel that having a wife in a manual job would be status-demeaning and of little economic advantage. In fact, many blue-collar families might feel the same way, given the extremely low-level manual jobs traditionally open to women. If the best jobs some women's educational attainment will qualify them for are those that their families would consider somewhat degrading, then this should depress such wives' work rates below the average for their socioeconomic group. Whether they do work is likely to be influenced by just how severe the economic pressures currently facing the family are rather than on any intrinsic relative advantage to the job itself.

The second type of occupation wives might obtain includes those that are compatible with the family's socioeconomic position as derived from the husband and which usually produce some positive economic contribution to the family's income. Wives qualified to work in the second type of occupation should be much more likely to be working than those whose occupational expectations fall into the first group. However, even here, the relative *advantage* of the wife working is not extremely high and, as such, whether a woman works should again be strongly influenced by economic pressures, home responsibilities, intrinsic work desires, etc. In short, whether the wife works might fluctuate considerably, depending on variations in other conditions.

The third category also consists of status-compatible occupations or jobs but, only those that provide a fairly considerable relative status and/or economic advantage to the family. Thus for families of many middle-level white-collar males, the relative advantage of a professional wife would be considerably above that of a wife in clerical work. Hence those wives with a potential for employment in a professional occupation would be more likely to enter the labor force and remain working at such jobs, even if economic pressures do not arise. Moreover, they should be especially responsive to *increases* in economic needs or aspirations because such jobs can provide a relatively attractive solution to economic difficulties, assuming, of course, that labor-market conditions are favorable. In addition, occupations of this type are often intrinsically more rewarding, though this is not particularly at issue in the present analysis.

Finally, we might distinguish a fourth type of potential occupational situation for the wife—one in which her occupational socioeconomic status so outstrips her husband's that it is not so much a question of the relative *advantage* of her working but the relative *disadvantage* her husband is placed in by her employment. This possible, though rare, situation may lead to all sorts of complications, one important one being maritial instability. However, it is not the kind of combination that can be adequately identified here, even wth the 3/1,000 PUS data.

As we have seen, particular educational transitions seem to have a considerable impact on working women's occupational levels and through this, on the relative socioeconomic advantage of their working. However, the educational (and occupational) transitions that will produce these changes in women's work propensities should vary, depending on, among other things, the husband's socioeconomic position. The higher the husband's general socioeconomic position, the higher will be the minimum occupational level not considered demeaning and the higher also will be the occupational level necessary to provide a distinct relative socioeconomic advantage to the woman and her family. Under these conditions, the educational differences that produce large increments in wives' labor-force participation for wives of men at higher socioeconomic levels may only start to occur at quite high absolute educational levels of the wife (e.g., graduating from college or completing some postgraduate work). However, for families of men at lower socioeconomic levels, the minimum educational level essential for a status-compatible occupation will be much lower. Lower too will be the point at which increasing educational attainments start to signify the possibility of working in occupations that represent a distinctly greater relative socioeconomic advantage to the family. Moreover, lower-level families can less afford the luxury of a threshold at all. Under such conditions, the employability of the wife may be the major factor involved. If so then a threshold effect might disappear and for low educational groups of husbands, each increase in the wife's educational level that increases her employability will have a positive effect on her labor-force participation.

In sum, the question at issue is whether, with rising educational level of the husband, an increasingly higher minimum educational attainment of the wife

II. Labor Force Impact of Advantage of Wives Working

is necessary for improvements in her educational level to have a substantial impact on her labor-force status. The results of the regression analysis exploring this issue are presented in Table 7.5. By and large, they support the notion that: (a) it is usually necessary to reach a certain threshold before improvements in the wife's educational level make much of a difference in her labor-force participation; and (b) the higher the husband's income level, the higher this threshold is.

For couples where the husband had achieved 18 or more years of schooling, improvements in the educational level of the wife had virtually no effect on her labor-force participation until the change from 13–15 years of schooling to 16–17 years had occurred. Thus the adjusted proportion of wives in the labor force varied between 33 and 34% for women in the 13–15-years-or-lower schooling categories. However, the adjusted rate for wives with 16–17 years of schooling went up to 41% and for wives who had attained 18 or more years of schooling, it rose all the way to 62%—a 21 percentage point increase! Where the husband had 16–17 years of schooling, the relationship between the wife's educational attainment and her labor-force participation was rather inconsistant for women in the three lowest educational categories. Once again, however, the first big jump in wives' adjusted rates occurred between the 13–15 and 16–17 educational attainment categories—an increase from 38 to 47% in the labor force. There is an even greater rise—to 63%—for wives with 18 or more years of school. In short, a similar pattern exists for wives of men with 16–17 and 18 or more years of schooling. It is not until 16–17 years of schooling is achieved by the wife that educational improvements start to have a marked effect on these wives' work propensitities.

In the case of husbands with 13–15 years of schooling (1–3 years of college), although the increases in wives' labor-force participation were greater for educational changes between upper schooling levels rather than between lower levels, a marked threshold effect was not really observable. In fact, 18 or more years of schooling did not lead to as big a jump in wives' labor-force participation as was characteristic of men with 16–17 years of schooling and, in particular, those with 18 or more years. For men with 12 years of schooling only, increases in wives' educational attainment had a positive impact on the wives' work propensties throughout the entire range of educational attainments under consideration and not just primarily at the upper levels. This was also the case for husbands with less than 12 years of schooling.

In sum, for fairly extensively educated men, a relatively high educational attainment on the part of their wives was also necessary before increases in a wife's educational attainment had a substantial positive effect on her work propensity. However, as we move to couples with the husband in lower

TABLE 7.5
Effect of Joint Educational Attainment of Husbands and Wives on Wife's Labor-Force Participation: 1970

Joint educational attainment of husbands and wives	Distribution of sample		Percentage in labor force	
	Number	Percentage	Unadjusted	Adjusted VI [a]
Total	91,937	100.0	43.0	
Husband 18+				
W 18+	548	.6	62.4	62.0
W 16–17	1,671	1.8	38.8	41.1
W 13–15	1,223	1.3	31.2	33.9
W 12	957	1.0	30.5	32.7
W under 12	121	.1	33.1	33.3
Husband 16–17				
W 18+	194	.2	65.0	62.7
W 16–17	3,093	3.4	47.7	46.9
W 13–15	3,240	3.5	37.5	37.6
W 12	3,366	3.7	33.0	34.1
W under 12	745	.8	39.2	39.6
Husband 13–15				
W 18+	92	.1	72.8	69.3
W 16–17	893	1.0	60.4	57.7
W 13–15	3,312	3.6	50.0	47.7
W 12	4,956	5.4	43.4	43.4
W under 12	2,995	3.3	40.0	40.2
Husband 12				
W 18+	111	.1	76.6	74.3
W 16–17	893	1.0	61.0	58.6
W 13–15	3,021	3.3	50.8	49.6
W 12	19,126	20.8	44.3	44.8
W under 12	7,711	8.4	37.1	37.6
Husband under 12				
W 18+	40	.0	62.5	60.9
W 16–17	332	.4	71.4	70.3
W 13–15	1,405	1.5	56.3	55.0
W 12	7,745	8.4	48.2	48.2
W under 12	24,147	26.3	40.1	39.8
F				54.0*

Source: 1970 Public Use Sample of White Couples. The adjusted participation rates were derived from the partial regression coefficients in Regression VI listed in Appendix D.

[a] Adjusted for the effect of family-cycle stage, spouses' previous marital experience, and husband's age.
*Significant at the .01 level.

educational attainment categories, the effect of wives' educational improvements at the lower attainment levels was more pronounced. All this is consistent with the notion that status compatibility is more readily achieved by lower-level educational improvements among such socioeconomic groups and that the relative socioeconomic contribution of the wife can have a more significant positive impact.

EFFECT OF THE WIFE'S EDUCATIONAL LEVEL RELATIVE TO HUSBAND'S OCCUPATION

Let us now consider the effect of the wife's educational attainment as it interacts with the husband's peak median occupation. Such an interaction analysis should be valuable since, as we saw in Chapter 3, a man's educational attainment is a rather imperfect indicator of his peak median occupational level. Moreover since so much of the study has been devoted to an investigation of the socioeconomic characteristics of men in these 18 occupational groups, it is important to undertake an analysis comparing the effect of wives' potential relative socioeconomic contribution among the different peak median occupational groups.

Basically, the question is the same as that for interaction analysis involving the joint educational attainments of husbands and wives. Is there evidence that with a higher socioeconomic level of the husband, there is a higher absolute educational threshold for the wife before changes in educational attainment have a pronounced impact on her labor-force participation? In investigating how a wife's educational attainment interacts with her husband's peak median occupation in its effect on work propensities, I have used a regression model including the variable measuring the ratio of husband's earnings to the median for men in the same occupation and age group. Given the occupational heterogeneity occuring within peak median occupational groups, there is considerable reason to believe that educational differences among wives will be indicative of variations in the husband's socioeconomic position within his assigned occupational category. If so, an unmeasured income effect will offset the effect of changes in the wife's educational attainment. Therefore, the husband's relative economic status variable was introduced into the equation in an effort to try to control for this problem and, this regression model provides the basis of the discussion to follow.[9]

---

[9]However a regression model with*out* the relative economic status variable was also run, though not reported here. Its results indicate that, within peak median occupations groups, the husband's socioeconomic position is correlated with the wife's educational attainment. For example, within Group I and II occupations, the adjusted work rates of less educated wives were higher for the shorter equation and lower for the more educated wives.

However, the inclusion of the relative economic status variable will best control for differences in the husband's *earnings* position, leaving some important variability in social status characteristics of men's occupations that might also vary with the wife's educational attainment.[10] Hence, educational differences and any associated social or status characteristics that may affect what is defined as a socially compatible occupation for the wife are very likely to vary within peak median occupational groups in spite of controlling for intragroup differences in earnings.[11] This may alter the nature of any hypothesized threshold effects of education on the wife's labor-force status.

Table 7.6 presents the adjusted work rates for this interaction analysis. It is important to point out as a preliminary, however, that despite the overall large sample size for the 1970 couples, cell sizes for some of these interaction dummy variable regressions become quite small. This is especially the case where we are looking at high educational levels for wives of men in blue-collar occupations and very low educational levels for wives of men in Group I and II white-collar occupations. Hence, in those situations the results are likely to become rather unstable. However, the table will indicate where this is the case. Let us proceed with the discussion of the results of the interaction analysis by looking first at Group I and II white-collar occupations, then at the Group III and IV white-collar groups, and finally at blue-collar occupations.

There seems to be little doubt that some sort of educational threshold effects are operating for the wives of Professional I and Managerial I men. In the case of the wives of Professional I males, there are only two educational transitions that have a substantial positive impact on wives' adjusted work rates. The first is the considerable increase in the rate for wives with 9–11 years of schooling over that for those with only 8 years—a rise from 16 to 28% in the labor force. This is probably indicative of a threshold effect. If holding down a white-collar job tends to represent the status minimum for a working wife of men in these high-level socioeconomic groups, then the shift from 8 to 9–11 years of schooling marks a critical educational step facilitating such white-collar employment. It is true that the adjusted rate for women with less than 8 years of schooling was about the same as for women with 9–11 years. However, the sample size for the lowest educational group was so small (28 cases) that this rate is undoubtedly highly unstable.

The second important educational transition for the wives of Professional I

[10]For example, both electrical engineering technicians and secondary-school teachers were placed in the Professional III group. Males in both these occupations has similar 1969 median earnings—$9,036 for the teachers and $9,361 for the technicians. However, the median school years completed for these two occupations were very different—17+ for the teachers compared to only 12.8 for the technicians (U.S. Bureau of the Census 1973b:Table 1).

[11]Life-style aspirations may vary as well, of course.

males is the very substantial rise in the adjusted work rate for wives with 17 years of schooling rather than 16—an increase from 35 to 51%. Having 18 or more years of schooling increased the adjusted rate still further to 57%. By and large, the differences between other educational categories were not nearly as large. Having some college compared to just 12 years of schooling did result in a moderate increase of about 4 percentage points, however.

For the wives of men in the Managers I group, there is also evidence that increases between lower educational attainment groups made rather small differences in their adjusted rates—only a 10 percentage point rise from the lowest attainment group to those with 16 years of schooling. However, there was a 23 percentage point increase between 16 and 17 years of schooling— from 36 to 59% in the labor force. Achieving 18 or more years of schooling as opposed to 17 increased the adjusted rate by another 12 percentage points.

Where the husband was in a Group II white-collar occupation, the pattern shifts. In the case of the wives of Professional II males, for example, there is certainly a fairly substantial increase in the adjusted work rate when comparing women with 16 years of schooling to those with 17 years—a rise from 48 to 56% in the labor force. But this increase was not nearly as large as that exhibited by the wives of Professional I males. Moreover, rising educational attainments at lower levels had a more positive effect on wives' work probabilities. The pattern appears to be that there are stepwise increments rather than there being a smooth progression. Thus, in the case of Professional II wives, it seemed to make little difference whether a woman had 8 years of schooling or less than 8. However, an increase to 9–11 did have a positive impact. Similarly, it made little difference if a woman had 9–11 or 12 years of schooling. However, 1–3 years of college led to another modest rise and 4 years of college had a further positive effect. Having 17 years of schooling had a relatively large impact, but no greater than the change occuring between the categories of 8 and 9–11 years of school.

The reason for this stepwise pattern is probably that certain educational increments seem to have a geater effect on some occupational attainments than others. As we have seen different educational levels qualify women for different types of occupations. However, the progression is not smooth. For example, the difference between graduating or not graduating from elementary school does not appear to be decisive in qualifying a woman for most clerical jobs whereas having at least some high-school experience is much more important. Similarly, the difference between 9–11 and 12 years of schooling is not strategic in qualifying a woman for a professional or semiprofessional job but varying degrees of college do make the crucial difference. Seventeen years of schooling may be especially important in preparing women for certain professions, such as teaching.

The pattern for the wives of men in the Managers II and Sales II groups

TABLE 7.6
Effect of Wife's Educational Attainment on Her Labor-Force Status, by Husband's Occupation: 1970

Husband's occupation	Total[b]	Adjusted rates[a]							
		Less than 8	8	9–11	12	13–15	16	17	18+
Total[b]		27.7	33.2	39.5	44.2	48.2	52.9	66.4	71.8
Professionals									
I	29.6	27.0**	15.7	28.1*	28.2	32.6	34.8	51.0	56.7
II	38.5	28.1**	29.2	38.6*	38.9	43.5	48.4	55.6	63.2
III	46.4	28.7	33.7	43.4*	46.5	48.1*	62.7	73.3	78.2
Managers									
I	33.5	26.3**	29.8*	30.7*	34.7	36.1*	36.4*	59.1	71.5
II	38.1	27.0	24.6	35.0	39.3	42.6*	45.0	59.4	61.8
III	45.2	35.0	38.2	43.7*	45.8	48.1*	46.4*	57.5**	78.8
Sales									
II	39.4	15.3	22.0	34.5	40.2	42.4*	46.8	62.5	72.8
III	47.0	38.1	36.8	43.5	48.6	50.4*	57.9	64.0	78.3
Clerical									
III	45.6	33.8	38.2	43.0	47.2	52.2	58.4	66.7	68.3
IV	52.2	38.5	41.4	48.9	56.3	68.4	58.1**	75.9**	—[c]

282

Craft								
II	38.9	30.0*	26.7	36.3	41.9	44.6*	57.7	72.9**	78.8**
III	43.2	27.9	31.3	39.2	45.2	50.3	61.0	74.4	71.6
IV	43.6	26.7	34.0	40.0	44.0	55.0	68.8	86.0	77.0
Operatives								
III	45.4	28.7	37.6	42.9	45.9	56.3	65.2	61.9**	45.2**
IV	46.0	31.8	36.3	41.6	47.9	52.7	66.8	80.1	69.6
Service								
III	44.9	17.5	32.8*	42.7*	44.0	51.1*	69.9	64.8**	55.6**
IV	52.3	39.1	46.4	47.1	54.8	65.5	56.6*	87.2	62.7**
Laborers								
IV	43.9	27.0	36.0	39.8	45.4	48.5*	57.2	58.4**	47.9**

Source: 1970 Public Use Sample of White Couples.
^aAdjusted for husband's intraoccupational relative economic status, previous marital experience of spouses, family-cycle stage, and husband's age.
^bThe adjusted rates for the "Total" columns were derived from the regression equation including the husband's peak median occupation group, husband's intraoccupational relative economic status, previous marital experience of spouses, wife's education, family-cycle stage, and husband's age—Model IV.
^cNo wives observed with this education attainment.
* means the partial regression coefficients from which these adjusted rates were calculated did not achieve a significant difference, at the 5% level, from the omitted category which in all cases was an educational attainment for the wife of 12 years.
** means in addition to a lack of statistical significance for the partial regression coefficients, the sample size was less than 60. In the case of high levels of schooling for the wives of most blue-collar workers, the sample size was usually below 30.

also exhibits stepwise features though they are not as pronounced as in the case of the wives of Professional II males. Furthermore, in the case of Sales II wives educational increments at the lower levels had a greater impact than for other Group II wives.

Among Group III and IV white-collar occupations, there really is no observable single marked threshold, though there is usually a stepwise pattern. This certainly seems to be the case for wives of Professional III, Managerial III, and Sales III males, though the stepwise patterns are not always identical. For the wives of Professional III males, educational increments had an important positive effect on their work rates at the lower as well as the higher educational levels.[12] On the one hand, the adjusted work rates for women with 9–11, 12, or 13–15 years of schooling were very similar. On the other hand, having finished college produced a great boost in their adjusted work rates—from 48 to 63%. This contrasts markedly with the situation for wives of Group I and II men, with 4 years of college producing little additional impetus to the labor-force participation of their wives. However, in light of the relative advantage theory, it certainly makes sense that 16 years of schooling would constitute a greater relative asset to the wives of Professional III than to those of Profession I or II males. For Professional III wives, having 17 years of schooling also produced a major increase in their work rates.

The pattern for Manager III wives was somewhat similar to that of Professional III wives except that 16 years of schooling did not have a positive impact on their work propensities. Nevertheless, 17 and 18 or more years of schooling did raise their work rates considerably. However, the sample sizes were small in these upper educational groups. Moreover, the Managers III group may be rather atypical in its patterns because it includes all self-employed men in retail trade and hence the employment of the wife in the family business may complicate the pattern. Sales III wives also showed something of a stepwise pattern, with larger increments first occuring between the 8 and 9–11 transitions and, second, in the transitions starting with the shift from 13–15 to 16 years of schooling.

Clerical III and IV wives do not really exhibit a particularly strong stepwise pattern. For example, for Clerical III wives, each increment in the wife's educational level produces at least a moderate increase in her work propensity. Increments are larger, however, in the transition from 12 to 13–15 years of school, from 13–15 to 16 years, and from 16 to 17 years. Nevertheless, given the lower white-collar squeeze that has been

[12]This is understandable, given the heterogeneity of this peak median group. For example, it includes men in occupations as diverse as secondary-school teachers, actors, athletes, technicians, funeral directors and embalmers, chemists, etc.

II. Labor Force Impact of Advantage of Wives Working

hypothesized for these couples, it is to be expected that any possible rise in the women's potential socioeconomic contribution might increase her probability of working. Substantial increments due to educational increases from the lowest educational categories are also characteristic of Clerical IV wives.

Service III wives also showed a substantial rise in their adjusted work rates due to increases in educational attainments at the low educational levels, combined with little difference in the rates for wives with 9–11 and 12 years of schooling. Some college once again made a difference and so did 16 years of schooling. Sample sizes for the two highest educational groups are so small that it is probably not wise to attach much importance to their associated rates.

In general, then for the white-collar occupations, we observed a pronounced and very high threshold effect of education for wives of Group I men. For wives of Group II and III males, a stepwise pattern was more common. A major difference was that for Group II wives the transition from 16 to 17 years of schooling was particularly important (as was the case for Group I wives) whereas for Group III wives the transition from 13–15 to 16 years was also significant. In the case of Clerical IV wives, it was the 12 to 13–15 transition that marked an important step up in their adjusted rates. In sum, then these data support the hypothesis that the potential *relative* advantage of the wife working is an important factor in her labor-force behavior. If so, the higher the women's derived socioeconomic position, the greater must be her potential contribution for it to have an important effect on her labor-force participation.

Turning to the wives of men in blue-collar occupations, there was little evidence of a single educational threshold. However, this may be because all those with less than 8 years of schooling were combined into one category. Such a broad grouping could obscure the kind of thresshholds that might be more common among families of men in blue-collar occupations. There is, however, sometimes though not always evidence of a stepwise effect to educational attainment. By and large, there are few educational transitions that made very *little* difference in wives' labor-force participation although, once again, transitions at the higher educational levels usually have the largest impact—except in the very highest groups where sample sizes are probably too small to produce statistically reliable results. It is significant that in several cases the "higher" educational levels which produce bigger increases in wives' adjusted work rates are lower than is typical for white-collar occupations. For example, the change from 12 to 13–15 years of schooling had a bigger effect on work rates for the wives of Craft III and Operative III workers and Craft IV and Service IV males than for any white-collar occupational group with the partial exception of wives of Clerical III and IV men. The difference some college made was particularly marked for Operative III, Craft IV, and Service IV wives.

In sum, this interaction analysis indicated that it is not just the *absolute* level of the wife's educational attainment that affects her work propensities. Which levels of educational attainments make an important impact on wives' labor-force participation depends to some extent on the occupation of the husband. For men at the upper occupation levels, it is primarily only when the wife has achieved a relatively high level of educational attainment herself that educational improvements make a considerable impact on her labor-force participation. As we turn to occupations at lower socioeconomic levels, however, substantial educational effects are also noted for women at lower educational attainments. All this supports the view that the socioeconomic meaning of a given potential occupational position will vary, depending on the husband's socioeconomic position. Hence, it is the wife's *relative* socioeconomic contribution to the family that is often strategic in whether or not she will work.[13]

---

[13]These findings suggest tht the interaction analysis using the joint education attainments of husbands and wives (reported in Table 7.5) is not as good a measure as one would desire of the impact of the potential relative socioeconomic contribution of the wife on her work propensities. Unfortunately, the joint education variable was set up and included in the correlation matrix along with the variable on the wife's educational attainment alone. Fewer educational categories had to be used for the joint variable to make the analysis manageable. I had surmised that many women who went into teaching would have had either 16 or 17 years of schooling and hence the transition to 17 years of schooling would not be very critical. Rather, I had anticipated that transitions involving more advanced postgraduate work would make a much bigger difference in wives' work propensities. Obviously, the regression results in Table 7.4 indicate that I was greatly mistaken. Achieving 17 years of schooling led to a large increase in wives' work propensities over just 16 years of schooling. This is also evident in the analysis of the interaction of wives' absolute educational attainment with their husbands' occupations. A major reason for these results is probably that going to graduate school tends to select out women with higher work aspirations.

Because women with 16 and 17 years of schooling were combined into one category, the regression analysis utilizing the joint educational attainment of both spouses may somewhat distort the effect of different amounts of college work on women's labor-force rates. Given the results from the analyses using women's educational attainment alone, it seems likely that: (*a*) for the upper educational groups of the husband, 17—not 16—years of schooling for the wife brings about the big increase in her work propensities, for men in medium or lower educational groups, 16 as opposed to 13–15 years of schooling may also be quite important as an impetus to higher work rates by the wife; (*b*) if, for more highly educated husbands, 17 years of schooling for the wife makes the strategic difference in her propensity to work, then combining women with 16 and 17 years of schooling into one category greatly understates the effect of having achieved 17 years of schooling.

III. CONCLUSION

This chapter has been devoted to the investigation of the impact of wives' potential economic contribution to the family on their labor-force status. As with earlier studies, we found that the higher women's potential *absolute* socioeconomic contribution (as measured by their educational attainment), the higher their propensity to be in the labor force in 1970. However, the main emphasis was on the effect of the potential *relative* socioeconomic impact of wives' employment. Here my reasoning was that the probability of a wife working partly depended on whether her employment would make a positive contribution to the family's socioeconomic status. This, in turn, was not only a function of the wife's occupational position (and its associated rewards), but of how these rewards compared to other sources of the family's socioeconomic status—mainly that of the husband. In general, the data analysis supported this view. Whichever the measure of the husband's socioeconomic position used—his educational attainment or his peak median occupational group—there was evidence of a relatively strong threshold effect. For husbands at a high socioeconomic level, it was primarily only when the wife had achieved a relatively high level of educational attainment herself that educational improvements made a considerable impact on her labor-force participation in 1970. As the husband's socioeconomic position declined, substantial educational effects on wives' labor-force participation were also observed for women at lower educational attainments. In short, the interaction pattern of wives' educational attainment with either their husbands' education or his occupation provided considerable support for the hypothesis that the relative socioeconomic impact of women working was an important factor in their labor-force behavior.

8

Socioeconomic and Demographic Implications of Wives' Employment

A major theme of this study has been that certain economic squeezes are an inherent feature of the socioeconomic organization of our society and, as a result, lead to a variety of compensatory patterns of social behavior. One such adaptive response is the labor-force participation of wives. However, wives' work behavior is not just a response to economic pressures but is, in addition, a function of a variety of other factors. One of these, as the data analysis of Chapter 7 indicates, is the relative socioeconomic *advantage* of wives' working. The present chapter will further explore the implications of these findings by examining some of the characteristcs of the PUS wives in greater detail. The goal is to achieve a fuller understanding of the actual and potential nature of women's socioeconomic contribution to their families, the extent this has changed over the short run, and the implications for possible long-term changes in women's economic roles and their related deomographic behavior. I shall attempt to do this by examining, first, the educational characteristics of the PUS wives and, second, the pattern of their 1959 and 1969 earnings and its implications for their families' socioeconomic position.

A relatively high potential socioeconomic contribution may promote wives' labor-force participation, as Chapter 7 indicates, but how many wives found themselves in such a position? Did this vary by the peak median occupational group of the husband, indicating the existence of substantial group differentials in the positive socioeconomic impact wives could make via paid employment? Moreover, What changes have been occurring over time? Since wives' potential socioeconomic contribution to their families was measured by means of their educational attainment, we will explore this issue by comparing the educational levels of husbands and wives.

Regarding earnings characteristics, I will attempt to document the nature of wives' actual economic contribution to the family in some detail. This is partly to consider the implications of their earnings position for the alleviation of various types of economic squeezes. There is the further question, however, of whether increases in women's labor-force participation might be producing important feedback effects which promote still further rises in their level of economic activity, labor-demand conditions permitting.

I. EDUCATIONAL ATTAINMENT

While considering the educational characteristics of husbands and wives in these 1960 and 1970 PUS it is important to keep in mind the relevant historical context. Most of these women, were making critical (though not necessarily final) decisions about their education, on-the-job training, and other career matters long before we observe them in 1960 and 1970. Hence, the women under study are by no means representative of young women currently making some of the same major career decisions. Today's decisions are being made within the context of a radically different normative and behavorial climate regarding women's social and economic roles than existed in the mid 1960s or earlier. In fact, most of the women in the 1970 and 1960 Public Use Samples were making important career decisions at a time when it was not very clear how much women's work behavior actually was changing. These, after all, are the very wives who pioneered most of these changes. For them, there was no clear-cut behavior pattern on which to model their actions. For some time, at least, much of the extensive postwar increases in women's work rates may have appeared as a temporary improvisation in response to shifting opportunities and needs, not as a possible permanent transformation in the nature of women's socioeconomic roles. Hence, in using these PUS data it is important to avoid making simplistic projections, either backward or forward. On the one hand, there is sometimes the tendency to project backward the normative (or ideological) conditions of the present or even of the period under observation when the conditions of a still earlier period are actually most relevant. On the other hand, it is equally unwise to assume that younger cohorts today will simply pick up from the point where older cohorts left off. This ignores the fact that very different social and economic conditions will have been operating at similar critical points in the life-cycle. However, these are not necessarily the points to which our observation refer.

One must also remember that major postwar changes have been occurring in the level of the demand for workers in different occupations, especially in predominantly *female* occupations. As I have argued elsewhere, sharp postwar increases in the demand for workers in predominantly female occupations encouraged the rapid rise in female labor-force participation after the war (Oppenheimer 1970, 1973). However, more recent trends indicate that such a rapid rise in the demand for female workers cannot and has not continued at the same pace as in the period up to the mid 1960s. Declining fertility and the possible slowing down of the expansion of government are two factors that can affect employment opportunities in traditionally female jobs such as teaching, social work, clerical jobs. (Oppenheimer 1972). The question to consider later on in this chapter involves the implications of these possible shifts in demand on women's economic roles, given changes in the socioeconomic characteristics of women and their families.

Occupational Comparability and Status Compatibility: 1960 and 1970 Similarities

Tables 8.1 and 8.2 show that wives' educational attainment is highly related to their husband's peak median occupation. Those most likely to have graduated from college were married to professionals or to Manager I males. Furthermore, the great majority of wives of white-collar men were high-school graduates, especially in 1970, and among the wives of Group I and II males at both dates (Table 8.1). But in the case of the blue-collar occupational groups of husbands, the majority of wives had not finished high school. In fact, a substantial proportion had no high-school experience at all—34% for wives of Operative IV males and 40% for the wives of Service IV men in 1960, for example (Table 8.2).

In short, and not surprisingly, the wives of higher-level men were more employable than the wives of lower-level men and at occupations of a higher socioeconomic status. However, not only the position of these wives relative to other *wives* but also what their potential socioeconomic position would be relative to their *husbands* and hence to their own derived socioeconomic position is at issue. In this comparison a very different picture emerges.

There are two somewhat different perspectives from which to view the significance of wives' potential relative occupational level as indicated by

TABLE 8.1
Selected Comparisons of the Cumulative Educational Attainments of Husbands and Wives, for Couples Where the Husband Was in a White-Collar Occupation: 1960 and 1970

	Percentage at specified educational level								
	High school				College				
	1+		4+		1+		4+		5+
Husband's occupation	W	H	W	H	W	H	W	H	W	H
---	---	---	---	---	---	---	---	---	---	---
1960[b]									
Total[a]	78	71	54	49	16	23	6	12	1	5
Professionals										
I	98	98	89	95	57	86	28	74	8	51
II	95	97	82	90	38	70	18	45	4	16
III	94	96	80	86	40	68	19	51	5	31
Managers										
I	95	94	79	80	35	55	16	31	2	8
II	87	82	69	63	24	33	9	16	2	4
III	84	80	63	59	22	27	8	10	1	2
Sales										
II	93	93	77	78	33	45	13	22	2	5
III	86	83	65	60	20	28	6	9	1	2
Clerical										
III	87	87	67	68	18	27	6	9	1	3
IV	75	69	46	42	9	10	2	3	1	2
Service										
III	87	86	62	58	12	15	2	3	—	2
1970									
Total[a]	88	82	61	63	22	30	9	16	3	8
Professionals										
I	98	99	90	97	60	88	34	75	12	54
II	97	99	82	94	42	71	18	46	5	17
III	97	97	82	92	49	73	26	57	10	37
Managers										
I	96	96	82	89	40	62	19	40	5	13
II	94	92	72	77	29	42	11	21	3	6
III	92	89	69	72	25	33	8	14	2	4
Sales										
II	97	97	81	88	39	56	15	30	3	7
III	92	91	70	74	25	34	8	13	2	3
Clerical										
III	93	94	69	80	24	36	7	14	2	4
IV	83	80	53	56	11	16	2	3	1	1
Service										
III	93	92	65	77	15	22	4	4	2	1

Sources: 1960 and 1970 Public Use Samples of White Couples.
[a]Includes blue-collar and white-collar occupational groups.
[b]Includes some families where the husband was not the household head.

educational data. One is what a wife's educational attainment can reveal about her ability to qualify for an occupation that is *comparable* to her husband's. For example, if the educational level of Manager I or Professional I wives, as a group, is much below that of their husband's then, as far as the *number* of years of school is concerned, such wives would probably not qualify for a comparable occupation.[1]

A second question is whether wives' educational attainment seems to qualify them for occupations that are status *compatible,* if not comparable, and that may also make a net positive socioeconomic contribution to the family. In part, this is a function of the nature of the economic pressures the family experiences. Depending on the extensiveness of women's work behavior over their life course, different types of occupations may represent status compatible jobs that also make a significant economic contribution to the family. Presumably, temporary jobs will have to conform to some minimum standard of acceptability but need not meet the same standards, nor be expected to pay as well, as jobs involving more long-term work commitments. Thus, to the extent economic pressures for the wife to work typically vary in their extensiveness among socioeconomic groups, the occupations to which such women are attracted will also vary. And, consequently, so may their level of human-capital investment.

Finally, when comparing the educational attainments of husbands and wives, it is important to remember that similar educational achievements have not traditionally qualified women for the same types of jobs as men because of institutionalized sex-segregated labor markets (Oppenheimer 1970). This may be changing in recent years but the impact of these changes on the 1960 and 1970 PUS cohorts was probably minimal.

WIVES OF GROUP I AND II WHITE-COLLAR MEN

As we have seen, the major economic stress point for Group I and II families seems to be during the first life-cycle squeeze since this is a period when the husband's earnings are low, especially relative to those of somewhat older men in the same occupational group, but also compared to older men in almost any other occupational group. Given the steep age-

---

[1]This approach is very crude, of course, because not just the *number* of school years attained is at issue but what subjects are studied—whether it is English literature or electrical engineering makes a considerable difference, to say the least. There is, in addition, the role of past on-the-job training. Furthermore, since occupations at similar socioeconomic levels often involve different amounts of formal schooling, the inability to function in exactly the same type of occupation as the husband does not necessarily imply that a wife cannot work at another occupation at the same general socioeconomic level but requiring less formal schooling. Nevertheless, just comparing husbands and wives on the number of school years attained should provide some idea of the proportion of wives whose educational level alone seems to preclude employment in jobs of a similar level or type to their husbands'.

TABLE 8.2
Selected Comparisons of the Cumulative Educational Attainments of Husbands and Wives, for Couples Where the Husband Was in a Blue-Collar Occupation: 1960 and 1970

	1960[b]						1970					
	High school				College		High school				College	
	1+		4+		1+		1+		4+		1+	
Husband's occupation	W	H	W	H	W	H	W	H	W	H	W	H
Total[a]	78	71	54	49	16	23	88	82	61	63	22	30
Craft												
II	81	76	54	48	14	15	90	86	59	63	12	19
III	76	68	48	40	9	9	86	78	54	54	11	11
IV	68	56	39	30	6	5	80	70	46	41	9	8
Operatives												
III	69	59	41	32	7	6	81	71	46	44	8	7
IV	66	53	36	25	5	4	79	68	44	39	8	7
Service												
IV	60	48	36	26	8	7	76	65	45	41	12	11
Laborers												
IV	59	43	30	19	4	4	74	64	41	38	8	8

Sources: 1960 and 1970 Public Use Samples of White Couples.
[a]Includes white-collar and blue-collar occupational groups.
[b]The 1960 data include some families where the husband was not the household head.

I. Educational Attainment 295

earnings profile of men in Group I and II occupations, the second life-cycle squeeze period would probably not represent the same economic difficulties for such men as for couples where the husband's age–earnings profile is flatter (e.g., Group III white-collar families) Nevertheless, the high postwar fertility certainly seems to have increased the severity of the second squeeze for many white-collar families and especially for families of men in Group I and II occupations who experienced some of the sharpest increases in fertility.

Focusing just on the impetus provided by life-cycle variations in economic stress, one might anticipate that if these Group I and II wives worked at all during their married life, it was usually at relatively temporary types of occupations. These need not meet the same high standards necessary for a more serious career commitment but would nevertheless offer status-compatible types of jobs that would make a relatively positive economic contribution to the family at difficult life-cycle squeeze points. For the wives of White-Collar I and II males, the types of occupations that seem to fit into this general scenario are, at a minimum, white-collar jobs. Within that group, clerical and sales occupations provide an easy, though not always a very appealing, option. However, women's professions have been particularly attractive as they are usually better paid than clerical jobs, frequently involve more flexible hours, are often intrinsically more rewarding, and may provide something of an insurance policy for women in case they do not marry or, if they do, become widowed or divorced. Their social status is typically higher as well.

Although the career goals of most women who became wives of Group I and II white-collar males were likely to have been rather limited, given the basic socioeconomic circumstances of their lives and the historically low labor-force participation of married women when many of these cohorts were young, a minority probably had more extensive occupational aspirations and achievements. Some women of middle-class origins may have adopted the occupational goals specific to their *"class"* rather than their *sex* and had the family backing to pursue atypical occupational careers. For other women with the necessary ability and opportunities, high occupational achievements may have provided an important means of upward mobility otherwise barred to them. Whatever the case, if such women married, they were most likely to marry men like themselves and hence we shall observe them as wives of men who are also at relatively high occupational levels.

Given such a range of hypothesized occupational "goals," certain educational attainment levels are essential and the question is the extent to which these women achieved such levels of schooling. What the data reveal, however, is that wives of high-level men were much less well educated than their husbands (Table 8.1). As a result, a very small proportion seemed educationally qualified for an occupation which would be status comparable to their husbands'. Neither is there evidence that the educational gap closed appreciably between 1960 and 1970. The educational differential is most marked in the professions where extended formal training is so important. For example, whereas 51% of the Professional I husbands had 5 or more years of higher education in 1960 and 54% in 1970, this was true for only 8% of their wives in 1960 and 12% in 1970.[2] However, a relatively high proportion of those wives of Professional I men who were working were actually employed in a professional occupation—47% in 1970 (Tables 8.3 and 8.4). In both 1960 and 1970 fully 74–75% of the Professional I husbands had at least graduated from college whereas in 1960 only 28% of their wives had done so and even in 1970 it was only 34%. Smaller, but still substantial, differences in the proportions achieving different levels of higher education between husbands and wives were also characteristic of other Group I and II occupations. However, years of schooling may be a less meaningful measure of potential occupational level in such occupations given the importance of on-the-job training. Nevertheless, considering the historically very limited opportunities for on-the-job training open to women in high-level sales or in management, it seems unlikely that a large number of highly qualified women have gone undetected by this analysis of educational characteristics.

A second important finding is that the proportion of wives who were qualified for relatively high-level female occupations was also relatively small, although increasing. Hence, comparatively few seemed to be eligible for positions in a status *compatible* occupation that, while not comparable to their husband's, would nevertheless represent a significant socioeconomic asset to the family—especially at certain times in the life-cycle.[3]

Although educationally handicapped for higher-level occupations, a majority of wives of Group I and II males did seem to be educationally qualified for Clerical III or Sales III occupations. Hence, most would have

---

[2]Moreover, a number of women who have achieved master's degrees in such fields as education or social work are included in this category. Thus it is impossible to distinguish those with higher-level professional degrees (mostly men) from those with lower-level degrees (where the women are concentrated).

[3]How much of a socioeconomic advantage such occupations represent depends on the husband's socioeconomic level, and we have not really been making very fine distinctions here. Thus the relative socioeconomic advantage of having a wife who is an elementary-school teacher is likely to be much greater for a college professor than for a physician (both of whom were placed in the Professional I grouping). So, for some of these families such types of professional occupations may represent a fairly attractive possibility for wives throughout the life-cycle, but for many others their attractions may be limited to life-cycle squeeze periods or other times of economic stress and to periods where the wife has fewer demands on her time and can work for rewards other than the socioeconomic advantages such an occupation may entail.

been able to get jobs that met a rough minimum standard of compatibility. And, indeed, of those actually employed, 10% or less were in blue-collar occupations in either 1960 or 1970. However, given their high derived socioeconomic position, the appeal of such occupations would probably depend on other life circumstances (e.g., the severity of the first or second life-cycle squeezes). Moreover, a percentage of women—sometimes a fairly substantial one—were not even high-school graduates and might have had considerable difficulty in obtaining white-collar positions. For example, in 1960, such women accounted for 31% of the wives of Manager II males and 28% in 1970. This would reduce the potentiality of their making a positive socioeconomic contribution to the family through paid employment. For some, the potential contribution might even have been negative.

In sum, focusing on the types of occupations in which Group I and II wives might be qualified to work and the socioeconomic rewards such employment might bring, the evidence indicates that the relative socioeconomic advantage of paid employment was low—at least on a regular basis as opposed to particular distinct periods in the life-cycle.

WIVES OF GROUP III AND IV WHITE-COLLAR MEN

I have hypothesized that many families of men in Group III and IV white-collar occupations are subject to a lower white-collar squeeze—a squeeze which probably intensified in the postwar period because of the much greater increase in white- than blue-collar fertility. Compared to Group I and II wives, this should have created greater economic pressures for a fairly regular labor-force attachment as well as increases in such pressures at the two life-cycle squeeze points. It is therefore particularly interesting to consider the educational qualifications of Group III and IV white-collar wives and, through this, their potential occupational position. Moreover, in contrast to Group I and II wives, not as high an occupational level is necessary for Group III and IV white-collar wives, either for status compatibiity or to exert an important positive economic impact on the family. Nevertheless, to the extent many of these families have a strong attachment to a white-collar status and to white-collar life-styles, the nonmanual status of different jobs should be an important factor in their desirability.

Keeping these considerations in mind, for what types of occupations do the educational attainments of white-collar Group III wives seem to qualify them? First, the educational disparity between husbands and wives is much less for them than for Group I and II couples, with the major exception of Professional III couples (Table 8.1). Hence, most human capital related differences in the potential occupational position of these Group III couples would not have depended as much on the *quantity* of schooling attained as on

TABLE 8.3
Occupation of Employed Wives, by Occupation of Husband: White Couples, 1960 (Percentage Distribution)

Husband's occupation	Total	Wife's occupation[a]							
		Professionals		Managers	Sales			Clerical	Blue collar	Service
		I, II	III		II	III				
Total	100	2	11	4	1	9	36	21	16
Professionals									
I	100	13	30	2	1	2	40	3	8
II	100	9	23	5	1	6	44	6	8
III	100	2	41	2	—	6	34	6	9
Managers									
I	100	4	16	4	1	7	53	5	9
II	100	1	11	7	3	8	52	9	10
III	100	2	11	13	2	17	34	11	11
Sales									
II	100	4	18	7	3	9	45	7	7
III	100	1	13	4	1	17	40	12	12

Clerical							
III	100	1	15	4	1	7	52	9	11
IV	100	—	11	2	—	4	45	26	12
Craft							
II	100	3	12	4	1	10	35	25	11
III	100	1	8	4	—	8	38	25	15
IV	100	1	5	3	1	14	28	26	23
Operatives							
III	100	1	7	3	—	9	28	36	16
IV	100	1	6	3	1	8	28	35	19
Service							
III	100	4	7	3	2	5	55	11	12
IV	100	1	7	2	1	5	22	24	37
Laborers							
IV	100	—	5	2	1	10	22	36	25

Source: 1960 Public Use Sample of White Couples.
[a]The occupational classification system for wives was collapsed to simplify presentation.

TABLE 8.4
Occupation of Employed Wives, by Occupation of Husband: White Couples, 1970 (Percentage Distribution)

Husband's occupation	Total	Professionals I, II	Professionals III	Managers	Sales II	Sales III	Clerical	Blue collar	Service
Total	100	4	14	4	1	7	38	18	15
Professionals									
I	100	13	34	3	2	4	34	4	6
II	100	9	24	3	1	6	44	5	7
III	100	4	43	2	1	5	32	6	7
Managers									
I	100	5	21	6	1	7	46	9	6
II	100	5	16	7	2	8	45	10	9
III	100	3	11	13	—	10	43	8	12

Wife's occupation[a]

Sales								
II	100	4	20	4	3	8	47	6	8
III	100	4	15	4	1	11	44	9	11
Clerical								
III	100	4	14	4	1	7	47	12	13
IV	100	3	8	2	—	8	46	22	12
Craft								
II	100	2	11	3	1	8	38	25	13
III	100	2	8	3	1	8	39	22	16
IV	100	1	8	3	1	8	33	26	20
Operatives								
III	100	2	7	2	1	8	31	31	18
IV	100	2	6	2	—	7	32	32	19
Service								
III	100	1	14	4	—	6	47	12	16
IV	100	3	9	3	—	6	27	21	31
Laborers								
IV	100	2	6	2	—	6	31	29	23

Source: 1970 Public Use Sample of White Couples.

[a] The occupational classification system for wives was collapsed to simplify presentation.

substantive differences in the type of formal schooling. Moreover, educational attainment is undoubtedly an imperfect indicator of the ability of women to obtain jobs in many male managerial, sales, or professional Group III occupations for other reasons as well. For example, limited opportunities for on-the-job training and employment discrimination are two important factors about which census data have little to tell us.

What about the educational qualifications of Group III wives for status compatible occupations at various levels? To begin with, where do they stand with regard to the professional and technical occupations? Professional III wives fared the best in this respect. In 1970, 49% had achieved 1 or more years of college-level schooling and 26% were college graduates. This showing is better even than that of wives of Professional II males. And, indeed, a relatively high proportion of the employed Professional III wives were actually in one professional group or another—43% in 1960 and 47% in 1970 (Tables 8.3 and 8.4). This heavy a concentration in the professions was matched only by the wives of Professional I men.[4] Turning to other Group III wives, a much smaller proportion had the minimum amount of schooling necessary for a professional or semiprofessional job. In 1970, for example, less than 10% of the wives of men in all the other Group III white-collar occupations had graduated from college and 25% or less had attained 1 or more years of college.

Once again, the majority of wives seemed to have achieved enough schooling to qualify for clerical occupations and, if not that, sales work. However, a fairly substantial percentage were only marginally qualified for lower-level white-collar jobs, although improvements were observed between 1960 and 1970. For example, in the case of wives of Managers, Sales, and Clerical III men, between 33 and 37% had not even graduated from high school in 1960 and between 30 and 31% were still in this position in 1970. A higher proportion had, of course, at least some high-school experience.

WIVES OF BLUE-COLLAR MEN

How do blue-collar husbands and wives compare with respect to their educational attainments? Given the husband's relatively low socioeconomic level, it is possible that even without very extensive schooling, a wife could still obtain a job that was both status compatible and represented a significant positive contribution to the family's socioeconomic position. However, it is also possible that many of these wives were at too low an educational level to

---

[4]Of course marital selection is probably a major factor in the high proportion of these wives in the professions.

I. Educational Attainment

obtain a relatively attractive job, particularly in view of the fact that the better blue-collar jobs—such as the crafts—have traditionally been male preserves. Hence job opportunities for wives of blue-collar workers have tended to be dichotomized into medium-lower-level white-collar jobs, on the one hand, and lower-level manual and service jobs, on the other.

In sharp contrast to white-collar wives, blue-collar wives had typically achieved more schooling than their husbands (Tables 8.1 and 8.2). This was especially the case in 1960 and was observable both in the proportions attaining 12 or more years of schooling and 9 or more years. Moreover, the differential was greater for Blue-Collar IV than Blue-Collar III couples. Hence, the number of years of formal schooling does not appear to be a factor in any blue-collar husband–wife differences in potential occupational comparability. Those human capital differences that would play an important role had to be related to childhood and adolescent differences in socialization, substantive differences in formal schooling, and the nature and extent of available on-the-job training taken advantage of.

Since the educational attainments of blue-collar wives compared quite favorably to those of their husbands, for what occupational levels did these women have the educational qualifications? Just how variable was their potential relative socioeconomic contribution to the family? As it turns out, quite a substantial proportion had achieved an educational level high enough to qualify for a white-collar occupation (i.e., a job that might represent a considerable status and economic asset to the family). This was particularly true in 1970, of course. At that time, for example, 54% of the wives of Craft III men had graduated from high school and only 14% had never been to high school at all. For Craft IV and Operative III and IV wives, the proportions with either 9 or 12 or more years of schooling were similar—between 44 and 46% having finished high school or better and between 79 and 81% having at least had some high school. Service and Laborers IV wives did not lag very far behind.

Since a substantial proportion of blue-collar wives probably qualified for white-collar positions of one sort or another, the relative advantage of their working ought to have been considerable. Whether it was greater than in the case of wives of Group III white-collar males is somewhat difficult to determine, however, from schooling data alone. On the one hand, the Group III blue-collar wives, at least, were presumably not subject to the lower white-collar squeeze. Furthermore, the relative *economic* advantage of the wife working may often have not been any greater (in fact sometimes less) because of the frequently superior earnings position of males in Blue-Collar III occupations. On the other hand, economic pressures in many blue-collar families—especially those in the Blue-Collar IV groups—must still have been considerable and hence one could hardly suppose that pressures for an additional income did not exist for these groups as well as for lower-level white-collar families. In any event, of those blue-collar wives who were employed, high proportions were to be found in white-collar jobs.

Although most blue-collar wives had attained 1 or more years of high school, it was also the case that a significant minority had never attended high school at all, especially in 1960. This was true for about one-third of the wives of Operative III and Craft IV and Operative IV males in 1960. The proportions with such low educational attainments was even higher for the wives of Laborers and Service IV men. By 1970 about 20% of the Operative III and IV and Craft IV wives still had not attended high school. Hence, these still constituted a significant though rapidly shrinking proportion that might have encountered difficulties in obtaining work. In the case of Group III white-collar wives, in contrast, only between 3 and 8% had never attended high school in 1970.

In sum, compared to wives of White-Collar III workers, a higher proportion of blue-collar wives seemed to have run a greater risk of unemployability at any occupational level or to be qualified for a job only at a level that might have been considered demeaning. However, a substantial proportion were in the position of being able, through paid employment, to make a significant impact on their family's socioeconomic position.

Implications of Changing Educational Attainment

As Tables 8.1 and 8.2 show, the educational attainment of wives rose considerably between 1960 and 1970. Table 8.5 gives a more expanded view of the magnitude of these changes by comparing the educational attainment of these couples across age cohorts for all occupational groups combined.[5] The increases in educational attainment it reveals are enormous. For example, the proportion of wives with 12 or more years of schooling increased from 36% for wives of men who were 55–64 in 1960 to 70% for the wives of 25–34-year-olds in 1970. The comparable rise in the proportions with 1 or more years of college was from 14 to 27%. In short, the proportion of wives who appeared educationally qualified for a white-collar job had changed from a minority to a majority. Hence, as younger and more extensively educated cohorts come to predominate among American couples, the employment prospects of American wives as a group should be greatly improved. And if the ability to find a clerical, professional, or

[5]Medians were not used as these tend to obscure important changes at the upper educational levels. Moreover, the comparisons were not broken down by husband's occupation because of the uncertainties introduced by occupational mobility into comparisons of different age cohorts in the same occupational group.

TABLE 8.5
Selected Educational Attainments of Husbands and Wives, by Husband's Age: 1970

	\multicolumn{10}{c}{Percentage with specified number of school years completed}
	9+		12+		13+		16+		17+	
Husband's age[a]	W	H	W	H	W	H	W	H	W	H
25–34	95	92	70	76	27	37	11	21	3	10
35–44	91	85	64	66	22	32	9	20	3	10
45–54	86	80	59	59	20	27	8	15	3	7
55–64	74	66	48	44	17	21	7	11	2	5
65–74[b]	57	47	36	30	14	16	5	7	1	3

Sources: 1960 and 1970 Public Use Samples of White Couples.

[a] Educational data were not presented for couples where the husband was aged 18–24. This is because many young adults will not have finished their schooling yet in this age group, especially the wives of such young men. In addition, because of the delayed marriage associated with school enrollment, couples where the husband is 18–24 years old will be particularly atypical of young people in these age groups.

[b] These are 1960 data for couples where the husband was aged 55–64 years old. They were included to give a broader picture of the rapid educational changes occurring between various cohorts.

semiprofessional position signifies the ability to work at a relatively socioeconomically advantageous job, and hence increases the likelihood of wives working, then such a transformation has certainly been taking place.

If more and more women are qualifying for female white-collar jobs, the question is whether these occupations can expand sufficiently to absorb such a large potential influx. This issue has added significance when one remembers the extent to which women have been concentrated in a relatively small number of predominantly female occupations (Oppenheimer 1970, 1972). Recent fertility trends indicate, however, that at least some of the traditionally female occupations have not and will not be expanding as rapidly as in the postwar baby-boom period and its aftermath. A prime example of this is the case of teaching, an occupation that is particularly dependent on fertility trends. It is also an especially interesting case because it has been such an important job source for college-educated women. For example, in 1960 and 1970 48–49% of women in the labor force who had achieved 4 or more years of higher education were concentrated in teaching below the college level (U.S. Bureau of the Census 1963b: Table 9; 1973b: Table 5). However, given the long-term decline in fertility, it seems unlikely that teaching will be an expanding occupation, even if student-teacher ratios should fall. Between 1970 and 1978 alone, there was a 15% decline in the number of children enrolled in kindergarten and elementary school. Although numbers enrolled in high school still rose during this period (slowly, by 5%) it is inevitable that high-school enrollments will start to decline as the smaller cohorts move into their teens (U.S. Bureau of the Census 1979b; Table 1).

In short, although the postwar baby boom encouraged the rapid expansion of occupations such as teaching, the more recent baby bust is having just the opposite effect—and at a time when the number of college-educated women is expanding. Hence, the continued growth of the female labor force will rest, in part, on the expansion of other traditionally female occupations—such as nursing and medical–technical specialities—combined with the penetration of women into more traditionally male occupations. However, unless job opportunities in all these occupations are expanding fairly rapidly, recent trends may have important implications for the relationship of women's family and economic roles—especially, perhaps, among more educated women.

Let us use the case of teaching to develop some of the implications of this situation. College-educated American women have historically gravitated towards certain female professions, not only because these professions were traditionally female but also because, in much of the postwar period, several of them had provided satisfactory ways of combining a career, even if a somewhat abbreviated one, with marriage and children. Teaching has been particularly practical in this respect. For one thing, the training is not so onerous or so extensive that it is not worthwhile making the necessary human-capital investment, even if the woman quits after marriage or the first child and *never* returns to work. It provided many women with their ace in the hole in case they did not marry or their marriages ended in widowhood or divorce. It was also possible to combine the process of acquiring the necessary human capital for teaching with that of finding a suitable mate since universities and colleges tend to have a higher concentration of eligible young men than almost any other work or nonwork context in which a young woman might become involved. Another advantage of teaching has been that earnings are higher than in most other major women's occupations. Furthermore, job opportunities were so plentiful for many years in the aftermath of the baby boom that teachers could often plan to take off a few years while their children were preschoolers and then return to work, if it was necessary, feeling relatively assured of being able to find a job. Teaching has also been ideal for the woman with schoolage children because she does not have to work summers when they are not in school and, frequently, she can get home earlier than the person with an ordinary full-time job. In addition, a number of the other female professions have permitted part-time, if not part-year work—for example, nursing, librarianship.[6] And, in an expanding labor

---

[6]In some cities with nursing shortages (e.g., Los Angeles) nursing registries exist that supply hospitals with temporary staff. This makes it possible for many women to maintain their level of human capital investment—or even improve on it—but work less than full time during family-cycle periods of extensive home responsibilities.

I. Educational Attainment

market, many female jobs could be dropped and picked up again without too many difficulties (e.g., clerical and sales work).

In sum, the rapid postwar expansion in job opportunities in traditional female professions, such as teaching, probably created a certain climate of expectations among many young women that a college education would pay off with a relatively high-status occupation that could easily be meshed with a woman's traditional familial role. This, in turn, involved both periodic variations in the family's need for an additional income and in the demands family responsibilities make on a woman's time. If such a climate of expectations did develop and was a factor encouraging increasing educational attainment among women and rising labor-force participation, what effect will the shifts in the demand for such workers have? What is likely to happen if these traditional higher-level female occupations—especially teaching—are not expanding as rapidly as is the supply of college-educated women? One likely result is that the opportunity cost of leaving the labor force will rise considerably. Not only will it become increasingly difficult for young women fresh out of school to find a job but these occupations will less and less provide jobs one can leave at inconvenient points in the family cycle and return to as circumstances permit or require. If job opportunities are relatively few and the supply of women who desire to work is large, then at every point it will be difficult to get placed. Furthermore, if women respond to this situation by holding on to jobs they might have been more casual about in a previous time, this will reduce the number of job openings resulting from turnover.[7] All this should intensify the difficulties of the young and of those who thought they were only retiring from the labor force temporarily. Both will have a harder time breaking into—or *back* into—the system. As a consequence, one advantage of a number of female occupations—to be able to leave them and return to them without having lost too much ground—will tend to disappear if changes in job opportunities fail to keep up with the supply of qualified women.

There are other possible responses to the sluggish growth in several female occupations. One is that an increasing number of women may attempt to enter into more traditionally male occupations. When they do that, however, the opportunity costs of leaving the labor force are also likely to rise. Some

---

[7]Unfortunately, CPS data on job tenure are not particularly helpful in trying to ascertain whether, once working, women are increasingly likely to stick to a particular job (U.S. Bureau of Labor Statistics 1979c). The problem is that trends in job tenure and labor-force participation become confounded. The CPS measure of job tenure is the tenure of currently employed workers rather than longitudinal data on the proportion of women working at a previous time period who are still with the same employer. Hence, the job tenure of current workers will be pulled down by new entrants or recent reentrants to the labor force in a period of rising labor-force participation among women.

jobs may become feminized and gain certain characteristics of the more typically female occupations—low amounts of on-the-job training and few paths of upward mobility. However, such a shift often involves low wages as a concomitant. But if the occupation remains sexually integrated, then such women should be under competitive pressures to behave more like mature males workers—that is, maintain a more permanent labor-force and job attachment. Another possibility is that some better-educated women will move into lower-level traditionally female occupations—especially, perhaps, those women who do not plan to maintain a long-run labor-force attachment. This might operate to displace adequately but less well-educated women who, in response, may try to establish more permanent job ties in order to achieve the job security that seniority often provides.

In short, a slow-down in the growth of many traditionally female occupations should promote a more regular and permanent labor-force attachment among adult women because the opportunity costs of dropping out of the labor force will rise. This process, in turn, will intensify the pressure to develop regular job attachments because one source of job openings, those due to high turnover rates, will be reduced by increases in long-term job attachments.

CHANGES IN WIVES' RELATIVE EDUCATIONAL STATUS

Although the PUS data show that the educational attainment of wives was increasing rapidly, the tables also reveal that the increases for their husbands were even more rapid, so that where in some socioeconomic groups women had once held an educational advantage over their husbands, this was greatly reduced or lost entirely. In other cases, where the educational attainment of husbands exceeded that of wives, there was little or no evidence of a reduction in the husband–wife differential. If anything, it tended to increase. Hence, on the basis of educational attainment alone, these PUS data suggest that little or no improvement had occurred in the ability of women to qualify for occupations *comparable* to their husbands'. More recent data, however, indicate that an improvement in the relative educational position of women does appear to be occurring. For example, there has been a substantial decline in the sex gap in college enrollments. Thus in 1978, 37% of white 18–19-year-old females were enrolled in college and 26% of 20–21-year-olds. This compares quite favorably to the comparable proportions for white males—36% for 18–19-year-olds and 31% for 20–21-year-olds (U.S. Bureau of the Census 1979b: Table 1). Moreover, enrollments of women in professional schools of, for example, medicine, dentistry, and law, have been increasing rapidly since 1965 (see Parrish 1974; U.S. Bureau of the Census 1977b: 106–161).

Another problem encountered in using education data is how well school years completed is indicative of similar levels of human capital attainment. In manual occupations, for example, the significance of educational similarities is ambiguous because on-the-job training is so important a feature of human capital investments. Thus, the educational advantage typical of blue-collar wives—in the past, at least—was certainly not indicative of an equal probability of employment in higher-paying Group III blue-collar occupations for both human capital and institutional reasons. Hence, a more complete evaluation of the total differential between spouses in human capital attainment and any trends in this differential would require information about on-the-job training that is simply not available in the PUS—or in most other data sets. If, as seems likely, a significant proportion of men's total human capital investment is made on the job, then, given women's increasing work experience, perhaps there was some unmeasured decline in human capital differentials for the cohorts included in this study. However, to the extent human capital investments in the form of on-the-job training are an important factor in men's occupational and earnings levels, this suggests that if wives do start to close the gap between themselves and their husbands it will be due to their developing not only a more long-term attachment to the labor force in general but also, to particular work organizations or sets of organizations operating within roughly the same internal labor market.

II. ECONOMIC IMPACT OF WIVES WORKING

What was the actual economic contribution of these PUS wives to their families and can this tell us anything about the *potential* economic contribution of women with similar socioeconomic characteristics if they too should work? Although this discussion will be phrased primarily in terms of *economic* impacts, a wife's earnings will undoubtedly also affect the general *status* position of the family via a modification of its consumption patterns, that is, its life-style (see also Barth and Watson 1967; Duncan 1961: 118).[8]

There are two major facets to the analysis of the economic impact on their families of wives working. First, there is the question of how this varied among wives of men in different peak median occupational groups, regardless of family-cycle stage. What effect did or could their working have on income

[8]Parsons, for example, stresses the importance of money as a criterion of status, especially in view of the fact "that its expenditure is largely for other symbols of status in turn [Parsons 1954a 85]."

differentials among the families in these 18 occupational groups? Might this have any implications for future changes in women's economic behavior and what changes were actually observed, if any, in women's economic contribution between 1960 and 1970?

A second major issue raises a number of questions having to do with the actual and potential impact on the severity of the two life-cycle squeezes. One concerns the general role wives' employment can play in alleviating the difficulties of the life-cycle squeezes. Another is whether the economic role of women in moderating the squeezes might not involve feedback effects so that certain self-generating mechanisms are set in motion that promote further increases in wives' labor-force participation. Finally, what is the nature of differences among occupational groups in the capacity of wives to affect the severity of the squeezes and does this change over time?

The Economic Impact of Wives of Men in Different Occupational Groups

VARIATIONS IN WIVES' EARNINGS

In Chapter 7 we saw that the employed wife's educational attainment was related to her occupational position. Her occupation, in turn, affected her annual earnings. Moreover, the propensity of wives to work was related to their educational attainment, in such a way as to indicate that the greater their absolute and relative potential socioeconomic contribution to the family, the greater the probability of being in the labor force. However, in this chapter we have found that although wives of higher-level men had achieved more schooling than other wives, there was considerable overlap in the educational attainments of these different groups of women. This was accompanied by substantial occupational overlaps among the employed wives of men in the various peak median occupational groups. Regardless of the husband's occupational group, between 33 and 58% of employed wives were in clerical or sales work in 1970 and between 28 and 63% were in 1960. Even among families of men in blue-collar occupations, the lowest proportions of employed wives in a white-collar occupation of one sort or another was 48% in 1970 and 38% in 1960 (Tables 8.3 and 8.4). All this suggests that the earnings of these wives might also be rather similar. And this is just what was actually observed.

Looking at women by the occupational group of their husbands, Table 8.6 presents the median earnings of all wives with some earnings in 1959 and 1969 as well as for those wives who worked "full time" (at least 40 weeks in

TABLE 8.6
Median 1959 and 1969 Earnings of Husbands and Wives, by Husband's Occupation and Wife's Work Experience (1969 Dollars)[a,b]

	1959			1969		
		Wives[c,e]			Wives[c]	
Husband's occupation	Husbands[d]	All	Full-time	Husbands[d]	All	Full-time
Total	6,926	2,505	4,179	8,926	3,298	4,933
Professionals						
I	11,284	2,628	4,856	14,489	3,483	6,212
II	8,980	3,249	4,943	11,431	3,569	5,696
III	7,167	2,756	4,652	9,627	3,909	5,993
Managers						
I	10,919	2,873	4,604	13,286	3,524	5,510
II	9,442	2,555	4,374	11,537	3,429	5,152
III	7,527	2,984	4,475	9,800	3,479	5,003
Sales						
II	8,596	3,005	4,778	11,372	3,750	5,652
III	6,633	2,546	4,300	8,772	3,655	5,152
Clerical						
III	6,859	2,854	4,482	8,609	3,536	5,156
IV	5,898	2,863	4,010	7,404	3,636	4,755
Craft						
II	9,097	2,698	4,443	10,838	3,460	5,009
III	7,215	2,613	4,221	8,989	3,204	4,831
IV	5,905	2,019	3,609	7,530	3,014	4,423
Operatives						
III	6,423	2,427	3,954	8.049	3,060	4,675
IV	5,792	2,166	3,685	7,425	3,029	4,440
Service						
III	6,840	2,916	4,507	9,234	3,438	5,242
IV	4,892	2,511	3,646	6,325	3,333	4,665
Laborers						
IV	5,082	1,847	3,641	6,475	2,736	4,328
Range	6,392	1,402	1,334	8.164	1,173	1,884
as a percentage of total median	92.3	56.0	31.9	91.5	35.6	38.2

Sources: 1960 and 1970 Public Use Samples of White Couples.

[a] Median income in dollars of those with net positive earnings.

[b] The medians for 1959 were inflated into 1969 dollars using the 25.8% increase in the Consumer Price Index in the 1959–1969 period.

[c] Two groups of wives with net positive earnings were considered: (a) *All*—all wives with earnings; and (b) *Full-time*—those wives who worked 40–52 weeks in 1959 or 1969 and 35 or more hours in the census reference week. Forty weeks was selected as the minimum for "full-time" employment in order not to exclude teachers.

[d] These are the median earnings of all husbands, not just those with earning wives.

[e] 1960 data for wives include some families where the husband was not the head of the household.

the year and 35 or more hours during the census reference week).[9] Median earnings of husbands are included for the sake of comparison. One outstanding feature of the table is how low the wives' earnings were. For all wives who had earnings, the 1959 median earnings were, with two exceptions, always below $3,000 (in 1969 dollars) and in 1969 they were, without exception, below $4,000. The earnings of wives working full time were also quite low. In fact, they were so low that even the medians of the wives of very high-level professionals or managers were below those of men in the Blue-Collar IV occupational groups.[10]

A concomitant of the low level of these women's earnings was the small variation in the median earnings among wives of men at radically different occupational levels. The 1969 median earnings of husbands in the 18 occupational groups ranged from a high of $14,489 for Professional I males to a low of $6,325 for Service IV males, a difference of $8,164. This range amounts to 92% of the median earnings of husbands in all occupational groups combined. In the case of their full-time-working wives, however, the range was from a high of $6,212 to a low of $4,328—a difference of only $1,884 or 38% of the median for all full-time wives combined. The pattern for 1959 was very similar.

RELATIVE ECONOMIC IMPACT OF WIVES WORKING

Since there was little variation in earnings among wives of men in different occupational groups, their relative economic impact must have varied inversely with the husband's peak median earnings level. That this was so is shown in Table 8.7 which presents the median of the ratios of wife's/husband's 1959 and 1969 earnings. Whether we consider all couples where the wife had earnings or just those where she was a full-time worker, there is a fairly strong tendency, within major occupational groups, for the median ratio to vary inversely with the husband's peak median earnings group. However, for most occupational groups, a decline occurred in the median ratio of wife/husband's earnings between 1959 and 1969 despite substantial increases in the labor-force participation of the wives of men in a number of occupational groups (Table 8.8).[11]

---

[9]Forty weeks was taken as the lower limit of "full time" in order not to eliminate teachers. Median earnings of wives who worked 50–52 weeks were also calculated but did not change the results significantly.

[10]It is, of course, not appropriate to use these data for an analysis of sex differentials in earnings as these husbands and wives are not matched on a number of important characteristics.

[11]This finding may be artifactual, however. The size of the earnings intervals for wives were larger in 1959 than in 1969. If women's earnings were somewhat negatively skewed within

TABLE 8.7
Median of the Ratios of Wife's/Husband's 1959 and 1969 Earnings, by Husband's Occupation and Wife's Work Experience[a,b]

Husband's occupation	All wives with earnings 1959[c]	All wives with earnings 1969	Wives working full time 1959[c]	Wives working full time 1969
Total	45	40	68	63
Professionals				
I	30	28	52	54
II	45	35	62	61
III	49	46	76	67
Managers				
I	33	30	50	52
II	33	32	54	52
III	46	38	64	59
Sales				
II	46	35	72	60
III	49	44	74	65
Clerical				
III	52	45	74	65
IV	58	53	75	67
Craft				
II	35	34	53	52
III	45	38	62	60
IV	43	42	76	64
Operatives				
III	46	42	66	63
IV	45	44	72	65
Service				
III	49	40	68	63
IV	58	56	78	78
Laborers				
IV	47	47	79	71

Sources: 1960 and 1970 Public Use Samples of White Couples.

[a] The ratios of wife's/husband's earnings were only computed for those couples where both husband and wife had net positive earnings.

[b] Two groups of wives with net positive earnings were considered: (*a*) *All*—all wives with earnings; and (*b*) *Full time*—those wives who worked 40–52 weeks in 1959 or 1969 and 35 or more hours in the census reference week. Forty weeks was selected as the minimum for "full-time" employment in order not to exclude teachers.

[c] The 1959 data include some families where the husband was not the household head.

---

intervals—as seems very likely in the broad higher earnings categories—their 1959 median earnings would be overstated. This, in turn, would produce an apparent, though not real, decline in their relative earnings.

TABLE 8.8
Wives' Standardized Work Rates, by Husband's Occupation: 1960 and 1970[a]

Husband's occupation	Percentage of wives in labor force		
	1960[b]	1970	Percentage change
Total	33.3	43.0	29
Professionals			
I	21.9	35.1	60
II	33.2	42.4	28
III	38.9	51.8	33
Managers			
I	22.2	36.5	64
II	28.3	39.5	40
III	36.9	45.0	22
Sales			
II	32.1	41.4	29
III	38.6	47.8	24
Clerical			
III	37.6	47.0	25
IV	39.2	52.1	33
Craft			
II	31.9	38.9	22
III	31.5	42.1	34
IV	30.7	41.2	34
Operatives			
III	34.3	43.5	27
IV	35.2	43.6	24
Service			
III	41.3	44.7	8
IV	42.1	50.5	20
Laborers			
IV	30.0	40.5	35

Sources: 1960 and 1970 Public Use Samples of White Couples.
[a] The standard used was the age distribution of all husbands in 1970.
[b] The data for 1960 include some families where the husband was not head of the household.

All this provides additional support for the view that the relative economic advantage of a wife working is an important factor in her labor-force participation since work rates were higher for those groups where the relative earnings position of working wives was greater. However, these couples are a select group as the husbands of working wives typically have lower earnings than the husbands of nonworking wives, since wives' work propensities are inversely related to husband's earnings (Table 8.9).[12] Moreover, as we have seen, working wives tend to be more highly educated and probably have other socioeconomic characteristics that would qualify them for a higher wage than nonworking wives. Hence the *actual* relative economic impact of the working wives of Table 8.7 will probably exaggerate the *potential* relative impact of all wives with similar socioeconomic characteristics. However, some idea of this potential impact can be obtained by examining the ratios of the median earnings of wives to the medians for *all* husbands and not just those with working wives. These data are presented in Table 8.10.

The ratios in Table 8.10, as in Table 8.7, show that the relative earnings position of working wives varied inversely with husbands' occupational earnings group. This indicates that the higher relative earnings position of wives of men in lower peak median occupations was not just a function of the particularly low incomes of those husbands with working wives. In this table too, we observe that the earnings ratios consistently declined between 1959 and 1969 for the wives who worked full time. The pattern was not as consistent for all wives with earnings.

WIVES' EARNINGS AND UPWARD SOCIOECONOMIC MOBILITY

Given the relatively low earnings of wives, how do we evaluate the importance of their socioeconomic contribution to their families? Could such low earnings really have a "status-determining" impact? The implications of Parsons's argument, for example, was that the wife's earnings are not important because they do "not produce a comparable proportion of the family income [Parsons 1949: 194]." Furthermore, the traditional absence of concern regarding wives' earnings in studies of stratification indicates that (until quite recently), this view has been generally shared. However, such an approach is inconsistent with the criteria usually employed in stratification research to determine socioeconomic status and social mobility. No scholar has maintained, for example, that social mobility only occurs when a man moves from one occupation to another paying at least twice as much. Hence to assume that the wife's income must be equal to her husband's for it to have an effect is confusing the difference between making an impact on the family's socioeconomic status and making the *same* impact as the husband

---

[12]Husbands with no net positive earnings were omitted from these tables. These amounted to about 3% of husbands in 1970 and about 4% in 1960. However, some of these men were located in occupational groups not analyzed in this study or some had no occupation given (in 1960 only). Hence, an even smaller proportion of the sample of husbands actually studied fell into this "no net positive earnings" group.

TABLE 8.9
Median 1959 and 1969 Incomes of Husbands with an Earning Wife as a Percentage of the Median Incomes of Those without an Earning Wife, by Husband's Occupation

Husband's occupation	1959[a]	1969
Total	87.0	86.2
Professionals		
I	71.8	78.3
II	82.8	83.4
III	85.9	87.1
Managers		
I	78.1	75.5
II	79.9	82.9
III	83.6	86.3
Sales		
II	78.2	77.3
III	82.4	83.6
Clerical		
III	91.3	90.3
IV	93.2	90.7
Craft		
II	87.4	90.1
III	93.1	90.2
IV	89.7	91.4
Operatives		
III	92.5	93.7
IV	90.4	91.6
Service		
III	92.1	91.1
IV	92.3	92.7
Laborers		
IV	94.6	95.4

Sources: 1960 and 1970 Public Use Samples of White Couples.
[a] Includes some families where the husband was not the head.

does. If not, though, how can we gauge whether the wife's economic contribution is indeed significant? One approach is to ask whether the addition of her earnings to the family income provides a functional substitute for the rise in earnings that might result from upward occupational mobility of the husband. If it does, then we can interpret this as one criterion of a "significant" contribution to the family's socioeconomic status.

Tables 8.11 and 8.12 are crude efforts to measure the socioeconomic contribution of wives in these terms. They compare the median income of families where the wife had earnings to those where she did not to provide a

II. Economic Impact of Wives Working

TABLE 8.10
Wives' 1959 and 1969 Median Earnings as a Percentage of the Median Earnings of Husbands, by Husband's Occupation and Wife's Work Experience[a,b]

	1959		1969	
Husband's occupation	All wives	Wives working full time	All wives	Wives working full time
Total	36	60	37	55
Professionals				
I	23	43	24	43
II	36	55	31	50
III	38	65	41	62
Managers				
I	26	42	26	41
II	27	46	30	45
III	40	59	36	41
Sales				
II	35	56	33	50
III	38	65	42	59
Clerical				
III	42	65	41	60
IV	48	68	49	64
Craft				
II	30	49	32	46
III	36	58	36	54
IV	34	61	40	59
Operatives				
III	38	62	38	58
IV	37	64	41	60
Service				
III	43	66	37	57
IV	51	74	53	74
Laborers				
IV	36	72	42	67

Source: Table 8.6.
[a]These ratios are based on the median earnings of all husbands, not just those with earning wives.
[b]The data for 1960 include some families where the husband was not the head of the household.

rough indication of the impact of wives' earnings on their families. Focusing on Table 8.11 first, median family income was higher for families of Professional III men *with* earning wives in 1969 (even if they were not full time workers) than for the families of Professional II males with*out* earning wives. Families of men in the Manager III group who had an earning wife all but closed the gap between themselves and the families of men in the

TABLE 8.11
Median 1959 and 1969 Income of Families, by Husband's Occupation and by the Earnings Status and Work Experience of the Wife (1969 Dollars)[a,b]

	1959[c]			1969		
Husbands occupation	Families without an earning wife	Families with an earning wife Total	Full time	Families without an earning wife	Families with an earning wife Total	Full time
Total	7,888	9,275	10,862	10,369	12,302	13,585
Professions						
I	15,121	12,094	14,483	16,834	17,065	18,516
II	10,022	11,352	13,887	13,156	14,683	16,331
III	8,201	9,552	11,196	10,930	13,578	15,048
Managers						
I	12,884	12,965	14,746	16,587	15,978	17,000
II	11,029	11,508	12,683	13,616	14,996	16,072
III	8,440	10,288	11,732	11,326	13,423	14,415
Sales						
II	10,176	11,090	12,389	14,064	14,620	15,824
III	7,776	8,976	10,621	10,438	12,573	13,568
Clerical						
III	7,628	9,692	11,165	10,098	12,423	14,085
IV	6,538	9,092	10,019	8,466	11,109	12,738
Craft						
II	10,483	11,804	13,541	12,477	14,356	15,773
III	7,943	9,839	11,303	10,037	12,258	13,668
IV	6,533	8,051	9,331	8,411	10,596	11,760
Operatives						
III	7,163	9,025	10,698	8,866	11,221	12,865
IV	6,496	7,979	9,572	8,293	10,555	11,842
Service						
III	7,514	9,592	11,322	10,189	12,484	14,295
IV	5,758	7,558	8,603	7,399	10,023	11,268
Laborers						
IV	5,552	6,906	8,702	7,055	9,452	10,955

Sources: 1960 and 1970 Public Use Samples of White Couples.

[a]Median income in 1969 dollars of families with net positive incomes. The medians for 1959 were inflated into 1969 dollars using the 25.8% increase in the Consumer Price Index in the 1959–1969 period.

[b]Two groups of wives with net positive earnings were considered: (*a*) *All*—all wives with earnings; and (*b*) *Full time*—those wives who worked 40–52 weeks in 1959 or 1969 and 35 or more hours in the census reference week. Forty weeks was selected as the minimum for "full-time" employment in order not to exclude teachers.

[c]The 1960 data for this table include some couples where the husband was not the head of the household.

TABLE 8.12
Economic Upward Mobility Index for Families, by Husband's Occupation and by Earnings Status and Work Experience of the Wife[a,b]

	Median family income as a percentage of the median income of families of men in the next higher-paying occupation and without an earning wife					
	1959			1969		
Husband's occupation	Families without an earning wife	Families with an earning wife		Families without an earning wife	Families with an earning wife	
		Total	Full time		Total	Full time
Professionals						
II	66	75	92	78	87	97
III	82	95	112	83	103	114
Managers						
II	86	89	98	82	90	97
III	76	93	106	83	99	106
Sales						
III	76	88	104	74	89	96
Clerical						
IV	86	119	131	84	110	126
Craft						
III	76	94	108	80	98	110
IV	82	101	117	84	106	117
Operatives						
IV	91	111	134	94	119	134
Service						
IV	77	101	114	73	98	111
Laborers						
IV[c]	78	96	121	80	107	124

Source: Table 8.11.

[a]This index is an effort to measure the extent to which wives' employment is a functional substitute for upward occupational mobility of the husband. For each major occupational group, the ratio was computed of the median family income to that of the next higher peak-median earnings group for families with*out* an earning wife. For example, ratios were computed of the median family incomes of Professional II families without an earning wife, for families with an earning wife, and for families with a wife working "full-time" to median family income of Professional I families without an earning wife. The ratios for the median incomes of Professional III families without an earning wife is another example. The same procedure was followed within each major occupational group. The goal was to see how much better an approximation to the income of higher-level families with*out* working wives was achieved in lower-level families *with* working wives.

[b]Two groups of wives with net positive earnings were considered: (*a*) *All*—all wives with earnings; and (*b*) *Full-time*—those wives who worked 40–52 weeks in 1959 or 1969 and 35 or more hours in the census reference week. Forty weeks was selected as the minimum for "full-time" employment in order not to exclude teachers.

[c]Since there was only one earnings group in the Laborer occupational group, these medians were divided by the median family income of Operative III families without an earning wife.

Manager II group who did not have wives with earnings. This is the case generally: The earnings of the wife usually put the family in the next higher income group. If the wife worked 40–52 weeks in the year and 35 or more hours in the week before the Census, her impact was even greater, of course. For example, for such families, if the husband was a Craft III worker, the family income went up to $13,668 in 1969—more than the income of families of Professional II men who did not have wives with earnings.

Table 8.12 puts these comparisons in ratio form. Within each major occupational group, the median income of three different types of families was made a percentage of the median income of families who did not have a working wife and who were in the next higher peak median earnings category. Thus the median income of families of Professional II men was made a ratio of the median income of families of Professional I males without an earning wife. The three types of families that formed the numerators of these ratios were those families without an earning wife, those with an earning wife regardless of the extent of her labor-force involvement, and those families with a full-time working wife. The ratios reveal more precisely the extent to which working wives put their families into the income category of higher paid occupations, despite the wife's low earnings. For example, in 1969, the median income of families of Professional III males without an earning wife was only 83% of the median for Professional II families who were also without an earning wife. However, for Professional III families with earnings wives, the ratio of their median income to that of Professional II families without an earning wife rose to 103%. If the Professional III wife was a full-time worker, the ratio rose to 114%. Upward mobilities on this rough order were observed for families with earning wives in most of the Group II, III, and IV occupational groups.

Table 8.12 can also give us a somewhat clearer picture of 1959–1969 changes in the extent to which a working wife seemed to provide a functional alternative to upward occupational mobility of the husband. By and large, in more occupational groups in 1969 than in 1959, the income ratios for all families with an earning wife were closer to parity or higher than that of the comparison families. In some cases this is at least, partly, true because the ratios for groups where neither family had an earning wife were higher in 1969 than in 1959 but the opposite was also frequently observed.

It is important to remember that these figures actually *under*state the impact of the wife's earnings on her own family's income because the income of husbands of nonworking wives was typically higher than that of husbands of working wives. For all occupational groups combined, the median 1969 income of husbands of wives with earnings was only 86% of the median income of husbands of wives without earnings (Table 8.9).

In sum, the evidence indicates that whether or not wives worked extensively during the year, and despite low earnings, they had a considerable impact on family income—enough in many cases to eliminate the income difference between a working wife's family and the family of a man in a much higher-paying occupational group whose wife did not work at all. Furthermore, even though the proportion of family income contributed by the wife often declined between 1959 and 1969, this did not appear to diminish the ability of wives' earnings to reduce or eliminate interoccupational differences in family income—largely, it seems, by working more extensively during the year.

IMPLICATIONS

If various reference groups are influential in setting life-style standards, these finding have at least two important implications—one for *within*-group comparisons and one for *between*-group comparisons. The first is based on the notion that families of men at a *similar* occupational level tend to provide important reference groups for each other. When some families have wives working this may put other families within the same reference group but with*out* an earning wife at a comparative economic disadvantage. This should then put pressure on such families to increase their income to keep up with the proverbial Joneses. One obvious way of accomplishing this is for *their* wives to go out to work. Hence, to the degree such competitive consumption motivations have an important influence on work behavior, the more wives who work extensively, the more families without working wives there are who will be put at a socioeconomic disadvantage. As a consequence, pressures for wives to work should increase considerably as the proportions who do work rise. Furthermore, the more families *with* working wives, the more difficult it becomes to maintain that they are "deviant" and such families will be less willing to see their life-styles so labeled. In addition, other types of social pressures should start to operate on nonworking wives. For example, the higher the proportion of wives in one's own social set or neighborhood who are working, the fewer nonworking women there are around to socialize with, share child-care responsibilities with, etc. In these ways, behavioral changes can lead to major revisions of norms regarding women's socioeconomic roles, in addition to the contribution of other factors such as the diffusion of feminist ideology.

In short, the rising labor-force particpation of wives disrupts previous socioeconomic similarities and social support groups among families of men at similar occupational levels and hence promotes a process of continually rising work rates among wives within the same reference group.[13]

A second kind of "destabilizing" influence suggested by these data is that

---

[13]This same process would be expected to operate in other reference-group comparisons as well—neighbors, friends, kin, etc.

inter- as well as *intra*group comparsions are affected by changes in wives' work behavior. If social stratification has some *subjective* meaning to people, then working wives can change the "traditional" (i.e., historical) hierarchical pattern of socioeconomic positions. For example, if a working wife of a lower-level professional can earn enough to make her family's income greater than that of a higher-level professional with*out* a working wife, then socioeconomic differences based on the rankings of families by the husband's socioeconomic characteristics become blurred. This raises the possibility that the higher-level families with nonworking wives may start to feel that their socioeconomic position is somewhat threatened. Although people are notoriously inventive in creating social-status signals or clues that are not just dependent on income, an increase in family income will often be required in order to maintain a certain social distance. Hence, the ability of families traditionally at a lower level—as measured by the husband's socioeconomic position—to approximate the life-style of higher-level families should exert some pressure on the latter groups to increase their income. And this is often accomplished by *their* wives also going out to work.

In sum, to the extent we are a competitively consuming society, and one in which upward mobility aspirations are considered a virtue rather than a vice, increases in the number of wives working, and the extensiveness of their employment, may have set in motion a chain reaction.[14] The more wives who work, the more families with*out* a working wife find themselves at a socioeconomic disadvantage. This increases pressures for *their* wives to work. If they so respond to such pressures, this, in turn, extends and probably intensifies the pressures on the remaining nonworking wives to go out to work. The possibility of feedback effects is thus intrinsic to the reference-group perspective. If people modify their behavior according to feelings of relative deprivation, this may lead to changes in the conditions providing the objective basis of reference-group comparisons, thereby fostering further behavioral adaptations.

Economic Impact of Wives Working and the Life-Cycle Squeezes

What can the PUS data tell us about the economic impact of working wives on the two life-cycle squeezes? This question also has two important facets. What general role can wives' employment play in alleviating the two squeezes and how may this vary among occupational groups? What feedback

---

[14]This is not to say that some asymptote well below 100% does not exist for wives' work rates. Even if one argued that Americans, *in general*, are competitive consumers, a substantial proportion may not conduct themselves in this manner. In some communities, and for some segments in many communities, nonpecuniary goals may be paramount.

effects might wives' employment have—effects which might alter the basic objective conditions underlying perceptions of relative economic status? An exploration of both these complimentary perspectives should provide a clearer idea of the forces affecting women's changing economic and demographic behavior. In addition, it will give us another opportunity to examine the Easterlin hypothesis and, as a result, somewhat modify the critique of it presented in Chapters 3, 4, and 5.

OCCUPATIONAL DIFFERENCES IN THE
ECONOMIC IMPACT OF WIVES WORKING

Our consideration of the impact of wives' employment on the two life-cycle squeezes will initially ignore the cost-of-children factor. This is unfortunately necessary for occupational comparisons because of the inability to estimate child-care expenditures by the husband's occupation. Hence the discussion will be limited to income comparisons among various groups without being able to take into account group differences in child dependency. In addition, even the type of abbreviated cohort analysis attempted in Chapter 5 seems unwise once the husband's occupation is involved because of the unknown effect of selective occupational mobility on the composition of members of any given birth cohort in the same occupation at two census dates.[15]

Wives' Work and the Amelioration of Life-Cycle Squeezes

We will explore the possible role of wives' employment in easing the life-cycle squeezes in two steps. First, within the same age and occupational groups, how much improvement in income was actually achieved by those families with a working wife? Second, how did wives' work affect the economic position of the families in the age groups going through the first and second squeezes compared to those at presumably less intrinsically stressful ages?

Basically at issue is not just how much improvement wives' earnings made on their *own* families' incomes but also how well the two-earner family did compared to some standard of family income based on husband's income

---

[15] Furthermore, I will only present data from the 1970 PUS although an identical analysis was conducted on the 1960 data. There are two main reasons for just concentrating on the 1970 sample. First, the 1970 data are more complete since small sample sizes in the 1960 sample in some occupation and age groups precluded a comparison of a number of types of families in several occupations—at the younger ages in particular. Second, by and large, the 1960–1970 overall pattern is similar and it would be very cumbersome to present both sets of census data in tabular form. Moreover, the simple statistical form of presentation used here does not readily lend itself to an analysis of the reasons for the small 1960–1970 differences observed. This would involve a much more elaborate analysis than is possible here and one that would not significantly change the overall thrust of my argument.

alone. Hence, as before, I have used the combined median income of husbands with and without earning wives as a basis for comparison. Conceptually, this is roughly equivalent to assessing how much income advantage is achieved by families with an earning wife compared to families living in a hypothetical world where only husbands work, assuming that working wives do not depress their husbands' earnings. This will, of course, lead to an understatement of the actual relative improvement in family income achieved by working wives within their own families.

Even though the income of husbands in families with an earning wife tended to be lower than average, the addition of the wife's income more than compensated for this (Table 8.13). As a result, the median 1969 family income of such couples was higher than that of all husbands in the same age and occupational group. Furthermore, the relative advantage of having a working wife varied by the husband's age. It was greatest for those couples where the husband was under age 25 or in the 45–65 age groups. This can be partly traced to the very depressed earnings of young men as well as the somewhat lowered earnings of older males in contrast to men in the middle years. In addition, however, although wives' age–earnings profiles were relatively flat, the earnings of wives of older men were somewhat higher than those of younger men (Table 8.14).

There are also occupational differences in this age pattern. By and large, when the husband was in the 18–24 age group, the advantage of a working wife was higher for white-collar than blue-collar families and for those in Group I rather than Group III and II white-collar occupations (Table 8.13). In the case of older age groups, however, the relative income advantage of the two-earner families declined sharply for Group I occuptions and, in general, the lower the peak median earnings level of the occupation, the greater the income advantage of the two-earner family. All this reflects, in large part, the much more favorable earnings position of older versus younger men in Group I and II occupations compared to the poorer relative position of older men in the lower-level occupations, particularly within the manual group. It was also a function of the somewhat steeper age–earnings profile of wives of blue-collar than white-collar workers. This, in turn, was due to the exceptionally low earnings of the wives of young blue-collar men.

Wives' Work and Relative Economic Status

Interage comparisons provide an additional valuable perspective on the economic impact of wives working (Table 8.15). Focusing first on those in the first-squeeze stage, families with husbands aged 18–24 and with an earning wife practically eliminated the income differential between themselves and that of all husbands aged 25–34. Thus, for all occupational groups combined, the median 1969 income of all husbands aged 25–34 was 51%

TABLE 8.13
Median 1969 Family Income of Couples with an Earning Wife Compared to the Median 1969 Income of All Husbands, by Husband's Age and Occupation[a]

Husband's occupation	\multicolumn{5}{c}{Husband's age and percentage by which family income was greater than husband's income}
	18–24	25–34	35–44	45–54	55–65
Total	38	29	29	44	52
Professionals					
I	72	20	11	23	31
II	40	26	22	30	43
III	48	38	33	42	59
Managers					
I	54	22	17	20	15
II	43	22	23	34	39
III	35	31	29	42	46
Sales					
II	41	27	18	27	38
III	50	32	34	43	58
Clerical					
III	39	30	39	55	54
IV	58	37	42	55	67
Craft					
II	—[b]	19	27	40	38
III	34	28	29	49	49
IV	40	28	56	46	57
Operatives					
III	29	28	38	51	49
IV	32	32	39	54	60
Service					
III	24	26	32	52	57
IV	63	34	46	63	72
Laborers					
IV	33	35	44	57	62

Source: Appendix Tables F.1 and F.2.
[a] Includes those with and without an earning wife.
[b] Medians were not computed because of small sample sizes.

greater than the median for 18–24-year-old husbands. However, when wives worked in the younger families, the median income of 25–34-year-old husbands was only 9% higher. In short, work by young wives could, in large part, compensate for the much lower income of their husbands compared to husbands in the next older age group. This was particularly the case for most

TABLE 8.14
Wives' Median 1969 Earnings, by Husband's Age and Occupation

Husband's occupation	Husband's age				
	18–24	25–34	35–44	45–54	55–64
Total	2,533	3,009	3,127	3,640	3,772
Professionals					
I	2,938	3,560	2,886	3,406	5,000
II	3,333	3,564	3,039	3,828	6,092
III	3,202	3,724	3,590	4,222	5,938
Managers					
I	3,438	3,175	3,156	3,864	4,100
II	3,362	3,097	3,084	3,561	4,074
III	2,433	3,010	3,028	3,800	4,045
Sales					
II	3,222	3,660	3,310	3,902	4,611
III	3,182	3,417	3,500	3,870	4,018
Clerical					
III	2,804	3,321	3,244	4,059	3,986
IV	3,354	3,361	3,315	4,032	3,968
Craft					
II	—[a]	2,857	3,407	3,914	3,667
III	2,580	2,826	2,977	3,531	3,666
IV	2,200	2,438	3,055	3,352	3,404
Operatives					
III	1,852	2,553	3,014	3,500	3,611
IV	1,985	2,665	3,092	3,474	3,288
Service					
III	2,500	3,043	3,333	4,300	3,667
IV	1,926	2,582	3,397	3,668	4,565
Laborers					
IV	1,817	2,472	2,984	3,310	2,929
Range	1,621	1,286	704	990	3,163

Source: 1970 Public Use Sample of White Couples.
[a]Medians were not computed for the sample size below 40 cases.

blue-collar occupations and for the two clerical occupations. It was much less true for Professional I and II couples where the age effect on men's earnings greatly exceeded the earning capacity of the wives of younger men.

What do these data reveal about the apparent impact of wives' earnings on the second squeeze? By definition, families in the second squeeze are those for whom child-care costs have risen considerably, often in a relatively brief period of time. However, husbands' incomes have probably not been

II. Economic Impact of Wives Working

increasing commensurately—especially relative to somewhat younger men in the same occupational reference group, but at an earlier stage of the family cycle. However, although the *dollar* costs of children may be rising rapidly for such families, the time demands children make are presumably declining. Hence, it is easier for wives to work and thereby help compensate for the economic squeeze associated with this stage of the family cycle. In the case of younger families the costs of children have probably not yet started to escalate whereas the time demands they make remain relatively high. Furthermore, it is a period in the husband's career cycle when earnings having typically been rising fairly rapidly, due to the age effect on earnings if nothing else. Hence wives are presumably more likely to remain at home, devoting much of their time to the home production of goods and services.

To the extent this pattern of social adjustment to life-cycle rhythms in husband's income, desired expenditures, and home production demands has been a common one, it makes sense to compare the *family* income of older families with an earning wife to the income of just husbands in younger families and, in this way, try to assess how well such a social pattern "copes" with at least some of the second-squeeze problems (Tables 8.16 and 8.17). Such comparisons do, in fact, show that an earning wife tends to put the older families well ahead of the younger families without an earning wife. Furthermore, in the comparison of 35–44- to 24–34-year-olds, this pattern varied inversely with the husband's peak median earnings group. For example, take the case of Craft III workers and their families. The median income of Craft III 35–44-year-old husbands was only 10% higher than that of 25–34-year-olds. On the basis of our overall estimates of interage differences in the costs of children in Chapter 5, it seems unlikely that, if we could take this into account, such a small income differential in favor of the older Craft III husbands would survive. However, in those families of 35–44-year-old Craft III workers where the wife worked, the combined family income was 42% higher than the median 1969 income of younger Craft III husbands. In the case of Craft IV husbands, the 5% greater median income of 35–44-year-olds compared to 25–34-year-olds turned into a 64% advantage if the older men's wives was working. In the case of men who were 45–54 years old, the addition of wives' earnings also greatly tipped the scales to the advantage of the two-earner family over that of a younger family without an earning wife. In sum, the evidence suggests that the earnings of wives could easily compensate for a relatively unfavorable economic situation based on husbands' incomes alone.

Wives' Economic Contribution: Feedback Effects

Although these findings imply that the employment of wives can help ameliorate the economic disadvantages of the two life-cycle squeezes, the

TABLE 8.15
1969 Income Comparisons for Couples Where the Husband Was 25–34 and 18–24, by Husband's Occupation

| Husband's occupation | Percentage by which the median income of husbands aged 25–34 was greater than the median income of: || Percentage by which the median income of families with a husband aged 25–34 and an earning wife was greater than the median income of: ||
	Husbands aged 18–24	Families with the husband aged 18–24 and an earning wife	Families with the husband aged 18–24 and an earning wife	Husbands aged 18–24
Total	51	9	41	95
Professionals				
I	122	29	55	166
II	64	17	48	107
III	63	11	52	125
Managers				
I	55	1	23	90
II	51	6	29	84
III	45	8	41	90
Sales				
II	50	6	35	90
III	62	8	42	113

Clerical			
III	46	5	36	89
IV	38	−13	20	89
Craft[a]			
III	34	1	28	72
IV	37	−?	25	75
Operatives			
III	29	—	28	66
IV	36	4	37	81
Service			
III	32	7	34	66
IV	70	4	40	128
Laborers			
IV	45	−26	18	132

Source: Appendix Table F.1 and F.2.
[a] Craft II couples were ommitted from the table because of small sample sizes.

TABLE 8.16
1969 Income Comparisons for Couples Where the Husband Was 35–44 and 25–34, by Husband's Occupation

	Percentage by which the median income of husbands aged 35–44 differed from the median income of:		Percentage by which the median income of families with a husband aged 35–44 and an earning wife differed from the median income of:	
Husband's occupation	Husbands aged 25–34	Families with the husband aged 25–34 and an earning wife	Families with the husband aged 25–34 and an earning wife	Husbands aged 25–34
Total	15	−11	15	49
Professionals				
I	38	15	28	53
II	21	− 4	17	47
III	23	−11	19	64
Managers				
I	35	11	30	59
II	25	3	26	54
III	14	−13	12	46
Sales				
II	26	− 1	16	48
III	17	−12	19	57

Clerical				
III	11	−14	20	55
IV	10	−20	13	56
Craft				
II	11	−7	18	40
III	10	−13	12	42
IV	5	−18	28	64
Operatives				
III	6	−18	14	46
IV	7	−19	12	49
Service				
III	10	−12	16	46
IV	12	−17	21	62
Laborers				
IV	5	−34	−6	50

Sources: Appendix Tables F.1 and F.2.

TABLE 8.17
1969 Income Comparisons for Couples Where the Husband Was 45–54, 35–44, and 25–34, by Husband's Occupation

Husband's occupation	Percentage by which the median income of husbands aged 45–54 differed from the median income of:		Families with an earning wife and the husband aged:				Percentage by which the median income of families with a husband aged 45–54 and an earning wife differed from the median income of:			
	Husbands aged:						Families with an earning wife and the husband aged:				Husbands aged:	
	25–34	35–44	25–34	35–44			25–34	35–44	25–34	35–44
Total	12	−3	−13	−25			25	8	62	40
Professionals										
I	48	8	24	−3			53	19	83	32
II	27	5	1	−14			31	12	65	36
III	32	7	−4	−19			36	15	88	52
Managers										
I	52	12	25	−4			50	16	83	35
II	24	−1	2	−19			36	8	66	33
III	16	2	−12	−21			25	12	64	44

Sales							
II	29	3	2	−13	30	11	64	31
III	15	−1	−12	−26	25	5	65	41
Clerical							
III	10	−2	−15	−29	31	10	70	53
IV	11	1	−19	−29	25	10	72	57
Craft							
II	11	−[a]	−6	−21	31	11	56	40
III	7	−3	−16	−25	25	12	60	44
IV	4	−2	−19	−37	18	−8	51	44
Operatives							
III	4	−1	−19	−28	22	8	57	49
IV	4	−4	−22	−31	21	7	60	49
Service							
III	12	1	−11	−23	36	17	70	54
IV	1	−10	−25	−38	23	2	65	48
Laborers							
IV	3	−2	−35	−32	2	8	62	55

Sources: Appendix Tables F.1 and F.2.
[a]There was no appreciable difference in the median earnings between these two age groups.

333

same patterns can also be interpreted as being indicative of rising economic pressures because of the feedback effects of wives' working. Once again, we need to ask whether there is evidence that the responses of such couples to perceived economic deprivation changes the reference-group reality other couples use as their standard. If so, what are the implications of such changes?

First, many of the families of husbands in one or the other of the two squeeze periods, but with*out* a working wife, probably found themselves at a considerable economic disadvantage compared to the families of men in the same age group but *with* an earning wife—even families of men who earned more than the median for their age. In the case of the first squeeze, unless the 18–24-year-old husband who was the sole support of his family had an income at least 38% higher than the median for his age group, his family would have had a lower income than the median for families with an earning wife (Table 8.13). The family that planned to get by on the 45–54-year-old husband's income alone would be at a disadvantage relative to the median for those with an earning wife unless their income was 44% greater than the median for the same age group.[16] For older couples, the amount by which the husband's income would have to exceed the median to maintain parity with two-earner families was the greatest for blue-collar families whereas for younger couples it was the greatest for white-collar families. Hence, if working wives' income contribution *more* than compensates for a life-cycle squeeze disadvantage, this will probably increase the relative economic disadvantage of those families in the same squeeze period but who do not—or do not yet—have their wives working.

Just how much of an impact this alteration of the relative economic position of various families may have on the work behavior of wives not currently in the labor force will again depend on how many wives are working at any point in time—that is, as emphasized earlier, it will be influenced by the size of the various reference groups involved in such comparisons. As long as relatively few wives worked, there would not be enough two-income families around to form important social reference groups for other families. However, the higher the proportion of families with a working wife, the more salient such families should become and hence the more widespread will be the development of perceptions of relative deprivation among families without working wives. In short, if relative economic deprivation is a significant factor in affecting wives' employment, then increases in wives' labor-force participation should have something of a snowball effect. Furthermore, census and CPS data indicate that labor-force participation

---

[16]However, these comparisons do not take into account the "cost" of wives working—higher taxes and the cost of the substitution of goods and services for the wife's previous home production.

II. Economic Impact of Wives Working

rates for wives have risen enormously in recent years. Table 8.18 documents this just for the 1960 and 1970 Public Use Samples. Even in 1960, and far more so in 1970, families with working wives were so large a proportion of all families—in all occupation and age groups—that it seems unlikely that they would not have constituted an important element in reference-group comparisons.

With regard to interage comparisons of income, families with an earning wife could largely compensate for the lower income of 18–24-year-old-husbands as compared to 25–34-year-old husbands. However, if the wives of these older men also worked, the younger families once again found themselves at a considerable economic disadvantage. For example, for all occupational groups combined, the median 1969 income advantage of 25–34-year-old husbands over that of 18–24-year-olds was cut down to just 9% if the younger couple had an earning wife. However, if the wives of 25–34-year-olds also worked, then the older family once again achieved a sizable income advantage—this time, of 41% (Table 8.15). Nor was the employment of wives of 25–34-year-old males such an uncommon occurrrence in 1970—38% were in the labor force compared to only 27% in 1960 (Table 8.18).[17] Hence, the relative compensatory value of the younger wives' working was almost entirely neutralized if somewhat older wives also entered the labor force in large numbers. This was particularly true for some occupational groups, though a clear-cut pattern is not readily observed. The relative advantage of the younger wife working was almost completely lost in comparison to somewhat older families with an earning wife for couples where the husband was a laborer, and operative, or a Service III worker. However, the ability of young wives to reduce the relative income disadvantage of their families compared to older two-earner families persisted for most other occupational groups, but the disadvantage was not eliminated and remained quite large in some cases.

Poor as the relative income position of younger husbands is compared to those in the 25–34 age group, their situation was considerably worse if they did not have an earning wife but the older family did. For all occupational groups combined, the median 1969 income of two-earner families of 25–34-year-old husbands was 95% greater than the median 1969 income of 18–24-year-old husbands (Table 8.15). For some occupational groups, the differential was even larger. For example, among Professional III couples, the median 1969 family income of two-earner couples where the husband was aged 25–34 was 125% larger than the median income of 18–24-year-old husbands. Especially large discrepancies were also noted for the other

---

[17]The proportions are much higher now, of course. For example, in March 1979, the CPS found that 56% of white married women aged 25–34 and living with their husbands were in the labor force (U.S. Bureau of Labor Statistics 1981: Table B-1).

TABLE 8.18
Percentage of Wives in the Labor Force, by Husband's Occupation and Age: 1960 and 1970

Husband's occupation	1960[a] 18–24	25–34	35–44	45–54	55–64	1970 18–24	25–34	35–44	45–54	55–64
Total	34	27	34	39	32	49	38	42	48	41
Professionals										
I	—[b]	19	18	22	22	62	34	30	35	33
II	41	25	30	39	37	56	38	38	48	41
III	44	36	38	46	31	62	46	50	56	52
Managers										
I	—[b]	17	20	29	24	54	34	36	37	33
II	—[b]	24	26	35	27	52	36	36	45	36
III	29	29	37	43	41	47	41	43	48	48
Sales										
II	—[b]	20	41	36	32	53	35	36	47	44
III	41	30	37	46	40	59	41	45	53	47

Clerical									
III	44	31	38	46	32	52	42	46	55	42
IV	36	31	38	53	32	60	47	52	56	50
Craft									
II	—[b]	31	35	33	24	38	34	42	45	34
III	32	23	33	39	30	45	36	43	48	40
IV	23	25	37	35	28	45	36	42	46	40
Operatives									
III	28	29	38	40	31	43	38	46	49	41
IV	35	29	37	41	33	43	38	46	47	42
Service									
III	—[b]	40	46	54	26	44	38	48	52	39
IV	36	40	44	45	41	56	43	52	56	48
Laborers									
IV	29	24	32	36	27	42	36	42	46	37

Sources: 1960 and 1970 Public Use Samples of White Couples.
[a]Includes some families where the husband was not the head.
[b]Percentages not shown when sample size was below 40.

337

professions, Sales III couples, Service IV, and Laborer IV families. Hence, if the labor-force participation of wives in these somewhat older families rises, this may greatly increase the relative economic deprivation of younger families who attempt to make a go of it on the basis of the husband's income alone. As a result, having a nonworking wife may become a luxury few young families can afford. If so, it is hard to believe that delayed childbearing and small family sizes will not become a relatively permanent feature of our society.

In sum, the severity of the first squeeze is not only a function of the relative income of young men or of inflation, but of the economic activity of older wives as well. If their labor-force participation is high and/or rising then the reference-group standard older families represent will be "inflated" by a second income, thus increasing the relative disadvantage of young couples in the first squeeze stage. Hence, even if reversals should occur in the relative earnings position of young men, they will probably be insufficient to counteract the income disadvantage of young families compared to older two-earner families. Only if the economic activity of older wives decreases will this be likely to occur. The question is, however, whether this is a realistic possibility.

We can also extend this reasoning to other interage comparisons. If the earnings of wives in the second squeeze period *more* than compensate for age differentials in child-care costs, this will change the relative economic position of other age groups, particularly of families who may wish to live on the husbands' earnings alone. As an illustration, if the wife of a 35–44-year-old was working, the 1969 median income of the family was 49% greater than the median income of husbands aged 25–34 compared to the 15% differential based on a comparison of husbands' incomes alone (Table 8.16). The relative advantage reaped by the older two-income family over the younger one-income family was even more pronounced in the comparison of 45–54-year-olds with 25–34-year-olds (Table 8.17). In addition, families of 45–54-year-old men also achieved a decided income advantage over the median of 35–44-year-old husbands. The lower the peak median occupation, the greater the advantage reaped by such two-income families. Since it is unlikely that the families of these 45–54-year-old men had considerably higher child-dependency burdens than families of 35–44-year-olds, the increasing prevalence of older wives' working probably put the somewhat younger families' wives under still greater economic pressure to work as well. To the extent all this is true, it implies that reductions in sex differentials in earnings should enhance feedback effects of this nature. They will increase the marginal economic advantage of wives working and thereby increase the relative disadvantages families with nonworking wives will experience in comparing themselves to two-income families.

II. Economic Impact of Wives Working

In sum, if families attempting to use the wife's employment to compensate for a relative economic disadvantage actually turn that *dis*advantage into an *ad*vantage, their behavior affects the relative position of various reference groups. Families who have not yet availed themselves of this option may be put at a substantial disadvantage unless the husband's income is well above average. Furthermore, somewhat older families who traditionally may have been at an economic advantage compared to those just starting out then find this advantage evaporating unless they too maintain a two-income family. Moreover, the same couples who had working wives early in marriage may find that the "age effect" on men's earnings is not enough to compensate for the loss of the wife's income if she should completely drop out of the labor force after the worst hurdles of the first squeeze are past. This is especially likely to be the case when the growth in men's earnings due to period effects, such as inflation, is not very rapid. That, of course, increases the difficulties of establishing a household early in life. However, it also increases the chances that rises in young husbands' income due to age and period effects will not entirely compensate for the loss of the wife's earnings. In that situation, the family may experience an actual decline in income if the wife quits working.[18] Similarly, if a high proportion of wives in somewhat older families work and raise their families' levels of living, this puts young couples without a working wife at a greater disadvantage.

One is tempted to call this whole phenomenon the "Red Queen Dilemma."[19] Considerable changes occur in people's behavior and in their *absolute* economic position. However, whether the long-run *relative* economic position of couples changes is another matter. Families who turn their comparatively economically *dis*advantaged position into a relatively *ad*vantageous one by the wife working may, in the process, encourage other families to do likewise, especially those whose relative position is negatively affected by such changing behaviors. As a consequence, over time, the *relative* advantage achieved may prove to be somewhat ephemeral, though substantial absolute changes in socioeconomic and demographic behavior will have probably occurred. Moreover, to the extent such a process really gets going, the price of wives dropping out of the labor force may rise enormously. In addition, not only does the behavior of two-earner families temporarily, at least, rearrange the relative economic position of other

---

[18] Depending on their occupations, interage differences in men's earnings can be equal to, greater than, or less than wives' earnings at either age. To the extent the interage differences in husbands' earnings are less than wives' actual (or potential) contribution, this suggests that period effects on men's earnings should increase in importance.

[19] "Now, *here*, you see, it takes all the running you can do, to keep in the same place. If you want to get somewhere else, you must run at least twice as fast as that! [Lewis Carroll, *Through the Looking Glass*, Chapter 2]."

families, as well as their own, but also it provides a behavioral model for the families so affected to follow in order to achieve an apparent improvement in their own economic position.

ANOTHER LOOK AT THE EASTERLIN HYPOTHESIS

Because of the difficulty of constructing estimates of child-care costs by the husband's occupation, we have been examining the possible impact of wives working on couples at different squeeze stages without explicitly allowing for age differences in the dependency burden. In addition, only data from the 1970 PUS have been used to illustrate the effect of wives' earnings on various reference-group comparisons. A further question is the effect of wives' work on 1960–1970 *changes* in the severity of the two squeezes, a problem that requires us to take into account estimated equivalent child-care expenditures but, perforce, to ignore occupational differences. However, this approach has the advantage of permitting a reconsideration of Easterlin's hypothesis to see whether the economic impact of working wives would require any modification of earlier criticisms.

In Chapter 5 the Easterlin hypothesis was examined by looking at the possible effect of changes in child-care costs on the relative economic status of young men. The data indicated that although the 1959–1969 income position of young husbands deteriorated considerably relative to older husbands, interage shifts in the child-dependency burden seemed to have largely compensated for these changes. Thus, on the basis of the husband's income alone, the households in which the baby-boom cohorts were raised were not so affluent if one allows for the rise in the adolescent dependency burden of families producing the baby boom. However, the analysis of Chapter 5 did not consider the possible influence of wives' working on changes in the relative economic status of younger and older families and hence on the severity of the two life-cycle squeezes. It is this question that concerns us now.

Conceptual Approach

As a preliminary to examining Easterlin's hypothesis in greater detail, it is essential to consider certain aspects of his conceptualization and measurement of relative economic status and how this affects a proper assessment of the economic impact on the two squeezes of wives' working. One problem is that there seems to be some ambiguity in Easterlin's discussion of whose relative economic status is being compared over time. Consequently, ambiguities arise about the nature of wives' economic role in the family. These ambiguities are probably partly due to measurement problems for, as Easterlin points out, the ideal economic indicators are simply not available

(Easterlin 1973: 182–185, 192). Nevertheless, some conceptual ambiguity seems to creep in too. To begin with, then, it is important to focus on what economic statuses should ideally be compared, given Easterlin's conceptualization of the problem. Second, there is the issue of what, in actuality, really gets measured. Finally, we can consider the implications of some of the ambiguities involved in the measurement of relative economic status for a theoretically satisfying understanding of wives' economic role in the family and the significance of this, in turn, for the Easterlin hypothesis as a whole.

The logic of Easterlin's hypothesis—and indeed his basic statement of it—indicates that the appropriate comparison of relative economic statuses should be the *son's* market position (as measured by unemployment levels, earnings, etc.) versus the income of his *family* of orientation while he was in his teens—the period during which his consumption aspirations are presumably being formed (Easterlin 1973: 181). This particular comparison seems appropriate because, on the one hand, the *total* income of the family of orientation while the youth was a teenager, and not just the *father's* income, will presumably be the income determining consumption levels and the development of consumption aspirations. On the other hand, the income of the young man alone is probably the major factor determining whether he can support a childbearing and childrearing wife at home and in the style to which they had both become accustomed during adolescence. Of course, if pregnancy and the presence of small children come to provide little or no deterrent to wives' labor-force participation then this reasoning loses its cogency, but this does not seem to be a major invalidating fact, as yet, despite increasing labor-force participation of mothers of young children.

In reality, however, Easterlin does not seem to try to approximate this ideal comparison of relative economic statuses. Instead, his main measure is a comparison of the *family* income of young households (rather than the husband's income) with the family income several years previously of households with heads estimated to be of an age equivalent to that of the young husbands' fathers. In his book, Easterlin uses the incomes of households where the head was 35–44 years old as the measure of the level of economic prosperity during young men's adolescent years (Easterlin 1968: 125–126). In more recent articles, he uses households where the head was 45–54 years old instead (Easterlin 1973: 184–185). One problem with this approach is that when Easterlin theorizes in terms of the son's economic position as a young adult vis-à-vis the position of his family of orientation while he was a teenager, but actually measures this comparison in terms of the family income of younger relative to older families, he is glossing over the nature of the wife's economic contribution—both in the family of orientation and in the family of procreation.

This ambiguity in Easterlin's conceptualization and measurement of relative income status can have serious consequences. First, women's labor-force participation has been increasing enormously since the war—first among older women and then younger. Hence, the relative contribution of women to family income has presumably been changing over time and not at the same rate for older and younger families. As a result, the trend in relative *family* incomes may not be the same as the trend in the relative incomes of sons–fathers or younger–older males or of the income of younger males to that of older families. This suggests that it is preferable to first establish the trends in the income position of younger *men* versus older *men* and then to consider the economic contributions of other family members as well. This is the procedure actually followed in Chapter 3 of this book.

Second, wives' labor-market behavior, as well as their fertility behavior, are possible responses to the income position of their husbands. As such, to include wives' income—especially *young* wives' income—in the relative income variable seems to be confounding cause and effect. If a young wife works to compensate for the relatively low income position of her husband, the combined family income will tend to understate the relatively poor position of young husbands because this has been offset by the wife's earnings. In short, a distorted measurement of the kind of relative economic deprivation that may lead to postponed fertility, entry of wives into the labor force, or both, may occur when one consequence (wife's income) of the response of young wives to their husbands' relatively poor income position is included in the measurement of relative income. So, it is important to distinguish between the relative economic position of families at different life-cycle stages, based on the husband's income alone, and the position as it is then modified by other sources of income—most notably, the wife's.[20] It is to this problem we now turn.

PUS data permit both cross-sectional interage comparisons of income and an abbreviated cohort analysis. But even the severely truncated cohort analysis allowed by these data can provide some information on the extent to which the economic position of families has, on average, improved over time. This is relevant to the severity of both the first and second life-cycle squeezes. With regard to the second squeeze, a comparison of 1959–1969 changes in family income, net of changing child-care costs (net of CCC), with the changes in husband's income, also net of CCC, can provide a rough idea of the extent to which wives' economic contribution more than compensated for the rapid rise in child-care expenditures occasioned by the baby-boom children reaching expensive adolescence. Hence, this reveals something about the severity of the second squeeze relative to the overall economic

---

[20]Ideally, one should also focus on other sources of family income, but that complication was not attempted in the present, admittedly exploratory, study.

position of these cohorts earlier in their family cycle. However, to the extent the addition of other sources of income did offset the increase in child-care costs, family income may have risen fairly substantially in this period. Such a rise would affect the difficulty of the first squeeze if, as Easterlin argues, adolescents' families of orientation are an important socializing influence on their life-style aspirations in young adulthood. If the incomes of the baby boom's families of orientation were rising significantly, despite rising child-care costs, these large cohorts may have developed high consumption aspirations after all.

Cross-sectional comparisons, however, provide information on the kinds of economic pressures that arise out of single moment-of-time comparisons among reference groups. That is, they will be indicative of economic pressures arising out of the "current" economic status of various groups and changes in this over time rather than pressures arising out of comparisons with the family's own past.[21]

The 1960–1970 Experience of Cohorts

This cohort analysis will simply add to the data originally presented in Table 5.10 and repeated in Table 8.19. In general, Table 8.19 suggests that if one takes into account the economic contribution of wives, the relative economic position of older cohorts probably did not deteriorate in the 1959–1969 period, despite their high fertility. The median income of the cohorts of husbands who were aged 25–34 in 1960 and 35–44 in 1970 rose by 47% during the decade. However, when the increase in the child-dependency burden was taken into account, the rise in income dropped to 18% because of the high fertility of these cohorts. However, the increase in the median *family* income, net of CCC, was 32%. Assuming the wife's earnings were the most important other factor in family income, these calculations suggest that the families of these men were able to achieve a fairly substantial improvement in their economic position over the decade, despite sharp rises in child-care responsibilities.

The situation for cohorts who were aged 35–44 in 1960 and 45–54 in 1970 was less clear-cut because of the difficulties of measuring changes in the costs of older children no longer in the home. Child-care expenditures seemed to have eased up for these cohorts by 1970 so that, although the gross increase in the husband's income over the decade was only 29%, the increase net of CCC was 43%. However, this does not mean that these cohorts did not

---

[21]Unfortunately, we do not, of course, have microdata on individual families' incomes over time. Therefore, this is very much a macropicture—with all the problems this involves in drawing inferences about individual-level data.

TABLE 8.19
Gross and Net 1959–1969 Percentage Increases in Husbands' Median Income and Total Median Family Income for Three Cohorts of Husbands

	1959–1969 percentage change in income		
	Cohorts and their age in 1960		
	(1926–1935) 25–34	(1916–1925) 35–44	(1906–1915) 45–54
Change in median income of husband			
Gross	47	29	16
Net of changes in expenditures on children	18	43	40
Changes in total median family income			
Gross	58	46	21
Net of changes in expenditures on children	32	58	39

Sources: Table 5.8 and 8.20.

experience an intensification of the second squeeze—only that our 1960 and 1970 snapshot views did not readily capture the problem.

In sum, if Easterlin's reasoning about the influence of the parental household on the consumption aspirations of the young is correct, the impact of older wives working on family incomes should have fostered the development of relatively high consumption aspirations among baby-boom cohorts, despite their large numbers.

Cross-Sectional Comparisons

What impact did wives' economic contribution have on the relative economic position of different age groups if rough estimates of child-dependency are taken into account? Did the rise in the *family* income of older husbands continue to put older couples at an advantage relative to younger couples, once child-care expenditures are considered? Table 8.20 suggests that this was probably the case, though the results are not as straightforward as one might wish. If we assume, as seems appropriate for the moment, that child-care costs remained constant for 18–24-year-old husbands (since reduced fertility is the presumed response to a decline in relative economic status), then their median income would have risen by only 22% during the decade. However, the median *family* income of men aged 35–44, net of

II. Economic Impact of Wives Working

CCC, rose by 28% and for men aged 45–54 the rise was 39%. Hence, the economic position of *husbands* aged 18–24 declined slightly compared to the income of *families* of men aged 35–44 and considerably compared to those of men aged 45–54.

It is also revealing to compare changes in the economic position of young married men to slightly older men who might provide consumption models for the family-cycle stage the younger men presumably aspire to enter in the near future. In this comparison, there is no doubt that men aged 18–24 were lagging behind (Table 8.20). Their median income rose by 22% during the decade compared to the 28% rise for those aged 25–34. The situation is far worse, however, when total family income is taken into account for the older group and not just husband's earnings alone. When this is done, the gross increase in family income of those aged 25–34 is to 35%, and the increase, net of CCC, was 36%.

All this has important implications for future trends in fertility. If declines in the relative economic position of young males helped promote the start of a fertility decline, further conditions then developed that promoted additional fertility declines on the part of young cohorts. These arose out of the compensatory responses to perceived relative (and absolute) deprivation by young people—postponement of marriage and children to cut down on expenses and the entry of wives into the labor force to increase income. This, in turn, permitted young families to better approximate preferred levels of material life-style, though at the cost of children and child-oriented kinds of consumption. However, as still younger cohorts reached early adulthood, they found that, in addition to their relative economic disadvantage compared to their parents, they had a relative economic disadvantage compared to slightly older, but still young cohorts. By virtue of wives' labor-force participation and reduced fertility, this slightly older group had been able to achieve a relatively affluent life-style far beyond what younger couples could attain without similar "sacrifices." Hence, whether the young couples looked to models representing their recent past (their parental households during adolescence), their near future (slightly older couples), or their more distant future (couples where the husband was at his career peak), they were losing ground over the decade. Once established, this pattern of increased wives' labor-force participation and reduced fertility should help perpetuate itself among each new group reaching childbearing age, unless major changes in the husband's economic status are experienced.

In sum, the trend towards the fuller integration of women into the economic system may be still another factor creating rather permanent dampening effects on fertility swings. As long as wives' labor-force participation was very limited, fertility was more likely to vary markedly in response to mechanisms such as those posited by Easterlin. For example, in the past,

TABLE 8.20
Changes in Equivalent Expenditures on Children under Age 25 in Relation to the 1959–1969 Increases in Median Income of Husbands and of Total Median Family Income, by Age of Husband[a,b]

	Age of husband				
	18–24	25–34	35–44	45–54	55–64
Median income of husband					
1959	4,787	6,905	7,673	7,197	6,484
1969	5,846	8,820	10,174	9,871	8,365
Increase					
Absolute	1,059	1,915	2,501	2,674	1,881
Percentage	22	28	33	37	29
Median total family income					
1959	5,816	7,871	9,006	9,248	8,300
1969	7,492	10,495	12,258	13,109	11,172
Increase					
Absolute	1,676	2,714	3,252	3,861	2,872
Percentage	29	35	36	42	35
Change in total cost of children[c]	−270	−119	+743	+218	−46
Increase in median income of husband, net of change in total equivalent expenditures on children					
Total	1,329	2,034	1,758	2,456	1,927
As a percentage of 1959 income	28	30	23	34	30
Increase in median family income, net of changes in total equivalent expenditures on children[d]					
Total	1,946	2,833	2,509	3,643	2,918
As a percentage of 1959 income	33	36	28	39	35

Sources: 1960 and 1970 Public Use Samples of White Couples, Tables 5.7, 5.9, and Appendix Table C.4.
[a] Includes only those families where the husband was the head of the household.
[b] Incomes for 1959 are presented in 1969 dollars.
[c] For husbands aged 18–34, child-care costs are for children under 18. For husbands aged 35–54, child-care costs are estimated for children under age 25.
[d] In computing this figure, the estimated income of children 18–24 was not deducted from their estimated "cost" because their income is already included in total family income. This resulted in changes in the cost of children of +$843, +$379, and −$2 respectively for fathers aged 35–44, 45–54, and 55–64.

II. Economic Impact of Wives Working

partly due to limited employment opportunities, wives in older families in the second life-cycle squeeze were less able to enter the labor force to help establish or maintain the high standards of affluence that the next generation, in turn, would find difficult to attain on the husband's earnings alone. Hence following Easterlin's own argument, now that older wives do work in larger numbers, this pattern should permanently intensify the difficulties of the first squeeze and increase the likelihood of young wives working and postponing births.

Even though the addition of wives' earnings (as well as other sources of income) led to considerably greater increases in the income of older families between 1959 and 1969 (net of CCC) than was exhibited by husband's income alone, in the cross-section it is obvious that economic pressures for wives to work remained. Whatever the reasons for the growing work involvement of younger wives as well as the decline in their fertility, these trends produced rises in family income (net of CCC) that either equalled or greatly outstripped that of the families of men who were aged 35–44—the age group for which the dependency burden is best documented. Thus, for 35–44-year-old husbands, the rise in family income, net of CCC, was 28% in the 1959–1969 decade (Table 8.20). However, the comparable rise for families of 25–34-year-old men was all the way up to 36% and for 18–24-year-olds it was 33%. Moreover, when we compare the increase in family income for 35–44-year-olds (net of CCC) with the *gross* increase for 25–34-year-olds (and thus do not "credit" them with their lowered fertility), the older males still come off more poorly. Hence, even allowing for the growing economic role of wives in older families, the rise in income (net of CCC) was not comparable to the next youngest age group.

In the case of families of men aged 45–54 years old, the situation is, once again, less clear-cut because of the difficulty of measuring the full extent of child-dependency. Nevertheless, although the 1959–1969 growth in the median family income of this age group (net of CCC) is considerably better than that experienced by families of 35–44-year-olds (39 compared to 28%), it still was only slightly better than that exhibited by the families of 25–34-year-olds (36%). Hence, even when comparing income of families (and thus including wives' contributions), families of 45–54-year-old men did not seem to have come out much better than families of 23–34-year-olds, though they did experience substantially greater improvements than families of either 35–44- or 18–24-year-olds.

In sum, economic pressures for older wives to work did not appear to be on the wane, despite the much more rapid increase in the income of their husbands. This was offset, on the one hand, by the rises in child-care costs due to the higher fertility of the cohorts who were 35–44 and 45–54 in 1970 and, on the other hand, by a combination of declining fertility and greater increases in the labor-force participation of the wives of men who moved into the 18–24 and 25–34 age groups in 1970.

III. CONCLUSION

Chapter 8 culminates the empirical analyses of this study. Rather than summarizing its general findings, I will incorporate them into an overview of the most important theoretical and empirical conclusions of the study as a whole. Two questions are at issue. First, what are the major findings and how do they tie together? Second, what are their overall implications for demographic behavior and women's changing economic roles in the latter part of the twentieth century?

A major thesis of the study has been that certain structural sources of relative economic deprivation are intrinsic to the socioeconomic organization of our society. These are related to our occupational system and to the interaction of certain career and family-cycle patterns. I have focused, particularly, on two types of economic squeezes—the lower white-collar squeeze and the life-cycle squeezes. The nature and potential severity of the two life-cycle squeezes should vary among different types of occupational groups. The first squeeze should be relatively more severe for families of men in Group I and II occupations because of the very low absolute and relative earnings of young men going into such occupations. However, the potential severity of the second squeeze should be greater for those in Group III and IV occupations because of the loss of the positive age effect on earnings relatively early in adulthood at just about the time child-care costs are peaking.

A considerable proportion of Chapters 3 through 5 have been devoted to an empirical documentation of the existence of these squeezes through an analysis of age–earnings profiles and the educational characteristics of men in different occupational groups, age-related expenditure patterns of consumption items that are important for setting up an independent household, and age and occupational variations in the child-dependency burden. In general, the data have provided considerable support for the hypothesized squeezes and the potential variability in their character among occupational groups.

The major impetus for developing the economic-squeeze appoach was, of course, to use it as a means of conducting a social–demographic analysis of certain types of behavior that would presumably be affected by such squeezes. My initial interest was in using the squeeze concept to study wives' economic behavior but it gradually became apparent that other behavioral

III. Conclusion

patterns were also involved—particularly certain types of demographic patterns. In short, as microeconomic models stress, there is a whole package of behavioral responses that, in one combination or another, will be used by people to deal with certain exogenous economic constraints. Hence, I have also paid some attention to marriage and fertility patterns, as well as to wives' economic behavior.

As anticipated, a number of demographic patterns were associated with occupational differences in the nature of the life-cycle squeezes, operating either to forestall or alleviate them. This certainly seemed to be the case for men going into Group I and II white-collar occupations. Age at marriage was later for these men, a pattern consistent with the major vulnerable point in their career cycle—the first squeeze. However, early marriage was more characteristic of males going into manual occupations where marriage postponement might have just pushed the second squeeze into another unfavorable stage in the husband's occupational career. Occupational differences in the relationship of family-cycle stage to age also showed that at each age (up to ages 55–64) men in white-collar occupations—particularly Groups I and II—were at an earlier point in the family cycle than manual workers. Families of blue-collar men appeared to have reached the launching stage for their children much earlier in life, despite their higher fertility which, logically, should have prolonged the childrearing period. Moreover, the marriage and fertility of white-collar families seemed particularly sensitive to variations in the economic position of young men, as is consistent with the disproportionate difficulties the first squeeze represents for these couples and the less severe constraints operating during the second squeeze period.

Finally, the analyses of Chapter 6 indicated that wives' work propensities were sensitive to the economic difficulties of the lower white-collar squeeze and the two life-cycle squeezes. Moreover, as other research has also found, wives' labor-force participation is not only responsive to economic pressures but also to the socioeconomic advantage of their working. In this study, I have particularly stressed the *relative*, in addition to the absolute, advantage of wives working and the relative *status* as well as *economic* implications. The analyses in Chapters 7 and 8 showed that the potential relative socioeconomic advantage of wives' working was an important factor in their labor-force participation and that this relative advantage varied inversely with the husband's socioeconomic level. Moreover, the addition of wives' earnings appeared to more than compensate for the economic disadvantage of those in the two life-cycle squeezes and in the lower white-collar squeeze. In fact, wives' earnings, low as they were, provided a functional substitute for upward occupational mobility of the husband.

If the potential for various economic squeezes is an inherent feature of modern industrial America and if certain adaptive behaviors appear to prevent or at least ease their difficulties, then two important issues to consider are how this "system" of economic pressures and behavioral responses has been changing in recent years and what the prospects are for the near future. The answer to these questions is understandably complex and at this point we can, at best, only "see through a glass, darkly."

The empirical analyses of Chapters 3, 4, and 5 certainly indicate that the life-cycle squeezes could and did vary over time. With regard to the income component of the first squeeze, young men's relative earnings position had clearly deteriorated between 1959 and 1969. Part of this was undoubtedly a result of large cohort size. However, the decline in the relative economic position of young men has not just been limited to the baby-boom cohorts. Two major period effects appear to be important factors in this decline. First there is the rising skill composition of the labor force which produces a steeper age–earnings profile with higher peak earnings but relatively low earnings early in the career cycle when formal and on-the-job human capital investments are being made and paid for by foregone earnings. Second there is the growing institutionalization of labor markets, providing greater job security for middle-aged workers via seniority rules and other provisions. As a consequence, the relative income position of older workers was improving and that of younger males was declining.

To the extent the decline in young men's relative earnings position has resulted from long-run secular changes and not just from the cyclical effect of cohort size, the severity of the first squeeze is not about to be greatly alleviated by the advent of baby-bust cohorts to the labor market. Hence, for these reasons alone, it appears unlikely that we are soon to experience another baby boom, accompanied by a declining rate of increase—or even an actual decrease—in young wives' labor-force participation.

That there are changes in the cost component of the life-cycle squeezes also support this conclusion. For one thing, the recent acceleration in the rate of inflation places economic pressures on all families but probably particularly on those in the two life-cycle squeeze periods. As long as inflation remains high, substantial pressures for wives to work should persist, with all the associated demographic behaviors this seems to entail. Second, fertility fluctuations, via relative cohort size, not only affect the labor-market position of young men but, before that, the child-dependency burden of their parents, especially in the second-squeeze period. Hence, the apparent deterioration in the relative earnings position of younger versus older *men* was largely offset by the increasing child-care burdens of older families. However, the rising labor-force participation of older wives, presumably partly in response to the second squeeze and its increasing severity, *has* produced a decline in the income position of young *husbands* relative to the total *family* income of

III. Conclusion

older husbands, net of changes in child-care costs. To the extent this is the case and the work rates of older wives remain high, there is yet another reason why it is unlikely there will soon be a significant reduction in the severity of the first squeeze. Hence, there probably will be a persistence of the pattern of delayed childbearing and smaller families combined with a more extensive life-time work involvement for a rising proportion of American women.

A major thrust of this chapter has been that there are important feedback effects of changes in the many types of behaviors that can, in part, be considered adaptive responses to economic squeezes. In particular, I have focused on the feedback effects of wives' rising labor-force participation. First, the more common it and the associated demographic behaviors become, the more these represent a behavioral model of how to deal with economic squeezes. This, in turn, encourages the further proliferation of this behavioral pattern rather than some alternative response to economically stressful situations. Concomitant with such major behavioral changes, the normative climate should become more supportive of the changing life-styles these behavioral patterns represent. Moreover, fewer women will be treating employment as simply a temporary activity sandwiched between the more important family-oriented segments of their life-cycle. As work becomes a more long-range activity, they will start to invest more of their time and effort into making it more rewarding. And to the extent their families come to rely on their economic contribution, women's work behavior should increasingly resemble that of men.

In addition, however, the increasing employment of wives has an impact on important reference-group comparisons and hence on the aspirational and income components of economic squeezes. For one thing, it puts those couples in a similar squeeze position but without a working wife at an even greater disadvantage, increasing the likelihood that they too will adopt this behavioral pattern. Second, it affects inter- as well as intragroup comparisons. Thus, if the life-style aspirations of young couples are partly a function of the socialization process in their parental household and partly due to contemporaneous reference-group comparisons, the frequent employment of wives in families comprising these reference groups "inflates" the aspirational level of young couples, making it extremely difficult for them to achieve comparable life-styles on the basis of the husband's earnings alone. Similarly, if work by the wife can be a functional substitute for upward mobility, this disrupts traditional socioeconomic differentials of families based on the husband's characteristics alone. This, in turn, will put economic pressure on families whose position in the stratification system is thereby threatened. Finally, when wives' employment makes it possible to *more* than compensate for a life-cycle-squeeze disadvantage, this disrupts interage comparisons of relative economic status and puts pressure on the families so disadvantaged to engage in some form of compensatory behavior.

In sum, one implication of a relative economic status model, combined with the notion of competitive consumption as a common behavioral pattern, is the strong possibility of rapid social change. This is because of the feedback mechanisms that seem intrinsic to such a model. The cumulative impact of responses of certain types of couples to perceived relative deprivation is likely to alter the reference-group reality of other couples. If these couples also respond, their actions may, in turn, alter an important reference group reality for still more families. And so on. In the case of women's economic behavior, it appears that, for better or for worse, the increase in the labor-force participation of wives past the very early life-cycle squeeze has helped create a self-generating process that tends to lead to continued increases in the extensiveness of wives' economic role outside the home, with all the demographic concomitants this may involve. If that is true, then the postwar changes in women's socioeconomic behavior and the more recent declines in fertility do not merely represent a fleeting departure from their age-old devotion to domesticity but, rather, a profound transformation in our way of life.

IV

EPILOGUE

9

Life-Cycle Squeezes and Adaptive Family Strategies

I. CONCEPTUALIZATION

A major theme of this study has been that socioeconomic differences in the career-cycle effect on men's earnings can influence the timing and severity of life-cycle squeezes. These, in turn, promote adaptive behavioral responses which vary significantly among families of men in different types of occupations. For those going into higher-level occupations, the first squeeze seems to be the most intrinsically stressful, given their steep age–earnings profiles. Marriage postponement and the employment of the wife early in marriage appear to represent important types of coping mechanisms developed to deal with these problems. However, the historically flat age–earnings profile of men in manual occupations suggests that delayed marriage and childbearing would just increase the severity of the second squeeze. Hence early marriage and childbearing appear to be the more adaptive responses.

In this closing chapter I will develop a more general theoretical statement about family strategies as adaptive responses to temporal and/or socioeconomic differentials in the nature of life-cycle squeezes. Such an endeavor seems particularly appropriate given the growing scholarly concern with family strategies, especially in the field of historical family studies (Tilly

1979a, 1979b; Bourdieu 1976; Cain 1978; Modell and Hareven 1973; Goldin 1979, 1980; Friedlander 1973; Haines 1979). Moreover, the idea of different adaptive responses to socioeconomic variations in the nature and severity of life-cycle squeezes seems readily generalizable to the study of nineteenth-century families as well as contemporary families in American and European societies

Basic Assumptions

When socioeconomic subgroups or whole societies regularly encounter a particular set of circumstances over which they have little or no control, adaptive strategies should evolve over time. In this instance it is family strategies that are of interest. Not only might these strategies develop in response to certain external constraints, but any particular strategy that is adopted will impose its own additional constraints on behavor as well. Moreover, one might expect all strategies to have certain vulnerabilities. By looking at the vulnerabilities of different strategies as well as the constraints they impose, we hope to achieve a better understanding of both the sources of stress that lead to change and the direction this change is likely to take.

An immediate question that comes to mind when the issue of adaptive family strategies is raised is just what is meant by the term *adaptive*. In general, I will roughly define an adaptive family strategy as one that on average, promotes the replacement (or even the multiplication) of the family unit over generations at the same or a higher socioeconomic level. In doing so, it safeguards the family against crises by either preventing them or, in some way, ameliorating their negative consequences. As a corollary, such an adaptive strategy promotes the maintenance or improvement of the customary level of living of the family unit and its individual members over the "life" of the unit. Such strategies will, of course, vary in their success as adaptations. Some, or most, will be relatively "imperfect" adaptations and hence will have internal stresses that increase their vulnerability to change.

Another concomitant of successful strategies, in the sense I have just outlined, is that, on a group basis, the population as well as the family unit is also being replaced or expanded. Thus, I am talking about both social and biological reproduction. It may be possible, of course, to have a family strategy that produces population replacement or even population growth—and thus achieves some measure of demographic "success"—but at a *declining* socioeconomic level over the generations.[1] However, such

---

[1] Basically, this is Malthus's argument, of course. See also David Levine (1977) for a rather similar position.

strategies are probably intrinsically unstable. To the extent parental households form important reference groups for children, a situation that chronically leads to a deterioration in the younger generation's socioeconomic position should generate considerable dissatisfaction and pressure for change. Even if it did not, such a strategy should ultimately jeopardize the survival chances of population groups following it since eventually the level of living will fall below that necessary for physical survival. In sum, groups utilizing such strategies will either disappear or they will adopt more successful strategies. In either case, the particular strategy that has produced such a phenomenon will tend to disappear. For this reason, and also because it seems more sociologically interesting, I have chosen to focus on the analysis of the reproduction of families at a given or higher socioeconomic level rather than to stress just biological replacement. By doing so, it is always possible to analyze strategies that are less successful and hence are presumably unstable.

The notion of adaptive family strategies used here is essentially macro in nature. It does not imply that the utility of some individuals in the family or even of the family unit as a whole, is being maximized. Nor does it necessarily imply that all or even most of those conforming to such a strategy have individualistically planned it in a rationalistic decision-making process. Rather, I am using the concept more in the way that biologists do when they discuss adaptive behaviors. Hence the evolutionary success of certain social patterns is really at issue rather than utility, happiness, or the chances for the development of a just society. Many individuals may follow a given strategy for entirely nonrational reasons or rational reasons unconnected with the adaptive value of the strategy. However, if certain strategies involve considerable "disutilities" for various (or all) family members, this will be a source of considerable stress that may lead to behavioral modifications. Hence, the structurally based disutilities of any strategy provide one of the sources of vulnerability to which it is subject. Nevertheless, I assume that, as in the behavior of other living things, it is possible to have adaptive responses that are not motivated by a conscious desire to change an overall strategy or behavioral pattern.[2] In other words, the notion of an "adaptive (or nonadaptive) family strategy" refers to its contribution to the evolutionary success of groups and does not necessarily imply that the individual actors involved perceive of it as a "strategy" though some or many may do so, of course.

Finally, it is recognized that strategies that might be highly adaptive for individual families may, if they become widespread, have long-run collective

---

[2] However, the concept of evolved social strategies utilized here does not incorporate any notion of genetic evolution, though it is possible that genetically related behaviors or characteristics have a socially adaptive value.

consequences that ultimately reduce the effectiveness of the strategy in question. Thus, as I stressed in Chapter 8, when people adapt to changing circumstances, their adaptations may often have feedback effects that promote still further changes. Hence, observed changes are often hard to interpret. They may be permanent or they may be temporary shifts to be followed by a return to a previous pattern. However, they may be temporary in the sense of representing transitions to still another type of social behavior.

The rough typology of family strategies that follows makes no pretense of being exhaustive and hence applicable to all societies at whatever point in time we may observe them. Indeed, it represents a very preliminary effort to develop a particular kind of analytical approach. A major limitation on its generalizability, for example, is that it will focus only on those societies where wage and salary earnings of males are the norm rather than nonmarket-based subsistence economic activities. Nevertheless, the discussion should have historical relevance in European and American societies though it will only be possible to deal somewhat superficially with the historical implications of this conceptual approach.

Given these limitations, the analysis of different types of family strategies focuses on what I see as problems intrinsic to age-related patterns of both male earnings and family behavior. For one thing, as we have seen, the earnings of young males are usually relatively (and absolutely) very low. This is one major factor in the first life-cycle squeeze in that low earnings make it difficult to set up an independent adult existence at a young age. Alternatively, too extensive a postponement of marriage and children also entails certain risks. One is that such delays may result in the heaviest child-care cost occurring when the career-cycle effect on husband's earnings is no longer positive but may actually be neutral or even negative, thereby intensifying the *second* squeeze. So of great interest is how family strategies deal with the competing risks of the various life-cycle squeezes.

Although it has not been explored in this book, at least one additional life-cycle squeeze seems intrinsic to the socioeconomic organization of Western society. This is the economic squeeze that often occurs when the husband and his wife, if she has been working, retire from market employment. This is the third squeeze of old age when income may drop precipitously because of the loss of earnings. The severity of the third squeeze should, like that of the first two, vary markedly among socioeconomic groups. As a consequence, it should engender different types of behavioral modifications, not only at the time of its occurence but earlier as well, in anticipation of the potential economic difficulties of the postretirement period.

Before launching into a discussion of how particular family strategies may be more adaptive to families of men in occupations with different types of age–earnings profiles, however, it is important to consider the two types of

I. Conceptualization

components that provide the framework of the analysis. One concerns some of the important exogenous factors influencing the development of one strategy or another. The other deals with the types of behavioral responses that will form the substance of these strategies. In neither case have I attempted to construct an exhaustive list. Rather, at this preliminary stage, I have been concerned with keeping the analysis tractable by considering a relatively few factors and behaviors that I think of particular significance or interest.

Adaptive Behaviors

There are nine types of behaviors that I think are especially important to consider in an analysis of adaptive family strategies though not all can be discussed in the present chapter.

1. *Nonmarriage:* The "success" of certain family strategies in maintaining living levels may sometimes rest on the nonmarriage of one or more offspring. Thus, in preindustrial Europe those children who did not stand to inherit much under an impartible inheritance system, in some cases, remained in the household of orientation and maintained a constant level of living—but at the price of never marrying. By so doing, they also did not form families that would operate at a lower socioeconomic level than did the parental generation. Or the success of some family strategies in providing care for the elderly might often have depended on the nonmarriage of one child in the family who would remain with the parent(s) and take responsibility for their care, if not also their economic support. Since the discussion in this chapter stresses the role of husbands' age–earning profiles in family strategies, I will focus on married couples and hence will not really go into the issue of nonmarriage as one possible component of an adaptive family strategy. Nevertheless, historically, it appears to have been a relatively important behavioral pattern in many European societies.

2. *Age at marriage:* Since age at marriage (by either men or women) can be thought of as one possible response to variations in the severity of the first squeeze, this is obviously a potentially important behavioral component of any family strategy. Its significance is further enhanced by the strong relationship of age at marriage to fertility patterns and directly or indirectly, via fertility, to women's economic roles and the timing of child-dependency burdens.

3. *Age at the birth of the first child:* It is essential to consider this for both fathers and mothers. The father's age at the start of childbearing will influence when in his career cycle the heaviest child-care responsibilities will

occur; hence behavioral modifications affecting when family formation commences may affect the severity of the life-cycle squeezes. Therefore, the focus on life-cycle squeezes attaches a previously unrecognized significance to the analysis of the *husband's* age at the birth of children. Since the age of the *mother* at the birth of the first child may be related to her ultimate family size and her economic role in the family, this too is an important factor to consider.

4. *Spacing of subsequent children:* Spacing differences may also affect the severity of squeezes. For example, under certain conditions close spacing can greatly intensify the second squeeze for some families if it leads to a bunching of costs (e.g., three children in college at the same time). Since spacing is often subject to modification, it forms one potential behavioral strategy for dealing with the difficulties of maintaining the same standard of living within and across generations. In addition, the spacing of children will affect the nature of women's economic role outside the home given their major role in the care of young children within the home.

5. *Total number of children born:* This too has obvious implications for the severity of squeezes and for women's economic and children's roles.

6. *Economic role of children:* The economic "burden" of children depends, in part, on the nature of their economic role in the family and the timing of this role over the family cycle. If children make a relatively significant contribution while they are still young, then this obviously eases the difficulty of the adolescent dependency burden or even eliminates it entirely. It may also, however, affect the ability of families to transmit or improve on socioeconomic status across generations. In any event, it is important to consider what role children's economic behavior may have in a variety of adaptive family strategies—especially among preindustrial and industrializing societies.[3]

7. *Economic role of wives and its timing:* Wives' economic role and its timing throughout the family cycle is a potentially important factor in the maintenance of socioeconomic status within and across generations. Therefore, it provides another type of behavioral component of an adaptive family strategy.

8. *Economic role of husbands and its timing:* Since the starting point of this analysis of family strategies is how occupational variations in the age effect on men's earnings affects families' socioeconomic position within and

---

[3] Unfortunately, I failed to include variables in my PUS files that would have enabled me to study the economic role of children in their families of orientation. However, I have come to believe that understanding the changing economic role of children in families is essential to achieve a greater understanding of the nature of the changes occurring in family strategies in the second half of the twentieth century.

I. Conceptualization

across generations, the importance of considering this behavioral component need not be stressed.

9. *Migration of individuals or families:* The success of a given family strategy in maintaining living levels within a particular area may depend on the possibilities of out-migration of individuals or families whose economic position would be precarious if they remained. One obvious example is the long-standing emigration of the Irish in the late nineteenth and early twentieth centuries away from rural areas in which impartible inheritance was practiced—and which led to a surplus of economicaly marginal young men and women (Arensberg and Kimball 1968). Although migration may be an important behavioral component of family strategies, I will not attempt to deal with it here.

Not all combinations of these different adaptive behaviors are possible, of course, thus the types of patterns likely to occur under any given set of exogenous constraints are limited. For example, early marriage and low fertility under conditions of little control over fertility seem to be a rather unlikely combination. These limitations on the combination of behaviors that will form successful adaptations are formed by the constraints imposed partly by the strategy itself rather than purely by exogenous factors.

Exogenous Constraints

Upon reflection, one could undoubtedly come up with a very long list of exogenous factors that affect the kinds of adaptive family strategies that evolve over time in social groups. I will briefly specify six classes of factors, assuming that any particular factor may operate independently of the others or jointly (either in an additive or multiplicative fashion) with the others to affect the strategies that evolve. How these constraints vary over time is also important to consider.

1. *Prevailing mortality and morbidity conditions:* These may refer to those conditions prevailing in the society in general or that especially affect particular subgroups (e.g., variations in mortality by age, sex, occupation, income, locale).

2. *Fertility control capabilities:* The extent to which people can control their fertility behavior obviously affects adaptive behaviors with regard to family size and timing of children.

3. *Family's standard of living:* This refers to the aspect of a family's standard of living that is socially determined in some way. Thus it partly involves the normative constraints under which many families operate and that push them to try to achieve and maintain certain life-styles.

4. *Cost of raising children:* By this is meant the cost of raising children so that their socioeconomic standing is roughly equal to or greater than that of their parents. It includes not only the total costs but their distribution over the life-cycle of the children.[4]

5. *The structure of economic opportunities for earnings:* This includes the structure of opportunities for men, women, and children and how they vary over the life-cycle, by socioeconomic groups, etc.

6. *Nonfamilial sources of income and their relationship to the life-cycle:* Included here would be transfer payments such as those from kin outside the household, government subsidies of one sort or another, unearned sources of income such as inherited wealth or interest on investments.

While labeling these factors as typically *exogenous,* one must maintain a certain theoretical flexibility regarding their causal status. For example, if one assumes that exogenous variables, and/or the information available about them, are often subject to change, then one would expect adaptive responses to be frequently occurring. That is, behavioral changes will be a regular feature of all but the most static societies. As a consequence, the causal status of many variables can become exceedingly complex. Given changes in one or more exogenous factors, the possible adaptive responses open to people will depend, in part, on their life-cycle stage (i.e., how many options have already been eliminated, or created, by past actions of varying degrees of reversability). Thus, one can no longer decide to marry early when one is 30, have two children after three have been born, respace the children already born, etc. In short, some behaviors (and often the consequences that ensue) cannot be undone and though others can, the probability of changing them declines with age. As a consequence, many variables that were once endogenous can achieve a more exogenous status over time. In short, past decisions, once carried out, tend to limit one's future options and all dynamic models of human behavior must somehow deal with this problem. Furthermore, as already emphasized, adaptive responses to change may have collective feedback effect. In this way, many adaptive behaviors essentially have the potential of operating as exogenous factors at some future date.

Using the age–earnings profiles associated with different types of peak median occupations as a basic starting point, let us now go on to consider a number of possible family strategies that, under a variety of external

---

[4]This does not imply that all "successful" family strategies require that every child be treated equally and given the same opportunity to emulate or exceed the standing of their parents. For example, a successful strategy may involve investing more in one particularly promising child who is then obligated to help others in the family after he has, they hope, achieved a measure of success far greater than that of his parents.

constraints, might be "appropriate" to different career trajectories.[5] In the process of doing this we can consider what different kinds of vulnerabilities and sensitivities to change each type of strategy may involve.

There are three types of peak median occupational groups that I think are important to consider separately. One is the Group I and II white-collar occupations (i.e., high-level white-collar occupations). These exhibit a steep age–earnings profile and families of men who spend much of their working life in such occupations presumably hold relatively high life-style aspirations. Second, at the other end, are Group III and IV blue-collar occupations, exhibiting what seems like a very different age–earnings profile. This is not only characterized by lower earnings at almost every age group but by a rather flat age–earnings profile with an early and relatively low peak. One might also expect that life-style aspirations are more modest for the families of men in these occupational groups. Finally, we shall examine Group III and IV white-collar occupational groups. These are the families who are often involved in what has been called the lower white-collar squeeze—caught between relatively high consumption aspirations and relatively flat and low age–earnings profiles.

II. GROUP I AND II WHITE-COLLAR FAMILIES

Period and cohort effects aside, men going into Group I and II white-collar occupations experience a career trajectory where the most economically vulnerable time occurs early in adult life. What types of family strategies might be adaptive for such a career trajectory, keeping in mind that, by definition, one goal of an adaptive family strategy is to maintain or improve on socioeconomic status across generations? How would these strategies vary depending on the influence of some of the other types of exogenous factors outlined above?

Economic Role of Children

The type of adaptive strategy that might evolve as a necessary concomitant of a career trajectory typical of high-level occupations depends, in part, on

[5]Which career trajectory an individual actually follows will not necessarily be predetermined, of course, For example, the type of family strategy a man starts to follow in his youth may, in fact, have a considerable impact on his occupational career. Thus a very early marriage and early births of unplanned children can make it impossible for some men to undertake the human capital investments they had originally planned. In that case, they may not end up in a high-level job after all. Hence, the career trajectory is not necessarily an exogenous variable.

whether the man's family of procreation is usually entirely dependent on his occupationally-derived income or whether (and when) additional sources of income are also available—such as from the wife or children or in the form of transfer payments of one sort or another.

Ignoring for the moment wives' possible income contribution, it seems rather unlikely that the children of such men make a significant socioeconomic contribution to their families of orientation while they are still children or even when they are young adults. If socioeconomic status is to be maintained across generations then the children, like their fathers, will typically follow a career trajectory characterized by relatively low youthful earnings. One reason for this is the extensive investments in human capital that are often prerequisite to a high-level occupational career. Moreover, even if the parents do not plan to make extensive investments in human capital for all their children—(e.g., for the girls) their potential relative economic contribution would be correspondingly very low because of low levels of human capital attainments. This is entirely aside from any problems they might have in finding a status-compatible occupation with a low skill level. In the case of daughters, moreover, the costs of ensuring that they marry well is not necessarily minor for high socioeconomic groups.

Data on just how much later the school-leaving age of men in higher-level occupations has been compared to other occupational groups and how this has been changing over time are not directly available. However, it is possible to make a rough estimate of these differentials, and any changes over time, by utilizing the 1960 and 1970 PUS data on educational attainment for different cohorts of white husbands, by occupation. By assuming that the average age in first grade is 6, the age at which boys would complete eighth grade is approximately 13 and they would then graduate from high school at about age 17 and from college at about age 21. These findings will undoubtedly be somewhat biased by the process of occupational mobility which distorts interage comparisons. Another probable problem, particularly in the Professional II category, is that new occupations may be developing, recruiting younger workers with somewhat different educational attainments than those of older men in the same peak median occupational group but in different specific occupations. Nevertheless, the data should be adequate to make general interoccupational comparisons and to track overall trends in the school-leaving age.

Table 9.1 presents the estimated school-leaving age for men in Group I and II white-collar occupations compared to the estimates for all husbands and white-collar husbands as a group. By and large, as expected, the estimated school-leaving age of men in every Group I or II occupation was later than for all occupation groups combined. Furthermore, this difference persisted for all the cohorts represented in the table. Second, there was considerable variation within the Group I and II occupations in the estimated school-leaving age. It was the latest, of course, by a wide margin, for Professional I husbands. For example, only 56% of the Professional I husbands who were aged 55–64 in 1960 (the cohort of 1896–1905) had finished school by age 21 compared to 97% for men in that cohort for all occupational groups combined and 93% for all white-collar husbands. In the case of the youngest cohort in the table—those 25–34 in 1970—the proportion who had left school by age 21 or earlier was only approximately 41% for Professional I husbands compared to 90% for all husbands and 79% for all white-collar husbands in this cohort. Professional II males were considerably more likely to have left school earlier but nevertheless had a much later school-leaving age than all husbands combined.

The estimated school-leaving age of Managers I and II and Sales II husbands was well below that of professionals, though above that of all husbands. However, it was sometimes similar to the figures for white-collar husbands as a group. In sum, a lower proportion of Group I and II husbands had left school at a younger age than husbands in all occupational groups combined and compared to many white-collar husbands as a group. This was particularly characteristic of Professional I and then Professional II men.

A final observation to make is that for all groups represented in the table, the school-leaving age was rising from older to younger cohorts, indicating a progressive delay in the age at full-time entry into their permanent high-level career-type positions.

The Husband as the Main Source of Income

When men going into higher-level, late-peaking occupations are expected to be the sole support of their families, marriage postponement seems like one obvious adaptive mechanism for dealing with the low–earnings period of youth. This not only postpones the heavy economic responsibilities involved in setting up a household until the man is more established (thus reducing the severity of the first squeeze) but may also lead to a postponement of the second-squeeze period until the husband's earnings are at their peak. What effect such marriage postponement by the man may have on completed fertility is another matter, however, and depends on a number of other factors as well. One is the age of the wife he ultimately marries and another is the use and effectiveness of marital fertility control measures. If little marital fertility control is exercised and the man marries a relatively young woman, then the couple's ultimate surviving family size might be quite large—just how large being partly a result of fecundity levels and the mortality risks faced by the husband, wife, and children at the time period in question. However, if

TABLE 9.1
Estimates of the School-Leaving Age of Selected Age Cohorts of Husbands in Group I and II White-Collar Occupations: 1960 and 1970

Percentage leaving school at or before a given age

Occupation and estimated maximum age at leaving school[a]	Birth cohort and age in 1960[b]			Birth cohort and age in 1970			
	1926–1925 25–34	1916–1925 35–44	1906–1915 45–54	1896–1905 55–64	1936–1945 25–34	1926–1935 35–44	1916–1925 45–54	1906–1915 55–64
Total								
13	17	22	37	53	8	15	20	34
15	33	38	53	66	19	28	34	50
16	40	46	59	71	24	34	41	56
17	71	76	81	84	63	68	74	79
20	84	87	90	93	79	80	86	89
21	93	94	95	97	90	90	93	94
White collar[c]								
13	4	7	15	30	2	4	7	14
15	12	16	27	43	5	10	14	25
16	17	22	34	48	8	13	19	31
17	45	54	61	68	37	43	52	58
20	65	72	77	84	60	62	71	75
21	85	86	89	93	79	81	86	88
Professional I								
13	—	1	3	7	—	1	1	3
15	2	2	5	8	—	2	2	6
16	3	2	7	12	1	2	2	8
17	12	14	14	20	9	12	14	17
20	26	24	25	29	20	23	29	29
21	48	48	45	56	41	45	50	45

Professional II							
13	1	3	5	9	1	1	2	5
15	3	7	9	15	2	3	6	10
16	5	12	12	20	3	5	8	13
17	21	34	32	40	23	28	33	38
20	44	56	61	68	48	50	58	62
21	78	83	87	95	78	81	86	88
Managers I							
13	2	2	9	16	1	2	4	8
15	7	7	19	29	3	6	8	17
16	11	12	26	37	5	8	12	21
17	39	38	51	56	34	32	39	51
20	59	62	75	81	60	51	61	72
21	91	90	91	96	87	83	87	90
Managers II							
13	7	9	22	37	3	6	9	16
15	20	21	37	52	10	14	17	30
16	27	26	42	56	14	20	24	37
17	60	63	70	76	51	53	62	67
20	75	83	86	91	76	75	82	84
21	94	96	97	96	94	92	94	96
Sales II							
13	2	6	5	24	1	2	4	9
15	9	13	17	40	2	6	11	20
16	12	19	25	45	5	9	14	28
17	39	57	58	68	34	39	49	58
20	60	81	85	89	63	65	76	79
21	94	94	96	98	92	91	94	96

Sources: 1960 and 1970 Public Use Samples of White Couples.

[a]Estimated ages at leaving school were based on the data on educational attainment. It was assumed that the average age of first-grade children was 6 and that the average at completing 8 years of elementary school is 13 and 17 for high school.
[b]Includes some men who were not heads of households.
[c]Includes Service III husbands.

marriage postponement for such men also involves a relatively late marriage for their wives, then completed family size may well be reduced. Finally, if marital fertility can be reliably controlled, then ultimate family size might be quite moderate, whatever the age of the wife at marriage. Furthermore, since high "quality" children—the kind necessary to maintain status over generations—are expensive, the cost of such children should promote family size restrictions by couples in higher-level socioeconomic groups except for the very wealthy.

Historical, as well as contemporary, examples of some of these strategies are not hard to find. Bank's fascinating description of the Victorian middle classes is actually a description of two of the strategies described. He pointed out that for these socioeconomic groups, it was considered imperative for newly married couples to set themselves up in a style appropriate to their social station in life. However, the only way of accomplishing this feat was to postpone marriage until the husband's income was sufficiently high (Banks 1954: Chapter 3): In this way, the difficulties of the first life-cycle squeeze could be avoided. In fact, Banks essentially captures the logic of my life-cycle squeeze argument.

> This calculation of life chances, so typical of the middle classes at this time, was directly related to the career structure of the older professions. At twenty-two or twenty-five years of age a middle-class lawyer or doctor could predict with a fair degree of accuracy what sums of money the men of his profession were likely to earn at various periods of their lives. Unlike the working man whose maximum was reached early on in adulthood, the middle-class man could anticipate a steady series of income increases in the future stretching out before him at least until middle age; and at the same time he need not expect to be susceptible on the income side to considerable fluctuations of an adverse kind due to the cycle of trade. Postponement of marriage, therefore, was a judicious policy, for a higher income would almost certainly be his in the course of time [Banks 1954: 199].

Banks goes on to point out, however, that although marriage postponement was a long-accepted family strategy, historically this had not also involved a limitation of births within marriage. However, he argues, the cost of children rose considerably in the latter half of the nineteenth century—especially due to the need to educate them more extensively as well as more expensively (Banks 1954: Chapter 11). Thus, during the nineteenth century, numerous changes led to the expansion of different types of occupational opportunities for middle-class sons. However, this expansion in opportunities had its price, creating considerable increases in the cost of children to parents. For example, the abolition of patronage in the Civil Service provided newly affluent middle-class families with the opportunity to place their sons in positions previously barred to them because of their lower socioeconomic backgrounds. To take advantage of the new opportunities, however, these sons had to receive the education of a gentleman and also survive through several lean years early in the occupational career (Banks 1954: 183). It thus became increasingly difficult to maintain the high standard of living to which the middle classes had become accustomed, prepare their children for a similar or higher station in life, and have large families as well. For these reasons, among others, Banks argues, in the English middle classes, control of marital fertility became more common in the later nineteenth century (Banks 1954: Chapter 12).[6]

As far as twentieth-century patterns are concerned, the analysis of the PUS couples in Chapters 4 and 5 indicated that a later timing of marriage and childbearing by higher as compared to lower occupational groups persists, although there was undoubtedly a considerable decline in the age at marriage and family formation since the late nineteenth and early twentieth centuries. As Chapter 4 showed, the median age at marriage of Group I and II males was typically well above that of blue-collar husbands. This was especially characteristic of the professions, of course, but involved other higher-level occupational groups as well. Furthermore, as we saw in Chapter 5, Group I and II men tended to be in an earlier stage of the family cycle than men in blue-collar occupations, in spite of the higher fertility of the latter. Moreover, recent CPS data indicate that, after a decline in age differences at the birth of the first child for white-collar as compared to blue-collar mothers, they have again increased (U.S. Bureau of the Census 1978e: Table 12).

Income from Multiple Sources

Other family strategies seem possible when the burdens of the first-squeeze period do not rest on the husband's shoulders alone. Thus marriage postponement may be less essential if the couple is able to delay having children until the husband's economic position is more financially secure, with the wife working in the interim. One possible result of such a strategy, however, is that family size is likely to be smaller than if childbearing had begun soon after marriage. However, there should be a limit to the extent to which such a strategy can permit early marriage. If the wife is expected to

---

[6] One might also speculate that in a historical period when mortality is relatively high, there was a greater necessity for a reliance on capital or wealth as a cushion for the families of such men in the event of their death. Hence, dowries might have been of great importance and the acquisition of a certain amount of wealth as well as high annual earnings might have become a prerequisite for marriage. This would have the double advantage of helping the couple set up a household suitable for their station in life and providing some economic provision for the wife in case of widowhood. For a discussion of several of these issues, see George Alter (1978: Chapter 7).

make an economic contribution in the first few years of the marriage, then some minimum level of human capital investments on her part will be necessary. Hence, this implies that such a pattern is incompatible with a very early school-leaving age for women—at least in a modern industrial society.

The success of such a strategy of a medium-young age at marriage combined with postponed childbearing and the employment of the wife depends both on the degree to which couples can effectively prevent early births and the state of the job market for young women. Where contraceptive efficiency seems rather uncertain or abortions are difficult to obtain, and suitable job prospects for young women are also uncertain, then the wide use of such a strategy might be discouraged as being too risky.

Still another family strategy that men going into late-peaking occupations might adopt would also involve medium-young ages at marriage but not include delayed childbearing by the wife. Such a strategy would be encouraged by the availability of sources of income other than from the husband or wife—income transfers from parents, the G.I. bill, subsidized housing, student loans and scholarships, etc. Relatively early marriage and childbearing, however, may hinge on a willingness to function at a low level of living for a number of lean years. Nevertheless, the availability of transfer payment should facilitate this pattern and perhaps promote the larger completed family size which often accompanies early childbearing.

It is also possible for the last two strategies to be combined. If some favorable conditions for each exist, then one strategy can provide a backup for the other. For example, if transfer payments are available to young couples so that a contraceptive failure is not a complete socioeconomic disaster, then more might attempt to follow a tactic of marrying at a fairly young age combined with the young wife working and efforts to postpone childbearing. Then if the first child is conceived earlier than planned, there are still other sources of income which can help pull the couple through the difficult early stages of the husband's career cycle, without jeopardizing his long-run economic prospects.

One question is whether such strategies promote or discourage the employment of wives later in life. Once past the first-squeeze period, strong economic pressures to work may not exist for wives of high-level men. However, trends in inflation and unanticipated costs of raising children may increase the severity of the second squeeze for these couples as well as for less affluent families. In addition, working later on in the life-cycle will be partly a function of whether the wife worked earlier and what type of job. Wives who have had little work experience, especially if combined with relatively modest educational attainments, might not view entering the labor force in the middle years as a realistic option. Late investments in human capital would have to be made and, given a lack of economic pressures plus the availability of alternate nonwork activities, then working at this stage of the life cycle may seem relatively unattractive. Wives of higher-level white-collar men who were employed early in the marriage at fairly low-level occupations such as many clerical jobs, might also be less inclined to reenter the labor force. If their previous jobs hold little appeal, then they are basically in a somewhat similar position as wives who never worked. Thus whether the wives of such men work at a later stage in the family cycle will depend in part on their level and type of early human capital investment—both in school and during their previous employment experience. However, if the couple followed a pattern of delayed childbearing with the wife working at a fairly attractive job—teaching, for example—then the labor force responsiveness of such wives to later economic pressures might be very marked indeed. In fact, if her occupational position is sufficiently attractive, her attachment to the labor force may be permanent, whether or not economic pressures ever arise.

The period after World War II in the United States seems, on the face of it, to provide an example of conditions that favored a number of these strategies. Long-run job prospects in higher-level occupations were good for men. In addition, the labor market for women was expanding rapidly and a variety of income subsidies became available to veterans—the G.I. bill, FHA low-interest home loans, and subsidized student housing provide three outstanding examples. Furthermore, as we have seen, after an initial period of readjustment in the economy, the inflation rate was quite moderate and hence the cost of setting up a household was by no means prohibitive. All this should have encouraged the much earlier marriage and childbearing exhibited by these cohorts of men going into the higher peak median occupations although the ultimate price of this shift, and the higher fertility that accompanied it, was an intensification of the second squeeze.

In sum, given the age–earnings profile of men in high-level occupations, strategies that involve postponements of marriage and childbearing have considerable adaptive value. However, this is partly because of the favorable age effect on earnings for middle-aged and older males in these occupations. Postponed childbearing not only eases the severity of the first squeeze but does not, in the process, increase the severity of the second squeeze. In fact, it probably leads to a more optimal timing of the second squeeze. Nevertheless, there is a limit on the extent to which family life can be postponed if it is to be experienced at all, especially by women. The greater the postponement, the greater the possibility of the development of strong attachments to alternative sources of gratification that compete with children and the less able are people to adjust to the major shifts in life-style that may accompany marriage and are certainly a concomitant of childbearing.

Another advantage of a postponement strategy for these couples is that where such wives have fairly extensive human capital investments, this may make it possible for the family to respond to economic pressures later on by her reentry into the labor force, depending, of course, on the job market.

III. GROUP III AND IV BLUE-COLLAR FAMILIES

The Nature of the Constraints

The age–earnings profile of manual workers—especially those in the lower-level blue-collar and service occupations—places very different constraints on the types of family strategies that have been historically feasible. The basic problem is that their age–earnings profiles exhibit sharp earnings increases only in youth. Earnings peak early, therefore, and may actually deteriorate with increasing age if depreciation in human capital occurs or if a man loses his job and hence, with it, the accrued advantages of operating in a stable internal labor market. As a consequence, whether earnings increase over time rests more heavily on such factors as upward occupational mobility and/or positive period or cohort factors that would offset a neutral or even negative age effect on earnings—and one that starts relatively early in adulthood. However, many of these possible sources of improved earnings seem less predictable at the early career stage than the age effect on earnings which can be roughly estimated by individuals on the basis of inter-age comparisons. In fact, over time, some cohort factors may have systematically worked to the the economic disadvantage of older men. For example, the long-run trend in increased educational attainment has meant that older men were usually at a considerable educational disadvantage compared to younger men.

In sum, from the point of view of developing an adaptive family strategy, an early-peaking and rather flat age-earnings profile creates certain rather severe constraints. The basic problem is that such men are caught in the dilemma that the period between the very low and uncertain earnings of youth and the start of a possibly negative age effect can be rather short. If, in response to the first squeeze difficulties, marriage and childbearing are considerably delayed, then the costs incurred by raising a family will also be postponed and to a point in the husband's career cycle when his earnings position may be relatively poor—and more importantly perhaps, much more uncertain. In addition, postponement may increase the economic vulnerability of elderly couples or the widowed. To the extent the elderly are heavily dependent on their children for economic and other types of aid, child postponement increases the risk that no or few children will be sufficiently launched economically to provide much assistance. In short, marriage and child postponement in response to the first squeeze may exact a price among these men and their families that it does not for those in occupational careers that regularly involve a steeper age–earnings profile, including greater income security in the middle and older years.

Given the continuing process of industrial development, historical shifts have undoubtedly occurred in the kind of penalties lower-level manual workers risk as a consequence of delays in family formation. For one thing, the nature of manual employment has been changing considerably over the years. In the nineteenth century, unskilled and semiskilled workers were a more substantial segment of the labor force. They were also more commonly employed in jobs where physical strength was of much greater importance than it is today, thus placing somewhat older men at a disadvantage. In addition, the more highly skilled manual labor force typical of the latter half of the twentieth century is one that has probably achieved a greater amount of firm-specific human capital training. Such training increases the employer's investment in the worker and hence presumably helps provide greater job security.[7] Furthermore, as educational attainment gradually approaches an asymptote, we are starting to observe fewer intercohort differences in educational attainment. As a result, in contrast to earlier in the twentieth century, and perhaps the nineteenth century as well, somewhat older males are now at much less of an educational disadvantage compared to younger ones (see Chapter 3).

Another important change to consider is the considerable improvement in both adult as well as childhood morbidity and mortality conditions. The working conditions under which blue-collar workers labored were, by and large, much more dangerous and more unhealthy in the past than they are at present. Furthermore, general adult levels of morbidity and mortality were much higher in the nineteenth and early twentieth centuries as well. For example, Jacobson estimates that of the cohort of white males born in 1840 in the United States, just 66% of those who survived to age 20 also survived until age 55; only 59% survived to age 60 (Jacobson 1964: 44). The current U.S. life table for white males indicates that under the mortality conditions of 1978, 88% of those surviving to age 20 will live to age 55 and 82% to age 60 (U.S. National Center for Health Statistics 1980: 5–10). However these are mortality figures for all white males and hence will overstate the survivorship chances of lower socioeconomic groups (see Rowntree 1922:

---

[7]However, rapid technological development may make some previous on-the-job training obsolete.

243; Young and Willmott 1962:22; Anderson 1971: 34; Kitagawa 1977; Kitagawa and Hauser 1973).

As a consequence of the higher mortality conditions of the nineteenth century and early twentieth centuries, there was a much greater chance then than now that husbands would die or be disabled for manual work while they were still supposedly in the prime economically productive years. For example, Uhlenberg estimates that of those children surviving to age 15, 28% of the cohort of 1870 were likely to have lost one or both parents by that age compared to 4% for the cohort of 1950. The chances of losing just a father to children surviving to age 15 was 18% for the cohort of 1870 but only 3% for the cohort of 1950 (Uhlenberg 1978: 79). Of course, these are national figures and hence do not accurately reflect the experience of working-class families—especially the poorer segments of this group.

A third historical trend that will have operated to increase the job—and hence the economic—security of older workers has been the growth of large protected internal labor markets plus other sources of institutionalized job protection for workers over age 35 or 40 as discussed in Chapters 2 and 3.

A final important factor to consider has been the increase in the sources of income other than the current earnings of family members. These include, in the United States, the growth of the Social Security system, unemployment insurance, health insurance, disability compensation, and pension plans as well as a variety of public welfare measures. Such sources of income provide support for at least two types of economic squeeze periods—during crises that occur while in the prime economically productive years and during retirement when earnings are very low or nonexistent. Hence, they provide a type of economic cushion that was largely unavailable to most manual workers in the earlier stages of industrialization.

As a result of all these factors improving the economic position of blue-collar men in the middle and later years, the penalties of postponed marriage and childbearing, and of low fertility as well, should have been declining over the years, though some of the benefits of this decline may not have been apparent until well after the Great Depression. Whether these trends also indicate a rise in the *advantages* of postponement is another matter, however.

Adaptive Strategies

Let us now go on to consider a variety of family strategies that would represent adaptive responses to an early-peaking and relatively flat earnings profile. In general, as emphasized earlier in this volume, a pattern of relatively early marriage and early childbearing seems like the most adaptive family strategy, given the age–earnings profile of many blue-collar workers.

This would be particularly true the earlier the age at peaking and the more uncertain the income-producing capabilities of men over age 35 or 40. However, how young an age at marriage is possible will depend, in part, on the extent to which young men can achieve some employment security and this will vary according to the business cycle and long-run trends affecting the full-time entry of males into stable occupational careers. The advantage of early marriage and early childbearing, once the young man can settle down to a regular job, is that his heaviest childcare responsibilities may be over before the age effect on the husband's earnings becomes neutral or even negative.

CHILDREN'S ECONOMIC ROLE

Within the general strategy of early marriage and childbearing, there are several variant patterns, depending on a number of factors such as mortality conditions, family size and the economic role of children and wives. In one variant, children provide an important source of family income, especially if they stay in the home until they marry. In that case, relatively large families are functional. This seems like a pattern most appropriate to the nineteenth- and early twentieth-century period of industrialization. Given such a strategy the work of children while they are adolescents or in young adulthood, could compensate for both large family size and the waning abilities of the father to be the economic mainstay of the family. As a consequence, the family's economic position would be relatively favorable when adolescent and young adult children are in the home, despite the low earnings of the young and possibly deteriorating earnings of the father. Several incomes plus economies of scale could produce a level of living for all above that which individual workers could produce for themselves independently. Under these circumstances, the *second* squeeze of peak child-dependency cost will not occur when children are adolescents, as is currently the case, but when they and their parents are much younger.

If children are an important source of family income, then high infant and childhood mortality would also favor a strategy of *early* childbearing as well as a large completed family size. High mortality among the young reduces the reproductive efficiency of families in the sense of their ability to produce a given number of surviving children within a relatively brief time period thus leading to delays in the time when enough children have survived to make a contribution. Furthermore, to the extent there were sex differentials in earnings, the survival of male children to working age may have been especially important (Anderson 1971: 23, 124–125).

Multiple-earner families would also have had the advantage of reducing the vulnerability of the family to severe income loss should the father die or be incapacitated. However, the greater the postponement of childbearing, the more likely the family would experience the loss of the husband's earnings before many of the offspring had reached working age. This, in turn, would have an extremely negative effect on the family's economic position.

In sum, in a family economy where nonfamilial sources of income are few and not very adequate, where childhood and adult mortality is high, and where children make an important economic contribution, early marriage and childbearing will probably increase the chances of families raising their children to economically productive ages while the husband is still alive and capable of employment himself or, at the least, before the probability of his making a significant income contribution greatly diminishes. However, such a strategy does not seem highly conducive to the employment of married women outside the home as their home productivity would be fairly high throughout the family cycle.

A number of historical studies have paid considerable attention to many of these issues and provide substantial support for the idea that such strategies were common. The data from England are particularly illuminating as they show an early awareness by scholars of life-cycle variations in the economic situation of families. Rowntree's 1898 study of working-class families in York and the more recent study by Anderson of families in nineteenth-century Lancashire are especially noteworthy (Rowntree 1922; Anderson 1971).

Rowntree divided up the population studied using a measure of poverty based on an estimate of a minimum budget for the basic necessities for families of different sizes and composition (Rowntree 1922: Chapter 4). All families with an income below the amount appropriate to their size and composition were considered to be in a state of poverty. Approximately 15% of the working-class population in his study (10% of the whole population of York) were classified as below the poverty line (Rowntree 1922: 144). After classifying the population by its relationship to the poverty line, Rowntree attempted to determine the reasons for their poverty. He estimated that for about 44% of the families it was because the husband was dead or not working regularly for one reason or another. For 13% of the families, it was because of a family size of five or more children.[8] However, in 44% of the cases it was simply because the husband's wages were low (Rowntree 1922: 153). Most of such men were laborers (73%) and other unskilled workers (Rowntree 1922: 165–166).[9]

What is particularly pertinent about Rowntree's analysis is that he looked

---

[8]Nevertheless, these children may have turned into an economic asset once they reached working age.

[9]According to Rowntree:

> Allowing for broken time, the average wage for a labourer in York is from 18s. to 21s.; whereas ... the minimum expenditure necessary to maintain in a state of

III. Group III and IV Blue-Collar Families

at poverty in life-cycle terms (see also Tilly and Scott 1978). Thus he argued that

> The life of a labourer is marked by five alternating periods of want and comparative plenty. During early childhood, unless his father is a skilled worker, he probably will be in poverty; this will last until he, or some of his brothers or sisters, begin to earn money and thus augment their father's wage sufficiently to raise the family above the poverty line. Then follows the period during which he is earning money and living under his parents' roof; for some portion of this period he will be earning more money than is required for lodging, food, and clothes. This is his chance to save money. If he has saved enough to pay for furnishing a cottage this period of comparative prosperity may continue after marriage until he has two or three children, when poverty will again overtake him. This period of poverty will last perhaps for ten years, i.e., until the first child is fourteen years old and begins to earn wages; but if there are more than three children it may last longer. While the children are earning, and before they leave the home to marry, the man enjoys another period of prosperity—possibly, however, only to sink back again into poverty when his children have married and left him, and he himself is too old to work, for his income has never permitted his saving enough for him and his wife to live upon for more than a very short time [Rowntree 1922: 169–71].[10]

Even more importantly, he points out that those observed to be in poverty at the time of the study only represented

> *merely that section who happened to be in one of these poverty periods at the time the inquiry was made.* Many of these will, in course of time, pass on into a period of comparative prosperity; this will take place as soon as the children, now dependent, begin to earn. But their places below the poverty line will be taken by others who are at present living in that prosperous period previous to, or shortly after, marriage. Again, many now classed as above the poverty line were below it until the children began to earn. The proportion of the community who at one period or other of their lives suffer from poverty to the point of physical privation is therefore much greater, and the injurious effects of such a condition are much more widespread than would appear from a consideration of the number who can be shown to be below the poverty line at any given moment [Rowntree 1922: 171–172].

Rowntree's study provides a picture of a socioeconomic group whose economic fortunes, both positive and negative, are closely related to the

---

> physical efficiency a family of two adults and three children is 21s. 8d, or, if there are four children, the sum required would be 26s. It is thus seen that *the wages paid for unskilled labour in York are insufficient to provide food, shelter, and clothing adequate to maintain a family of moderate size in a state of bare physical efficiency* [Rowntree 1922: 116].

[10]However, Rowntree did not explicitly deal with the arrangements made for the care and support of the aged. As we shall discuss, Anderson's study indicates that children and kin bore the major responsibility of the elderly (Anderson 1971: 139–147).

number and ages of their children. If they do marry and have children they must, as a consequence, pass through a period of considerable absolute deprivation until several of the children are old enough to work and make an income contribution themselves. When that point is reached, however, the family may achieve a relatively favorable income position. Moreover, given the high mortality of the period, considerable delays in family formation incur the risk of the loss of the husband's income. Hence, we would expect to observe a fairly early age at marriage and childbearing in order for such families to get over the difficult economic squeeze period when all the children are economically dependent and before the husband's earnings position becomes too precarious. Using information on marriages registered in York in 1898 and 1899, Rowntree did, in fact, observe differentials in the age at marriage between skilled workers and laborers. Unfortunately, he did not compare these to other groups. However, he found that, for example, 32% of the marriages of laborers were to men below the age of 23 while this was only true for 19% of the marriages of skilled workers (Rowntree 1922: 174).[11, 12]

Anderson's study of mid-nineteenth-century Lancashire presents a somewhat similar picture of variations in the economic position of working class families over the family cycle as well as of the important role of children in the family's well-being (Anderson 1971). Using Rowntree's primary poverty line, Anderson estimated the proportion of Preston families at various levels in relation to the poverty line. His general findings were that poverty status varied sharply by family-cycle stage. The highest proportion of families *at or below* the poverty line were those with several children at home but none employed (52% below the poverty line) and those where some, but less than half, of the children were employed (31%). The highest proportions of families who were well *above* the poverty line were those where half or more (82%) of the children were employed. Anderson thus concluded that the earnings of children were essential to the family's standard of living (Anderson 1971: 31–32).

Anderson also pointed out that the earnings of wage workers of various sorts tended to peak early in life (Anderson 1971: 23, 128ff). For example, he maintained that in the cotton industry "peak earnings for men were reached by the mid-twenties at the latest [Anderson 1971: 201]." As a consequence, he argued that

[11] Unfortunately, it is impossible to ascertain the role of second marriages in possibly inflating the overall ages at marriage and any differences in this between the skilled and unskilled.

[12] Rowntree remarked that the younger marriage ages of the laborers "no doubt indicates how the exercise of prudence and forethought increases as you advance in the social scale [Rowntree 1922: 174]." However, this overlooks the risks such lower-level workers incurred by waiting and it is this risk which I think is essential to keep in mind.

III. Group III and IV Blue-Collar Families

> this early independence, coupled with the fact that subsequent expectations were likely to be of a fall rather than any much greater rise, of wages, seems to have persuaded most that it was safe and even best to marry young [Anderson 1971: 132].

As evidence supporting this interpretation, Anderson cites the considerable differentials in the age at marriage of males in Preston, a manufacturing town, compared to rural areas where coming into property was more important. For example, in 1851, whereas 94% of males aged 20–24 had never been married in rural Lancashire only 69% of Preston males in this age group had not yet married. For 25–34-year-olds, the proportion who had never married was still 50% for rural men but only 27% for Preston males (Anderson 1971: 133). Furthermore, he found that

> early marriage was not just a matter of rural–urban differences. Areas where most of the population were agricultural labourers, and where, therefore, independence, such as it was ever likely to be, was attained quite young, had marriage ages only a little higher than those of the Lancashire towns. Conversely, rural areas like those of Lancashire, where independence came late because their agriculture was based on small farms, had delayed marriage ... while towns relying on traditional artisan and trade occupations had more delayed marriage, and higher non-marriage rates [Anderson 1971: 134].

Concerning the position of the aged, in his Preston sample of 1851 Anderson found that most of those noninstitutionalized persons aged 65 and older were living with one of their children—68% were living with a child, 13% with a spouse, and 5% with other kin. Only 6% were living alone (Anderson 1971: 139).[13] Furthermore, it was primarily the widowed who lived with children—there was little evidence of both parents residing with children (Anderson 1971: 140). An advantage of such an arrangement was that it saved on housing costs, on the investment in furniture, (and thus eased both the first and third squeezes) and, in some cases, it provided the young mother with someone to look after her children if she worked (Anderson 1971: 141).

In sum, Anderson's study is consistent with the notion that for men in early peaking, low-income occupations, early marriage and childbearing was a common adaptive strategy. A pattern whereby the economic role of adolescent and young adult children was extremely important in helping families achieve a certain measure of prosperity in the latter party of the family cycle was also common. Finally, adult children were a major source of

---

[13]The addition of the institutionalized to the table from which these figures came would hardly have changed the picture since Anderson estimated that only about six elderly people from Preston were in institutions.

support for the widowed aged who, in exchange, often still provided some useful functions in the household. All this implies, of course, that, contrary to the position of Malthus, "moral restraint" was primarily a middle-class virtue. It might reward its *middle-class* practitioners with improved chances for prosperity but it promised few benefits for the *laboring classes* and probably entailed numerous risks, given the rising economic uncertainties of their middle and later years.

Although both Rowntree and Anderson focused particularly on poverty and its relationship to the family cycle, it ought to be possible to treat their analyses more generally. If the number and ages of children present have income and cost implications, changes in family composition over the family cycle will signify variations in the family's economic position, even if the process does not involve falling into or rising out of a state of poverty, however this is defined. Hence, the literature on how *poverty* is related to the family cycle can also tell us something about how economic *affluence* can vary over the life-cycle, even for families who never experience poverty.

Demographic and economic historical research on American society has only recently begun to concern itself with a detailed examination of some of the factors involved in the type of family strategies under discussion here. The study by Michael Haines is a case in point (Haines 1979; see also Goldin 1979, 1980). The main focus of Haines's book is an investigation of the theory that a number of particular factors led to the earlier marriage and higher fertility observed among mining and heavy industrial populations in nineteenth-century Europe and America. However, many of his findings, and the causal factors he saw as important, would hold for a large variety of manual occupations, not just those involved in heavy industry or mining. Of particular interest is his analysis of the United States Commissioner of Labor Survey in 1889–1890 which obtained information on the demographic characteristics, occupations, incomes, and expenditure patterns of 8,544 families and their family members in these nine industries for 24 states in the United States and five European countries—Belgium, France, Germany, Great Britain, and Switzerland. Of the families in the sample, 98% were male headed (Haines 1979: Chapter 6).

Haines stressed the importance of the nature of the age–earnings profile, arguing that an early-peaking pattern would tend to promote early marriage and early childbearing and a large completed family size. This is for two major reasons: (*a*) young men could afford to marry and have children earlier and in greater numbers; and (*b*) since the husband's income prospects in later life were probably unfavorable or, at least, uncertain, large numbers of surviving children would act as an insurance policy, contributing to the support of the family while they were teenagers (Haines 1979: 225).

III. Group III and IV Blue-Collar Families

Furthermore, Haines found from the labor survey that the economic role of children increased considerably in importance for older families. For example, in the United States sample of the 1889–1890 survey, the proportion of families with income from children rose from 12% for families with the head aged 30–39 to 51% where he was 40–49 and on up to 59% where he was 50–59. It was still 58% when the head was 60 and over (Haines 1979: 227). As a consequence of the increase in the likelihood of children contributing income as they reached working age, combined with the declines in income of heads past age 40, the proportion of family income contributed by husbands was less for older men whereas that by children was greater. The results from the European samples were similar except that the relative contribution of the children was even greater (Haines 1979: 226–227).

Other adaptations to the declining income-producing ability of older men was the taking in of boarders, providing 9 and 13% respectively of the income of families headed by men aged 50–59 and 60 and over. Of course, this can be viewed, in part, as an increase in the production of money income by wives as they shifted home production activities to those that provide some income rather than concentrating only on those contributing to the maintenance of family members alone (Haines 1979: 227; see also Model and Hareven 1973). However, the data show that the income contribution of wives via paid employment outside the home was minor, though this varied somewhat by industry. It was higher, for example, for wives of men in textiles (Haines 1979: 234–235).

As a consequence of variations in the sources and relative importance of income among members of families with heads at different ages, the study indicates that the age pattern of total mean *family* expenditures as well as the age pattern of total mean *family* income was very different from the age pattern of *husband's* income. Although husband's income peaked in the 30–39 age group, family expenditures and family income peaked in the 50–59 age groups (Haines 1979: 224).

In sum, historically, in the United States as well as in Europe, the middle-aged period of blue-collar male heads of families was, because of multiple earners, often one of relative prosperity for working-class households. But this was primarily because of the income contribution of children. Without that contribution and solely on the basis of the husband's income, the relative income position of older families would have been well below that of families of men in their thirties.

Some of Katz and Davey's findings in their study of families in Hamilton, Ontario between 1851 and 1871 give additional insights into the nature of children's important economic role in industrializing societies—at least those in Europe and the North American continent (Katz and Davey 1978). They argue that during the industrialization there was a major change in the residence pattern of young people. Before industrialization got well under way children had typically left home when they started work, often at an early age (see also Anderson 1971: 84ff). However, in the early industrial city young people remained home for much longer, frequently until the time they married (Katz and Davey 1978: S88). In the case of Hamilton, Katz and Davey found that between 1851 and 1871 a sharp increase occurred in the proportion of teenage and young adult males (and females to a lesser extent) living with their parents. For example, the proportion of 18-year-old males living at home rose from 38 to 70%; for 20-year-olds it rose from 24 to 61% and for 22-year-olds it increased from 28 to 44% (Katz and Davey 1978: S88). During the same period, however, the age at starting work did not increase. In fact, in some cases it declined. Thus, for 18-year-old males, the proportion employed rose from 76 to 85% between 1851 and 1871; for 20-year-olds it changed from 76 to 91% and for 22-year-olds from 85 to 94% (Katz and Davey: S90).

In sum, as Katz and Davey point out, "the period between the onset of work and departure from home had been extended in two decades from at most a year to about seven years, a radical shift [S92]." This then not only provides evidence that young people made an important economic contribution to their parental households at that time but that there was a considerable increase in the proportion of working-class families where such a contribution was being made during the early period of industrialization.

Another pertinent finding of Katz and Davey was that in the 1851–1871 period in Hamilton there was an increase in the age at marriage for those in professional, clerical, and commerical occupations whereas a decrease occurred for blue-collar workers, thus confirming the notion that early marriage was not only a common but an increasing behavioral pattern of manual workers in industrial occupations (Katz and Davey 1978: S112).

Given an early-peaking age–earnings profile involving a growing uncertainty about the income-producing capabilities of blue-collar males past the peak age, and given high mortality and morbidity conditions combined with few significant nonfamilial sources of income, I have argued that at least one type of family strategy would represent an adaptive response to such conditions. In terms of demographic behavior, such a strategy would involve relatively early marriage and childbearing combined with a moderate or high completed fertility. In terms of economic behavior, it would involve a considerable reliance on the income contribution of adolescent and young adult children but usually not including an extensive economic involvement of wives outside the home. Just how large a family size would be most beneficial depends, in part, on how much high fertility is offset by high infant and childhood mortality. But it also depends on the economic ability of the family to support its children during their early nonproductive years. Presumably, the more children a family has, given such a strategy, the greater the annual potential family income when a significant proportion of these children reach working age, and the longer the period in which the parents may be able to rely on having income-producing children in the home. The potential benefits of such a large number of progeny in the later stage of the family cycle are offset, however, by the cost of maintaining them earlier in the family cycle. In short, given a strategy of children making a significant economic contribution, the extent to which families can "maximize" their income *later* in the family cycle via high fertility is constrained by how much they are willing and able to live in a state of considerable relative, and sometimes absolute, deprivation *earlier* in the family cycle. Hence, a balance of some sort must be struck if the family is to survive at some minimum level of living before it can reap the rewards of its high fertility. Furthermore, the deprivations of the early dependency period must constitute a major disadvantage of this strategy and hence must be one of its major vulnerabilities.

Although it is obvious from this review of the historical literature that the income contribution of working-class children to their parental household used to be quite extensive, the exact character of their economic behavior is not entirely clear. Until its complexities are sorted out somewhat better, it will be difficult to achieve a full understanding of children's economic role in family strategies. For example, many authorities seem to argue that although young working children handed over all their earnings to the family, young adult children often only contributed an amount comparable to what they would have to pay for room and board elsewhere (Rowntree 1922: 56; Anderson 1971: 129). According to Anderson, this was usually less than what it cost the family to maintain the working offspring while it nevertheless provided the young person a more comfortable level of living than could be obtainable through boarding arrangements. Hence, both the young adult children and the rest of the family benefitted (Anderson 1971: Chapter 9). What is not entirely clear is how extensive the children's *obligations* were to their families of orientation beyond this contribution. However, the extent of their obligations has considerable importance in the analysis of family strategies, particularly with regard to the age at marriage. On the one hand, the arrangement can simply be one of mutual convenience and maintained as such by the children only until they can save enough to afford to set up their own household. Anderson, for example, seems to emphasize this pure economic exchange attitude and so does Roundtree, to some extent. If this is all that is involved, then age at marriage will, in large part, be a function of economic conditions and how well these have permitted young people to get an early start in marriage—particularly if early marriage and childbearing was truly the adaptive strategy I have hypothesized it was.

On the other hand, if the economic contribution of children in the parental household used to be significant, then it is also likely that certain normative constraints had developed to make this arrangement more dependable than that which would be implied in a purely self-interested short-run cost–benefit analysis by the children themselves. This too is a theme that seems to run through the literature—namely, that children had certain *obligations* to contribute to the family, especially if the husband had died or was incapacitated (Tilly and Scott 1978; Ankarloo 1978; Modell, Furstenberg, and Hershberg 1978: 214). The notion of economic obligation on the part of children to their families of orientation is also consistent with the idea of a family strategy that promotes a stable economic position of the family over time. However, as Anderson's analysis suggests, it also represents a vulnerable aspect of such a strategy because as children's earnings increase, so does their ability to operate independently (Anderson 1971: Chapter 9). Nevertheless, to the extent children's economic role in the working-class family had a normative element, age at marriage did not just depend on how fast economic conditions permitted them to obtain a stable job and save enough to set up their own households. In addition, it should also be influenced by the extent to which their economic contribution was essential to their families of orientation. Hence, some children might have to delay— and sometimes end up foregoing—marriage to help support households which have lost the earnings of the male head or to care for young children and the chronically ill if the mother has died or become incapacitated. Thus, although an early marriage strategy might be optimal, later ages at marriage for some is implied in family strategies that placed a heavy economic reliance on children, especially as back-up earners or home producers. Hence, this strategy may result in an average younger age at marriage for working-class men and women compared to those in middle-class occupations. However, it will not lead to the young ages at marriage that have often been observed in other parts of the world. The need to be able to set up an independent household and to fulfill economic obligations to the family of orientation will prevent very young ages at marriage.[14]

STRATEGY VULNERABILITIES

This discussion of blue-collar adaptive family strategies implies certain inherent stresses. One is the cross pressures in which young adult children

---

[14]In some cases, however, young couples were able to or were forced to double up with kin though this did not appear to be the preferred arrangement (see Anderson 1971: Chapter 5; Model, Furstenberg, and Strong 1978: 135–137).

often find themselves—caught between the obligation to continue to contribute earnings to the parental household and the need to start their own families relatively early in life. Another stress lies in the incompatibility between short-term and long-term family welfare goals that is a consequence of the extensive reliance on children as a source of income. The earlier children enter employment, the less schooling they tend to achieve, reducing their life-time income. In this way, a familial goal of *improving* the family's socioeconomic position within and especially across generations is incompatible with the extensive employmemt of children in an industrial society. This should provide an additional source of intergenerational tension since it tends to promote the welfare of the parents at the expense of the children.

A family economic strategy relying heavily on the work of children is also at variance with the premium put on formal schooling by industrial societies. Increasingly, however, laws governing the minimum school-leaving age have limited the ability of families to choose such strategies, and improvements in the economic position of blue-collar males in the middle and older years have greatly reduced if not eliminated the importance of the earnings of adolescents.[15] The resulting rise in the school-leaving age for blue-collar children therefore signals a major shift in the timing of the greatest child-dependency burden—from the preteen years to the period of adolescence. All this extends the burden on parents to a later point in their own life-cycle, how much later depending on changes in completed family size.

It is well known that the school-leaving age has been rising over time for populations in industrial societies. Just how much change has occurred for blue-collar families in particular is more uncertain. However, it would be very valuable to attempt to examine this in trying to pin down the changing potential economic role of children in their parental households. Once again, I will try to estimate the school-leaving age—and changes in this over time—by using age data on the educational attainment of husbands in different occupational groups. Estimated changes in the school-leaving age will, in turn, be taken as a very rough indication of changes in the prevalence of the second squeeze.[16]

There are a variety of possible biases which may somewhat distort the extensiveness of the apparent increase in the school-leaving age for manual workers. Continuing school at night, etc., will tend to produce overestimates of the school-leaving age. This will lead to an understatement of the declines

[15]For a brief discussion of trends in laws governing the school-leaving age and the use of child labor with the resulting changes in children's economic roles in the family in England and Europe, see Tilly and Scott (1978: Chapter 8).

[16]It is very rough because information on the school-leaving age of groups of *individuals* does not necessarily correctly indicate to us the prevalence among groups of *families* in their experience of the second squeeze. This is because of differential fertility and the high probability that the school-leaving age varied among different children within the same family.

in the proportions leaving school at a young age. Dropping out of the labor force earlier than usual or out of the married status because of factors associated with low levels of educational attainment will also lead to an understatement of the change in the proportions leaving school at a young age (because of an overstatement of the school-leaving age for older cohorts). If these biases are significant, they should produce 1960–1970 declines in the proportions leaving school at a young age for any given cohort. However, occupational mobility should have the opposite effect as it will be positively related to educational attainment. If it does provide a major distortion, there will be a 1960–1970 *increase* in the proportions of middle-aged and older cohorts who left school at a young age for these manual occupations—especially the lower-level ones.

As we can see from Table 9.2, these biases do not appear to be very large—or, at least, they seem to cancel each other out. All things considered, the educational attainment of husbands from the same cohorts in any given occupation (with the exception of Laborers IV) are remarkably similar at the two census dates. Furthermore, the biases which lead to an apparent or real increase in the educational attainment of a cohort over time seemed to have outweighed the reverse bias. In general, then, we ought to be able to obtain an overall idea of long-run changes in the school-leaving age of men in manual occupations from these PUS data, imperfect though they may be.

If the school-leaving age is a rough predictor of economic dependence on parents, the intercohort comparisons of Table 9.2 indicate that, in general, there was an extensive growth in adolescent dependency during the first 70 years of the twentieth century. Take, for example, the proportions leaving school by approximately age 13. This declined from 53% (in 1960) for the cohort of 1896–1905 husbands to only 8% (in 1970) for the 1936–1945 cohort. In the case of the proportions leaving at age 16 or younger, the decline was from 71 to 24%.

This shift in the school-leaving age was much more marked, of course, for manual workers. For example, in the case of Craft III husbands, most of the cohort of 1896–1905 had left school by age 13—61%. This proportion declined all the way to 10% for the cohort of 1936–1945. Although 80% of the cohort of 1896–1905 had left school by age 16, only 30% had done so for the cohort of 1936–1945. The age at leaving school was generally younger for operatives than for craftsmen. Nevertheless, even for operatives, despite the fact that an early school-leaving age used to be extremely common, it is now relatively rare. For the Operative IV group (by far the larger of the two operative groups), 78% of the cohort of 1896–1905 husbands had left school by about age 13 and 93% by age 16. But for the cohort of 1936–1945, only 18% had left by age 13 and 47% by age 16.

In sum, then, these data indicate that, for blue-collar families, the nature

III. Group III and IV Blue-Collar Families

and timing of the child dependency squeeze has undergone a major shift in the twentieth century. If this also indicates that the economic role of children and young adults—in the normative as well as the behavioral sense of the term—has declined, then age at marriage will have become less influenced by economic obligations to the family of orientation. Other things being equal, this should have led to a reduction in the age at marriage if an early-marrying strategy is desirable. Moreover age at marriage certainly did decline for males as well as females in the twentieth century, especially after 1940.

Another important concomitant of this shift in the timing of the second squeeze is the increased possibility of a pileup or overlapping of squeezes. It is very unlikely that in one family the experience of the first squeeze by the younger generation will coincide with the third (i.e., old-age) squeeze of their parents and greatly impede strategies of mutual aid. However, there is a much greater possibility that middle-aged parents in the *second* squeeze period may also have elderly parents in the *third* squeeze period. Since, in working-class households, the middle years are a time when the husband's earnings are not rising rapidly, at least due to the career-cycle effect on earnings, then middle-aged couples with elderly parents and dependent or semidependent adolescent children may find themselves in quite an economic crunch. Furthermore, the couple's ability to prepare for its own third squeeze may be greatly hampered by extensive and simultaneous socioeconomic obligations to both parents and children.

WIVES' ECONOMIC ROLE

If the twentieth century has seen major changes in the nature of child dependency for blue-collar families, then adaptive family strategies should be evolving that somehow compensate for the increased cost and decreased economic contribution of children. An important question is whether marriage postponement and the postponement of the first child might, initially at least, represent an important adaptive change since early childbearing would no longer result in the same early contribution of money wages from children. Although there is some merit in this argument, the early-peaking flat age–earnings profile of blue-collar men still seems to promote a pattern of relatively early marriage and childbearing. Other adaptive responses to the changing squeeze situation would, however, evolve. Thus limiting family size (though still having one's children early) would reduce the adolescent dependency burden. An early end to childbearing also has the advantage of making it easier for wives to make a significant and extended income contribution to the family economy after childbearing and the heaviest child-care activities are completed. Hence, one possible adaptation to the emer-

TABLE 9.2
Estimates of the School-Leaving Age of Selected Age Cohorts of Husbands in Group III and IV Blue-Collar Occupations: 1960 and 1970

Percentage leaving school at or before a given age

Occupation and estimated maximum age at leaving school[a]	Birth cohort and age in 1960[b]			Birth cohort and age in 1970			
	1926–1935 25–34	1916–1925 35–44	1906–1915 45–54	1896–1905 55–64	1936–1945 25–34	1926–1935 35–44	1916–1925 45–54	1906–1925 55–64
Total								
13	17	22	37	53	8	15	20	34
15	33	38	53	66	19	28	34	50
16	40	46	59	71	24	34	41	56
17	71	76	81	84	63	68	74	79
White collar[c]								
13	4	7	15	30	2	4	7	14
15	12	16	27	43	5	10	14	25
16	17	22	34	48	8	13	19	31
17	45	54	61	68	37	43	52	58
Craft II								
13	10	13	29	56	8	10	14	26
15	25	32	51	75	16	27	31	43
16	30	42	60	82	21	33	40	55
17	77	82	89	93	73	78	84	88
Craft III								
13	19	23	43	61	10	19	24	42
15	38	46	64	76	24	38	43	61
16	46	55	71	80	30	46	52	69
17	88	90	92	94	86	90	91	93

Craft IV								
13	27	36	56	69	18	25	35	50
15	50	57	73	83	38	47	56	70
16	59	65	80	86	46	56	64	77
17	93	94	96	97	89	93	94	94
Operatives III								
13	27	36	51	65	15	28	34	50
15	50	58	70	83	33	51	55	69
16	58	66	76	87	40	58	63	75
17	93	96	94	96	91	93	94	96
Operatives IV								
13	35	43	60	78	18	33	40	55
15	57	65	79	89	38	56	62	75
16	68	74	83	93	47	62	70	80
17	95	96	97	98	92	95	95	96
Service IV								
13	28	36	55	76	16	26	35	53
15	45	59	73	86	30	45	55	71
16	54	66	80	90	38	51	61	77
17	87	92	96	97	82	90	93	94
Laborers IV								
13	43	53	74	82	20	37	44	64
15	68	75	86	92	41	58	62	79
16	72	81	91	94	48	64	72	83
17	96	97	99	98	90	94	96	97

Sources: 1960 and 1970 Public Use Samples of White Couples.

[a] Estimated ages at leaving school were based on the data on educational attainment. It was assumed that the average age of first-grade children was 6 and that the average age at completing 8 years of elementary school is 13 and 17 for high school.

[b] Includes some men who were not heads of households.

[c] Includes Service III husbands.

gence of a later second squeeze for blue-collar families is for the market work of wives to substitute for the market work of their children. In fact, even though declining mortality and increased job security for older males has reduced the economic vulnerability of families dependent on a single income, the risks of such an economic arrangement still seem great where the main source of that income is in the form of earnings. Even if the chances of the husband dying, being incapacitated, or losing his job have declined, there is still some chance of these events occurring—and the risk is probably higher in blue-collar families. Furthermore, if the marriage breaks up, an event whose probability has been rising rapidly over time, the wife and children are extremely vulnerable economically. Hence, this would greatly increase the importance of the wife being able to make a monetary contribution to the household, given the declining economic importance of children.

Early marriage and early completion of childbearing combined with a more extensive involvement of wives in the latter part of the family cycle, is a strategy that has become really practical as a widespread social pattern relatively only recently. For one thing, it depends on a successful early completion of childbearing requiring, in turn, reliable methods of fertility control.

Second, relying on the wife to make an important economic contribution after the children are in school presumes some minimum level of human capital investment on her part. This, in turn, should involve a later age at the initiation of childbearing than would be necessary if the family were not planning for her to have a later economic role outside the home. As a result, it may be difficult for many families to switch to such a strategy midway through the family cycle. Thus this probably puts certain breaks on the speed with which a strategy of this kind might evolve over time, even if it is destined to become very widespread.

Finally, families of men in work careers involving flat age–earnings profiles may opt for a delayed-childbearing and also, perhaps, a delayed-marriage strategy. However, this makes the second squeeze occur later in the husband's career and this may operate to intensify its severity. Hence, such a strategy is most feasible when men are assured of employment and income stability later on in their career cycle. This security may have been on the increase in recent years but has probably not been historically characteristic for workers in lower-level occupations. And in recent years the value of such security has been threatened by rising inflation. However, if the strategy includes the wife working before children are born and later on in the family cycle as well, then the penalties of fertility postponement would probably be effectively offset.

IV. GROUP III AND IV WHITE-COLLAR FAMILIES

Let us close with a brief consideration of the situation of middle- and lower-level white-collar workers, the constraints under which they operate, and the type of adaptive strategies that are likely to develop.

In the course of this volume I have been arguing that the socioeconomic position of the families of men in medium and lower-level white-collar occupations is unique in some respects. If one assumes that they desire their offspring to achieve a socioeconomic position comparable to or better than themselves, then children must typically remain in white-collar occupations.[17] If so, then the educational attainment of offspring should at least equal that of their parents. In fact, it should probably be greater since there is evidence that a higher educational attainment is increasingly necessary just to replicate the status of the parental generation. That the educational attainment of Group III white-collar males—even Clerical and Sales III males—has typically been much higher than that of blue-collar males (Tables 3.6, 8.1, and 8.2) implies a relatively late school-leaving age for the children of such families. Although this school-leaving age may have been increasing over time, there is reason to believe that a somewhat late age at school completion was also characteristic of an earlier stage of industrialization (see Banks 1954: 192–193; Kaestle and Vinovskis 1978: 171; Katz and Davey 1978: S110–S111). Moreover, some evidence of this is found in the estimated school-leaving ages for peak median white-collar groups presented in Table 9.3.

Although the school-leaving age has increased for all Group III white-collar cohorts, as for all occupational groups, even the oldest cohorts for which we have information—those born in 1896–1905—completed school at a considerably later age than did men in blue-collar occupations (Table 9.3). This is particularly true for Professional III husbands, as one would expect, but it is not limited to them. For example, in the case of the oldest cohort, only 54% of Clerical III husbands and 63% of Sales III men had left school by about age 16. This compared to 87% for all blue-collar workers combined. In the case of husbands from the 1906–1915 cohort (those aged 45–54 in 1960), only 40% of the Clerical III males had left school by approximately age 16 and 76% by age 17. The proportions were 50 and 82%

---

[17]This is true, if one takes status as well as income into consideration. Also maintaining a white-collar status may be considered important in order to provide a stepping stone to higher level white-collar occupations, if not for oneself then for one's children.

TABLE 9.3
Estimates of the School-Leaving Age of Selected Age Cohorts of Husbands in Group III and IV White-Collar Occupations: 1960 and 1970

Percentage leaving school at or before a given age

Occupation and estimated maximum age at leaving school[a]	Birth cohort and age in 1960[b]					Birth cohort and age in 1970			
	1926–1935	1916–1925	1906–1915	1896–1905	1936–1945	1926–1935	1916–1925	1906–1915
	25–34	35–44	45–54	55–64	25–34	35–44	45–54	55–64

Total

13	17	22	37	53	8	15	20	34
15	33	38	53	66	19	28	34	50
16	40	46	59	71	24	34	41	56
17	71	76	81	84	63	68	74	79
20	84	87	90	93	79	80	86	89
21	93	94	95	97	90	90	93	94

Blue collar

13	28	34	53	70	14	26	32	49
15	49	56	71	83	32	46	52	68
16	58	64	78	87	39	53	61	74
17	92	93	95	96	88	92	93	94
20	98	98	99	99	98	98	98	99
21	100	100	100	100	99	99	100	100

Professionals III

13	2	4	5	20	1	2	5	8
15	5	10	15	25	3	5	10	14
16	8	14	20	26	4	7	13	17
17	24	37	36	41	22	26	36	32
20	43	50	49	57	39	41	50	44
21	70	66	62	71	63	54	63	61

Managers III								
13	9	15	22	39	3	8	11	22
15	23	25	35	55	10	19	20	36
16	30	33	42	61	15	24	28	44
17	67	71	73	81	58	66	69	74
20	87	90	88	95	83	83	86	89
21	98	98	98	99	94	96	96	96
Sales III								
13	6	11	23	40	3	6	10	19
15	14	24	39	56	10	17	22	33
16	22	33	50	63	14	23	30	42
17	58	68	82	84	56	65	71	76
20	86	87	92	98	82	85	89	93
21	97	97	99	100	95	97	98	98
Clerical III								
13	6	8	17	33	2	5	7	14
15	15	17	32	46	7	13	14	28
16	21	23	40	54	10	18	23	36
17	67	74	76	77	54	63	71	72
20	90	89	92	93	83	84	90	88
21	97	96	96	98	94	95	97	97
Clerical IV								
13	25	26	30	58	8	17	25	36
15	46	49	44	73	24	34	47	50
16	57	54	61	74	29	44	56	60
17	87	92	92	90	81	90	86	88
20	96	98	96	96	95	97	99	99
21	98	98	99	97	99	100	100	100

(continued)

TABLE 9.3 (Continued)

	Percentage leaving school at or before a given age									
	Birth cohort and age in 1960[b]					Birth cohort and age in 1970			
Occupation and estimated maximum age at leaving school[a]	1926–1935	1916–1925	1906–1915	1896–1905	1936–1945	1926–1935	1916–1925	1906–1915
	25–34	35–44	45–54	55–64	25–34	35–44	45–54	55–64
Service III								
13	3	8	26	c	2	7	15	22
15	18	30	49	c	8	20	29	38
16	27	42	61	c	10	23	38	46
17	82	88	84	c	74	81	82	77
20	98	96	96	c	96	97	97	93
21	98	98	98	c	99	99	100	98

Sources: 1960 and 1970 Public Use Samples of White Couples.
[a]Estimated ages at leaving school were based on the data on educational attainment. It was assumed that the average age of first-grade children was 6 and that the average age at completing 8 years of elementary school is 13 and 17 for high school.
[b]Includes some men who were not heads of households.
[c]Percentages not computed because sample size was less than 40.

394

IV. Group III and IV White-Collar Families

respectively for Sales III husbands. This compares to a high of 78% of this cohort of blue-collar husbands leaving by age 16 and 95% by age 17. In sum, even older cohorts of males in white-collar occupations (in 1960 or 1970) had a later school-leaving age than men in blue-collar occupations.

A relatively late school-leaving age delays the entry of lower-level young white-collar men into full-time work until later in the life-cycle than is the case for semiskilled or unskilled workers. This implies that even in times past a relatively late second life-cycle squeeze was characteristic of lower-level white-collar occupations, though not necessarily of blue-collar occupations. That is, young white-collar sons (and daughters too probably) would be able to make much less of an early contribution to their families than the blue-collar children of blue-collar families. The contribution such white-collar offspring could make would start later and probably only achieve significance if there was later marriage.[18] Marriage delays were also likely if on-the-job training and achieving a secure position added more time to the late job-entry stage before a sufficient measure of economic security was achieved.

In short, the child-dependency burden of white-collar families—even those at moderate or lower-paying levels—was quite prolonged and the relative economic contribution these children would make was probably small. At the very least, it was delayed. However, the age–earnings profile of Group III white-collar workers does not appear to favor very late childbearing since earnings peak early in these occupations, as in blue-collar occupations, though there is probably greater late-career security for white-collar than for blue-collar males. However, the earnings of white-collar males are often below that of men in several of the blue-collar occupations. Hence, implied in the interaction of the age pattern of child-care costs and that of the husband's earnings, is a relatively severe second squeeze that, if anything, has intensified over time.

What types of family strategies might represent an adaptive response to the constraints under which these medium- and lower-level white-collar couples have been operating? First, given the late school-leaving age, we should observe a later age at marriage than that observed for manual workers but not as late as for the professions, whatever the level. Second, wives would probably have a more significant economic role than the wives of either Group I and II white-collar men or of manual workers. In addition to the other reasons for this cited earlier in the study (for example, their potentially greater *relative* socioeconomic contribution) one would expect that since children's economic role was limited, wives might be expected to have a more significant role themselves. Otherwise, the family's socioeconomic position

---

[18]For evidence that there probably were marriage delays among lower-level white-collar workers in the past, see Katz and Davey (1978: S112–S113).

would rest entirely on the husband's earnings, with all the risks this might entail. In an earlier historical period, this may have involved relatively lengthy employment by the wife before marriage and/or before childbearing to help set up the family in a style deemed appropriate. More recently, it also involves the extensive employment of the wife after children are in school, if not before. We certainly observed that the labor-force participation of Group III white-collar wives was among the highest of all peak median occupational groups—overall and net of other factors such as education and husband's income (Chapters 6 and 7).

Certain fertility patterns should also be characteristic of families of men in such lower-paid white-collar occupations. Given the relatively high cost of children and their limited economic value during childhood and adolescence, combined with the flat age–earnings profile of the father, this socioeconomic group should be most highly motivated to limit family size, in general, and to be particularly sensitive to changes in apparent economic life chances or the cost of children. Certainly the data on the mean number of children ever born to the wives of 35–44- and 45–54-year-old-men cited earlier support this (Table 5.13).

Timing is a more difficult question. However, some delays in childbearing, when fertility control is possible, should permit a greater economic contribution by the wife and the setting up of an independent household at a desired standard of living. But, if fertility is low, then childbearing might best be completed soon if the wife expects to return to the labor force to maximize her economic contribution. However, since delays in childbearing combined with small family size and possibly close spacing tend to offset each other, it is difficult to ascertain whether such a spacing pattern was actually followed by the wives of such men in the PUS.

V. IMPLICATIONS

There are a number of tentative implications to be drawn from this preliminary discussion of family strategies, the constraints under which they operate and which they impose on family and economic behavior. First of all, the growing importance of extensive schooling for children has undoubtedly intensified and prolonged the child-dependency burden while also opening up opportunities for upward mobility. This should have affected families of men throughout the occupational spectrum. At the lower occupational levels, a growing premium on graduating from high school has considerably raised the school-leaving age of young people and, in the process, has probably postponed entry into the labor force except in a fairly casual manner. As one rises in the occupational scale, attending and graduating from college has become increasingly important in the United States. And for some socioeconomic groups, professional or postgraduate training of some sort is considered essential for an occupational career.

In the case of families of men in white-collar occupations, all this has probably postponed still further an already late launching date for their children and, in the process, increased the costs of raising children. For working-class families, however, the prolongation of the child-dependency burden has probably had a somewhat different effect on the nature of intergenerational transfers of income at this stage of the family cycle. For these families, if "older" children have increasingly become an economic drain on parents, then the historically common family strategy of having adolescent and young adult children remaining at home, working, and contributing to the support of the family has ceased to be viable.

At the same time that child dependency has become more prolonged, however, the economic position of middle-aged men has probably been improving and growing more secure—at least for native, white middle-aged men in America. This has occurred due to a number of reasons—the declining importance of physical strength, increased job security because of greater institutionalization of internal labor markets and rising investments in human capital, better health, and so on. As a consequence, this improvement in the economic position of middle-aged men has partly offset the intensification of the second squeeze. On the other hand, declining adult mortality has increased the prevalence of the third squeeze of old age.

Another important factor has been the growing capability of controlling both the number and timing of children in industrial societies. Such control greatly increases the feasibility of attempting to follow certain types of family strategies. For example, it makes it possible to marry and realistically plan to postpone the first birth while the young wife works in order to ease the passage through the first-squeeze period. Moreover, by being able to limit completed family size, the overall child-care burden can be reduced, especially during the expensive adolescent period. Being able to end childbearing fairly early in the family cycle, in turn, permits wives to have a more active economic role outside the home during the time of the second as well as the first squeeze. This then is another factor that can help offset the growing burdens of the second squeeze.

However, if more extensive work involvements by women increasingly become incorporated into a popular family strategy, then this has certain implications. For one thing, the feedback effects discussed in Chapter 8 suggest that in a competitively consuming society it may be difficult to keep wives' employment limited to distinct segments of the life-cycle. For another, if women are to make an important socioeconomic contribution to the family, it becomes more important for them to achieve higher levels of human capital attainment. Otherwise, their potential relative economic contribution to the family may not be great enough to warrant working. This can partly be achieved by women increasing their educational attainment and levels of training via other types of formal schooling as well. However, another way to make additional human capital investments is on-the-job training. But if women wish to take advantage of such training, their work habits must become more regular as firm-specific training is often not highly transportable. As a consequence, women may have to adopt work patterns that increasingly resemble those of men.

Second, the more frequent family strategies relying on income from the wife are used, the more vulnerable families become to the nature and extent of job opportunities available to women. This has several important ramifications. The higher the proportion of women who want to work regularly—or, at least, regularly work at certain periods in their life-cycles—the less adequate will be the traditional female occupations as a source of job opportunities. American women, at least, have been so heavily concentrated in just a few types of female-dominated occupations, that it is inconceivable that these occupations could expand sufficiently to provide jobs for the rapidly rising proportion of women who are entering the labor force. In fact, in some of the more attractive female occupations, job oportunities for women have actually been declining recently. One major example is elementary- and secondary-school teaching which for many years were the most important occupations for working female college graduates.[19] This is because a number of typically female occupations are service oriented and with lagging population growth, demand for new workers will necessarily flag. Hence, even if couples only plan to have wives work outside the home at certain periods of the family cycle and not on a regular basis, women will, as a result, probably have to penetrate into occupations that have been traditionally male. Otherwise, it is difficult to see how this strategy can become very widespread (see Oppenheimer 1972). As a consequence, such women workers will be under pressure to behave somewhat more like male workers in order to remain competitive and to qualify for similar rewards. Maintaining job stability may be one of the most important ways of doing this.

In general, any family strategy that becomes a widespread pattern in the society and that involves a reliance on paid employment by wives late as well as early in the family cycle should lead to a more *continuous* work

---

[19]For example, in 1970, 45% of the female experienced civilian labor force with 4 or more years of college were in elementary- or secondary-school teaching (U.S. Bureau of the Census 1973b: Table 5).

V. Implications

history for women rather than a stable pattern of intermittent labor-force participation. The major reason is that family strategies that involve planned behaviors later in the family cycle entail different sorts of risks than those that plan behaviors at the early family-cycle stages because there is greater flexibility and more options earlier in life. Particular risks seem attendant upon strategies that involve embarking on irreversible actions, such as having children, but that also depend for their "success" on the *future* reemployment of the wife some 10 or 15 years hence. This is because of the unpredictability of the future labor-market conditions facing a women who has not worked for a number of years. Hence, it seems likely that the inherent uncertainties of such a strategy introduce a basic instability into life-time plans involving too great a temporal separation of work and maternal activities. This will lead, I suspect, to one of two alternatives. Either such a strategy will not be widely adopted as a regular social pattern or the work commitments of wives will tend to increase. However, increased work commitments would undoubtedly require a more stable and continuous labor-force involvement in order to guarantee greater employment security rather than an employment pattern characterized by one or more long gaps between jobs. Leaving and returning to the labor force at will is fundamentally something of a luxury and one that requires rapidly expanding job opportunities of a particular type. There is little evidence, as yet, that the number of such jobs will expand so rapidly in the future that this kind of a work pattern will be encouraged on a scale very much larger than exists at present.

In sum, then, in this chapter, as in past chapters, we have seen that there are a variety of theoretical and empirical reasons for believing that wives' work behavior will increasingly become more continuous throughout their life-cycle and, as such, will not be highly sensitive to long-run or short-run cyclical conditions. However, if that is the case, then marriage and fertility behavior will also probably be undergoing some rather permanent changes. The notion of adaptive family strategies should be a heuristically valuable tool for exploring how these diverse but interconnected behavior patterns will evolve over time.

APPENDIXES

APPENDIX A

Occupations Classified by Peak 1959 Median Earnings within Major Occupation Groups

This occupational classification system took the highest or peak 1959 median earnings among the different age groups in an occupation as the means of subclassifying occupations within major occupational groups. One issue was how detailed an occupational classification system should be used to create the 18 peak median occupational groups. I have attempted to use a system that roughly approximates the detailed occupational groups in published census reports. However, such a system involves occupational categories that often included information on industry and sometimes class of worker as well. Such detail appeared important to include because the evidence indicated that peak median earnings often differed significantly among the "same" occupations depending on the industry and whether the man was self-employed or a wage and salary worker. For example, the peak 1959 median earnings of male salaried managers in manufacturing was $10,861 whereas it was only $8,596 for self-employed managers in manufacturing (Table A.3). In sales work, peak median earnings varied substantially among various industries. In general, it was most important to distinguish industry (and class of worker for the managers) for occupational categories that were very broad and hence extremely heterogeneous (e.g., "managers, n.e.c.," "sales workers, n.e.c."). And this is what the Census Bureau does in its published tables involving detailed occupational groups. Hence, I attempted to partially replicate this practice by cross-classifying a select number of occupations in the managers, sales, craft, operative, and laborer major occupational groups by industry and, in the case of managers, by class of worker as well. The codes developed to distinguish these multidimensional occupational categories are presented in Tables A.1 and A.2.

One main problem encountered in creating the peak-median occupational classification system was to ascertain the peak median earnings for the detailed occupational groups. Most were obtained from Subject Report PC(2)-7A, *Occupational Characteristics* from the 1960 Census (U.S. Bureau of the Census 1963b). Table 31 in that report gives 1959 median earnings by occupation and age for all males in the United States. Unfortunately, the occupational classification system was not extremely detailed. It was possible to calculate medians for all the professional occupations not listed separately in PC(2)-7A from earnings data by age in another Subject Report, PC(2)-7E, *Characteristics of Professional Workers* (U.S. Bureau of the Census 1964a: Table 10). Median earnings were also available for a few additional detailed occupations in Subject Report, PC(2)-7B, *Occupations by Earnings and Education*(U.S. Bureau of the Census 1963g: Table 1). The peak median earnings of the remainder of the occupations had to be estimated from the median earnings for all ages combined (U.S. Bureau of the Census 1963b: Table 29). The resulting estimates and the classification of the occupations by peak median earnings are presented in Table A.3. The frequency distributions for the peak median occupational groups are presented in Tables A.4 and A.5.

One problem with estimating the *peak* median earnings of an occupation on the basis of the median earnings for all age groups combined is that the latter provides an *under*estimate of the peak medians. This underestimate had to be corrected in some way. I set about this by first analyzing the differences between the peak median earnings and the overall median earnings for those detailed occupations where earnings data by age were available. It was immediately apparent that the discrepancy between the peak median and the total median was not the same among the different major occupational groups. The differences tended to be largest for managers and sales workers. Rough correction factors were estimated, based on the differences in the medians for occupations where the data were available.

Appendix A

These correction factors are as follows:

Managers, officials, and proprietors	+$1,000
Sales workers	+ 1,000
Clerical workers	+ 600
Craftsmen and foremen	+ 500
Operatives	+ 500
Service workers	+ 500
Laborers	+ 500

The correction factor was added on to the median earnings for all age groups combined to arrive at an estimate of peak median earnings.

TABLE A.1
CLOCCIN6: Industry and Class of Worker Recode for Selected Occupations: 1960

| Industry | Occupation and class of worker[a] |||||||
	1	2	3	4	5	6	7
Construction: 196	1	11	21	31	41	51	61
Manufacturing, durables: 206–296	2	12	22	32	42	52	62
Manufacturing, nondurables: 306–459	3	13	23	33	43	53	63
Transportation, communications, and utilities: 506–579	4	14	24	34	44	54	64
Wholesale trade: 606–629	5	15	25	35	45	55	65
Retail trade: 636–658, 666–698	6	16	26	36	46	56	66
Retail trade, eating and drinking places: 659	7	17	27	37	47	57	67
Finance, insurance, and real estate: 706–736	8	18	28	38	48	58	68
Business serivces: 806–807	9	19	29	39	49	59	69
Other nonmanufacturing: 808–936, 016–018, 126–156, 999	10	20	30	40	50	60	70

Sources: U.S. Bureau of the Census no date.

[a] The following are the occupations used in this code (with their three-digit code numbers in parentheses):

1—Managers (290), salaried
2—Managers (290), self-employed
3—Managers (290), other
4—Salesmen (394)
5—Foremen (430)
6—Operatives (775)
7—Laborers (985)

TABLE A.2
CLOCCIN7: Industry and Class of Worker Recode for Selected Occupations: 1970

Industry	Occupation and class of worker[a]									
	1	2	3	4	5	6	7	8	9	10
Construction: 067–078	1	11	21	31	41	51	61	71	81	91
Manufacturing, durables: 107–267	2	12	22	32	42	52	62	72	82	92
Manufacturing, nondurables: 268–399[b]	3	13	23	33	43	53	63	73	83	93
Transportation, communications, and utilities: 407–499	4	14	24	34	44	54	64	74	84	94
Wholesale trade: 507–599	5	15	25	35	45	55	65	75	85	95
Retail trade: 607–699	6	16	26	36	46	56	66	76	86	96
Finance, insurance, and real estate: 707–719	7	17	27	37	47	57	67	77	87	97
Business Services: 727–749	8	18	28	38	48	58	68	78	88	98
Other nonmanufacturing industries: 757–767, 769–947, 017–029, 047–058	9	19	29	39	49	59	69	79	89	99

Source: U.S. Bureau of the Census 1972a.
[a]The following are the occupations used in this code:
 1—Managers (202), salaried
 2—Managers (202), self-employed
 3—Managers (220, 233, 245, 246), salaried
 4—Managers (220, 233, 245, 246), self-employed
 5—Managers (230), salaried
 6—Managers (230), self-employed
 7—Sales (296)
 8—Foremen (441)
 9—Operatives (612, 614, 635, 641, 650, 652, 653, 656, 660, 665, 681, 690, 692, 694, 695, 696)
 10—Laborers (751, 753, 762, 780, 785, 796)
[b]Includes nonspecified manufacturing industries.

TABLE A.3
Codes for the Classification of Occupations by 1959 Peak Median Earnings for Samples of All White Males and for White Husbands and Their Wives: 1960 and 1970[a]

Occupation	1959 peak median earnings[b] (dollars)	Occupational code numbers for males[c] 1960	1970
Professionals			
Professionals Ia (1959 peak at $10,000+)			
Airplane pilots and navigators	13,897	012	163
Architects	10,664	013	002
Dentists	14,993	071	062
Aeronautical engineers	10,560	080	006
Chemical engineers	10,931	081	010
Lawyers and judges	13,844	105	030, 031
Physicians and surgeons (including osteopaths)	15,256	162, 153	065
Veterinarians	10,987	194	072
Optometrists	9,260	152	063
Professionals Ib (1959 peak at $9,000–9,999)			
College presidents, professors, and instructors	9,196	030–060	102–122, 125–130, 132–140, 235
Electrical engineers	9,435	083	012
Mechanical engineers	9,165	085	014
Metallurgical and mining engineers	9,750	090, 091	015, 020
Sales engineers	9,850	092	022
Engineers, n.e.c.	8,998	093	023
Natural scientists, n.e.c.	9,425	130–145	035, 042–044, 051–054
Public relations men and publicity writers	9,551	163	192
Social scientists	9,342	172–175	091–094, 096
Other specified professionals	n.a.[d]		036, 164

408

Professionals IIa (1959 peak at $8,000–8,999)		
Authors, editors, and reporters	8,030	020, 075	181, 184
Civil engineers	8,679	082	011
Industrial engineers	8,298	084	013
Personnel and labor relations workers	8,532	154	056
Pharmacists	8,271	160	064
Professionals IIb (1959 peak at $7,000–7,999)		
Accountants and auditors	7,615	000	001
Artists and art teachers	7,234	014	190
Chemists	7,993	021	045
Designers and draftsmen	7,134	072, 074	152, 183
Other specified professional and technical workers in the Professional IIb group[e]	n.a.	010, 070, 195	003–005, 055, 095, 182, 193, 195, 196
Professionals IIIa (1959 peak at $6,000–6,999)		
Funeral directors and embalmers	6,629	104	165, 211
Musicians and music teachers	6,027	120	123, 185
Photographers	6,548	161	191
Social and welfare workers, including group and recreation workers	6,140	165, 171	100, 101
Athletes, sports instructores, and officials	6,771	015, 180	124, 180
Secondary-school teachers	6,961	183	144
Teachers, other	6,278	184	145
Electrical and electronic technicians	6,780	190	153
Technicians, other	n.a.	191, 192	150, 151, 173, 154–156, 162
Other specified professions in the Professional IIIa group	n.a.	022, 073, 101, 102, 111, 150, 164, 170, 193	024, 026, 032, 061, 071, 073–076, 090, 131, 141, 170–172, 174, 194, 240, 923
Professionals IIIb (1959 peak at $5,000–5,999)		
Foresters and conversationists	5,596	103	025
Surveyors	5,496	181	161
Teachers, elementary school	5,931	182	142
Medical and dental technicians	5,442	185	080–085, 426
Other specified professions in the Professional IIIb group[f]	n.a.	151	143, 175

(continued)

TABLE A.3 (Continued)

Occupation	1959 peak median earnings[b] (dollars)	Occupational code numbers for males[c] 1960	1970
Managers			
Managers Ia (1959 peak at $10,000+)			
Managers, salaried, manufacturing	10,861	CLOCCIN6: 2, 3	CLOCCIN7: 2, 3, 22, 23, 42,43
Managers, self-employed, finance, insurance, and real estate	11,425*	CLOCCIN6: 18	CLOCCIN7: 17, 37, 57
Managers Ib (1959 peak at $9,000–9,999)			
Managers, salaried, finance, insurance, and real estate	9,671	CLOCCIN6: 8	CLOCCIN7: 7, 27, 47
Managers, salaried, business services	9,340*	CLOCCIN6: 9	CLOCCIN7: 8, 28, 48, 212
Health administrators	n.a.		
Managers IIa (1959 peak at $8,000–8,999)			
Managers, salaried, construction	8,632*	CLOCCIN6: 1	CLOCCIN7: 1, 21, 41
Managers, salaried, wholesale trade	8,339*	CLOCCIN6: 5	CLOCCIN7: 5, 25, 45
Managers, self-employed, manufacturing	8,596	CLOCCIN6: 12, 13	CLOCCIN7: 12, 32, 52, 13, 33, 53
Managers, self-employed, wholesale trade	8,045	CLOCCIN6: 15	CLOCCIN7: 15, 35, 55
Railroad conductors	8,179*	252	226
Officers, pilot, ship	8,119*	265	221
Officials, lodge, society, union	8,187*	275	223
Managers IIb (1959 peak at $7,000–7,999)			
Managers, salaried, transportation, communications and utilities[g]	8,566*	CLOCCIN6: 4	CLOCCIN7: 4, 24, 44
Managers, salaried, other	7,211*	CLOCCIN6:10	CLOCCIN7: 9, 29, 49
Managers, self-employed, construction	7,189	CLOCCIN6: 11	CLOCCIN7: 11, 31, 51
Managers, self-employed, transportation, communications and utilities	7,509*	CLOCCIN6: 14	CLOCCIN7: 14, 34, 54
Buyers and department-store heads	7,945	250	205, 231
Credit men	7,039*	253	210
Postmasters	7,105*	280	224
Purchasing agents and buyers	7,839*	285	225

Managers IIIa (1959 peak at $6,000–6,999)		
Managers, salaried, retail trade	6,731	CLOCCIN6: 6, 7
Managers, self-employed, other	6,332	CLOCCIN6: 19, 20
		CLOCCIN7: 6, 26, 46
		CLOCCIN7: 18, 19, 38, 58, 39, 59
Inspectors and public administrators	6,129	260 201, 213, 215
Officials and administrators, public administration	6,998	270 222
Managers IIIb (1959 peak at $5,000–5,999)		
Managers, self-employed, retail trade	5,748	CLOCCIN6: 16, 17
Buyers and shippers, farm products[h]	5,622	CLOCCIN7: 16, 36, 56 203
Sales		
Sales IIa (1959 peak at $8,000–8,999)		
Stock and bond salesmen	8,118	395 271
Sales IIb (1959 peak at $7,000–7,999)		
Manufacturing	7,553	CLOCCIN6: 32, 33
Advertising agents and salesmen	7,286*	380 281, CLOCCIN7: 62, 63
Insurance agents and brokers	7,201	385 260
Real estate agents	7,337	393 265
		270
Sales IIIa (1959 peak at $6,000–6,999)		
Wholesale trade	6,764	CLOCCIN6: 35 282, CLOCCIN7: 65
Other industries	6,340	CLOCCIN6: 31, 34, 38, 39, 40	285, CLOCCIN7: 61, 64, 67, 68, 69
Sales IIIb (1959 peak at $5,000–5,999)		
Retail trade	5,219	CLOCCIN6: 36, 37	CLOCCIN7: 66, 283, 284
Other specified sales	n.a.	381–383, 390	261, 262, 264, 266, 280
Clerical Workers		
Clerical IIIa (1959 peak at $6,000–6,999)		
Agents, n.e.c.[i]	6,702*	301	—
Insurance adjusters and examiners	6,272	321	326
Express messengers and clerks[j]	6,219	315	—
Ticket, station and express agents	6,168	354	390

(continued)

TABLE A.3 (Continued)

Occupation	1959 peak median earnings[b] (dollars)	Occupational code numbers for males[c] 1960	1970
Clerical IIIb (1959 peak at $5,000–5,999)			
Bank tellers and bookkeepers	5,001*	305, 310	301, 305
Dispatchers and starters	5,979*	314	315
Mail carriers and postal clerks	5,924*	323, 340	331, 361
Office machine operators	5,850	325	341–355
Payroll and timekeeping clerks	5,644*	333	360
Secretaries and stenographers	5,934*	342, 345	370–72, 376
Telegraph operators	5,955*	352	384
Clerical workers, n.e.c.	5,492	370	394–396
Other specified clerical workers[j]	n.a.	304, 360	303, 311, 312, 314, 320, 323, 334, 362, 364, 375, 385, 391
		353	
Clerical IVa (1959 peak at less than $5,000)			
Collectors, bill and account	4,832	313	313
Shipping and receiving clerks	4,723	343	374
Stock clerks and storekeepers	4,627	350	381
Other specified clerical workers[k]	n.a.	—	332,392
Craftsmen and Foremen			
Craft IIb (1959 peak at $7,000–7,999)			
Foremen, durable goods manufacturing	7,665	CLOCCIN6: 42	CLOCCIN7: 72
Locomotive engineers	7,728	454	455
Electrotypers and photoengravers	7,534*	423, 503	434, 515
Craft IIIa (1959 peak at $6,000–6,999)			
Foremen, nondurable goods manufacturing	6,744	CLOCCIN6: 43	CLOCCIN7: 73

		CLOCCIN6: 41, 44–50	CLOCCIN7: 71, 74–79
Foremen, nonmanufacturing industries	6,472	414	422
Compositors and typesetters	6,348	421	430, 431
Electricians	6,302	424, 512	530, 531
Engravers, pressmen, and plate printers	6,466*	453	433, 552, 554
Linemen and servicemen, telegraph, telephone and power	6,533	460	456
Locomotive firemen	6,446	471	471
Mechanics and repairmen, airplanes	6,293	491	502
Millwrights	6,188	510	522, 523
Plumbers and pipe fitters	6,059	520	545
Stationary engineers	6,890	530	561, 562
Toolmakers and diemakers	6,816	n.a.	475
Data processing machine repairmen	n.a.		
Craft IIIb (1959 peak at $5,000–5,999)			
Blacksmiths, forgemen, and hammermen	5,470	402, 431	403, 442
Boilermakers	5,723	403	404
Masons, tile setters and stone cutters	5,254	405, 521	546, 560
Cabinet makers and pattern makers	5,845	410, 502	413, 514
Plasterers and cement finishers	5,084	413, 505	421, 520, 521
Cranemen and derrickmen	5,433	415	424
Excavating, grading and machine operators	5,236*	425	412, 436
Glaziers	5,816*	434	445
Heat treaters, annealers, and temperers	5,917	435	446
Machinists and job setters	5,808	452, 465	454, 461, 462
Mechanics and repairmen, n.e.c.	5,311	461, 470, 473, 475, 480	470, 480, 481, 482, 483, 484, 486, 491, 492, 495
Molders, metal	5,068	492	503, 504
Rollers and roll hands	5,764*	513	533
Structural metal workers	5,857	523	550, 540
Tinsmiths, coppersmiths	5,876	525	535, 536
Other specified craftsmen and foremen	n.a.	404, 420, 444, 451, 490, 493, 494, 545	405, 420, 425, 450, 453, 501, 505, 506, 571, 572, 575, 586

(continued)

413

TABLE A.3 (Continued)

Occupation	1959 peak median earnings[b] (dollars)	Occupational code numbers for males[c] 1960	1970
Craft IVa (1959 peak at $4,000–4,999)			
Bakers	4,982	401	402
Carpenters	4,832	411	415, 416
Tailors and furriers	4,567	432, 524	551, 444
Inspectors, n.e.c.	4,753*	450	452
Mechanics and repairmen, auto	4,854	472	472–474
Mechanics and repairmen, radio and TV	4,949	474	485
Painters, construction, and maintenance	4,295	495	510, 511, 543
Upholsterers	4,616	535	401, 563
Other specified craft	n.a.	—	440
Craft IVb (1959 peak at less than $4,000)			
Other specified craftsmen and foremen	n.a.	501, 504, 514, 515	512, 516, 534, 542
Operatives			
Operatives IIIa (1959 peak at $6,000–6,999)			
Asbestos and insulation workers	6,421	630	601
Power station operators	6,454	701	525
Operatives IIIb (1959 peak at $5,000–5,999)			
Brakemen and switchmen, railroad	5,932	640, 713	712, 713
Bus drivers	5,032	641	703
Checkers and examiners, manufacturing	5,524	643	610
Metal workers, n.e.c.	5,560*	653, 670, 672, 721	621, 622, 626, 651, 680

Meat cutters	5,297	675	631
Oilers and greasers, except auto	5,164	692	642
Stationary firemen	5,280	712	666
Operatives, durable goods manufacturing	5,033	CLOCCIN6: 52	CLOCCIN7: 82
Other specified operatives	n.a.	635, 645, 691	701, 704
Operatives IVa (1959 peak at $4,000–4,999)			
Operatives, nondurable manufacturing	4,915	CLOCCIN6: 53	604, 633, 664, 670, 674; CLOCCIN7: 83
Operatives, nonmanufacturing industries	4,548	CLOCCIN6: 51, 54–60	CLOCCIN7: 81, 84–89; 615
Assemblers	4,922	631	602
Truck drivers, delivery men, and routemen	4,853	650, 715	705, 715
Mine operators and laborers	4,596	685	640
Packers and wrappers, n.e.c.	4,299	693	634, 643
Painters, except construction and maintenance	4,672	694	443, 644
Photographic process workers	4,841*	695	645
Sailors and deckhands	4,711	703	661
Sewers and stitchers, manufacturing	4,029*	705	663
Other specified operatives	n.a.	634, 651, 652	603, 613, 620
		671, 673, 690	624, 671, 710
			706, 726
Operatives IVb (1959 peak at less than $4,000)			
Attendants, auto service and parking	3,407	632	623, 711
Laundry and dry-cleaning	3,546	674	611, 630
Sawyers	3,197	704	662
Spinners and weavers	3,771	710, 720	672, 673
Taxicab drivers and chauffeurs	3,526	714	714
Other specified operatives[f]	n.a.	642, 654	605, 625, 636
Service workers			
Service IIIb (1959 peak at $5,000–5,999)			
Firemen	5,768	850	961
Marshals, constables, policemen, and sheriffs	5,556	852–854	963–965
Other specified service	n.a.	—	931

(continued)

415

TABLE A.3 (Continued)

Occupation	1959 peak median earnings[b] (dollars)	Occupational code numbers for males[c] 1960	Occupational code numbers for males[c] 1970
Service IVa (1959 peak at $4,000–4,999)			
Barbers	4,302	814	935
Bartenders	4,240*	815	910
Housekeepers and stewards	4,353	832	950
Hairdressers	4,731*	843	944
Guards and watchmen	4,823	851	962
Service IVb (1959 peak at less than $4,000)			
Attendants, hospitals, professional, and personal service	3,435	810, 812	921, 922, 924–926, 942, 952, 953
Charworkers and cleaners, janitors and porters	3,328	824, 834, 841	901–903, 934
Cooks	3,924	825	912
Counter workers, waiters	2,535*	830, 875	914, 915
Elevator operators	3,771	831	943
Kitchen workers, n.e.c.	1,945*	835	913, 916
Other specified service workers[m]	n.a.	813, 820, 821	911, 932, 933
		842, 860, 890	940, 941, 960, 976
Private household workers[n]	n.a.	—	—
Laborers			
Laborers IVa (1959 peak at $4,000–4,999)			
Manufacturing	4,070	CLOCCIN6: 62–63	CLOCCIN7: 92–93
Warehousemen, n.e.c.	4,896*	973	770
Laborers IVb (1959 peak at less than $4,000)			
Nonmanufacturing industries	3,493	CLOCCIN6: 61, 64–70	CLOCCIN7: 91, 94–99; 754
Fishermen and oystermen	2,890	962	752
Other specified laborers	n.a.	960, 963, 964, 970, 971, 972	740, 750, 755, 761, 763, 764

Miscellaneous occupations—cases omitted from sample

Professional workers			
Clergyman[o]	4,547	023	086
Nurses, student professionals[f]	n.a.	—	—
Managers			
Other (than salaried or self employed)	n.a.	CLOCCIN6: 21–30	—
Buyers and shippers, farm products[q]	5,622*	251	—
Floormen and floor managers, store	5,789*	254	—
Managers and superintendents, building	<5,000*	262	216
Clerical workers[r]			
Cashiers	3,610*	312	310
Attendants and assistants, library	<2,000*	302	330
Attendants, physicians' and dentists' offices	<4,000*	303	—
File clerks	<4,000*	320	325
Messengers and office boys	<3,000	324, 351	333
Other specified clerical workers	n.a.	—	382, 383
Craft workers			
Members of armed forces and former members[s]	n.a.	555	580
Operatives			
Apprentices[t]	n.a.	601–621	—
Service workers			
Ushers, recreation and amusement[u]	n.a.	874	—
Personal service apprentices	n.a.	—	945
Welfare service aides	n.a.	—	954
Private household workers[n]	<2,000	801–804	980–986
Laborers			
Longshoremen and stevedores[v]	5,168	965	760

(continued)

TABLE A.3 (Continued)

Occupation	1959 peak median earnings[b] (dollars)	Occupational code numbers for males[c] 1960	1970
Farmers and farm workers	n.a.	200–222, 901–903, 905	801, 802, 806, 821–824, 846
Occupation not reported[w]	n.a.	995	—
No occupation	n.a.	999	991

Sources: Tables A.1 and A.2; U.S. Bureau of the Census 1963b; Tables 29 and 31; 1963g; Table 1; 1964a; Table 10; No date; 1972a.

[a] By and large, the classification systems used for men and women were identical. However, a few predominantly female occupations were placed in the omitted category for males because of the small number of cases involved but were included within specified occupational groups for women—most notably, private household workers and several clerical occupations. A footnote will indicate where the classification system for wives differs from that of men.

[b] Based on published 1960 census data, the 1959 peak median earnings for any occupational group is defined as the highest of the median earnings for the following five age groups: 18–24, 25–34, 35–44, 45–54, and 55–64. For some occupations the peak median was estimated from the median earnings for all age groups combined. See the explanation accompanying the table for how these estimates were made.

[c] The code numbers for this occupational classification system have two major sources. One is the code numbers for the detailed occupational classification for the 1960 and 1970 censuses. The second is a created variable that cross-classified a select number of occupations by industry and, in some cases, by class of worker as well. See Tables A.1 and A.2 definitions of these codes. They are termed CLOCCIN6 for 1960 and CLOCCIN7 for 1970.

[d] n.a. is used when peak median earnings were not ascertained.

[e] By mistake, actors (code 010) were placed in the Professional IIIb group in 1960 for all males and for husbands. However, there were only three actors in the 1960 all white males sample and none in the husbands' sample. Actors and actresses were placed in the Professional IIIb category for wives in 1960 and for all samples in 1970.

[f] For wives in 1960, code category 151 was put in the omitted miscellaneous occupational group at the end. In addition, code category 010 was included in the Professional IIIb group for wives in 1960.

[g] Salaried managers in transportation, communications, and utilities should be in the peak median group $8,000–8,999 instead of $7,000–7,999. However, no error resulted in the analysis because these two income categories were then combined into one—the Manager II group. The more collapsed form of the variable has been used in the data analysis of the study.

[h] In 1960, this occupation was inadvertently placed in the miscellaneous occupational group which was omitted from the analysis. Since there were only 18 men in the 1960 all white males sample in this occupation, it did not appear worthwhile correcting the error.

[i] No such occupational category in 1970.

[j] In 1960, occupational category 341 was also included in this peak median occupational group for wives.

[k] In 1960, the following occupational code categories were also included in the Clerical IV group for wives: 302, 303, 312, 320, 324, 351. In 1970, the following occupational categories were included in this peak median group for wives: 310, 325, 330, 333, 382.

^{l}In 1960, occupational category 680 was also included in this peak median occupational groups for wives.

^{m}For wives in 1960, the following detailed occupational codes were also included in this peak median occupational group: 823, 840, and 874.

^{n}Since there were so few males in private household work, these men were placed in the miscellaneous category (i.e., omitted from the analysis). However, wives in private household work were included in a separate occupational category for this type of work. For 1960, this included occupations with the following code numbers: 801–804. In 1970, the code numbers were: 980–986.

^{o}Clergymen were excluded from the analysis since this was the only profession in which the 1959 peak median earnings was less than $5,000. Since there were only 179 males in the occupation in 1960, the number seemed too small to justify setting up a Professional IV category. In addition, since this occupational group includes celibate Catholic clergy, it did not seem appropriate to include it in an analysis of the family.

^{p}This occupation has the code of 151 and was omitted from the 1960 wives sample only.

^{q}These men were omitted from consideration in 1960 because the median earnings for all age groups combined (there were not data on earnings by age) was below $5,000. Due to the small number of managers in the earnings group below $5,000, it was decided not to analyze them. However, this was a mistake in these two cases because the *estimated* peak median earnings (using the correction factor of $1,000) would actually have put these occupations into the $5,000–5,999 range. However, in both 1960 samples fewer than 25 men were involved. These occupations, or similar ones, were placed in the Managers IIIb category for the 1970 samples.

^{r}In the case of wives, these occupations were placed in the Clerical IV occupational group.

^{s}The 1960 samples included people in various occupations which were omitted from the analysis—the armed forces and farm occupations. Men in these occupations were omitted from the 1970 samples when these were set up by DUALABS. Hence, there were no cases in the 1970 samples to be placed in the miscellaneous category.

^{t}Apprentices were not treated the same in 1970 as in 1960. In 1960 they were omitted from the analysis because of their somewhat marginal status. However, I later decided this was a mistake and that they should be grouped with the occupations in which they were apprenticing in order to achieve a more accurate representation of workers in the occupation at all stages of the career cycle. Hence, in 1970 apprentices were classified with their relevant occupation. However, this inconsistency in classification should not have much, if any, empirical consequence since so few cases were involved in 1960. There were only 84 apprentices in the all white males 1960 sample and 48 husbands who were apprentices in 1960.

^{u}This occupation was placed in the Service IV group for all samples with the exception of 1960 all white males.

^{v}Longshoremen and stevedores were omitted from the analysis because they were in the only Laborers occupation group with peak 1959 median earnings over $5,000. Since there were so few men in this occupational category—only 31 in the 1960 all white males sample—analyzing a Laborer III category did not appear feasible.

^{w}This category refers only to the 1960 samples since occupation was allocated in 1970 when it was not reported.

*Asterisk means peak median earnings were estimated on the basis of the median earnings for all age groups combined.

419

TABLE A.4
Absolute and Relative Frequency Distributions of Males, by Peak Median Occupational Group and Marital Status: 1960 and 1970

Peak median occupational group	Percentage				Number			
	All white males		Husbands		All white males		Husbands	
	1960	1970	1960	1970	1960	1970	1960	1970
Total	100.0	100.0	100.0	100.0	34,710	27,675	124,675	91,937
Professionals								
I	4.0	4.3	5.1	5.8	1,382	1,200	6,352	5,329
II	4.4	4.6	5.8	6.1	1,540	1,268	7,256	5,626
III	3.5	3.3	5.0	4.9	1,230	916	6,210	4,508
Managers								
I	2.7	3.1	3.0	3.6	941	864	3,759	3,320
II	4.7	5.4	4.9	5.8	1,632	1,491	6,157	5,309
III	4.9	5.6	3.8	4.4	1,713	1,552	4,760	4,069
Sales								
II	2.7	3.0	2.7	3.1	929	821	3,322	2,828
III	5.1	4.8	4.8	4.8	1,781	1,333	6,023	4,415
Clerical								
III	6.5	6.0	5.6	5.2	2,259	1,658	6,943	4,778
IV	1.6	1.3	1.8	1.4	546	372	2,190	1,308
Craft								
II	1.5	1.8	1.4	1.7	531	493	1,779	1,583
III	15.9	17.1	15.9	17.2	5,520	4,727	19,848	15,817
IV	6.6	6.7	6.2	6.4	2,291	1,861	7,729	5,869
Operatives								
III	8.6	8.7	7.5	7.5	2,997	2,406	9,334	6,869
IV	14.7	13.9	13.1	11.8	5,108	3,854	16,309	10,878
Service								
III	1.2	1.3	1.3	1.5	400	369	1,659	1,388
IV	4.6	3.7	5.7	4.3	1,609	1,033	7,175	3,957
Laborers								
IV	6.6	5.3	6.4	4.4	2,301	1,457	8,004	4,086

Sources: 1960 and 1970 Public Use Samples of White Males and of White Couples.

Appendix A

TABLE A.5
Peak Median Occupational Group of Employed Wives: 1960 and 1970[a]

Peak median occupational group	Percentage 1960	Percentage 1970	Number 1960	Number 1970
Total	100.0	100.0	8,480	37,574
Professionals				
I	.4	.8	38	312
II	1.5	2.8	123	1,040
III	11.4	14.1	970	5,301
Managers				
I	.7	.7	58	266
II	1.4	1.4	118	539
III	2.0	1.6	170	598
Sales				
II	.9	.8	73	297
III	8.9	7.3	756	2,750
Clerical				
III	32.2	33.1	2,727	12,438
IV	3.9	4.9	327	1,824
Craft				
II	.1	.1	11	49
III	1.0	1.2	82	444
IV	.3	.4	27	134
Operatives				
III	4.4	4.3	370	1,599
IV	15.1	11.1	1,277	4,175
Service				
III	.0	.1	3	26
IV	13.7	13.5	1,162	5,084
Private household	1.9	1.1	160	404
Laborers				
IV	.3	.8	28	294

Sources: 1960 and 1970 Public Use Samples of White Couples.
[a]Includes only those employed wives of men in the 18 peak median occupational groups listed in Table A.4.

TABLE A.6
Number of Cases Where Peak Medians Were Estimated, by Peak Median Occupational Group: All White Males, 1960

Peak median occupational group	Males in occupations with estimated peak medians Number	As a percentage of total in peak median occupational group
Managers		
Ia	60	9.7
Ib	33	10.2
IIa	402	58.9
IIb	569	59.9
IIIa	732	77.5
IIIb	—	—
Sales		
IIa	31	100.0
IIb	20	2.2
IIIa	—	—
IIIb	—	—
Clerical		
IIIa	234	100.0
IIIb	1,940	95.8
IVa	270	49.4
Craft		
IIb	24	4.5
IIIa	64	2.6
IIIb	302	9.9
IVa	136	6.1
IVb	—	—
Operatives		
IIIa	—	—
IIIb	587	19.9
IVa	127	2.8
IVb	—	—
Service		
IIIb	—	—
IVa	215	36.1
IVb	418	41.2
Laborers		
IVa	94	12.6
IVb	—	—

Source: 1960 Public Use Sample of White Males.

APPENDIX B

Total Male Population in Selected Age Groups

TABLE B.1
Total Male Population in Selected Age Groups: United States, 1947–1977 [a] (Numbers in 1,000s)

Year	18–19	20–24	25–34	35–64
1947	2,277	5,830	11,473	36,407
1948	2,254	5,837	11,576	36,870
1949	2,268	5,783	11,663	37,362
1950	2,215	5,794	11,804	37,939
1951	2,125	5,753	11,889	38,365
1952	2,072	5,658	11,947	38,769
1953	2,110	5,516	11,972	39,116
1954	2,149	5,407	11,982	39,453
1955	2,135	5,351	11,967	39,794
1956	2,193	5,299	11,905	40,128
1957	2,265	5,291	11,775	40,384
1958	2,296	5,372	11,628	40,537
1959	2,376	5,486	11,451	40,699
1960	2,524	5,569	11,327	40,900
1961	2,791	5,744	11,230	41,101
1962	2,894	5,985	11,149	41,296
1963	2,804	6,367	11,109	41,498
1964	2,785	6,649	11,101	41,703
1965	3,313	6,899	11,130	41.907

(continued)

TABLE B.1 (Continued)

Year	18–19	20–24	25–34	35–64
1966	3,709	7,056	11,257	42,202
1967	3,581	7,665	11,465	42,565
1968	3,586	7,937	11,876	43,095
1969	3,659	8,290	12,216	43,504
1970	3,792	8,645	12,521	43,916
1971	3,885	9,092	12,799	44,311
1972	3,978	9,064	13,587	45,215
1973	4,065	9,224	14,195	45,938
1974	4,129	9,427	14,777	46,646
1975	4,231	9,679	15,347	47,331
1976	4,313	9,880	15,912	48,109
1977	4,307	10,104	16,464	48,937

Sources: U.S. Bureau of the Census 1965f; 1974c: Table 1; 1978f: Table 1.

[a]Includes the total male population of the United States including Alaska and Hawaii and the District of Columbia and armed forces overseas.

APPENDIX C

Dollar Estimates of Expenditures on Children

Espenshade computed estimates of annual child-care expenditures by age of child and birth order for one-, two-, and three-child families and for three levels of after-tax family incomes—low, medium, and high. One might suppose that the medium income level would be most appropriate for the estimates of all families combined in the PUS sample as these would presumably represent the "average." However, Espenshade's estimates of his medium after-tax incomes seem to high for my sample, and his income estimates for the "low" level seem too low. For example, following Bowen and Finegan's method for deducting taxes, I estimated that the taxes amounted to 12.5% of gross family income and the total after-tax 1959 income for PUS couples where the husband was 35–44 years old was $6,273 (Bowen and Finegan 1969: 578). However, the range of *medium* incomes Espenshade gives for men 34.9–43.9 years old is $7,464–8,103 (Espenshade 1973: 38). Thus his lower limit of the medium range is above my estimate of after-tax income for families in the 35–44 age group. The same is true for the other age groups. However, his "low" estimates are too low. For example, for 35–44-year-old men again, he has a range of low after-tax family incomes of $5,511–5,879 which is below my estimate of $6,273 for this age group. Since neither low or medium estimates were appropriate, I averaged the expenditures of the two.

Espenshade also had separate estimates for birth orders (by family size, although this did not make a great deal of difference). Since I really did not know birth orders for my sample—at least on aggregate data—I needed an overall average estimate of the expenditures on a child by age. Hence, my first approach was to average the estimates for the various birth orders and family sizes. This seemed particularly appropriate to do since the estimates for the first child were so much higher than for second or third children (a ratio of about 2:1) that even Espenshade expressed doubts about their validity (Espenshade 1973: 66ff). However, there was one exception to this general procedure. For families where the head was 18–24, I assumed that all children were first-order births. This seemed like a reasonable assumption—especially as I also think that Espenshade's estimates do not give us a clear idea of the costs of setting up a child-oriented household.

In sum, then, in my first approximation, I estimated the expenditures on children in each age group for men in the 25–64 age range by averaging the expenditures for each of the birth orders for each family size and for low and medium income levels (i.e., 12 different expenditures estimates were averaged). For husbands 18–24 years old, however, I averaged expenditures for first-order children among the three family types and the two income levels (i.e., 6 different expenditure estimates were averaged). The results were estimates of the annual costs of a child 0–5, 6–11, and 12–17 years old in 1960 dollars. These, in turn, were adjusted for the 23.8% rise in the Consumer Price Index between 1960 and 1969 (U.S. Bureau of Labor Statistics 1976c:105). The estimates, in 1969 dollars, are presented in Table C.1.

Espenshade's estimates of expenditures were not really designed for the purposes to which I am putting them and my estimates based on his data left me somewhat dissatisfied—especially as it is so hard to bring in independent evidence to properly evaluate them. Three important reservations that I had were with regard to the expenditures on firstborn children and on children 0–5 and 12–17 years old. From a purely intuitive point of view, the estimates for firstborn children and those for 12–17-year-olds seemed too high. From a more objective point of view, they do not appear to lead to results that are entirely consistent with the Bureau of Labor Statistics (BLS) equivalence scales although both Espenshade's estimates and the equivalence scales are based on the assumption that equivalent levels of living are achieved when the same proportion of after-tax family income is spent on food (Espenshade 1973: Chapter 2; U.S. Bureau of Labor Statistics, 1968b). It is difficult to compare Espenshade's results with the equivalence scales because they are not reported in the same way. The equivalence scales use different age groups for children (0–5, 6–15 instead of 6–11, and 16–17 instead of 12–17). Furthermore, the BLS does not distinguish costs of individual children in

TABLE C.1
Preliminary Estimates of the Unit Expenditures on Children under Age 18, by Own Age and Age of Husband (1969 Dollars)[a,b]

Age of husband	Age of child	Preliminary expenditure estimates
25–64	0–5	$ 739
	6–11	1,842
	12–17	3,419
18–24	0–5	1,144
	6–11	2,748
12–17		4,264

Sources: Espenshade 1973: Chapter 3; U.S. Bureau of Labor Statistics 1976c: 105.

[a] Based on Espenshade's estimates of child-care expenditures. I estimated the expenditures on children in each age group for men in the 25–64 age range by averaging the expenditures for each of the birth orders for each family size and for low and medium income levels. For husbands aged 18–24, however, I averaged expenditures for first-order children among the three family types and the two income levels.

[b] Espenshade's expenditure estimates were for 1960. They were, therefore, adjusted for the 23.8% rise in the Consumer Price Index between 1960 and 1969.

families—it gives an index, for example, for two-child families where the father is 35–54 and the oldest child is 16–17 but no information on the age of the youngest child and, hence, what expenditures to allow for him or her. However, if we compare single-child families we can get some idea of how consistent Espenshade's results are with those of the BLS. According to the BLS, equivalence scales (U.S. Bureau of Labor Statistics 1968b: Table 1), the scale values for the families of interest are as follows. (Note, two-child couples, head 35–54, with oldest child 6–15 = 100.)

1. Childless couples, head under 35   49
2. Childless couples, head 35–54   60
3. One-child couples, head under 35, child under 6   62
4. One-child couples, head 35–54, child 6–15   82
5. One-child couples, head 35–54, child 16–17   91

If my understanding of these types of computations is correct, the equivalent expenditure on a child under 6 when the head was under 35 would be the difference between the "cost" to a childless couple with the head under 35 and the cost to a similar couple with one child under 6. The "cost" of a child 6–15 to a couple with a head 35–54 would be the difference between the cost to a similarly aged childless couple and a couple with a child 6–15. And so on. This reasoning and the BLS scale values imply that the ratios reported in Table C.2 should prevail between expenditures on older and younger children and these ratios are very different than those coming out of Espenshade's estimates.

TABLE C.2
Ratios of Costs of Children in Various Age Groups: Comparisons of Cost Estimates

Ratio of costs of children in various age groups	Bureau of Labor Statistics	Espenshade Low income	Espenshade Medium income
6–15/under 6	1.69		
6–11/under 6		2.50	2.38
16–17/under 6	2.38		
12–17/under 6		3.96	3.72

Sources: U.S. Bureau of Labor Statistics 1968b: Table 1; Espenshade 1973: Chapter 3.

If it is indeed true that the older they are the more expensive children are (until they start working and earning money themselves) then Espenshade's estimates for 6–11 and 12–17-year-olds seem very high compared to the BLS figures. Thus one would expect expenditures on children 6–15 years old (the age interval the BLS uses) to be greater than on 6–11-year-olds because 12–15-year-olds would be more expensive to maintain than 6–11-year-olds. However, the BLS ratio of "costs" of 6–15-year-olds to costs of children under 6 is much lower than the ratio of 6–11-year-old children to costs of children under 6 from Espenshade—1.69 versus 2.50.

As another test of the consistency of the BLS and Espenshade estimates I used the BLS equivalence scale on their own moderate 1967 budget for urban families. I estimated the expenditures on children under 6, 6–15, and

TABLE C.3
Various Estimates of the Unit Expenditures on Children, by Own Age and Age of Husbands (1969 Dollars)

		Oppenheimer First expenditure estimates		Oppenheimer Revised expenditure estimates	
		Age of husband		Age of husband	
Age of child	Bureau of Labor Statistics	18–24	25–64	18–24	25–64
0–5	1,296	1,144	739	1,273	1,036
6–11		2,748	1,842	1,903	1,549
12–17		4,264	3,419	2,943	2,397
6–15	2,192				
16–17	3,089				

Sources: U.S. Bureau of Labor Statistics 1968b: Table 1; 1969; Espenshade 1973: Chapter 3; Table C.1.

Appendix C

16–17 in single-child families and then inflated these "costs" to 1969 dollars. Table C.3 shows these estimates and my first approximation estimates based on Espenshade's data. My second approximation estimates are also presented and their derivation will be discussed shortly.

In the case of children under 6, my first approximation estimates for husbands 18–24 were almost identical to the estimates based on the BLS moderate budget. However, the estimates for children under 6 for men 25–64 appeared too low. For children 6–11 my estimates for men 25–64 are somewhat less than those of the BLS children 6–15, as they should be, because older children are left out. However, the difference amounts to only $350, which seems a little small, given the fact that the more expensive 12–15-year-olds are omitted from my age group estimates but are included in those of the BLS. For children 12–17 my first approximation estimates for men 25–64 seemed rather high considering the younger children included in my age group versus the BLS 16–17 age group. My estimates for older children of men 18–24 are much too high but this hardly matters because of the rarity of children in these age groups for young families. In sum, my first approximation estimates left me somewhat dissatisfied. The expenditures for older children seemed high in general and also high relative to the estimates for younger children. Finally, the estimates were not as consistent with the BLS data as I would have liked.

In a private communication, Dr. Espenshade suggested several ways in which I could modify the estimates and perhaps make them more suitable for my purposes. With regard to the high estimated expenditures on the first born children, he suggested that before I averaged the expenditures on children of various birth orders, I reduced the expenditures on firstborns by multiplying the original estimates by .75. This would result in a ratio of expenditures of firstborns to secondborn children of something on the order of 3:2. Moreover, this procedure is not as arbitrary as it may seem since the initial equation for estimating expenditures on children (Espenshade 1973: 29) quite possibly exaggerates expenditures on firstborn children (Espenshade 1973: 66). This I did as the first step in arriving at my second approximation of expenditures on children.

With regard to the distribution of total expenditures by age of the child, as we have seen, Espenshade's estimates seem to lead to an overestimate of expenditures for the 12–17 age group and an underestimate for the 0–5 age group. In Espenshade's data roughly 50% of all expenditures to age 18 for the first child occur in the last age interval, 12–17, whereas for the second and third child the percentage is even larger. This occurs, especially for children after the first, because Espenshade has estimated the *marginal* and not the *average* expenditures on children and it is the average expenditures that are the appropriate figures for my purposes (though not his). Since the marginal cost of the oldest child in the family exceeds that of younger siblings, when the second child is the oldest (i.e., at ages 16 and 17), a disproportionate share of child-related expenditures is attributed to him or her. This tends to further increase the proportion of total expenditures that are concentrated in the last age interval. The same general argument holds for the third child. With regard to the low estimates for children in the 0–5 age group, this may be because Espenshade does not appear to have made explicit allowances for expenses associated with childbirth and with setting up a child-oriented household.

To deal with these problems, I carried out the following procedures. After having calculated the average expenditures for each age group, I totaled and redistributed them according to the expenditure distribution implied by the Sydenstricker and King scale reported in Espenshade (1973: 4). Averaging the separate values for males and females, the scale indicates that 20.8, 31.1, and 48.1% of the total expenditures occurred in ages 0–5, 6–11, and 12–17 respectively as opposed to the Epenshade distribution of 14, 33, and 53% for ages 0–5, 6–11, and 12–17 respectively. These second estimates are also presented in Table C.3.

By and large, the second approximation estimates seem much more satisfactory than the original estimates, although the process by which they were obtained was somewhat arbitrary. Nevertheless, they do exhibit several advantages and provide a much more conservative test of my argument. For example, the very high estimates for 12–17-year-olds are greatly reduced— from the first estimate of $3,419 for fathers 25–64 to $2,397 for the second estimate. Second, the revised estimates seem much more consistent with the BLS data. For one thing, the estimates for children under 6 are improved— they are even closer for 18–24-year-old fathers and although still somewhat low for 25–64-year-old fathers, the discrepancy is much reduced over the first estimates. For children 6–11 (fathers 25–64) my second estimates are below the first and therefore seem more consistent with the BLS data which include the 12–15-year-old, more expensive, adolescent age group. In addition, my revised estimates for 12–17-year-olds are now below the BLS estimates for 16–17-year-olds ($2,397 versus 3,089) which was not the case before. Because my 12–17 age group includes the presumably less expensive 12–15-year-olds, my revised estimates seem to have achieved a decided improvement in this respect. Finally, the use of the distribution of expenditures of the Sydenstricker and King scale, although based on old data, is highly consistent with the distribution of expenditures based on the BLS data presented in Table C.3. Thus the relative expenditure scale implies that 20.8% of the expenditures occur in the 0–5 age group versus the 21.7% implied by the BLS data. The relative expenditure scale indicates that 60.2% of the expenditures occurred in the 6–15 age groups versus the 61.1%

Appendix C

implied by the BLS data and for 16–17-year-olds the estimates are 18.9% for the relative expenditure scale versus 17.2% for the BLS data. In general, then, these revised estimates of the expeditures on children by age seem to be more statisfactory in at least two ways—the extremely high cost of children 12–17 are reduced and the estimates are now much more in line with the BLS equivalence scales.

Once estimates of expenditures for each child by age group were achieved it was a relatively simple matter to estimate total expenditures for husbands in any given age group. First I computed the mean number of children in each of the three age groups (0–5, 6–11, and 12–17) for men in each of the four age groups under consideration (Table 5.3). Then I multiplied the mean number of children present in each age group by the estimated "cost" per child in the same age group. Then the "costs" for each age group were summed up to get the total expenditures (Table 5.7).

Dollar Estimates of Expenditures on Children 18–24

Espenshade's data on expenditures by the ages of children only provided a basis for estimating costs by age for children under 18. Since children over 18 were present in some households and since some of these children were partially dependent economically on their parents, it was important to estimate the extent of the economic burden such older children represented. The problem can be broken down into several steps:

1. Estimating the mean number of 18–24-year-olds in the household
2. Estimating the expenditures of parents on 18–24-year-olds, net of the earnings of these older children
3. Estimating the earnings of such young people

Left out of all these calculations is any estimate of the economic burden on their parents of young adults no longer in the household (e.g., attending school away from home). To estimate such costs is a very difficult and time-consuming task and may not, in fact, be possible at all—at least in the sense of getting results that would be usable for the couples in my public use samples. The reader must therfore realize that these estimates for expenditures on 18–24-year-olds are probably much too low.

THE ESTIMATING PROCEDURE

The goal is to measure first the number of 18–24-year-old children of heads in the households of fathers 35–44 and 45–54 years old and second the parents' share of the expenditures on youths in this age group. It is assumed that no appreciable number of men under 35 years old have children in the

18–24 age group. This is consistent with the 1970 PUS where 99.6% of husbands 25–34 had no 18–24-year-olds in the home.

A. Measuring the Presence of White 18–24-Year-Old Children of Heads Present in the Household in 1960

The version of the 1960 public use sample that I have used in this study only has data on the presence of *single* 18–24-year-old children of the head. I roughly estimated the total number of households with at least one 18–24-year-old present by using published data on the marital status of white children, aged 18–24, who were offspring of the household head. To be exact, I divided the number of families in the 1960 PUS with at least one single 18–24-year-old present by the proportion of 18–24-year-old children of heads, who were reported single in the published data (90.4%).

B. Measuring the Mean Number of White 18–24-Year-Old Children of Heads, Present in the Household in 1960

No information on the *number* of 18–24-year-old children of household heads was available in 1960—either in my public use sample or in the published data that detailed children under 18 only. I estimated the distribution by assuming that it was the same in 1960 as in the 1970 PUS where that information was available. This undoubtedly led to overestimates of the number present in 1960 because the number of children ever born to these families was lower than in 1970. However, such overestimates will tend to minimize the measure 1960–1970 increase in the number of children 18–24 present and this seemed like a conservative approach. The estimated mean number of 18–24-year-olds present in the household appears in Table 5.3 and in Table C.4.

C. Measuring Parental Expenditures on Children Aged 18–24 in the Household

It had been estimated previously that the expenditures on each child in the 12–17-year-old group were $2,397, using Espenshade's data. I assumed that the basic expenditures on children aged 18–24 would be the same. This seems like a conservative assumption since young adults are likely to have increased expenses. However, this basic estimate does not include higher educational costs which are likely to be a relatively significant factor for this age group. My next problem, then, was to try to estimate the educational cost of 18–24-year-old children in the home. This involved two steps: obtaining estimates of the educational costs of those enrolled and estimating the mean number of children enrolled in college. It is presumed that all of these will be in the 18–24 age group.

TABLE C.4
Estimating Parental Expenditures on Those 18–24-Year-Olds Present in the Home, by Age of Husband: 1960 and 1970 (1969 Dollars)

	\multicolumn{4}{c}{Age of husband}				
	\multicolumn{3}{c}{1960}		\multicolumn{3}{c}{1970}	
	35–44	45–54	55–64	35–44	45–54	55–64
(1) Base unit expenditure[a]	2,397	2,397	2,397	2,397	2,397	2,397
(2) Average number of 18–24-year-olds present[b]	.09	.28	.17	.15	.38	.20
(3) Preliminary expenditure estimates: (1) × (2)	216	671	407	360	911	479
(4) Estimated unit educational costs[c]	796	796	796	934	934	934
(5) Estimated mean number of 18–24-year-olds enrolled[d]	.023	.083	.053	.039	.113	.062
(6) Estimated educational costs: (4) × (5)	18	66	42	36	106	58
(7) Expenditures including educational costs: (3) + (6)	234	737	449	396	1,017	537
(8) Estimated income contribution of 18–24-year-olds[e]	160	497	302	260	658	346
(9) Total estimated parental expenditures on 18–24-year-olds: (7) − (8)	74	240	147	136	359	191

Sources: Unless where otherwise indicated, 1960 and 1970 Public Use Samples of White Couples.
[a]Table C.3
[b]Estimated for 1960. Table 5.3.
[c]Table C.5.
[d]It was assumed that the ratio of the mean number enrolled in college to the mean number of 18–24-year-olds in the household was the same in 1960 as in 1970 for each age group of husbands. The means for 1970 are the mean number of all children attending college for all households.
[e]This is the mean number of 18–24-year-olds in the home multiplied by $1,774 for 1959 and $1,731 for 1969 (U.S. Bureau of the Census 1964b: Tables 2, 5, and 22; 1973f: Table 10).

TABLE C.5
Estimating Educational Costs per Student Enrolled in College: 1960 and 1970

	1960		1970	
	Cost item	Enrollments (in 1,000s)	Cost item	Enrollments (in 1,000s)
Tuition and charges				
Public	200	1,929	323	5,194
Private	794	1,298	1,533	1,826
Weighted average[a]	439		638	
Books and supplies[b]				
1960: .225 × 439 =	99			
1970: .225 × 638 =			144	
Transportation[c]				
1960: .239 × 439 =	105			
1970: .239 × 638 =			152	
Estimated total educational costs per child enrolled in college:				
1960:	643			
Adjusted to 1969 dollars[d]	796			
1970[e]			934	

Sources: Becker 1975: 254; U.S. Bureau of the Census 1974d: Tables 221 and 225; 1970d: Tables 189 and 192.

[a] The weights were the numbers enrolled in public and private institutions.
[b] Based on Becker's estimate that the cost of books and supplies amounts to 22.5% of tuition (1975: 254).
[c] Based on Becker's estimate that the cost of transportation amounts to 23.9% of tuition (1975: 254).
[d] Adjusted for the 23.8% increase in the CPI between 1960 and 1969.
[e] Through an oversight, educational costs for 1970 were expressed in 1970 instead of 1969 dollars.

Educational Costs

1. *Educational costs per child enrolled:* The methodologies used for both 1960 and 1970 were the same. Educational costs were only computed for college students and hence do not include estimates for students in vocational schools. College and university costs were assumed to consist of three components: (a) tuition and fees; (b) books and supplies; (c) transportation. Tuition and fees were estimated by computing a weighted average of the charges listed in 1960 and 1970 of public and private institutions. The weights used were the appropriate enrollment figures in public and nonpublic colleges and universities for 1960 and 1970. Unfortunately, no allowance could be made for scholarships and other financial aids to students. Books and supplies and transportation were estimated using Becker's estimates that the cost of books and supplies amount to 22.5% of tuition and that transportation amounts to 23.9% (Becker 1975: 254). The calculations for the unit educational costs are presented in Table C.5.

Appendix C

2. *Number of children enrolled:* Only the number of children enrolled in *college* were to be estimated, as indicated above. The 1970 Public Use Sample supplied data on the number of children enrolled in college in each household. Using the estimated educational costs of $934 per student, I estimated the mean educational costs of 18–24-year-olds for families where the husband–father was in the 35–64 age groups (Table C.4).

In 1960, the estimates were harder to develop because of a lack of information on the number of children enrolled in college in the PUS analyzed. In order to construct the estimates, it was assumed that the ratio of the mean number enrolled in college to the mean number of 18–24-year-olds in households was the same in 1960 as in 1970 for each age group of husbands. This assumption will probably produce an overestimate of college enrollments in 1960 for children still in the home since enrollments went up between 1960 and 1970. However, such an overestimte will tend to minimize the increase in the cost of 18–24-year-olds for men in the same age groups between the two census dates. The estimated educational costs were then added to the preliminary expenditure estimates on 18–24-year-olds to arrive at total gross expenditure estimates. These estimates are also presented in Table C.4.

Income of Young Adults

Young adults in the 18–24 age group earn money. Hence their income had to be deducted from estimated expenditures on them to arrive at an estimate of expenditures by parents, net of the young persons' presumed economic contribution. There were no data on earnings of children available in my public use samples. Using published data for both the 1960 and 1970 censuses, I estimated the mean earnings of white 18–24-year-olds who lived in husband–wife families and were the children of the head (U.S. Bureau of the Census 1964b: Tables 2, 5, and 22; 1973f: Table 10).

Actually these published income data were for *14*–24-year-old children (in both 1959 and 1969) and hence would have greatly underestimated the income of *18*–24-year-olds. My strategy was to assume that children 14–17 were entirely concentrated at the low end of the income distribution for the 14–24 age group. In this way, I eliminated all youths with no income at all and a high proportion of youths with incomes in the $1–999 groups. Since it was probably true that some portion of the 18–24-year-olds had no earnings and that a higher proportion than I estimated had earnings in the $1–999 group, I am, as a result, probably *over*estimating the median income of 18–24-year-olds. I will therefore *under*estimate their net costs to the parents. Since this works against my argument, it seemed like a conservative approach to my estimation problems—perhaps too conservative but my options were limited.

These various estimation procedures yielded median earnings for 18–24-year-olds in 1959 of $1,774 (inflated into 1969 dollars) and $1,731 in 1969 which is really a remarkable similarity. Deducting these youthful incomes from the estimated total gross expenditures on each 18–24-year-old of $2,397 I arrived at an estimate of the mean net expenditure to parents for 18–24-year-olds in the household (Table C.4).

Where possible, I have tried to achieve conservative estimates of the increases in child-care expenditures as should be clear from the above discussion. Furthermore, as we have seen, it has not been at all possible to estimate increases in the economic burden of children no longer in the household but still partly or wholly dependent economically. That the number of children ever born and at an age to be in early adulthood rose significantly between 1960 and 1970 for men 35–54 and since school enrollments have also risen markedly, is another reason for believing that my estimates of increases in child-related expenditures for 18–24-year-olds are much too low. This should particularly affect the estimates of the expenditures burden on husbands 45–54 years old as they are more likely to have children in this age group than younger men.

APPENDIX **D**

Multiple Regression Models of Wives' Labor-Force Status in 1970

TABLE D.1
Multiple Regression Models of Wives' Labor-Force Status in 1970 (Partial Regression Coefficients as Percentages)[a,b]

Independent variables	I	II	III	IV	V	VI
Peak Median Earnings Group						
I	− 11.93					
II	− 5.63					
III	—					
IV	0.94*					
Peak Median Occupation Group						
Professionals						
I		− 9.84	− 10.56	− 13.62		
II		− 2.40	− 1.96*	− 4.71		
III		6.04	7.00	3.15		
Managers						
I		− 7.72	− 8.00	− 9.75		
II		− 4.04	− 3.89	− 5.12		
III		− 2.71	2.65	1.99*		
Sales						
II		− 2.85		− 3.85		
III		4.80		3.79		
Clerical						
III		3.16	3.82	2.41		
IV		8.90	10.31	8.93		
Craft						
II		− 3.79	− 2.94*	− 4.35		
III		—	—	—		
IV		.11**	.03**	.38**		

Operatives					
III		1.90	1.79*	2.12	—
IV		2.46	2.46	2.82	—
Service					
III		2.09**	1.71**	1.71	.81**
IV		8.60	9.32	9.06	1.69*
Laborers					
IV	—	.10**	−.35**	.68**	.61**
Relative economic status[c]					
Less than 0.50	2.71	2.56	4.82	3.42	—
0.50–0.74	8.05	7.84	9.21	8.55	—
0.75–0.99	4.67	4.56	5.04	4.90	—
1.00–1.24	—	—	—	—	1.22*
1.25–1.49	−5.47	−5.56	−6.41	−5.82	−1.18**
1.50–1.99	−10.24	−10.22	−11.32	−10.71	−1.33**
2.00+	−16.98	−17.01	−17.66	−17.78	—
Family-cycle stage					
No children present, husband less than 30	—	—	—	—	—
All children under 6: 1	−36.70	−36.54	—	−36.40	−36.96
All under 6: 2+	−47.35	−47.12		−46.98	−47.53
Under 6 and 6–11: 2	−36.37	−36.22		−36.04	−36.32
Under 6 and 6–11: 3+	−44.07	−43.81		−43.54	−43.79
2+ present: all under 6 and 12 or older	−26.26	−26.08		−25.88	−26.26
3+ present: under 6, 6–11, and 12–17, 18–24 (if present	−34.88	−34.58		−34.16	−34.68
All children 6–11: 1	−17.25	−17.07		−16.60	−17.41
All 6–11: 2+	−22.85	−22.67		−22.44	−22.65
6–11 and 12–17: 2	−16.19	−15.97		−15.69	−15.96
6–11 and 12–17: 3+	−18.32	−18.08		−17.77	−18.06
6–11 and 18–24: 2+	−12.78	−12.56		−11.94	−12.66

	−38.87
	−50.77
	−40.20
	−48.43
	−30.13
	−39.20
	−20.54
	−27.15
	−20.36
	−22.85
	−17.00

(continued)

TABLE D.1 (Continued)

Independent variables	Regression model					
	I	II	III	IV	V	VI
6–11, 12–17, and 18–24: 3+	−14.25	−13.97		−13.38	−14.05	−18.79
All 12–17: 1	−7.77	−7.61		−7.21	−7.64	−11.74
All 12–17: 2+	−8.20	−7.97		−7.76	−8.02	−12.68
12–17 and 18–24: 2	−5.58	−5.42		−5.10	−5.42	−10.10
12–17 and 18–24: 3+	−7.12	−6.89		−6.42	−7.00	−11.70
All 18–24: 1	−4.29	−4.27		−3.76	−4.33	−8.23
All 18–24: 2+	−6.28	−6.15		−5.49	−6.10	−10.27
No children under 25 present, husband 30 or older	−7.68	−7.60		−6.99	−7.69	−10.94
Previous marital experience of spouses						
Both in first marriage	—	—	—	—	—	—
Either or both widowed, no divorce	−2.70	−2.61*	−2.28*	−2.18	−2.59*	−1.45**
Husband in first marriage, wife previously divorced	1.60*	1.61*	2.83	1.70*	1.53*	2.00
Wife in first marriage, husband previously divorced	5.44	5.43	4.57	5.60	5.48	5.48
Both previously divorced	7.02	7.03	7.62	7.01	6.88	7.25
Husband previously divorced and wife previously widowed	.90**	1.07**	2.46**	1.40**	.91**	1.86**
Husband previously widowed, wife previously divorced	5.80	5.87	4.84*	5.79	5.81	6.38
Number of school years completed by wife						
Less than 8				−16.54		
8				−11.05		
9–11				−4.73		

440

12				—		
13–15				3.94		
16				8.69		
17				22.15		
18+				27.58		
Joint educational attainment of spouses						
Husband 18+						
W 18+	27.02	25.85	27.48		26.49	17.19
W 16–17	7.22	6.06	5.77		6.27	3.71
W 13–15	−.58**	−1.73**	−2.64**		−1.09**	−10.88
W 12	−3.06**	−4.41	−5.50		−2.98**	−12.14
W < 12	−5.11**	−6.44**	−7.13**		−5.06**	−11.52
Husband 16–17:						
W 18+	26.09	24.84	27.80		26.43	17.90
W 16–17	8.69	7.20	9.25		8.74	2.07*
W 13–15	−.81**	−2.16*	−1.16**		−.79**	7.20
W 12	−4.74	−5.94	−6.26		−4.39	−10.66
W < 12	−1.57**	−2.87**	−2.84**		−1.50**	−5.25
Husband 13–15						
W 18+	26.66	26.07	28.85		26.40	24.48
W 16–17	15.76	14.89	17.73		15.67	12.94
W 13–15	5.35	4.54	6.75		5.58	2.87
W 12	.54**	.10**	.13**		−.60**	−1.40*
W < 12	−3.37	−3.99	−4.19		−3.32	−4.61
Husband 12						
W 18+	29.72	29.38	30.35		29.33	29.53
W 16–17	14.73	14.50	17.03		14.74	13.76
W 13–15	5.69	5.58	6.88		5.79	4.81
W 12	—	—	—		—	—
W < 12	−8.16	−8.10	−8.79		−8.25	−7.18
Husband < 12						

(continued)

TABLE D.1 (Continued)

Independent variables	Regression model					
	I	II	III	IV	V	VI
W 18+	14.98*	15.39*	16.18*		14.77*	16.07*
W 16–17	24.06	24.22	24.92		24.18	25.53
W 13–15	8.98	9.14	9.84		8.88	10.18
W 12	1.42*	1.84	1.66*		1.24**	3.38
W < 12	− 7.72	− 7.25	− 7.51		− 7.80	− 4.98
Husband's age						
18–24	5.57	5.70	5.61	5.60	.67**	3.85
25–34	4.30	4.40	− 5.38	4.21	2.40	4.40
35–44	—	—	—	—	—	—
45–54	− 4.79	− 4.89	5.67	− 4.51	− 4.90	− 5.50
55–64	− 13.73	− 14.00	− .52**	− 12.92	− 14.77	− 15.05
Husbands earnings (in dollars)						
Zero or negative					− 6.57	
1–4,999					—	
5,000–6,999					2.22	
7,000–8,999					− .21**	

9,000–10,999				— 5.12
11,000–12,999				— 8.94
13,000–14,999				— 13.18
15,000–19,999				— 17.24
20,000+				— 24.71
Constant (× 100)	66.04	63.96	41.98	63.60	70.95
F	181.17	150.63	86.06	197.34	170.71

Source: 1970 Public Use Sample of White Couples.

[a]Regression coefficients are significant at the .01 level unless otherwise indicated:

*—significant at the .05 level
**—not significant

[b]The omitted reference category is indicated by a "—."

[c]Relative economic status is defined as the ratio of a man's earnings to the median earnings for men in the same age and occupational group.

9,000–10,999					— 5.12
11,000–12,999					— 8.94
13,000–14,999					— 13.18
15,000–19,999					— 17.24
20,000+					— 24.71
Constant (× 100)	66.04	63.96	41.98	63.60	70.95	69.03
F	181.17	150.63	86.06	197.34	170.71	169.51

Source: 1970 Public Use Sample of White Couples.
[a]Regression coefficients are significant at the .01 level unless otherwise indicated:
  *—significant at the .05 level
  **—not significant
[b]The omitted reference category is indicated by a "—".
[c]Relative economic status is defined as the ratio of a man's earnings to the median earnings for men in the same age and occupational group.

APPENDIX E

Time Demands of Children

Even though everyone recognizes that children—especially young children—make heavy time demands on their mothers and that all studies show that wives' labor-force participation is particularly sensitive to the presence of young children, our data on the actual hours mothers spend on child-care activities are rather poor. A relatively recent analysis of this problem has been made by Boone Turchi, an economist interested in the determinants of fertility (Turchi 1975a: Chapter 3). Turchi was concerned with how "time costs" of children might influence parents' fertility decisions. To estimate this he used two data sources: the Michigan 1965 Productive American Sample, and the Michigan 1970 Family Economics Survey. Both these studies collected data on hours spent on housework and it is on the basis of this kind of information—rather than data on hours actually spent in child care activities—that Turchi estimated the time costs of children. One problem with this approach, as Turchi himself points out, is that it may result in underestimates of the time actually involved in raising children since housework does not usually involve time spent on helping with school work, other educational activities, child-oriented recreational activities, chauffeuring children around, PTA, Scouts, and so forth.Furthermore, this underestimate of time spent in childrearing will not be distributed evenly among children by age. We would expect that much of the care of very young children would be included in "housework" kind of data but that as children get older, these other uncounted activities become increasingly significant. Hence, using hours-spent-on-housework data will result in our greatest underestimates of time spent on children occurring for older chidlren (Turchi 1975: 77, 89).

Unfortunately, the question of the time demands of older children is of major interest in the present study since we want particularly to test whether the time and cost demands of children are offsetting each other in households where young school-age and adolescent children are present (i.e., households where the direct expense might also be an important factor). If we can be assured that two adolescent children are more work, as well as more expensive, than one, then we can interpret little or no difference in adjusted work rates in these two situations as an indication of the cancelling out of the effects of the time demand and cost factors. However, that younger children make heavier time demands than older children on their mothers is relatively uncontroversial and not really at issue here. Our problem is that studies such as Turchi's, which are concerned with the analysis of fertility decisions, are most concerned with getting rough estimates of the total time demands children make. Here, hours spent on young children loom large and of much less substantive importance is the question of the time demands by different numbers of older children. As a consequence, for my purpose the studies Turchi reports on seem to yield rather unsatisfactory (and sometimes contradictory) data on time inputs into older children. However, since nothing else appears to be available, some discussion of Turchi's analysis is important.

Turchi esimtated time spent on children by regressing annual hours of regular housework on a number of variables, one of which was the number of children by age. For each data source (the 1965 and the 1970 Michigan surveys) he computed two different dummy variable multiple regressions— an ordinary least squares (OLS) and a two-stage least squares (2SLS) regression. All four regressions show, of course, that younger children take much more time than older children. Of greater interest here, however, are the effects of the *number* of children by age. In this respect, they all indicate that the greater number of children in families with at least one preschooler, the more hours of housework the mother does. When we come to families with their youngest child at least of grade-school age, however, the picture becomes more confused. For example, both the 2SLS and the OLS regressions on the 1965 Productive Americans sample show that more hours of housework result if, in households with grade-schoolers only, there are two children as opposed to one child present. However, in the 1970 Family Economics Survey, the 2SLS exhibited somewhat similar results, but the OLS regression showed a *reduction* in the number of hours on housework when going from one to two grade-schoolers. There is then a big jump up again when moving from two to three or more grade-schoolers. When only high-school students are in the home, we have similar anomalies. In the 1965 study, the 2SLS regression shows an increase in hours spent on housework as we moved from one, to two, to three or more high-school children in the home. However, the OLS regression shows a decrease as we move from one to two high-school children and then a relatively big increase as we move to three or more high-schoolers present. In the case of the 1970 study, the 2SLS again show an increase in hours spent on housework as the number of high-schoolers present increases—from 341 hours annually for one high-school student to 961 for three or more. However, the OLS regression shows a *decrease* in hours spent on housework as we move from mothers with two to three or more high-school-age children present and the coefficients for the two regressions are quite different (Turchi 1975: 84–87).

Turchi does not express a preference for either the 2SLS or OLS methods—each has advantages and disadvantages, he points out. Hence, for his purposes, it suffices to average them (Turchi 1975: 87–89). However, for my needs, this does not appear to be a satisfactory approach since the considerable impact of very young children is not at question here but rather whether a greater *number* of children (especially older children) make more time demands on the mother. With regard to this question—especially in the case of school-age children—the results of Turchi's analysis seem inconclusive, to say the least, and for me there seems to be no particular advantage in averaging contradictory results. To do so will not reliably give me an answer to the question, Do more grade-school or high-school children make heavier time demands on the mother than fewer such children? By and large, I will assume that they do, although I do not know of good data to support this assumption. I make it on the basis that (*a*) at least some of Turchi's regression estimates support this view; (*b*) the *under*estimate of the time demands of children occasioned by using housework as a proxy for time spent on childbearing activities will be greater for older children; and (*c*) it appears to be a common-sense approach.

There still remains another question, however, which might result in lower time demand on mothers occasioned by having older children in the home. This is the question of the housework and babysitting contribution of older children to the household. Bowen and Finegan, for example, suggest this might be important in their analysis (1969: 100). The logic of this argument, with regard to babysitting at least, has never been crystal clear to me, however, since older children tend to be in school longer hours than younger school children. Hence, the babysitting contribution of teenagers would probably be mainly limited to late afternoons, evenings, and weekends. Thus they might free some mothers for part-time working during these hours but do not seem to provide a major mother substitute to permit regular daytime employment. However, my main interest in the family-cycle regression was not so much the effect of having a teenager present with preschoolers (a relatively rare occurence) but whether, for example, two teenagers are more work than one. If so, then we can argue that a household where two teenagers are living involves greater expenses *and* more work than a household with just one teenager. As a result, the time demand and cost factors should offset each other. However, as far as I can tell, we know pitifully little about the housework contribution of older children. For one thing, I would suspect that the nature of their contribution would depend, to some extent, on the sex of the children involved. Male children are probably more likely to do chores that help their fathers more than their mothers (e.g., helping out in the yard). Female children might be more assistance to their mothers. But I do not know of any data on this issue.

In sum, we do not have adequate information on whether older children take up more time than they contribute. By and large, I will assume that they do take up more time. However, it seems to me that there would be probably be socioeconomic differences in this—adolescent children will be more time intensive as the socioeconomic status of the family rises. However, the lack of data on this issue precludes introducing such a nicety into the analysis.

APPENDIX F

Median Income of Husbands and Families by Age and Occupation

TABLE F.1
Median 1969 Income of White Husbands, by Occupation and Age: 1970

Husband's occupation	Husband's age				
	18–24	25–34	35–44	45–54	55–64
Total	5,846	8,820	10,174	9,871	8,365
Professionals					
I	5,364	11,897	16,422	17,652	17,250
II	6,465	10,590	12,848	13,480	12,392
III	5,431	8,870	10,923	11,703	10,973
Managers					
I	6,954	10,808	14,630	16,462	15,621
II	6,783	10,260	12,837	12,718	11,589
III	6,420	9,316	10,571	10,769	9,406
Sales					
II	6,816	10,222	12,836	13,200	12,236
III	5,362	8,660	10,096	9,995	8,342
Clerical					
III	5,865	8,562	9,536	9,384	8,810
IV	5,435	7,482	8,196	8,276	7,198

(continued)

TABLE F.1 (Continued)

Husband's occupation	Husband's age				
	18–24	25–34	35–44	45–54	55–64
Craft					
II	a	10,289	11,389	11,411	10,696
III	6,628	8,911	9,846	9,537	8,510
IV	5,653	7,750	8,150	8,026	6,835
Operatives					
III	6,310	8,165	8,631	8.511	7,734
IV	5,574	7,611	8,163	7,878	6,640
Service					
III	6,867	9,068	10,008	10,133	8,115
IV	3,946	6,721	7,494	6,773	5,995
Laborers					
IV	4,704	6,831	7,149	7,043	5,799

Source: 1970 Public Use Sample of White Couples.
[a] Medians were not computed where the sample size fell below 50 cases.

Appendix F

TABLE F.2
1969 Median Family Income, by Husband's Age and Occupation: Families Where the Wife Had Net Positive Earnings in 1969

Husband's occupation	\multicolumn{5}{c}{Husband's age}
	18–24	25–34	35–44	45–44	55–64
Total	8,085	11,405	13,153	14,249	12,755
Professionals					
I	9,200	14,241	18,237	21,725	22,647
II	9,059	13,376	15,610	17,467	17,667
III	8,016	12,222	14,517	16,656	17,423
Managers					
I	10,700	13,188	17,143	19,800	17,938
II	9,682	12,500	15,788	17,036	16,154
III	8,656	12,197	13,636	15,235	13,708
Sales					
II	9,636	12,981	15,100	16,810	16,929
III	8,045	11,418	13,573	14,261	13,154
Clerical					
III	8,128	11,096	13,294	14,553	13,565
IV	8,559	10,275	11,656	12,846	12,000
Craft					
II	[a]	12,200	14,458	16,000	14,750
III	8,846	11,369	12,696	14,211	12,708
IV	7,900	9,889	12,681	11,695	10,712
Operatives					
III	8,160	10,489	11,904	12,825	11,516
IV	7,340	10,086	11,350	12,159	10,608
Service					
III	8,500	11,380	13,200	15,444	12,714
IV	6,431	9,000	10,905	11,068	10,280
Laborers					
IV	9,250	10,900	10,277	11,088	9,365

Source: 1970 Public Use Sample of White Couples.
[a] Medians were not computed when the sample size fell below 50 cases.

References[1]

Ackers, Joan
   1973   "Women and Social Stratification: A Case of Intellectual Sexism." *American Journal of Sociology* 78(January): 936–945.

Akers, Donald S.
   1967   "On Measuring the Marriage Squeeze." *Demography* 4(1967): 907–924.

Alter, George
   1978   "The Influence of Social Stratification on Marriage in Nineteenth Century Europe: Verviers, Belgium, 1844–45." Unpublished doctoral dissertation. Philadelphia: Universty of Pennsylvania.

Anderson, Michael
   1971   *Family Structure in Nineteenth Century Lancashire*. Cambridge: Cambridge University Press.

Ankarloo, Bengt
   1978   "Marriage and Family Formation." Pp. 113–133 in Tamara K. Hareven (ed.), *Transitions: The Family and the Life Course in Historical Perspective*. New York: Academic Press.

Arensberg, Conrad M. and Solon T. Kimball
   1968   *Family and Community in Ireland*. Second edition. Cambridge, Mass.: Harvard University Press.

Bancroft, Gertrude and Stuart Garfinkle
   1963   "Job Mobility in 1961." *Special Labor Force Reports*. No. 35.

[1]Government documents are listed separately.

Banks, J.A.
　1954　*Prosperity and Parenthood: A Study of Family Planning among the Victorian Middle Classes.* London: Routledge and Kegan Paul.

Barth, Earnest A.T. and Walter B. Watson
　1954　"Social Stratification and the Family in Mass Society." *Social Forces* 45 (March) 392–402.

Bean, Frank D. and Charles H. Wood
　1974　"Ethnic Variations in the Relationship between Income and Fertility." *Demography* 11(November): 629–639.

Becker, Gary
　1975　*Human Capital.* Second edition. New York: Columbia University Press.

Bednarzik, Robert W.
　1975a　"Involuntary Part-Time Work: A Cyclical Analysis." *Monthly Labor Review* 98(September): 12–18.
　1975b　"The Plunge of Employment during the Recent Recession." *Monthly Labour Review* 98(December): 3–10.

Ben-Porath, Yoram
　1974　"Economic Analysis of Fertility in Israel." Pp. 189–220 in Theodore Schultz (ed.), *Economics of the Family: Marriage, Children and Human Capital.* Chicago: University of Chicago Press.

Berger, Joseph, Morris Zelditch, Jr., Bo Anderson, and Bernard P. Cohen
　1972　"Structural Aspects of Distributive Justice: A Status-Value Formulation." Pp. 119–146 in Joseph Berger, Morris Zelditch, Jr., and Bo Anderson (eds.), *Sociological Theories in Progress.* Vol. 2. Boston: Houghton Mifflin.

Bernhardt, Eva M.
　1972　"Fertility and Economic Status—Some Recent Findings on Differentials in Sweden." *Population Studies* 26(July): 175–184.

Blake, Judith
　1968　"Are Babies Consumer Parables? A Critique of the Economic Theory of Reproductive Motivation." *Population Studies* 22(March): 5–25.

Blau, Peter M. and Otis Dudley Duncan
　1967　*The American Occupational Structure.* New York: Wiley.

Bourdieu, Pierre
　1976　"Marriage Strategies as Strategies of Social Reproduction." Pp. 117–144 in Robert Forster and Orest Ranum (eds.), *Family and Society: Selections from the Annales: Economies, Societies, Civilisations.* Baltimore, Md.: Johns Hopkins University Press.

Bowen, Willian G. and T. Aldrich Finegan
　1969　*The Economics of Labor Force Participation.* Princeton, N.J.: Princeton University Press.

Bumpass, Larry L. and Charles F. Westoff
　1970　*The Later Years of Childbearing.* Princeton, N.J.: Princeton University Press.

Byrne, James J.
　1975　"Occupational Mobility of Workers." *Special Labor Force Report 176.* Washington, D.C.: Government Printing Office.

Cain, Glen G.
　1966　*Married Women in the Labor Force: An Economic Analysis.* Chicago: University of Chicago Press.

1975 "The Challenge of Dual and Radical Theories of the Labor Market to Orthodox Theory." Discussion Paper 255-75. Madison: Institute for Research on Poverty, University of Wisconsin.

Cain, Glen and Dooley, Martin D.
1976 "Estimation of a Model of Labor Supply, Fertility and Wages of Married Women." *Journal of Political Economy* 84(August): S179-199.

Cain, Mead T.
1978 "The Household Life Cycle and Economic Mobility in Rural Bangladesh." *Population and Development Review* 4(September): 421-438.

Carroll, Lewis
1979 *Through the Looking-Glass and What Alice Found There.* Kingsport, Tenn.: Kingsport Press.

Centers, Richard
1949 *The Psychology of Social Classes: A Study of Class Consciousness.* Princton, N.J.: Princeton University Press.

Chase, Ivan D.
1975 "A Comparison of Men's and Women's Intergenerational Mobility in the United States." *American Sociological Review* 49(August): 483-505.

Cramer, James C.
1979 "Employment Trends of Young Mothers and the Opportunity Cost of Babies in the United States." *Demography* 16(May): 177-197.

Crowley, Michael F.
1972 "Professional Manpower: The Job Market Turnaround." *Monthly Labor Review* 95 (October): 9-15.

David, Martin
1959 Welfare, Income, and Budget Needs. *The Review of Economics and Statistics* 41(November): 393-399.

Day, Lincoln
1961 "Status Implications of the Employment of Married Women in the United States." *The Amcrican Journal of Economics and Sociology* 20(July): 391-397.

DeJong, Peter Y., Milton J. Brawer, and Stanley S. Robin
1971 "Patterns of Female Intergenerational Occupational Mobility: A Comparison with Male Patterns of Intergenerational Mobility." *American Sociological Review* 36(December): 1033-1042.

Doeringer, Peter B. and Michael J. Piore
1971 *Internal Labor Markets and Manpower Analysis.* Lexington, Mass. Heath Lexington Books.

Duesenberry, James, S.
1960 "Comment." pp. 231-234 in National Bureau of Economic Research (ed.), *Demographic and Economic Change in Developed Countries.* Princeton, N.J.: Princeton University Press.

Duncan, Otis Dudley
1961 "A Socioeconomic Index for All Occupations." Pp. 109-138 in Albert J. Reiss, Jr. (ed.), *Occupations and Social Structure.* New York: Free Press.

Dunlop, John T.
1957 "The Task of Contemporary Wage Theory." Pp. 117-139 in George W. Taylor and Frank C. Pierson (eds.), *New Concepts in Wage Determination.* New York: McGraw-Hill.

Durand, John D.
1968 *The Labor Force in the United States: 1890–1960.* New York: Gordon and Breach. Science Publishers, Inc.

Easterlin, Richard A.
1968 *Population, Labor Force and Long Swings in Economic Growth: The American Experience.* New York: Columbia University Press.
1969 "Towards A Socioeconomic Theory of Fertility: A Survey of Recent Research on Economic Factors in American Fertility." P;. 127–156 in S. J. Behrman, Lesllie Corsa, Jr., and Ronald Freedman (eds.), *Fertility and Family Planning: A World View.* Ann Arbor: University of Michigan Press.
1973 "Relative Economic Status and the American Fertility Swing." Pp. 170–223 in Eleanor Sheldon (ed.), *Family Economic Behavior.* Philadelphia, Pa.. J. B. Lippincott.
1978 "What Will 1984 Be Like? Socioeconomic Implications of Recent Twists in Age Structure." *Demography* 15(November): 397–432.
1980 *Birth and Fortune: The Impact of Numbers on Personal Welfare.* New York: Basic Books.

Easterlin, Richard A., Michael L. Wachter, and Susan M. Wachter
1978 "Demographic Influences on Economic Stability: The United States Experience." *Population and Development Review* 4(March): 1–22.

Espenshade, Thomas
1973 *The Cost of Children in Urban United States.* Population Monograph Series No. 14. Berkeley: Institute of International Studies, University of California.
1977 *The Value and Cost of Children.* Population Bulletin. Vol. 32, No. 1.

Featherman, D. L. and Robert M. Hauser
1976 "Sexual Inequality and Socioeconomic Achievement in the United States, 1962–1973." *American Sociological Review* 41(June): 462–483.

Freedman, Deborah S.
1963 "The Relation of Economic Status to Fertility." *The American Economic Review* 53(June): 414–426.

Freedman, Ronald and Lolagene Coombs
1966 "Economic Considerations in Family Growth Decisions." *Population Studies* 20(November): 197–222.

Freedman, Ronald, Lolagene C. Coombs, and Larry Bumpass
1965 "Stability and Change in Expectations about Family Size." *Demography* 2: 250–275.

Freeman, Jo
1973 "The Origins of the Women's Liberation Movement." *American Journal of Sociology* 78(January): 792–811.

Frieden, Betty
1963 *The Feminine Mystique.* New York: Dell Publishing.

Friedlander, Dov
"Demographic Patterns and Socioeconomic Characteristics of the Coalmining Population in England and Wales in the Nineteenth Century." *Economic Development and Cultural Change* 22(October): 39–51.

Gallup, George
1969 "Opposition to Wives Who Work Declines." Part 1. *Los Angeles Times.* September 18.

Glenn, Norval D.
1976 "Cohort Analysts' Futile Quest: Statistical Attempts to Separate Age, Period and Cohort Effects." *American Sociological Review* 49(October): 900–904.

Glenn, Norval D., Adreain A. Ross, and Judy Corder Tully
1974 "Patterns of Intergenerational Mobility of Females Through Marriage." *American Sociological Review* 39(October): 683–699.

Glick, Paul C.
1977 "Updating the Life Cycle of the Family." *Journal of Marriage and the Family* 39(February): 5–13.

Glick Paul C. and Arthur J. Norton
1973 "Perspectives on the Recent Upturn in Divorce and Remarriage." *Demography* 10(August): 301–314.

Glick, Paul C. and Robert Parke, Jr.
1965 "New Approaches in Studying the Life Cycle of the Family." *Demography* 2: 187–202.

Goldberger, Arthur S.
1964 *Econometric Theory*. New York: Wiley.

Goldin, Claudia
1979 "Household and Market Production of Families in a Late Nineteenth Century American City." *Explorations in Economic History* 16(April): 111–131.
1980 "Family Strategies and Family Economy in the Late Nineteenth-Century: The Role of Secondary Workers." In Theodore Hershberg (ed.), *Toward An Interdisciplinary History of the City: Work, Space, Family and Group Experience in Nineteenth-Century Philadelphia*. New York: Oxford University Press.

Goodman, Leo
1972 "A Modified Multiple Regression Approach to the Analysis of Dichotomous Variables." *American Sociological Review* 3-7(February): 28–46.
1973 "Causal Analysis of Data from Panel Studies and Other Kinds of Surveys." *American Journal of Sociology* 78(March): 1135–1191.

Grabill, Wilson H., Clyde V. Kiser, and Pascal K. Whelpton
1958 *The Fertility of American Women*. New York: Wiley.

Haines, Michael
1979 *Fertility and Occupation: Population Patterns in Industrialization*. New York: Academic Press.

Hamilton, Richard F.
1964 "Income, Class, and Reference Groups." *American Sociological Review* 29(August): 576–579.
1966 "The Marginal Middle Class: A Reconsideration." *American Sociological Review* 31(April): 192–199.

Haug, Marie
1973 "Social Class Measurement and Women's Occupational Roles." *Social Forces* 52(September): 86–98.

Hedges, Janice Neipert
1976 "Youth Unemployment in the 1974–75 Recession." *Monthly Labour Review* 99(January): 49–56.

Hill, C. Russell and Frank P. Stafford
1974 "Allocation of Time to Preschool Children and Educational Opportunity." *Journal of Human Resources* 9(Summer): 323–341.

Hout, Michael
1978 "The Determinants of Marital Fertility in the United States, 1968–1970: Inferences from a Dynamic Model." *Demography* 15(May): 139–160.

Jacobson, Paul H.
1964 "Cohort Survival for Generations Since 1840." *Milbank Memorial Fund Quarterly* 42(July): 36–53.

Jasso, Guillermina and Peter H. Rossi
- 1977 "Distributive Justice and Earned Income." *American Sociological Review* 42(August): 639–651.

Kaestle, Carl F. and Maris Vinovskis
- 1978 "From Fireside to Factory: School Entry and School Learning in Nineteenth-Century Massachusetts." Pp. 135–185 in Tamara K. Hareven (ed.), *Transitions: The Family and the Life Course in Historical Perspective*. New York: Academic Press.

Katz, Michael B. and Ian E. Davey
- 1978 "Youth and Early Industrialization in a Canadian City." Pp. S81–S119 in John Demos and Sarane Spence Boocok (eds.), *Turning Points: Historical and Sociologicl Essays on the Family*. Chicago: University of Chicago Press.

Kerr, Clark
- 1954 "The Balkanization of Labor Markets." Pp. 92–110 in E. Wight Bakke, Philip M. Hauser, Gladys L. Palmer, Charles A. Myers, Dale Yoder, Clark Kerr (eds.), *Labor Mobility and and Economic Opportunity*. New York: Wiley.

Kiser, Clyde V., Wilson H. Grabill, and Arthur A. Campbell
- 1968 *Trends and Variations in Fertility in the Unites States*. Cambridge, Mass.: Harvard University Press.

Kitagawa, Evelyn
- 1977 "On Mortality." *Demography* 14(November): 381–89.

Kitagawa, Evelyn M. and P.M. Hauser
- 1973 *Differential Mortality in the United States: A Study in Socioeconomic Epidemiology*. Cambridge, Mass.: Harvard University Press.

Kreps, Juanita
- 1971 *Lifetime Allocation of Work and Income: Essays in the Economics of Aging*. Durham, N.C.: Duke University Press.

Kuznets, Simon
- 1974 "Demographic Aspects of the Distribution of Income among Families: Recent Trends in the United States." Pp. 223–245 in Willey Sellekaerts (ed.), *Economics and Economic Theory: Essays in Honour of Jan Tinbergen*. White Plains, New York: International Arts and Science Press.
- 1976 "Demographic Aspects of the Size Distribution of Income: An Exploratory Essay." *Economic Development and Cultural Change* 25(October): 1–94.

Lazear, Edward P. and Robert T. Michael
- 1979 "Family Size and the Distribution of Real per Capita Income." Manuscript.

Lee, Ronald D.
- 1980 "Aiming at a Moving Target: Period Fertility and Changing Reproductive Goals." *Population Studies* 34(July): 205–226.

Leibenstein, Harvey
- 1974 "An Interpretation of the Economic Theory of Fertility: Promising Path or Blind Alley?" *Journal of Economic Literature* 12(June): 457–479.
- 1976 "The Problem of Characterizing Aspirations." *Population and Development Review* 2(September–December): 427–431.

Leibowitz, Arleen
- 1975 "Education and the Allocation of Women's Time." Pp. 171–197 in F. Thomas Juster (ed.), *Education, Income and Human Behavior*. New York: McGraw-Hill.

LeRoy, Douglas R.
- 1978 "Scheduled Wage Increases and Escalator Provisions in 1978." *Monthly Labor Review* 101(January): 3–8.

Leshin, Geraldine
 1976 *Equal Employment Opportunity and Affirmative Action in Labor-Management Relations: A Primer.* Los Angeles: Institute of Industrial Relations, University of California.
 1978 *Update: Equal Employment Opportunity and Affirmative Action in Labor-Management Relations: A Primer.* Los Angeles: Institute of Industrial Relations, University of California.

Levine, David
 1977 *Family Formation in an Age of Nascent Capitalism.* New York: Academic Press.

Lindert, Peter H.
 1978 *Fertility and Scarcity in America.* Princeton: Princeton University Press.

Mackenzie, Gavin
 1973 *The Aristocracy of Labor.* New York: Cambridge University Press.

Mason, Karen Oppenheim
 1973 "Studying Change in Sex-Roles Via Attitude Data." Pp. 138–141 in *Proceedings of the American Statistical Association, Social Statistics Section.*
 1976 "Change in U.S. Women's Sex-Role Attitudes, 1964–1974." *American Sociological Review* 41(August): 573–596.

Mason, Karen Oppenheim and Larry L. Bumpass
 1973 "Women's Sex Role Attitudes in the United States, 1970." Working Paper 73–27, Revised Version. Madison: Center for Demography and Ecology, The University of Wisconsin.

Mason, Karen Oppenheim, John L. Czajka, and Sara Arber
 1976 "Changes in U.S. Women's Sex-Role Attitudes, 1964–1974." *American Sociological Review* 41(August): 573–596.

Mason, Karen Oppenheim, William M. Mason, H.H. Winsborough, and W. Kenneth Poole
 1973 "Some Methodological Issues in Cohort Analysis of Archival Data." *American Sociological Review* 38(April): 242–258.

McClendon, McKee J.
 1976 "The Occupational Status Attainment Process of Males and Females." *American Sociological Review* 41(February): 52–64.

Melichar, Emanuel
 1965 "Least Squares Analysis of Economic Survey Data." *1965 Proceedings of the Business and Economic Statistics Section of the American Statistical Association.* 373–385.

Merton, Robert K.
 1957 *Social Theory and Social Structure.* Glencoe, Ill.: Free Press.

Miller, Herman
 1965 "Lifetime Income and Economic Growth." *American Economic Review* 55(September): 834–844.

Mincer, Jacob
 1962 "Labor Force Participation of Married Women: A Study of Labor Supply." Pp. 63–105 in National Bureau of Economic Research (ed.), *Aspects of Labor Economics.* Princeton, N.J.: Princeton University Press.
 1963 "Market Prices, Opportunity Costs, and Income Effects." Pp. 67–82 in Carl F. Christ et al. (eds.), *Measurement in Economics: Studies in Mathematical Economics and Econometrics in Memory of Yehuda Grunfeld.* Stanford, Cal.: Stanford University Press.
 1974 *Schooling, Experience, and Earnings.* New York: National Bureau of Economic Research.

Mincer, Jacob and Solomon Polachek
  1974   "Family Investments in Human Capital: Earnings of Women." *Journal of Political Economy* 82(March–April): S76–108.
Mitchell, Daniel J. B.
  1980   "Does the CPI Exaggerate or Understate Inflation?" *Monthly Labor Review* 103(May): 31–33.
Modell, John and Tamara K. Hareven
  1973   "Urbanization and the Malleable Household: Boarding and Lodging in American Families." *Journal of Marriage and the Family* 35(August): 467–479.
Modell, John, Frank F. Furstenberg, Jr., and Theodore Hershberg
  1978   "Social Change and Transitions to Adulthood in Historical Perspective." Pp. 192–219 in Michael Gordon (ed.), *The American Family in Social-Historical Perspective*. Second edition. New York: St. Martin's Press.
Modell, John, Frank F. Furstenberg, Jr., and Douglas Strong
  1978   "The Timing of Marriage in the Transition to Adulthood: Continuity and Change, 1860–1975." Pp. S120–S150 in John Demos and Sarane Spence Boocock (eds.), Chicago: University of Chicago Press.
Morgan, James N. and Sandra J. Newman
  1976   "Changes in Housing Costs, 1968 to 1974." Pp. 219–256 in Greg J. Duncan and James N. Morgan (eds.), *Five Thousand American Families—Patterns of Economic Progress*. Vol. 4. Ann Arbor: Institute for Social Research, The University of Michigan.
Namboodiri, N. Krishman
  1972   "Some Observations on the Economic Framework for Fertility Analysis." *Population Studies*. 26(July): 185–206.
Norton, Arthur J. and Paul C. Glick
  1976   "Marital Instability: Past, Present, and Future." *Journal of Social Issues*. 32(Spring): 5–20.
Okun, Bernard
  1960   "Comment." Pp. 235–240 in National Bureau of Economic Research (ed.), *Demographic and Economic Change in Developed Countries*. Princeton, N.J.: Princeton University Press.
Oppenheimer, Valerie Kincade
  1970   *The Female Labor Force in the United States: Demographic and Economic Factors Determining Its Growth and Changing Composition*. Population Monograph Series, No. 5. Berkeley: Institute of International Studies, University of California.
  1972   "Rising Educational Attainment, Declining Fertility and the Inadequacies of the Female Labor Market." Pp. 305–328 in Charles F. Westoff and Robert Parke, Jr. (eds.), *Demographic and Social Aspects of Population Growth*. Vol. 1 of the Research Reports of the Commission on Population Growth and the American Future. Washington, D.C.: Government Printing Office.
  1973   "Demographic Influences on Female Employment and the Status of Women." *American Journal of Sociology* 78(January): 946–961.
  1977   "The Sociology of Women's Economic Role in the Family." *American Sociological Review* 42(June): 387–406.
  1979   "Structural Sources of Economic Pressure for Wives to Work: An Analytical Framework." *Journal of Family History* 4(Summer): 177–197.

References

Orshansky, Mollie
- 1965 "Counting the Poor: Another Look at the Poverty Profile." *Social Security Bulletin* 28(January): 3–29.

Parnes, Herbert S. and Randy King
- 1977 "Middle-Aged Job Losers." *Industrial Gerontology* 4(Spring): 77–95.

Parrish, John B.
- 1974 "Women in Professional Training." *Monthly Labor Review* 97(May): 41–43.

Parsons, Talcott
- 1942 "Age and Sex in the Social Structure of the United States." *American Sociological Review* 7(October): 604–616.
- 1943 "The Kinship System of the Contemporary United States." *American Anthropologist* 45(January–March): 22–38.
- 1949 "The Social Structure of the Family." Pp. 173–201 in Ruth Ansheu (ed.), *The Family: Its Function and Destiny*. New York: Harper and Brothers.
- 1954a "An Analytical Approach to the Theory of Social Stratification." Pp. 69–88 in *Essays in Sociological Theory*. Glencoe, Ill.: Free Press.
- 1954b "A Revised Analytical Approach to the Theory of Social Stratification." Pp. 386–439 in *Essays in Sociological Theory*. Glencoe, Ill.: Free Press.
- 1955 "The American Family: Its Relations to Personality and the Social Structure." Pp. 3–33 in Talcott Parsons and Robert F. Bales (eds.), *Family Socialization and Interaction Process*. New York: Free Press.

Preston, Samuel H. and John McDonald
- 1979 "The Incidence of Divorce within Cohorts of American Marriages Contracted Since the Civil War." *Demography* 16(February): 1–25.

Reed, Fred W., Richard J. Udry, and Maxine Ruppert
- 1975 "Relative Income and Fertility: The Analysis of Individuals' Fertility in a Biracial Sample." *Journal of Marriage and the Family* 37(November): 799–805.

Reed, Ritchie H. and Susan McIntosh
- 1972 "Costs of Children." Pp. 337–350 in Elliott R. Morss and Ritchie H. Reed (eds.), *Economic Aspects of Population Change*. Vol. 2 Research Reports of the Commission on Population Growth and the. American Future. Washington, D. C.: Government Printing Office.

Reis, Albert and George P. Schultz
- 1970 *Workers and Wages in an Urban Labor Market*. Chicago: University of Chicago Press.

Rindfuss, Ronald R. and James A. Sweet
- 1977 *Postwar Fertility Trends and Differentials in the United States*. New York: Academic Press.

Ritter, Kathleen V. and Lowell L. Hargens
- 1975 "Occupational Positions and Class Identifications of Married Working Women: A Test of the Asymmetry Hypothesis." *American Journal of Sociology* 80(January): 934–948.

Rosenfeld, Carl
- 1979 "Occupational Mobility During 1977." *Special Labor Force Reports*. No. 231.

Rossi, Peter H., William A. Sampson, Christine E. Bose, Guillermina Jasso, and Jeff Passel
- 1974 "Measuring Household Social Standing." *Social Science Research* 3(September): 169–190.

Rowntree, B. Seebohm
  1922   *Poverty: A Study of Town Life*. London: Longmans, Green and Company.
Runciman, W. G.
  1968   "Reference Grops and Inequalities of Class." Pp. 207–221 in Herbert H. Hyman and Eleanor Singer (eds.), *Readings in Reference Group Theory and Research*. New York: Free Press.
Ryder, Norman
  1965   "The Cohort as a Concept in the Study of Social Change." *American Sociological Review* 30(December): 843–861.
Saben, Samuel
  1967   "Occupational Mobility of Employed Workers." *Special Labor Force Report No. 84* Washington, D. C.: Government Printing Office.
Sampson, William A. and Peter H. Rossi
  1975   "Race and Family Social Standing." *American Sociological Review* 40(April): 201–214.
Scanzoni, John H.
  1975   *Sex Roles, Life Styles and Child-bearing*. New York: The Free Press.
  1976   "Gender Roles and the Process of Fertility Control." *Journal of Marriage and the Family* 38(November): 677–691.
Schaie, K. Warner
  1967   "Age Changes and Age Differences." *The Gerontologist* 7(June): 128–132.
Schmitt, Raymond L.
  1972   *The Reference Other Orientation*. Carbondale, Ill.: Southern Illinois University Press.
Schultz, T. Paul
  1975   "Understanding Labor Market Behavior of U.S. Women." Unpublished. Mineapolis: Department of Economics.
Schulz, James H.
  1976   *The Economics of Aging*. Belmont, Cal.: Wadsworth.
Sewell, William H., Robert M. Hauser, and Wendy Wolf
  1980   "Sex, Schooling, and Occupational Status." *American Journal of Sociology* 86(November): 551–583.
Sheppard, Harold L.
  1976   "Work and Retirement." Pp. 286–309 in Robert H. Binstock and Ethel Shanas (eds.), *Handbook of Aging and the Social Sciences*. New York: Van Nostrand Reinhold Company.
Smith, James P.
  1977   "Family Labor Supply over the Life Cycle." *Explorations in Economic Research* 4(Spring 1977): 205–276.
Smith, James P. and Finis Welch
  1981   "No Time to Be Young: The Economic Prospects for Large Cohorts in the United States." *Population and Development Review* 7(March): 71–83.
Spilerman, Seymour
  1977   "Careers, Labor Market Structure, and Socioeconomic Achievement." *American Journal of Sociology* 83(November): 551–593.
Stolzenberg, Ross M.
  1975   "Occupations, Labor Markets and the Process of Wage Attainment." *American Sociological Review* 40(October): 645–655.
Sweet, James A.
  1973   *Women in the Labor Force*. New York: Seminar Press.

Thompson, James D., Robert W. Avery, and Richard O. Carlson
    1968   "Occupations, Personnel, and Careers." *University Council for Educational Administration Quarterly* (Winter): 6–31.

Tilly, Louise A.
    1979a   "Individual Lives and Family Strategies in the French Proletariat." *Journal of Family History* 4(Summer): 137–152.
    1979b   "The Family Wage Economy of a French Textile City: Roubaix, 1872–1906." *Journal of Family History* 4(Winter): 381–394.

Tilly, Louise A. and Joan W. Scott
    1978   *Women, Work, and Family.* New York: Holt, Rinehart and Winston.

Treas, Judith and Robin Jane Walther
    1978   "Family Structure and the Distribution of Family Income." *Social Forces* 56(March): 866–880.

Treiman, Donald J. and Kermit Terrell
    1975   "Sex and the Process of Status Attainment: A Comparison of Working Men and Women." *American Sociological Review* 40(April): 174–200.

Triplett, Jack E.
    1980   "Does the CIP Exaggerate or Understate Inflation? Some Observations." *Monthly Labor Review* 103(May): 33–35.

Turchi, Boone
    1975a   *The Demand for Children.* Cambridge: Ballinger.
    1975b   "Microeconomic Theories of Fertility: A Critique." *Social Forces* 54(September): 107–125.

Turner, Ralph H.
    1956   "Role-Taking, Role Standpoint, and Reference-Group Behavior." *American Journal of Sociology* 61(January): 316–328.
    1964   "Some Aspects of Women's Ambition." *American Journal of Sociology* 70(November): 271–285.

Tyree, Andrea and Judith Treas
    1974   "The Occupational and Marital Mobility of Women." *American Sociological Review* 39(June): 293–302.

Uhlenberg, Peter
    1978   "Changing Configurations of the Life Course." Pp. 65–97 in Tamara K. Hareven (ed.), *Transitions: The Family and the Life Course in Historical Perspective.* New York: Academic Press.

van Velsor, Ellen and Leonard Beeghley
    1979   "The Process of Class Identification among Employed Married Women: A Replication and Reanalysis." *Journal of Marriage and the Family* 41(November): 771–778.

Wachter, Michael L.
    1974   "Primary and Secondary Labor Markets: A Critique of the Dual Approach." *Brookings Papers on Economic Activity* 3: 637–693.
    1977   "Intermediate Swings in Labor-Force Participation." *Brookings Papers on Economic Activity.* 2: 545–576.

Waite, Linda J.
    1976   "Working Wives: 1940–1960." *American Sociological Review.* 41(February): 65–80.

Warner, William L.
    1949   *Democracy in Jonesville.* New York: Harper.

Watson, Walter B. and Ernest A. T. Barth
  1964 "Questional Assumptions in the Theory of Social Stratification." *Pacific Sociological Review* 7(Spring): 10–16.
Watts, Harold W.
  1967 "The Iso-Prop Index: An Approach to the Determination of Differential Poverty Income Thresholds." *Journal of Human Resources* 2(Winter): 2–18.
Weiss, Yoram and Lee A. Lillard
  1978 "Experience, Vintage, and Time Effects in the Growth of Earnings: American Scientists, 1960–1970." *Journal of Political Economy* 86(June): 427–447.
Welch, Finis
  1979 "The Effects of Cohort Size on Earnings: The Baby Boom Babies." *Journal of Political Economy* 87(October): 565–597.
Westoff, Charles F., Elliott G. Mishler, and E. Lowell Kelly
  1957 "Preferences in Size of Family and Eventual Fertility Twenty Years After." *American Journal of Sociology* 62(March): 491–497.
Westoff, Charles F., Robert G. Potter, Jr., and Philip G. Sagi
  1963 *The Third Child: A Study in the Prediction of Fertility*. Princeton, N.J.: Princeton University Press.
Westoff, Charles F. and Norman B. Ryder
  1977 "The Predictive Validity of Reproductive Intentions." *Demography* 14(November): 431–451.
Wilensky, Harold
  1963 "The Moonlighter: A Product of Relative Deprivation." *Industrial Relations* 3(October): 105–124.
Willis, Robert J.
  1974 "Economic Theory of Fertility Behavior." Pp 25–75 in Theodore W. Schultz (ed.), *Economics of the Family: Marriage, Children, and Human Capital*. Chicago: University of Chicago Press.
Yahalem, Martha Remy
  1977 "Employee-Benefit Plans, 1975." *Social Security Bulletin* 40(November): 19–28.
Young, Michael and Peter Willmot
  1962 *Family and Kinship in East London*. Baltimore, Md.: Penguin Books.

REFERENCES TO GOVERNMENT DOCUMENTS

U.S. Bureau of the Census
  1943 *U.S. Census of Population: 1940. The Labor Force (Sample Statistics). Employment and Family Characteristics of Women*. Washington, D.C.: Government Printing Office.
  1953 *U.S. Census of Population: 1950*. Vol. 2. *Characteristics of the Population*. Part 1, U.S. Summary, Chapter C. Washington, D.C.: Government Printing Office.
  1955 *U.S. Census of Population: 1950*. Vol 4. *Special Reports. Fertility* P-E-5C. Washington, D.C.: Government Printing Office.
  1961 *Current Population Reports*. Series P-20, No. 105. "Marital Status and Family Status: March 1960." Washington, D.C.: Government Printing Office.
  1962 *Current Population Reports*. Series P-20, No. 114. "Marital Status and Family Status: March 1961." Washington, D.C.: Government Printing Office.
  1963a *U.S. Census of Population: 1960. Subject Reports. Employment Status and Work*

References

	Experience. Final Report. PC(2)-6A. Washington, D.C.: Government Printing Office.
1963b	*U.S. Census of Population: 1960. Subject Reports. Occupational Characteristics*. PC(2)-7A. Washington, D.C.: Government Printing Office.
1963c	*U.S. Census of Population: 1960. Detailed Characteristics. U.S. Summary*. Final Report. PC(1)-1D. Washington, D.C.: Government Printing Office.
1963d	*Statistical Abstract of the United States: 1963*. Washington, D.C.: Government Printing Office.
1963e	*Current Population Reports*. Series P-20, No. 122. "Marital Status and Family Status: March 1962." Washington, D.C.: Government Printing Office.
1963f	*U.S. Census of Population: 1960. Subject Reports. Employment Status and Work Experience*. PC(2)-6A. Washington, D.C.: Government Printing Office.
1963g	*U.S. Census of Population: 1960. Subject Reports. Occupations by Earnings and Education. Final Report* PC(2)-7B. Washington, D.C.: Government Printing Office.
No Date	*U.S. Censuses of Population and Housing: 1960. 1/1000, 1/10,000: Two National Samples of the Population of the United States, Description and Technical Documentation*. Washington, D.C.: Government Printing Office.
1964a	*U.S. Census of Population: 1960. Subject Reports. Characteristics of Professional Workers*. Final Report. PC(2)-7E. Washington, D.C.: Government Printing Office.
1964b	*U.S. Census of Population: 1960. Subject Reports. Persons by Family Characteristics*. PC(2)-4B. Washington, D.C.: Government Printing Office.
1965a	*Current Population Reports*. Series P-20, No. 138. "Educational Attainment: March 1964." Washington, D.C.: Government Printing Office.
1965b	*Current Population Reports*. Series P-20, No. 139. "Household and Family Characteristics: March 1964 and 1963." Washington, D.C.: Government Printing Office.
1965c	*Current Population Reports*. Series P-60, No. 47. "Income in 1964 of Families and Persons in the United States." Washington, D.C.: Government Printing Office.
1965d	*Current Population Reports*. Series P-20, No. 135. "Marital Status and Family Status: March 1964 and 1963." Washington, D.C.: Government Printing Office.
1965e	*Current Population Reports*. Series P-20, No. 144. "Marital Status and Family Status: March 1965." Washington, D.C.: Government Printing Office.
1965f	*Current Population Reports*. Series P-25, No. 311. "Estimates of the Population of the United States, by Single Years of Age, Color, and Sex: 1900 to 1959." Washington, D.C.: Government Printing Office.
1967a	*Trends in the Income of Families and Persons in the United States: 1947–1964*. Technical Paper No. 17. Washington, D.C.: Government Printing Office.
1967b	*Current Population Reports*. Series P-60, No. 51. "Income of Families and Persons in the United States." Washington, D.C.: Government Printing Office.
1967c	*Current Population Reports*. Series P-20, No. 159. "Marital Status and Family Status: March 1966." Washington, D.C.: Government Printing Office.
1968	*Current Population Reports*. Series P-20, No. 170. "Marital Status and Family Status: March 1967." Washington, D.C.: Government Printing Office.
1969a	*Current Population Reports*. Series P-60, No. 60. "Income in 1967 of Persons in the United States." Washington, D.C.: Government Printing Office.
1969b	*Current Population Reports*. Series P-60, No. 66. "Income in 1968 of Families and Persons in the United States." Washington, D.C.: Government Printing Office.
1969c	*Current Population Reports*. Series P-20, No. 187. "Marital Status and Family Status: March 1968." Washington, D.C.: Government Printing Office.

1970a *Current Population Reports.* Series P-20, No. 207. "Educational Attainment: March 1970." Washington, D.C.: Government Printing Office.
1970b *Current Population Reports.* Series P-60, No. 75. "Income in 1969 of Families and Persons in the United States." Washington, D.C.: Government Printing Office.
1970c *Current Population Reports.* Series P-20, No. 198. "Marital Status and Family Status: March 1969." Washington, D.C.: Government Printing Office.
1970d *Statistical Abstract of the United States: 1970.* Washington, D.C.: Government Printing Office.
1971a *Current Population Reports.* Series P60, No. 80. "Income in 1970 of Families and Persons in the United States." Washington, D.C.: Government Printing Office.
1971b *Current Population Reports.* Series P-20, No. 212. "Marital Status and Family Status: March 1970." Washington, D.C.: Government Printing Office.
1971c *Current Population Reports.* Series P-20, No. 225. "Marital Status and Living Arrangements: March 1971." Washington, D.C.: Government Printing Office.
1972a *Public Use Samples of Basic Records from the 1970 Census: Description and Technical Documentation.* Washington, D.C.: Government Printing Office.
1972b *1970 Occupation and Industry Classification Systems in Terms of Their 1960 Occupation and Industry Elements.* Technical Paper No. 27. Washington, D.C.: Government Printing Office.
1972c *Statistical Abstract of the United States: 1972.* Washington, D.C.: Government Printing Office.
1972d *Current Population Reports.* Series P-60, No. 85. "Money Income in 1971 of Families and Persons in the United States." Washington, D.C.: Government Printing Office.
1972e *Current Population Reports.* Series P-65, No. 40. "Household Ownership and Availability of Cars, Homes, and Selected Household Durables and Annual Expenditures on Cars and Other Durables and Annual Expenditures on Cars and Other Durables: 1971." Washington, D.C.: Government Printing Office.
1972f *Current Population Reports.* Series P-20, No. 242. "Marital Status and Living Arrangements: March 1972." Washington, D.C.: Government Printing Office.
1972g *U.S. Census of Population: 1970. General Social and Economic Characteristics. U.S. Summary.* PC(1)-C1. Washington, D.C.: Government Printing Office.
1973a *U.S. Census of Population: 1970. Detailed Characteristics. U.S. Summary.* Final Report. PC(1)-D1. Washington, D.C.: Government Printing Office.
1973b *U.S. Census of Population: 1970. Subject Reports. Occupational Characteristics.* PC(2)-7A. Washington, D.C.: Government Printing Office.
1973c *Current Population Reports.* Series P-60, No. 90. "Money Income in 1972 of Families and Persons in the United States." Washington, D.C.: Government Printing Office.
1973d *Current Population Reports.* Series P-20, No. 255. "Marital and Living Arrangements: March 1973." Washington, D.C.: Government Printing Office.
1973e *Current Population Reports.* Series P-20, No. 245. "Living Arrangements of College Students: October 1971." Washington, D.C.: Government Printing Office.
1973f *U.S. Census of Population: 1970. Subject Reports. Persons by Family Characteristics.* PC(2)-4B. Washington, D.C.: Government Printing Office.
1974a *Current Population Reports.* Series P-65, No. 47. "Household Expenditures on Cars and Selected New Household Durables: 1968–1972, Annual Data." Washington, D.C.: Government Printing Office.

References

1974b *Current Population Reports.* Series P-20, No. 271. "Marital Status and Living Arrangements: March 1974." Washington, D.C.: Government Printing Office.
1974c *Current Population Reports.* Series P-25, No. 519. "Estimates of the Population of the United States, by Age, Sex, and Race: April 1, 1960 to July 1, 1973." Washington, D.C.: Government Printing Office.
1974d *Statistical Abstract of the United States: 1974.* Washington, D.C.: Government Printing Office.
1975a *Historical Statistics of the United States, Colonial Times to 1970. Bicentennial Edition.* Part 1. Washington, D.C.: Government Printing Office.
1975b *Current Population Reports.* Series P-60, No. 97. "Money Income in 1973 of Families and Persons in the United States." Washington, D.C.: Government Printing Office.
1975c *Current Population Reports.* Series P-20, No. 287. "Marital Status and Living Arrangements: March 1975." Washington, D.C.: Government Printing Office.
1976a *Current Population Reports.* Series P-60, No. 101. "Money Income in 1974 of Families and Persons in the United States." Washington, D.C.: Government Printing Office.
1976b *Current Population Reports.* Series P-20, No. 297. "Number, Timing and Duration of Marriage and Divorces in the United States: June 1975." Washington, D.C.: Government Printing Office.
1977a *Current Population Reports.* Series P-60, No. 105. "Money Income in 1975 of Families and Persons in the United States." Washington, D.C.: Government Printing Office.
1977b *Statistical Abstract of the United States: 1977.* Washington, D.C.: Government Printing Office.
1977c *Current Population Reports.* Series P-20, No. 314. "Educational Attainment in the United States: March 1977 and 1976." Washington, D.C.: Government Printing Office.
1977d *Current Population Reports.* Series P-60, No. 105. "Money Income in 1975 of Families and Persons in the United States." Washington, D.C.: Government Printing Office.
1977e *Current Population Reports.* Series P-20, No. 306. "Marital Status and Living Arrangements: March 1976." Washington, D.C.: Government Printing Office.
1978a *Current Population Reports.* Series P-20, No. 319. "School Enrollment—Social and Economic Characteristics of Students: October 1976." Washington, D.C.: Government Printing Office.
1978b *Current Population Reports.* Series P-60, No. 114. "Money Income in 1976 of Families and Persons in the United States." Washington, D.C.: Government Printing Office.
1978c *Current Population Reports.* Series P-20, No. 326. "Household and Family Characteristics: March 1977." Washington, D.C.: Government Printing Office.
1978d *Current Population Reports.* Series P-20, No. 323. "Marital Status and Living Arrangements: March 1977." Washington, D.C.: Government Printing Office.
1978e *Current Population Reports.* Series P-20, No. 315. "Trends in Childspacing: June 1975." Washington, D.C.: Government Printing Office.
1978f *Current Population Reports.* Series P-25, No. 721. "Estimates of the Population of the United States by Age, Sex, and Race: 1970 to 1977." Washington, D.C.: Government Printing Office.

1979a *Current Population Reports.* Series P-20, No. 338. "Marital Status and Living Arrangements: March 1978." Washington, D.C.: Government Printing Office.
1979b *Current Population Reports.* Series P-20, No. 346. "School Enrollment—Social and Economic Characteristics of Students: October 1978." Washington, D.C.: Government Printing Office.
1980a *Current Population Reports.* Series P-20, No. 356. "Educational Attainment in the U.S.: March 1979 and 1978." Washington, D.C.: Government Printing Office.
1980b *Current Population Reports.* Series P-20, No. 349. "Marital Status and Living Arrangements: March 1979." Washington, D.C.: Government Printing Office.

U.S. Bureau of Labor Statistics
1960 "Labor Force and Employment in 1959." *Special Labor Force Report No. 4.* Washington, D.C.: Government Printing Office.
1961a "Labor Force and Employment in 1960." *Special Labor Force Report No. 14.* Washington, D.C.: Government Printing Office.
1961b "Marital and Family Characteristics of Workers, March 1960." *Special Labor Force Report No. 13.* Washington, D.C.: Government Printing Office.
1962 "Labor Force and Employment in 1961." *Special Labor Force Report No. 23.* Washington, D.C.: Government Printing Office.
1963 "Labor Force and Employment, 1960–1962." *Special Labor Force Report No. 31.* Washington, D.C.: Government Printing Office.
1964 "Labor Force and Employment in 1963." *Special Labor Force Report No. 43.* Washington, D.C.: Government Printing Office.
1965 "Labor Force and Employment in 1964." *Special Labor Force Report No. 52.* Washington, D.C.: Government Printing Office.
1966a "Labor Force and Employment in 1965." *Special Labor Force Report No. 69.* Washington, D.C.: Government Printing Office.
1966b *City Worker's Family Budget for a Moderate Living Standard.* Bulletin No. 1570-1. Washington, D.C.: Government Printing Office.
1967 "Occupational Mobility of Employed Workers." *Special Labor Force Report No. 84.* Washington, D.C.: Government Printing Office.
1968a *Retired Couple's Budget for a Moderate Living Standard, Autumn 1966.* Bulletin No 1570-4. Washington, D.C.: Government Printing Office.
1968b *Revised Equivalence Scale for Estimating Incomes or Budget Costs by Family Type.* Bulletin No. 1570-2. Washington, D.C.: Government Printing Office.
1969 *Three Standards of Living for an Urban Family of Four Persons: Spring 1967.* Bulletin No. 1570-5. Washington, D.C.: Government Printing Office.
1970a *Major Collective Bargaining Agreements: Seniority in Promotion and Transfer Provisions.* Bulletin No. 1425-11. Washington, D.C.: Government Printing Office.
1970b *Monthly Labor Review.* 93(March).
1970c "Employment and Unemployment Developments in 1969." *Special Labor Force Report No. 116.* Washington, D.C.: Government Printing Office.
1970d *Three Budgets for a Retired Couple in Urban Areas of the United States, 1967–1968.* Bulletin No. 1570-6. Washington, D.C.: Government Printing Office.
1971a "Employment and Unemployment in 1970." *Special Labor Force Report No. 129.* Washington, D.C.: Government Printing Office.
1971b *Monthly Labor Review.* 94(March).
1971c *Monthly Review.* 94(April).
1971d "Marital and Family Characteristics of Workers, March 1970." *Special Labor Force Report No. 130.* Washington, D.C.: Government Printing Office.

References

1972 "Employment and Unemployment in 1971." *Special Labor Force Report No. 142.* Washington, D.C.: Government Printing Office.
1973a *Manpower Report of the President—March 1973.* Washington, D.C.: Government Printing Office.
1973b "Changes in the Employment Situation in 1972." *Special Labor Force Report No. 152.* Washington, D.C.: Government Printing Office.
1973c *Handbook of Labor Statistics.* Bulletin No. 1790. Washington, D.C.: Government Printing Office.
1974a "Employment and Unemployment—A Report on 1973." *Special Labor Force Report No. 163.* Washington, D.C.: Government Printing Office.
1974b *Monthly Labor Review.* 97(September).
1975a *Characteristics of Agreements in State and Local Governments, January 1, 1974.* Bulletin No. 1861. Washington, D.C.: Government Printing Office.
1975b *Handbook of Labor Statistics 1975—Reference Edition.* Bulletin 1865. Washington, D.C.: Government Printing Office.
1975c "Employment and Unemployment in 1974." *Special Labor Force Report No. 178.* Washington, D.C.: Government Printing Office.
1975d *Characteristics of Major Collective Bargaining Agreements, July 1, 1974.* Bulletin No. 1888. Washington, D.C.: Government Printing Office.
1975e "Occupational Mobility of Workers." *Special Labor Force Report No. 176.* Washington, D.C.: Government Printing Office.
1975f "Marital and Family Characteristics of Workers, March 1975." *Special Labor Force Report No. 183.* Washington, D.C.: Government Printing Office.
1976a *Collective Bargaining Agreements for State and County Governments.* Bulletin No. 1920. Washington, D.C.: Government Printing Office.
1976b "Employment and Unemployment During 1975." *Special Labor Force Report No. 185.* Washington, D.C.: Government Printing Office.
1976c *Monthly Labor Review.* 99(January).
1977a *Handbook of Labor Statistics 1977.* Washington, D.C.: Government Printing Office.
1977b "Marital and Family Characteristics of the Labor Force in March 1976." *Special Labor Force Report No. 206.* Washington, D.C.: Government Printing Office.
1977c *Monthly Labor Review.* 100(February)..
1978a "Employment and Unemployment Trends During 1977." *Special Labor Force Report No. 212.* Washington, D.C.: Government Printing Office.
1978b *Monthly Labor Review.* 101(May).
1978c *Monthly Labor Review.* 101(February).
1979a "Employment and Unemployment During 1978: An Analysis." *Special Labor Force Report No. 218.* Washington, D.C.: Government Printing Office.
1979b "Occupational Mobility During 1977" *Special Labor Force Report No. 231.* Washington, D.C.: Government Printing Office.
1979c "Job Tenure Declines as Work Force Changes." *Special Labor Force Report No. 235.* Washington, D.C.: Government Printing Office.
1980 "Employment and Unemployment During 1979: An Analysis." *Special Labor Force Report* No. 234. Washington, D.C.: Government Printing Office.
1981a "Marital and Family Characteristics of the Labor Force, March 1979." *Special Labor Force Report No. 237.* Washington, D.C.: Government Printing Office.
1981b "Employment and Unemployment. A Report on 1980. *Special Labor Force Report No. 244.* Washington, D.C.: Government Printing Office.

U.S. Department of Labor. Employment Standards Administration
- 1978 "A Report Covering Activities under the Act During 1977." Submitted to Congress in 1978. (Mimeo)

U.S. National Center for Health Statistics
- 1973 *Remarriages: United States*. Series 21, No. 25. Washington, D.C. Government Printing Office.
- 1980 *Vital Statistics of the United States, 1978*. Vol. 2, Section 5. "Life Tables." Washington, D.C.: Government Printing Office.

Subject Index

A

Adaptive family strategies
  children
    number of, 200, 368, 377–378, 380, 387, 396
    timing of, 190–191, 200–201, 209–211, 369, 375–378, 380, 387, 380, 395, 396
  conceptualization of, 356–362
  exogenous constraints on, 361–362, 370–374
  marriage, timing of, 147–156, 190, 368, 374–375, 376, 379, 382, 390, 395
  occupational differences, 190–191, 200–201, 209–211
    blue-collar, 372–390
    white-collar, lower, 391–396
    white-collar, upper, 363–372
  vulnerabilities of, 357–358, 383–387, 397–399
  work of children, 363–365, 375–387, 395
  work of wives, 227, 230–231, 252–253, 369–372, 390, 395, 397–399

Age, period and cohort effects, 42–44
  age effect on earnings, 45–47, 97–103
  cohort effect on earnings, 53–59, 90–97
  period effect on earnings, 47–53, 97–103
Age Discrimination in Employment Act, 101–102
Age–earnings profiles, 11, 42, 47–50, 66–68, 71–74
  changes
    description of, 84–90
    reasons for, 90–103
  occupational comparisons, 74–78, 88–89, 449–451
  occupational mobility and, 68–71

C

Career-cycle stage, 9–12
  age at marriage and, 138–142, 147–162, *see also* Adaptive family strategies
  stop-gap jobs and, 142–147
Child-dependency
  changes in, 179–180, 191–209

471

Child-dependancy *(cont'd.)*
  measurement of, 173–177, 180, 182, 186, 188–189, 445–448
  number present and ages, 173–180
  occupational differentials in, 188–209
  total ever born, 179, 191, 204–205
Children, cost of, *see also* Child-dependency
  direct dollar costs, 172–173, 180–184, 425–436
  impact of changes on income, 184–187
  relative costs by age, 169–172
  Victorian England, 368–369
Cohort effects, *see* Age, period and cohort effects
Consumer Price Index, changes in, 130–135
Consumption aspirations, 6, *see also* Feedback effects
  life-cycle stage and, 10–12, 124–130
  occupation and, 7–9, 78–83

E

Earnings, *see also* Age–earnings profiles; White-collar squeeze
  occupational differentials in, 41, 81–83, 88–90
Easterlin hypothesis, 10, 15, 25–28, 87–88, 103–120, 168, 184–188, 340–348
Economic squeezes, 5–12, *see also* Life-cycle squeezes; White-collar squeeze
Educational attainment, 78–80, *see also* Wives' labor force participation
  men, trends in, 96–97, 104–106
  wives, implications of, 265–273, 286n, 291–305, 308–309

F

Family-cycle stages, 9–12, 244–252, *see also* Life-cycle squeezes
Family strategies, *see* Adaptive family strategies
Feedback effects, of wives' economic behavior, 27–28, 321–322, 327–340, 345–348, 351–352
First squeeze
  age at marriage and, 135–142
  cost component, 124–135
  economic impact of wives' working on, 324–325, 334–335, 338

H

Human capital theory, age–earnings profiles and, 45–46, 97–98

I

Institutionalized labor markets, age–earnings profiles and, 46–47, 99–103

L

Life-cycle squeezes, 293–295, *see also* First squeeze; Second squeeze
  inflation, impact on, 47–48
Lower white-collar squeeze, *see* White-collar squeeze

M

Marriage, age at, 136–142, 147–156
Microeconomic models of family decision making, 3–5, 20–25

O

Occupational mobility, 68–71

P

Peak median occupational group, measurement, 37–42, 403–422
Pension reform law of 1974, 102
Period effects, *see* Age, period and cohort effects

R

Reference groups, 7–9
  negative, 8
  occupational, 14–19
  positive, 7–9
Reference group theory, 12–19
Relative economic status
  changes, 84–87, 97–103, 113–118, 187–188
  see also Feedback effects

Subject Index

cohort size and, 58, 91–92, 106–113
fertility and, 14–15
occupations and, 81–83
recessions and, 92–95, 99
Remarriage patterns, selectivity of, 240–244

S

School-leaving age, 364–367, 385–386, 388–389, 391–395
Second squeeze
changes in severity of, 184–188, 191–211, 397
changes in timing of, 179–180, 191–209, 386–387, 397
cost of children, 167, 169–173, 180–184
economic impact of wives working on, 326–327, 334, 338–339, 343–348
occupational differentials in, 188–209
timing of, 174–178, 189–209
Seniority, age–earnings profiles and, 11, 99–102
Sex-role norms, 28–31
Sex-role segregation, functionalist position, 259–265
Stop-gap jobs, 142–147, 156–162
age at marriage and, 147–156

U

Unemployment
age differentials, 48–50
industry and occupational differentials, 50–53

W

White-collar squeeze, 65–66, 78–83, 226–227, 252–253, 297
Wives' economic role, *see also* Feedback effects
economic squeezes and, 5, 19–20, 295
female occupations and, 305–308
status compatibility and, 259–265, 293–304
status maintenance and, 261–265
traditional sociological perspectives of, 256–265
upward mobility and, 315–321
Wives' labor-force participation
cohort effects, 231–238
educational level and, 273
family-cycle stage and, 244–252
husband's earnings and, 220–222, 227–230, 314–316
husband's peak median occupation and, 223–231
past marital instability and, 238–240
relative educational level and, 274–286
Wives' occupation
earnings and, 271–273
educational attainment and, 266–271
Wives' working
economic impact of, 309–321, 323–327, 343–348, *see also* Feedback effects

STUDIES IN POPULATION

Under the Editorship of: H. H. WINSBOROUGH

Department of Sociology
University of Wisconsin
Madison, Wisconsin

Samuel H. Preston, Nathan Keyfitz, and Robert Schoen. **Causes of Death:** *Life Tables for National Populations.*

Otis Dudley Duncan, David L. Featherman, and Beverly Duncan. **Socioeconomic Background and Achievement.**

James A. Sweet. **Women in the Labor Force.**

Tertius Chandler and Gerald Fox. **3000 Years of Urban Growth.**

William H. Sewell and Robert M. Hauser. **Education, Occupation, and Earnings: Achievement in the Early Career.**

Otis Dudley Duncan. **Introduction to Structural Equation Models.**

William H. Sewell, Robert M. Hauser, and David L. Featherman (Eds.). **Schooling and Achievement in American Society.**

Henry Shryock, Jacob S. Siegel, and Associates. **The Methods and Materials of Demography.** *Condensed Edition by Edward Stockwell.*

Samuel H. Preston. **Mortality Patterns in National Populations:** *With Special Reference to Recorded Causes of Death.*

Robert M. Hauser and David L. Featherman. **The Process of Stratification: Trends and Analyses.**

Ronald R. Rindfuss and James A. Sweet. **Postwar Fertility Trends and Differentials in the United States.**

David L. Featherman and Robert M. Hauser. **Opportunity and Change.**

Karl E. Taeuber, Larry L. Bumpass, and James A. Sweet (Eds.). **Social Demography.**

Thomas J. Espenshade and William J. Serow (Eds.). **The Economic Consequences of Slowing Population Growth.**

Frank D. Bean and W. Parker Frisbie (Eds.). **The Demography of Racial and Ethnic Groups.**

Joseph A. McFalls, Jr. **Psychopathology and Subfecundity.**

Franklin D. Wilson. **Residential Consumption, Economic Opportunity, and Race.**

Maris A. Vinovskis (Ed.). **Studies in American Historical Demography.**

Clifford C. Clogg. **Measuring Underemployment: Demographic Indicators for the United States.**

Doreen S. Goyer. International Population Census Bibliography: *Revision and Update, 1945-1977.*

David L. Brown and John M. Wardwell (Eds.). New Directions in Urban–Rural Migration: *The Population Turnaround in Rural America.*

A. J. Jaffe, Ruth M. Cullen, and Thomas D. Boswell. The Changing Demography of Spanish Americans.

Robert Alan Johnson. Religious Assortative Marriage in the United States.

Hilary J. Page and Ron Lesthaeghe. Child-Spacing in Tropical Africa.

Dennis P. Hogan. Transitions and Social Change: *The Early Lives of American Men.*

F. Thomas Juster and Kenneth C. Land (Eds.) Social Accounting Systems: *Essays on the State of the Art.*

M. Sivamurthy. Growth and Structure of Human Population in the Presence of Migration.

Robert M. Hauser, David Mechanic, Archibald O. Haller, and Taissa S. Hauser (Eds.) Social Structure and Behavior: *Essays in Honor of William Hamilton Sewell.*

Valerie Kincade Oppenheimer. Work and the Family: *A Study in Social Demography.*